The Cold War and the New Imperialism

The Cold War and the New Imperialism
A Global History, 1945–2005

Henry Heller

MONTHLY REVIEW PRESS
New York

To Doctor Jack Fainman, hero.

Library of Congress Cataloging-in-Publication Data

Heller, Henry.
  The Cold War and the New Imperialism : a global history, 1945-2005 / Henry Heller.
    p. cm.
      Includes bibliographical references.
        ISBN 1-58367-139-0 (pbk.) — ISBN 1-58367-140-4 (cloth)

1. History, Modern--1945-1989. 2. History, Modern—1989- I. Title.
  D840.H443 2006
  909.82'5—dc22
      2005036713

Designed by Terry J. Allen

Monthly Review Press
122 West 27th Street
New York, NY 10001
www.monthlyreview.org

Printed in Canada

10 9 8 7 6 5 4 3 2 1

Contents

Preface

The end of the Cold War has not brought the end of history. On the contrary, as we move into the new millennium, the tempo of change is quickening. Global economic and cultural interdependence grow year by year. Economic expansion and the spread of industrialization continue, but most spectacularly so in the underdeveloped countries. The majority of the world's population now live in cities and work for wages. Women increasingly are freeing themselves from patriarchal control and, concomitantly, birth rates everywhere are in decline. Definitions of the family and, indeed, gender are being transformed in some countries, while in other places tribal, ethnic, and religious authorities desperately attempt to reassert control. Economic inequality and environmental degradation worsen. Representative democracy and capitalism are apparently dominant everywhere and everywhere are being questioned as never before. The United States has dramatically ruptured the post-Cold War order by brazenly trying to assert itself as the single and undisputed world power. Its bid for imperial dominance is being contested by rival states and regions in Europe and Asia, worldwide popular opposition, and its own internal social and economic weaknesses. China and the rest of Asia have begun to rival the economic and, increasingly, the political supremacy of Europe and the United States.

History clearly has not ended. Indeed, the future has never been of greater concern to humanity, and yet it appears more confusing, less certain, and more pregnant with change than ever. This historical narrative has been written in an effort to illuminate and clarify the momentous changes that have occurred and, hopefully, to shed some light on what may lie ahead. It looks at the major events and innovations of the last 50 years to provide some context for understanding the undeniably major transformations of the present age and to cast some light on the future.

Beginning such a historical narrative in 1945 is in a sense an arbitrary act. Urbanization of the world's largely peasant population, for example, began much earlier than the mid-twentieth century. Similarly, patriarchal authority over the family began to be challenged, not in 1945, but at the beginning of the twentieth century. It is, nonetheless, true to say that these two historical processes reached their turning points in the last 50 years. Indeed, most of the important transformations noted above either first appeared or reached their culmination in the last half-century. In other words, the last six decades have been ones of profound and unprecedented change.

In a work of history whose purpose is to order and explain the kaleidoscope of recent events, one must necessarily be selective. Those events and developments that seemed to me to have the greatest global impact have been stressed. Precedence has been given to political and economic history, with attention to cultural and social change where appropriate. Inevitably, this has meant the highlighting of certain states, events, and trends and the neglect of others. In this history, the politics and culture of the United States receives paramount attention. This follows not from some predilection on my part, but from the fact that it was the dominant world power from 1945. Its foreign policy, culture, and internal history were, therefore, of great importance. On the other hand, this work tries to give states and cultures in other Western and non-Western states their due. In particular, it tries to understand events from their perspective as much as possible.

Some states such as the Soviet Union and China, Cuba, Vietnam, and Korea are featured, while others such as Canada, Spain, the Philippines, Nigeria, and Colombia are not. East Asia is given more attention than South Asia. Secular ideologies are taken quite seriously, but religion only when it impinges on politics. The assassinations of President John F. Kennedy, President Ngo Dinh Diem (South Vietnam), and Prime Minister Patrice Lumumba (Congo) are duly registered, but those of Prime Minister S.W. Bandaranaike (Ceylon/Sri Lanka), King Abdullah (Jordan), and Prime Minister Indira Gandhi (India) are omitted.

This history begins at the end of the Second World War. This was the point at which the global popular and revolutionary aspirations born of the Russian Revolution reached their peak. The fate of these radical expectations at the hands of the United States and the Soviet Union form the main historical axis of the narrative. It was the Cold War between the superpowers that established the framework within which the popular upheavals of the last half-century played themselves out.

The Cold War, among other things, was a means of blocking internal social and political revolutions. It redefined them in terms of international ideological and state rivalry between East and West. This was obviously true in the sphere of influence controlled by the United States. But it was also true in the case of the Soviet Union. Revolutionary change certainly occurred in regions under Soviet control, but within the strict political limits imposed by communist bureaucratic dictatorship.

In Europe the Cold War quickly led to political division and military stalemate. But in the third world, ideological rivalry accelerated challenges to the traditional and colonial orders. The early postwar decades were marked by the proliferation of national liberation movements and revolutions in Asia, Africa, the Middle East, and Latin America. Indeed, the upheavals in the underdeveloped world, notably, the Cuban and Vietnamese revolutions, set off revolutionary convulsions in the 1960s that challenged established authority in the leading capitalist countries and in major communist states such as China and Czechoslovakia. Reverberations from these upheavals continued to shake nations throughout Latin America, Africa, and the Middle East through the 1970s.

In the East, West, and throughout the underdeveloped world, these years of political tumult were also years of major economic and social advance. But from the 1970s onward, economic growth faltered in both the capitalist and communist worlds. In the communist world, economic stagnation eventually led to challenges to the model of bureaucratic and centralized control itself. In the case of the Soviet Union and its allies, the outcome was the collapse of the system at the end of the 1980s. In China, where the crisis was more political than economic, ideological exhaustion led to the transformation of the system almost beyond recognition. The outcome in the West differed. As in Eastern Europe, the economy tended to stagnation and instability. The competitiveness and, indeed, solvency of the U.S. economy, the lynchpin of the global capitalist system, was increasingly in question. But the United States and its close allies were able to use these mounting economic difficulties as a means to recover control over the social and political upheavals that marked the 1960s and 1970s. Using neoliberal ideology as a policy lever, the working classes of the major capitalist countries and the states of the third world were brought to heel. The erstwhile communist world, meanwhile, was integrated into the capitalist global economy.

Yet at the dawn of the new millennium, things have never seemed so unstable. The poverty and instability created by neoliberalism have produced massive resistance in the advanced capitalist countries and among the impoverished populations of Latin America. There is pervasive disorder of one kind or another in Africa and Latin America, and also visible social and political decay within the fabric of advanced countries. Economically and politically, the United States appears increasingly hollowed out and socially polarized. Its attempts to impose its control on the Middle East are backfiring. Its dominance in the global market place is challenged by an emerging polycentric capitalism. The U.S. order seems not so much to be collapsing as unravelling.

The Cold War was a political dynamic or system that, while limiting the possibility of total war, maintained a state of permanent tension between the superpowers. As such armed conflict was allowed, but was confined largely to the periphery of the system. The origins of this Cold War system date back to the Russian Revolution and the imperialist wars of the first part of the twentieth century. The introduction of this narrative examines those roots. The establishment of the Cold War system in both East and West occurred during the years 1945–1960; this period is the subject of chapters one through three, a section entitled "Construction." In the Western world, the United States focussed on the construction of a liberal international political and economic order that included its erstwhile enemies Germany and Japan, the two key economies of Europe and Asia. The communist world saw the imposition of Stalinism, an order marked by fierce political repression and rapid economic development. Revolution in China, Korea, and Vietnam in this period expanded the communist sphere to virtually the whole of the Eurasian continent. The United States responded by constructing a global system of military bases and political alliances meant to contain communism, but also designed to project its own power worldwide. The decolonization and national liberation movements in the underdeveloped countries between East and West is the theme of the third chapter.

The second part of the narrative, "Crisis," begins (chapter four) with the development of populism and revolution in Latin America culminating in the Cuban Revolution. It continues (chapter five) with the Vietnam War and the development of revolutionary challenges to the Cold War system, both in the capitalist and communist world during the 1960s. Chapter six recalls the remarkable transition from third world revolution to neoliberalism that occurred during the 1970s.

The final part of the chronicle, "Devolution," suggests fall or descent (1980–2004). The Soviet Union collapsed, the Cold War as a system came to an end, political and economic power tended toward dispersal. Try as it might, the ability of the United States to control global events became doubtful.

Introduction

The Second World War ended in 1945 with the defeat of Germany and Japan. The German surrender on May 7 followed the suicide of Adolf Hitler as the Soviet army overran Berlin. In Asia, the Japanese government sued for peace at the beginning of August after nuclear weapons were dropped on Hiroshima and Nagasaki by U.S. bombers. With the surrender of these two so-called Axis powers, the greatest war in human history came to an end.

In response to German (1939) and then Japanese aggression (1941), Great Britain, the Soviet Union, and the United States had mobilized unprecedented industrial and military power against the Axis over the course of six years of war. The "weapons of mass destruction" of that age—including super bombers, aircraft carriers, and tank armies—were used on a vast scale. As a finale, the atomic bomb—the ultimate expression of the destructive potential of modern science and technology—was unleashed for the first time.

The titanic conflict produced a scale of violent death and mass destruction that was unspeakably large. The Soviet Union lost twenty-six million, almost three times more than its fearsome enemy Germany. In the principal theatres of the war, Poland, the Balkans, and elsewhere in Eastern Europe, perhaps ten million were wiped out. Included in these totals were millions of Jews who lived mainly in Eastern and Central Europe. Along with these estimates, the appalling death tolls in Asia have for too long been ignored. Three to four million Japanese perished. In China well over twenty million died. There were perhaps ten million additional deaths in the rest of Asia. The number of dead in all theatres totaled sixty to seventy million, more than seven times the mortality in the First World War.

To the nightmare of mass death must be added immense material devastation. At the end of the war, most of the cities of Germany and Japan lay in ruins. Much of their populations were left without a roof over their heads. Destroyed also were large parts of Poland, Russia, Yugoslavia, Italy, northern France, and the Low Countries. In these places, the passing and re-passing of armies and massive bombardments accounted for most of the damage. The Soviet Union alone saw 1,500 towns and cities and 70,000 villages annihilated. Allied bombing and naval blockade wiped out an estimated quarter of Japan's wealth including a third of all industrial machine tools, a quarter of rolling stock and motor vehicles, and much of the housing stock in 66 cities. The Japanese military had wreaked similar havoc through much of East Asia. Indeed, the full extent of Japanese carnage and destruction has yet to be accurately charted.

Homelessness was the plight of millions in Europe and Asia, but starvation was an even more immediate threat. Already in 1943, British emergency measures in Bengal had provoked a famine that led to the death of three million peasants. Two million Vietnamese died of hunger in the closing months of the war as a result of the failure of the rice harvest and the disruption of transportation. The threat of a similar shortfall and famine existed also in Japan and Europe. Japan had been gradually cut off from its customary Asian sources of rice by a U.S. naval blockade. With the end of the war, it lacked the financial wherewithal to import additional food stocks. Meanwhile, a severe drought struck Europe in 1945. It intensified problems in agriculture that had developed during the war. Farmers there had prospered during the early stages of the conflict. But as the hostilities continued, the agricultural sector experienced an increasingly serious shortage of labor power. A growing lack of spare parts, machinery, seeds, and fertilizer made the situation worse. The result was reduced harvests and declines in livestock holdings. In Western and Central Europe, the first postwar harvest fell to 31 million tons compared to a prewar average of 59 million.

All over Europe severe rationing continued or deepened. By 1946, 100 million people were living on 1,500 calories a day or less. In Germany the ration was reduced to 900-1,000 calories a day in the British and U.S. occupation zones. Fuel supplies were also extremely short. The coal industry of the Ruhr, for example, was able to produce only 25,000 tons per day compared to a prewar average of 400,000. Losses in transportation made the delivery of fuel, food, and raw materials extremely difficult. German railways had ceased to function altogether under Allied aerial onslaught. Only 35 percent of France's locomotives were operative. Inland canal and river traffic all over Europe was hampered by bombed out or dynamited bridges.

Amid such havoc, a massive contraction of industrial production occurred. In France at the end of the war, manufacturing output was a third of what it had been in 1938, a year of depression. The situation in Germany, Austria, and Greece was even worse. The shortages and economic disruptions caused runaway inflation and currency collapses in many European countries. Denmark had suffered little damage during the war and had plenty of foodstuffs available for export. But its chief prewar customers Germany and Great Britain did not have the wherewithal to buy Danish ham, butter, or cheese. Japan's cities had been reduced to rubble and its factories destroyed or idled. Runaway inflation and hunger imperiled the lives of millions of poverty-stricken urban dwellers.

It was true the U.S. economy was physically intact. Indeed, it had experienced unprecedented expansion and prosperity as a result of the war. But with the collapse of the European and Asian economies, the major trading partners of the United States had been ruined. In no position to buy U.S. exports, they were now living off U.S. charity. Indeed, the old European order based on politically and military competitive nation states seemed irretrievably ruined. In Asia and the rest of the third world, the future of both colonialism and the traditional social order appeared to be in question.

Imperialism

The world had never witnessed material and human destruction on the scale of the Second World War. The vast economic powers of the most important nations of the world had been set against one another in an extraordinary act of self-destruction. The global market had ceased to function. Its vestiges had to be sustained by all-encompassing government intervention and control. Why had this happened? We have to look back to the nineteenth century to answer this question.

Great Britain had dominated world politics during most of the century. The gradual breakdown of British military and economic dominance in the late nineteenth century precipitated a struggle among the great powers. International rivalries among the leading states—England, Germany, France, Russia, Austria-Hungary, Japan, and the United States among them—intensified from the 1880s. Antagonism took the form of intense economic competition and rising tariffs, festering territorial disputes, a growing armaments race, and heightened nationalism and racism. Enormous territories in Asia, Africa, the Near East, and Latin America were converted by these rival states into spheres of influence or colonies.

Political rivalry was heightened by economic competition. The fact is that capitalism decisively changed its character toward the end of the nineteenth century. Throughout most of the century the development of capitalism had been mainly founded on competition between rival firms in national markets and, at least in principle, free trade between nations. But from about 1880, the mature economies of the leading states of Europe and the United States were dominated by gigantic industrial and financial monopolies. National governments supported the existence of these trusts and cartels through the imposition of tariffs, the acquisition of colonies, and large-scale expenditure on armaments, increasingly discarding their commitments to laissez-faire and free trade policies. Indeed, international relations became more and more predatory and aggressive.

The evolution of national markets toward monopoly was inherent in the competitive nature of nineteenth-century capitalism. Under such circumstances, there could be only a limited number of winners and many losers. Under conditions of monopoly at the turn of the nineteenth century, competition at the national level was increasingly limited. It was displaced instead into international economic and political rivalries. Indeed, support from the state became indispensable to the pursuit of markets and tended to exacerbate international political conflicts. In each imperialist country, state policy became increasingly integrated with the economic strategies of the most powerful monopoly capitalists.

Monopolies and tariffs made it possible to extract higher profits in the home market as well as in the colonies. Such returns in protected markets enabled firms to compete more effectively in contested markets, including those of rival imperialist states. The search for protected markets, as well as for cheap raw materials and inexpensive labor, were openly acknowledged as reasons for backing colonialism. Indeed, the bountiful economic returns of colonialism enabled the rival capitalist states to buy the loyalty even of significant sections of the working class. But such late-nineteenth-century imperialism was driven, above all, by the need to export increasing amounts of surplus capital in search of profitable investment. Major capitalist financial institutions facilitated the export of capital through increasingly sophisticated credit operations.

The First World War

The First World War saw political and economic rivalries explode into a test of military will between the great European powers. The outcome of the war amounted to a reshuffling of the cards between imperialist winners and losers. In the aftermath of the conflict, two of the victorious states—England and France—sought to affirm their status as great powers at the expense of their defeated rivals. They arranged to cripple Germany economically, while liquidating its overseas empire. For good measure, the Austro-Hungarian and the Ottoman Empire—Germany's allies in the lost war—were dismembered and ceased to exist. France and England seized control of the Middle East including the newly important petroleum resources of Iraq and Iran. But the United States, now clearly a global economic and financial colossus, contented itself with its own sphere of influence in Latin America and its interests in the Philippines and China.

Depression and Fascism

The postwar pursuit of national self-interest as defined by banking and industrial monopolies, the resulting lack of international political and financial coordination, the weakening of consumer demand as a result of deflationary fiscal and monetary policies, and the accumulation of unpaid business debt then set the stage for global economic breakdown. After a brief return to economic growth fed by a wave of financial speculation during the 1920s, the world economy finally collapsed into the Great Depression (1929–39).

The struggle for the re-division of the world between the big powers almost immediately recommenced at the onset of the Depression. Socially and politically fragile, Italy had gone fascist as early as 1924. Economic crisis and the intensification of class conflict in the 1930s led to the triumph of fascism in Germany and Japan as well. The continued dominance of the middle class and a vestigial landlord class in these two countries was now founded on the virtual fusion of the state and monopoly capitalism. Authoritarian dictatorship, economic autarchy, militarism, territorial and colonial aggression, and mass mobilization and regimentation became hallmarks of these fascist regimes. Capital was obliged to accept a certain degree of forcible restructuring under state auspices. Germany under Adolf Hitler sought to militarily conquer the whole European continent. A major aspect of this scheme was the establishment of a new brutal colonial government over Eastern Europe including the territory of the Soviet Union. Japan's dream was to reorganize the whole of Asia into an area reserved for its exclusive economic exploitation. The refusal of England, France, and, ultimately, the Soviet

Union and the United States to accept these bold ambitions led to another conflict to redivide the world—the Second World War.

The End of European Hegemony

The world and, indeed, Europe would recover from the death and destruction of the Second World War. But the war represented a historic turning point marking the definitive end of European dominance. Europe—the Old Continent—had been the determining factor in world politics for centuries. The nations of Europe had long had the most powerful armies and navies. The European states dominated colonial Africa and Asia, the Near East and Latin America. Great Britain, France, and Germany made 83 percent of the world's investments prior to 1914. The cultural centers of the world were London, Paris, and Berlin, and most scientific advances were made in European laboratories and universities. A mood of optimism pervaded the European elites up to the outbreak of war in 1914. The idea of progress based on continued European ascendancy held sway over public opinion in the Western world.

The horrendous mortality of the First World War destroyed this sense of optimism. The upper classes in Germany, England, and France were gravely weakened by the conflict. Economic dominance passed from Europe to the United States. The Bolshevik Revolution, which was provoked by the war, alarmed the European upper classes even further. The mood of catastrophe deepened when, after a short period of prosperity, Europe was plunged into an unprecedented, deep economic crisis during the 1930s. Fascism flourished in reaction to the Depression, the growing economic strength of the Soviet Union, and the increasing threat of social revolution. In addition to those in Germany and Italy, fascist governments came to power in other eastern and southern European states. Much of the middle class in liberal democracies became openly sympathetic to the fascists. Economically and politically, nations barricaded themselves against one another and prepared for war once more.

Soviet and U.S. Isolationism in the Interwar Years (1917–41)

The Soviet Union initially was deeply interested in internationalizing its revolution. It saw the overthrow of the bourgeoisie in Russia in 1917 as the spark of an international working-class revolution. The Bolshevik leaders, Lenin and

Trotsky, believed that only through an international revolution could workers conquer the commanding heights of the capitalist system—heights that lay in advanced capitalist states like Germany and England. In Trotsky's view, Berlin, Paris, and London would soon replace Moscow as the capital of world revolution. But by 1924 the Soviet Union, led now by Joseph Stalin, abandoned this policy of promoting world revolution. Exhausted by war against external and internal enemies, the Soviet government resolved to concentrate for the immediate future on its own economic recovery and development. Pessimistic at the immediate prospect of international revolution, the leadership of the new Soviet state turned its gaze inwards. The Revolution's failure to seize the economic and cultural heights of the capitalist world would have fateful consequences on the emerging international communist movement. Autocratic, backward, and remote Russia would become the movement's headquarters and would shape its future. The tightly organized Soviet leadership expanded the party and state bureaucracy and carried out massive drives to industrialize and to collectivize agriculture during the 1930s. Its principal instruments were the carrot of social mobility and the stick of massive repression. By such means it transformed the still largely peasant population into workers.

The United States was also politically isolationist during the interwar period. Prior to 1914, the United States was already the largest and most productive economy in the world. During the First World War, the United States replaced Europe as the center of world finance. Entering the war in 1917 under the leadership of President Woodrow Wilson, it temporarily abandoned its long-standing policy of isolation from European affairs. It seemed to commit itself to a policy of political internationalism. Wilson fully participated in the Paris Peace Conference and insisted on the creation of the League of Nations to mediate future international conflicts. The subsequent refusal of the U.S. Senate to endorse U.S. entry into the League (1921) signified a return to the traditional policy of isolationism. Financially and economically, the United States was globally dominant. It refused, nonetheless, to assume political leadership. The political and economic consequences of this stance proved disastrous.

Origins of the Second World War

The isolation of the United States and Soviet Union left a power vacuum that other powers vainly attempted to fill. Globally, Great Britain and France clung on to their colonial possessions as tokens of their fading power. As the 1920s advanced, Germany cautiously reasserted its diplomatic influence led by liberal-democratic politicians. But with Hitler's seizure of power in 1933, Germany lost its inhibitions. The German dictator's unabashed goal was to dominate the whole continent of Europe politically and economically. Eastern Europe, including the territory of the Soviet Union, was to become Germany's Africa and Asia. Just as France, Great Britain, and the United States dominated the third world, Germany would conquer and exploit the raw materials and the labor of the Eastern Europe peoples. In order to carry out this plan, the Soviet Union or the so-called Red Menace to the East would have to be destroyed.

In pursuit of this goal, Hitler provoked war in September 1939. After the defeat of France and expulsion of Great Britain from Europe (May–June 1940), the conflict on the continent reduced itself to a fight to the death between Germany and the Soviet Union. At first the Soviet Union suffered terrible defeats, retreating deep into the Russian heartland. But as the fighting continued, not only did the Russians outfight the Germans, they outdid them in the mass production of tanks, planes, and artillery. The Russians by 1943 became masters of combined air and land offensive operations on a gigantic scale. The Germans were driven back.

During the interwar period, the United States vied with the other imperialist powers for hegemony in Asia. The Dutch continued to hold Indonesia, the French Indochina, and the British Malaysia, Burma, Ceylon, and India. Britain also sought to retain its important financial interests in south China. But it was the United States and Japan that became the ultimate contenders for supremacy in Asia, especially in China.

Japan had difficulty competing economically against the United States based on the free market or so-called open door. In the face of such stiff economic competition, Japan's military and economic elites fell back on political imperialism. Only by exclusive control of Asian natural resources, markets, labor, and investment opportunities could Japan survive. Prior to 1914, Japan had already acquired control of Korea and Taiwan and had gained significant influence in Manchuria. The First World War enhanced its political and economic position, particularly as European influence in Asia weakened. With the onset of the Depression, Japan's need for direct control through colonies and protectorates increased. In 1931 the Japanese army invaded Manchuria and in 1937 it occupied coastal China.

The United States refused to allow the markets of Asia to be closed to U.S. trade and investment. It retaliated against Japanese aggression in China by imposing increasingly stringent economic embargoes. With Dutch and British support, the United States made it difficult for Japan to gain access to spare parts, raw materials, scrap metal, and petroleum. The Japanese responded with the surprise attack on Pearl Harbor on December 7, 1941.

The Japanese assault on Hawaii represented a stunning setback for the United States, but it was also an act of desperation on the part of Japan. Its fundamental irrationality emerges in the face of the ten-to-one industrial advantage held by the United States over Japan at the beginning of the war. The United States would go on to build no less than 130 new air craft carriers between 1942 and 1945 compared to Japan's mere fifteen. Exactly as the Soviets became masters of land offensives on the continent of Europe, the U.S. perfected combined air and naval operations across the broad reaches of the Pacific. At the same time, the U.S. navy progressively cut off Japanese access to oil by a devastating campaign of submarine warfare.

Europe Exhausted

With the defeat of Japan in 1945, Asia lay at feet of the United States. Indeed, the United States held absolute dominance of the air and sea lanes of virtually the whole world. Across the Atlantic, the devastated states of Western Europe were reduced to economic supplicants. Germany had been beaten, France humiliated by years of wartime occupation, and Great Britain exhausted economically and financially. It was true that the great armies of the Soviet Union made it the pre-eminent power on the European continent. But it had been so damaged by the long and terrible conflict waged on its soil that it could not immediately challenge the United States in Europe let alone elsewhere. Meanwhile, the internecine warfare and mass murder of the Second World War left most of the European states politically and even morally bankrupt. The traditional political order based on the rivalries of the European states had ended. For the foreseeable future the states of Europe would be dependencies of the two great powers that loomed on the periphery of the continent—the Soviet Union and the United States.

Roots of the Soviet-U.S. Conflict

The Cold War between the Soviet Union and the United States broke out as soon as the war ended. The conflict would shape most of the rest of the twentieth century. Its origins can be directly traced to the nearly simultaneous

Bolshevik Revolution (October 1917) and U.S. entry into the First World War (November 1917). On the morrow of the Revolution, Leon Trotsky, the most prophetic of its leaders, declared: "Either the Russian Revolution will unleash a revolutionary movement in Europe or the European powers will crush the Russian Revolution." In other words, the revolution could not survive if confined to backward Russia. The revolution had to become international. It would become so if workers seized control of the heights of capitalism in war-torn Germany and the other major capitalist countries. Otherwise, these strong points of capitalist power would be used to organize a counter-revolution to overthrow the revolution in Russia. At almost the same moment, U.S. President Woodrow Wilson justified U.S. entry into the European war as establishing "...peace in the world on the tested foundation of political liberty." According to the U.S. president, international peace was possible only by establishing an international order based on national states that enjoyed political liberty as defined by U.S. conceptions.

As both Trotsky and Wilson made clear, liberal democracy and proletarian revolution were mutually exclusive ideas. Indeed, ideological hostility between the U.S. government and the new Soviet leadership existed from this point onwards. Certain historians have tried to minimize the ideological element of the Cold War. They have insisted that the real motives for discord lay in great power rivalry or even mutual incomprehension. One cannot entirely discount such factors. At the same time, it seems evident that the period 1917–89 was, indeed, an age of ideological conflict. In this respect, it resembles the period of the Protestant Reformation and Counter-Reformation or the epoch of the French Revolution and Napoleon. Passionate ideological conviction reinforced by rival material interest inflamed the struggle between the Soviet Union and the United States. However mistaken they may have been, other states and millions of people globally would line up on one side or another in a conflict between the principles of individual liberty and nationhood on the one hand and the principle of equality on the other. It would be folly to ignore this aspect of the conflict.

U.S. hostility toward the new Soviet state quickly became overt. In the immediate wake of the revolution, the Soviet Union withdrew from Russia's wartime alliance with the British and French. It made a separate and disadvantageous peace with Germany by signing the Treaty of Brest-Litovsk (March 1918). The reestablishment of a second or Eastern Front became an urgent strategic concern of the Western allies, now joined by the United States. Using this as a pretext, the

United States and its allies intervened in the Russian Civil War to try to crush the Bolsheviks. For three years, U.S., British, French, Canadian, and Japanese troops unsuccessfully endeavored to assist the counter-revolutionary Whites in overthrowing Soviet rule. With France in the lead, these allies attempted to establish anticommunist governments on the western frontiers of the Soviet Union in the aftermath of the war. Such a policy was thought of as a way of quarantining communist influence in the rest of Europe. With the exception of Czechoslovakia, these new governments on the western flank of the Soviet Union were clerical and reactionary in nature. Their semi-colonial economies made them dependent on Western Europe.

By common agreement, the allies sought to politically and economically isolate the new communist state. The Soviet Union made a virtue of necessity by adopting Stalin's policy of "socialism in one country" in 1924. It withdrew into virtual isolation from the rest of Europe. From the Soviet perspective, whatever now favored the survival and development of the beleaguered Soviet state coincided with the advance of international socialist revolution.

In line with this policy, the Soviets suspended efforts to foment revolution in Europe. However socialist the Soviet Union was—and in certain respects it was—by the late 1920s it was a bureaucratized state that in some aspects resembled the Russian governments of the Czarist period. As such, its foreign policy objectives echoed some of the motifs of the prerevolutionary period based on realpolitik: unfettered access to the Mediterranean, the extension of Russian influence in the Far East, and the protection of fellow Slavic states like Yugoslavia and Bulgaria. Harking back to the Slavophile traditions of the nineteenth century, the sense of the special destiny of the Russian people reappeared as a part of national ideology during the 1930s.

The United States, likewise, had a sense of its own unique destiny. From early days, the U.S. republic believed it was evident, even providentially ordained, that it would dominate the North American continent at the expense of the indigenous peoples, the Mexican state, and the British Empire. The enunciation of the Monroe Doctrine (1823) formed the basis for its later claim to hegemony over the whole of the New World. At the end of the nineteenth century, it acted on these claims through its short victorious war (1898) with Spain, the last European colonial state in the Americas. Puerto Rico was made a colony and Cuba a protectorate in the aftermath. By the eve of the First World War, the United States had established control to a greater or lesser degree over the other states of the Caribbean and Central America. Beyond the Americas, it sought to expand its economic reach across the Pacific to China. An enlarged U.S. military and political influence there had been assured through the annexation of Hawaii (1893) and the conquest of Guam and the Philippines during the Spanish American War.

During the nineteenth century, the respective political interests of Russia and the United States seldom clashed. The geographic distance that separated Russia and the United States kept friction between them to a minimum. State-to-state relations between the two powers were therefore largely cordial. U.S. public opinion was generally hostile to Czarist autocracy, but relations between the governments of the two countries remained friendly. The cession of Alaska by Russia to the United States (1863) represented the highpoint of the diplomatic relationship.

The first significant disagreement between the two states occurred at the beginning of the twentieth century. All the European powers as well as Japan were occupied with carving out spheres of influence in China. Russia was especially interested in dominating Manchuria and Korea. The United States opposed Russian imperialism as well as that of the other powers. Russia's ambitions in particular conflicted with those of the rising power of Japan. In the ensuing Russo-Japanese War (1904–05), the United States sympathized with Japan, the underdog.

Secretary of State William Hay had outlined U.S. aims with respect to China in 1899. His celebrated Open Door Policy called on the major powers to respect the territorial integrity of the Chinese state. The quest for colonies or spheres of influence should be renounced in favor of the freedom of all states to trade in the Chinese market. Hay's policy reflected the needs of the greatest and most competitive industrial economy in the world in quest for markets. Closed spheres of influence and colonies were inimical to it. More pragmatically, U.S. elites were confident that the disproportionate size of the U.S. economy would allow them to tip the scales on any otherwise level playing field. The policy of the open door was to become the foundation of twentieth-century U.S. foreign policy, not only with respect to China, but globally. To the astonishment of conventional Western opinion, little Asiatic Japan inflicted a humiliating defeat on Russia in 1905. President Theodore Roosevelt offered the good offices of the United States in negotiating the terms of peace at Portsmouth, New Hampshire.

Despite its tendency toward isolationism, the United States had opposed the Bolshevik Revolution, sending U.S. troops to Russia in support of the White armies. Throughout the 1920s, it refused to recognize the legitimacy of the new regime. Meanwhile, the European powers one-by-one opened diplomatic and economic relations with the socialist government, despite their ongoing ideological hostility. In 1933, U.S. President Franklin D. Roosevelt finally recognized the Soviet Union. Roosevelt acted to try to open foreign markets as U.S. exports had dramatically declined as a result of the global depression. In according recognition to the Soviet government, Roosevelt also sought to respond indirectly to the growing truculence of fascist Germany and Japan.

The United States attempted to remain neutral as Europe moved toward war. At the same time, it tried to bridle Japanese imperialism in Asia through increasing economic pressure. The Soviets, meanwhile, rebuffed Japanese military aggression by defeating its armies in Outer Mongolia (1938). They also believed that signing the notorious Hitler-Stalin Pact (1939) would ward off the immediate danger of war with Germany, freeing them to deal with further threats from Japan. As a result, Japan turned its ambitions southward and eastward against the interests of the United States, Britain, France, and the Netherlands in southeast Asia.

Stalin congratulated himself that, as a result of his astute diplomacy, the imperialist enemies of the Soviet Union would fight one another. Germany predictably went to war against Great Britain and France (September 1939), and Japan attacked the United States and the other colonial states in Asia. But the Soviets were unprepared for the sudden onslaught of German armies onto Russian soil in June 1941. The United States and the Soviets became allies with the attack on Pearl Harbor (December, 1941) and the following German declaration of war against the United States. The U.S. Lend-Lease program provided the Soviets with some $11 billion in military and economic aid over the following three years of war. The war years saw the development of an intense diplomatic relationship between the two states, but this political honeymoon was a late and brief flowering against an earlier background of hostility and suspicion. It remained to be seen whether such a relationship could endure. Given their past histories, their ideologies, and their ambitions, the future of their alliance after the Second World War was dubious.

1

The Cold War Begins

As the war in Europe ended in the spring of 1945, both the United States and the Soviet Union prepared for the peace that would follow. Each defined the future in terms of their existing political circumstances and long-term goals. Stalin and the Soviet leadership remained completely devoted to the ideology of Marxism-Leninism. The war had been an imperialist conflict aimed at redividing the world and destroying the Soviet Union. The defeat of Nazi Germany largely at the hands of Soviet armies demonstrated the superiority of socialism as a system. Eventually, capitalism would be overthrown worldwide and the Soviet Union, the capital of world socialism, would assist in the process in so far as possible. But the immediate task was the reconstruction of the Soviet Union, which had been devastated by the war.

From the Soviet perspective, a postwar period of peace and reconstruction was indispensable. Therefore, the continuation of cooperation and peaceful relations with its wartime allies, the United States and Great Britain, was greatly to be desired. The eradication of the remnants of Nazism and German militarism was a central objective, not only of the Soviet Union, but also of the United States and Britain. The agreement on the joint occupation and administration of Germany would, accordingly, be the keystone of the effort to maintain postwar cooperation between the allies. But Germany would have to pay a heavy price in reparations for its aggressive war against the Soviet Union.

After the First World War, the Western allies had established anti-Soviet governments in many of the Eastern European states bordering the Soviet Union. They became launching platforms for Nazi military offensives during the war

against the Soviet Union. Following its military victory over the Nazis, the Soviet
Union reinforced security on its western border through the support of people's
democracies friendly to the Soviet Union. These states were not exclusively
Communist, but rather coalitions of left-wing and centrist parties committed to
fostering mixed economies. Unimpeded access to the Black Sea through the
Dardanelles and continued influence in northern Iran were primary objectives of
Soviet foreign policy in the Middle East. In the Far East, control over the south
Sakhalin and Kurile Islands and a sphere of influence in Manchuria and northern
Korea were to be the reward for Soviet entry into the war against Japan in August
1945. Soviet foreign policy, then, was based on an amalgam of ideological com-
mitments and the political objectives of the Soviet state.

The United States, likewise, shaped foreign policy in terms of their own state
interests and ideology. The emerging Cold War quickly became an impasse based
on the rival ideological principles and conflicting national interests of the two giant
states. Roosevelt, whose days in 1945 were numbered, viewed the world from the
perspective of a president whose priority was still that of winning the war. He continued to think that friendship with the Soviet Union was essential to such a victory. Hence, Roosevelt allowed significant room to accommodate Soviet interests.

Fundamental to the outlook of the dying Roosevelt was a rejection of traditional U.S. isolationism once and for all. The repudiation of internationalism by the
United States that had followed the First World War was rightly perceived as a
disaster helping to lead to eventual economic depression and another world war.
As the leading economic and political power in the world, the objective of the
United States ought now to be the creation of a new international order based on
liberal democracy and open market capitalism.

The trading blocks, colonies, and spheres of influence of the interwar years
had led to economic catastrophe, militarism, and the outbreak of the Second
World War. The future dismantling of colonialism and the liberalization of world
trade based on multilateral agreements would ensure postwar reconstruction and
prosperity. To be sure, based on its naval and air power, the United States controlled the Seven Seas as well as the air space above them. Indeed, it planned to
keep the postwar peace by holding on to much of its worldwide system of military
bases. But the creation of the United Nations would, hopefully, allow the settlement of international disputes without resort to the predatory and aggressive militarism that marked the first half of the twentieth century. Under U.S. hegemony,
a new worldwide liberal and capitalist order was possible, one that could over-

come the political and military conflicts that had led to suicidal world wars. Cooperation, free trade, and multilateralism were to be the foundations of international relations under U.S. auspices.

In Roosevelt's eyes, there was ample place for the Soviet Union within this order of things. It was important to preserve the alliance that had been created between the United States and the Soviet Union as the basis for postwar peace. True, the Russians had not been officially informed of the secret of the atomic bomb. Yet the denazification and the demilitarization of Germany was a common goal. Soviet demands for war reparations and the legitimate security interests of the Soviet Union in Eastern Europe needed to be taken into account. The new world system ought to be founded on liberal democracy. By developing further political and economic ties with the Soviet Union, even it could be eventually absorbed into this overwhelmingly powerful liberal world order that would be dominated, but not unilaterally controlled, by the United States.

Roosevelt's death in April 1945 immediately changed the conciliatory approach of U.S. foreign policy toward the Soviet Union. Roosevelt's commitment to political and economic internationalism was maintained. But Roosevelt's successor, Vice-President Harry S. Truman, was an instinctually anticommunist politician. Endowed with a limited Midwest outlook, he was himself incapable of enunciating a sophisticated foreign policy after the manner of the patrician and independently minded Roosevelt. He immediately assented to the much more hard-line approach to the Soviet Union that surfaced among his advisers as early as the concluding months of the war in Europe. Key members of Truman's entourage, including his Secretary of State James Byrnes, Under Secretary of State Joseph C. Grew, ambassador to Moscow Averell Harriman, and the increasingly influential Secretary of the Navy James Forrestal were all proponents of this tough approach. Indeed, the virtual absence of conciliatory views toward the Soviet Union among the principal military and diplomatic advisers to Truman is striking. The anti-Soviet posture of U.S. policy under Truman represented a striking throw back to the hostile and uncompromising attitude of U.S. diplomacy of the 1920s.

The Polish and German questions soon divided the two wartime allies. True to their view that Eastern Europe properly lay in the Soviet sphere of influence, in 1944 the Soviets put into place a new Polish government dominated by Communist ministers. At the urging of the United States and Britain, the composition of the new government was somewhat broadened by Stalin at the Yalta

Conference (February 1945). But even so the Communists remained predominant in the restructured Polish government. As soon as he assumed office in April 1945, Truman decided to test this arrangement. Supported by British Prime Minister Churchill, he demanded that the composition of the restored Polish government be divided equally between the Communists and the so-called London government-in-exile backed by the British. Lend-Lease aid to the Soviet Union was temporarily suspended to strengthen Washington's hand. Stalin refused to budge and the emergent Polish government remained firmly orientated toward Moscow. This contretemps soon blew over amid the celebrations of the end of the war in Europe. Nonetheless, it already signaled the postwar refusal of Washington to accept a Soviet sphere of influence over Eastern Europe.

At the ensuing big power conference in July 1945, which unfolded in the Berlin suburb of Potsdam, further areas of tension between Washington and Moscow surfaced. Indeed, toward the close of the conference Truman unsuccessfully attempted to use word of the new U.S. monopoly over atomic weapons as a means of intimidating Stalin. Germany proved to be the principal focal point of discord. To be sure, the notion of joint allied administration of Germany was reaffirmed. As agreed at the Yalta Conference, furthermore, France was recognized as one of the occupying powers. But there were sharp arguments over the question of postwar reparations from Germany. Indeed, the Western powers insisted on their right to fix the level of reparations in their own zones of occupation. By spring 1946, they suspended further reparation payments to the Soviet Union from their zones of occupation in West Germany. In the meantime following the close of the Potsdam Conference, France had begun de facto to administer its zone of occupation independently of the other powers. The division of Germany had begun.

The struggle between the United States and the Soviet Union over Poland and then Germany emerged from competing views over the future of Europe. In the first place, the Soviets placed their highest priority on their future military security based on their ongoing political control of Eastern Europe. Secondly, in the Soviet view continuing inter-allied cooperation in the postwar occupation of Germany was indispensable to prevent a possible revival of German militarism. From the perspective of the Soviet Union, the commitment of the Western allies to joint control of Germany was to be measured by their continued willingness to hand reparation payments to the Soviet Union from their zones of occupation. The extraction of reparations from all of Germany was considered a guaranty of a common allied approach.

The United States believed that war-ravaged Germany should pay only what it could afford in making reparations. Germany ought not to be left permanently weakened. Reinforcing this view was the growing U.S. conviction that the Soviet Union had become too strong in Europe. There was no immediate danger of military aggression from the war-weary Russians, Truman and his advisers concluded. But the presence of vast Soviet armies on the Elbe was disquieting. The power of the Soviet Union needed to be offset and contained through the economic revival of Germany. Indeed, Truman was not prepared to concede a Soviet sphere of influence even over Eastern Europe.

The Soviets had never ceased to avow that they were Communists. During the war, the United States affected to ignore this assertion as much as possible. But now they were prepared to hold it against their erstwhile ally. Indeed, they blamed the Soviets for the rising popularity of the left in Europe and signs of growing unrest among third world peoples. In Europe the Communists appeared to be gaining political advantage from popular misery on a continent ravaged by war. The popularity of the Communists in France, Italy, and Greece was especially disturbing to the United States. Even the new Labour government in Great Britain might take things too far in the direction of state control of the economy. The possibility of a postwar Europe that was socialist was unacceptable to Washington. From its perspective, economically powerful Germany needed to be chastened, but it ought not to be unduly punished by excessive reparations. Over time its powerful economy needed to be reconstructed as the foundation of a stable capitalist Europe that could balance Russian power. The Soviet Union, furthermore, was bent on the creation of a sphere of influence in Eastern Europe. But the grain and natural resources of that region were essential to German and Western European economic recovery. Moreover, the United States was opposed to closed economies based on state control. It demanded the open door in Eastern Europe as much as in Asia.

The United States held some strong cards with its monopoly over nuclear weapons, powerful naval and air forces, and overwhelming economic strength. With these powers held in reserve, Washington sought to pressure the Soviet Union to abandon its grip on Eastern Europe by diplomatic means. In any case, Truman and his advisors were determined to build a worldwide Pax Americana. The empire they envisioned would be informal, as had been the British Empire in its early days.

Indeed, the word empire was eschewed, the concept denied. It was not a question of outright political imperialism or colonialism. Indirect control through economic power, strategic military bases, political pressure, and alliances would be the essential means by which Washington would exercise its newfound global power. The Europeans would have to be treated in a gingerly fashion, especially as they were forced to cede their former colonies. The sensibilities of the British and the French in particular had to be taken into account. They had to be consulted as well as managed. They along with the Belgians and the Dutch and the rest could console themselves by becoming loyal political allies and trading partners of the United States. The new multilateralism implied compromise and mutually satisfactory economic and political arrangements within a system that was, in the final analysis, dominated by the United States.

The character of U.S. global ambitions is revealed more starkly in Asia. There, its historic rival, Japan, had been defeated and occupied. Its future was to be decided by U.S. alone. Militarily and economically dependent, China under the Nationalists was U.S.'s grateful friend and supplicant and future great market. Over the long term, the British, French, and Dutch would step-by-step be forced to abandon their colonial possessions and depart Asia.

The results of the Potsdam Conference in the summer of 1945 proved inconclusive at best. The subsequent Foreign Ministers Conference in London (September 1945) and Moscow (December 1945) ended in impasse. Meanwhile, the the United States cancelled Lend-Lease to the Soviet Union altogether and shelved Soviet requests for a reconstruction loan. At the beginning of the next year, George Kennan, the U.S. chargé d'affaires in Moscow, sent his long telegram, which outlined a comprehensive view of Soviet belligerence, expansionist ambition, and worldwide conspiracy. Kennan, a proponent of the hard line against the Soviet Union since the 1920s, called for containment of Russia at certain points vital to U.S. interests. At which points, and by what means, the Soviet Union was to be held in check was not made explicit. Nonetheless, Kennan became the toast of Washington, now provided with a comprehensive analysis and blueprint for bridling the menace of Soviet power.

While the Washington elite was lending an ear to the words of Kennan, U.S. public opinion at large was being swayed by Winston Churchill's eloquence in a speech given at Fulton, Missouri, in March 1946. Playing Greek to the Romans, the former British Prime Minister showed the text of the speech to Truman several hours before its delivery and received his enthusiastic endorsement. Widely disseminated by the U.S. media, Churchill's speech portrayed the Soviet Union as a state bent on instigating trouble. Soviet influence, according to Churchill, lay behind the fifth columns of the left that seemed to be mush-rooming almost everywhere. More memorably, Churchill asserted that from "Stettin in the Baltic to Trieste in the Atlantic, an iron curtain had descended across the Continent." The United States and Great Britain should deal with the Soviet Union from a position of strength. The English-speaking powers should create a great new alliance that would force the Soviet Union to become a peaceful and responsible state.

From a historical perspective, the policy of containment elaborated by Kennan and Churchill represented a reassertion of the anti-Soviet and antileft policy pursued by Washington and London since 1918. The containment policy, nonetheless, now provided the rationale for post-isolationist Washington's assumption of the imperial role being ceded, willingly or not, by Great Britain. It held the Soviet Union responsible for the upsurge of revolutionary and anticolonial sentiment that followed the war. In doing so it served to justify U.S. intervention not only in Europe and Asia, but also against socially revolutionary and national liberation movements worldwide. In U.S. eyes they would all be linked to the Cold War struggle against Soviet influence.

Soviet Reconstruction (1945–1953)

Soviet victory in the Second World War reinforced the personal dictatorship of Joseph Stalin. But the cult of Stalin as omniscient leader of the Soviet people was born already in the 1930s. Such veneration was a concomitant of the monolithic authoritarianism of the period of collectivization, crash industrialization, and purges. By the time the war ended, worship of the great leader reached monumental levels. His image and words pervaded the whole public sphere of Soviet society. Acting as his own censor, Stalin personally supervised all of the major aspects of intellectual and cultural life. In turn, literature, theatre, the press, and movies treated him like a god. The Stalin cult was in effect a kind of religious worship that at a historical distance echoed the rule of autocratic Czars over a worshipful Russian peasantry.

Stalin and his entourage undoubtedly believed themselves to be orthodox Communists. Moreover, their enemies in the West at the beginning of the Cold War wholeheartedly agreed with them. After all, in the Soviet Union the means of production were public property, investment decisions were not determined by the possibility of profit, and a labor market based on a reserve of unemployed workers did not exist. Certainly the Soviet Union was not capitalist. But it was a highly bureaucratic and authoritarian country that had evolved in virtually complete political and economic isolation from the rest of the world. Its political practice was completely contrary to Marx's and even Lenin's notions of democracy. Since the 1920s it had step-by-step subordinated the material and intellectual producers to the state, denying them any real control over their workplaces or over political decisions. In so doing it ultimately denied the Soviet population the means of defending public control of the means of production. Far from the leadership aiming at the gradual dismantling of this setup, consolidating this system of bureaucratic domination internally and externally became the fundamental goal. The Soviet Union was a state that had seceded from the world of global capitalism. But if political democracy is part of the socialist project, it was not socialist in that sense, whatever Stalinists or their Western opponents believed.

In the eyes of Stalin and his entourage, the success of the Soviet system of rule was evident. In the first place, it had made possible rapid industrialization and urbanization. The victorious outcome of the war had then proven the extraordinary productive capacity and the political and military power of the Soviet Union. Such successes were real enough. But they tended to strengthen and confirm conservative tendencies that had become inherent in the system. The Communist Party and the state bureaucracy were seen as the system's foundations and as institutions essential to socialism. Other possibilities for organizing an alternative to capitalism were unacceptable deviations. Tampering with these monolithic bodies was tantamount to attacking the foundations of socialism itself. Both the party and the state were at the same time thoroughly subordinated to the will of Stalin. There were no Communist Party Congresses between 1939 and 1952. The Central Committee no longer met under Stalin. Even the Politburo, the highest political body, played only a minor role.

Party functionaries, economic planners, managers, bureaucrats, technical and professional intelligentsia, and army generals constituted a still insecure, but, nonetheless, privileged elite. The postwar promotion of a new generation of war veterans into important positions helped to infuse new energy into this dominant stratum. It was through this elite that Stalin and the top leadership controlled the white- and blue-collar workers who now constituted the majority of the Soviet population. In the immediate aftermath of the war, workers remained under military discipline, which was justified by the need to rebuild the country. Reduced to 45 percent of the population, the peasantry eked out a livelihood as the least favored part of Soviet society.

Postwar Soviet propaganda stressed the need for peaceful coexistence with the West. Indeed, a prolonged period of peace was the primary foreign policy objective of the Soviet Union. Peace was indispensable if the ravages of the war were to be made good. The Soviet leadership was determined, however, to hold onto its sphere of influence in Eastern Europe for which Soviet citizens had paid in blood. Otherwise, the Soviets sought good relations with the West, above all, in order to block the possibility of a rearmed and vengeful Germany.

Based on their achievements during the war, many Soviet citizens believed that life would be more free and open afterwards. But in fact, the late Stalin period (1945–1953) was perhaps the most repressive of the whole period of his rule. As a result of the war, the standard of living in 1947 was lower than it had been in 1928. Recovery, it was argued, would require discipline. Armed resistance to the Soviets in the Western Ukraine and the Baltic states continued into the early 1950s and demanded additional stern measures. The onset of the Cold War and the development of the U.S. policy of containment provoked still new fears of attack, subversion, and encirclement. The result was a renewal of the policies of repression and censorship that marked the 1930s. The secret police under Lavrenti Beria were given virtual carte blanche to suppress internal enemies. While one should rightfully dismiss the wild exaggerations of anti-Soviet scholars, one still must note that prisoners in the Siberian Gulag reached a zenith in 1950, more than 2.5 million compared to a prewar peak of 1.9 million.

Fuller understanding of Soviet cultural life is only now becoming possible. Who in the West during the Cold War heard of Andrei Platonov, a writer the equal of Franz Kafka and James Joyce? Such ignorance is not the consequence only of Stalinist repression. Still it seems clear that the late Stalin period was particularly severe on writers and intellectuals. Andrey Zhdanov, the party head of Leningrad, led the campaign to impose cultural uniformity on writers and artists. Those who were individualistic, formalistic, vulgar, and reactionary were condemned. Excessive servility toward Western culture was denounced. Instead, intellectuals were required to unstintingly praise Soviet and Russian achievement. A kind of proletarian classicism was confirmed as the norm of visual art. Gene theory, Freudianism, and quantum physics were denounced. Strict controls on all contact with the West were reinforced. Such policies were stultifying culturally, suggesting a petrified social and political order. They had a crippling effect on scientific and technological innovation. Toward the close of the Stalin period, this campaign toward imposing cultural conformity degenerated into an increasingly vehement anti-Semitic movement recalling the darkest days of Czardom.

The positive feature of the immediate postwar period was the rapid economic reconstruction of the Soviet Union. Hopes for loans or normal commercial relations with the West soon evaporated. Turning its back on the capitalist world, the Soviet Union returned to the autarchic development methods that had proved themselves during the 1930s. Sacrifices were once again demanded of the Soviet people. Once again they responded. As in the 1930s, savings on agriculture and on consumption were reinvested in heavy industry. The agricultural sector bore the brunt as before. The collective farms were paid low prices for their grain and were deprived of labor power and all but essential capital investment. Productivity suffered and the recovery of agricultural output from the war lagged. Housing and consumer goods for urban dwellers were not priorities of the regime either. Living conditions, while certainly better than during the war years, nonetheless remained below the prewar level.

The result was that industrial production, by 1950, surpassed prewar levels by 71 percent. Especially impressive was the development of manufacturing and hydro-electric capacity in the new industrial zones that had developed east of the Urals. Unfortunately, growing tension with the West forced rearmament and an increasing diversion of new manufacturing resources toward reequipping the Soviet military. The pace of growth of the civilian economy was slowed as major investments were made in the development of nuclear weapons, jet propulsion, and rockets.

Postwar United States: Stabilizing Global Capitalism

The foreign policy of the United States was conditioned by the commanding global status it enjoyed in 1945. Externally, all remaining rivals to U.S. dominance had been eliminated as a result of the conflict, with the exception of the Soviet Union. The oceans had protected the United States from any attack on its mainland, thus human losses and material damage from the war had been minimal. Its 300,000 dead were a fraction of that of other major combatants. Its view of the rest of the world was also conditioned by its internal realities. Military spending during the war spurred a rapid recovery from the devastating effects of the Depression. In 1942 alone, the U.S. government placed orders for military procurements of one hundred billion dollars. As a result of this government-induced growth, the capital assets of

U.S. manufacturing in 1945 were 65 percent higher than in 1939. The profits of U.S. business improved spectacularly, unemployment disappeared, and wages soared. Even inequality of income lessened somewhat.

Notwithstanding this renewed prosperity, there were abiding fears of another depression at the war's end. Government intervention during wartime had jolted the economy out of its slump. It was hard to say what would happen once the visible and guiding hand of government was removed. But given the forces in play in Washington, the removal of the hand of government intervention was a virtual certainty. Conservative influence was far from dead in the United States in 1945. Despite the New Deal, the propertied and wealthy still ran the country, as they had since the beginning of the republic. Indeed, large corporations, banks, and Wall Street financiers dominated twentieth-century U.S. economic life. It was true that the coming of the New Deal and, then, the Second World War created a new regulated framework within which such business institutions had to operate. Big government and organized labor were able to establish themselves as important elements of U.S. life alongside big business. But the latter ultimately called the shots.

As early as 1938 the reform impulse of the New Deal had exhausted itself. Republicans and conservative southern Democrats recovered control of the Congress. The federal government may have grown larger, but business advocates and corporate lawyers dominated the chief government posts and the upper echelons of the federal bureaucracy. As soon as the war came to an end, regulation of prices and wages and other economic controls were step-by-step dismantled at the behest of business as well as conservative politicians and government bureaucrats. In 1945 no less than 41 percent of GNP was generated in the public sector. Within three years, the percentage of GNP created by the public sector had fallen to a mere 9 percent. Unemployment temporarily increased as most of the 14 million men and women in uniform returned to civilian life. The Full Employment Act of 1946, the last measure of an exhausted New Deal, attempted to ease the pain. But the Truman government counted on pent up demand and private savings built up in wartime rather than government to sustain the postwar economy in the near term.

Whatever the fears of an ultimate relapse into depression, the immediate problem was handling inflation. The lifting of price controls, strong consumer demand, and problems of reconversion to non-military production led to rapid price hikes in 1946. Profits and business investment surged, while the purchasing power of workers shrunk. The labor movement responded with a massive strike wave. In the forefront of this upsurge were the big industrial unions led by the Congress of Industrial Unions (CIO). The CIO was born in 1938 from the great strike and organizing insurgencies of the Depression era. With the support of the New Deal, the new powerful union was able to organize the major sectors of U.S. industry. By wars end, its membership stood at more than five million workers. Of the thirty-eight affiliated unions at the CIO's national convention in 1946, almost half were led by left-wing or Communist leaders.

Postwar inflation and the buildup of grievances due to a no-strike pledge during the war engendered a militant mood in the rank-and-file. The result was a series of strikes that mobilized almost the entire union membership. U.S. industry was virtually paralyzed. In response, Truman legislated the railway men back to work. Faced with the defiance of the United Mine Workers, the U.S. president nationalized the coal industry and forced the workers back into the pits. Taking advantage of the public backlash to the runaway postwar inflation and the strike wave, the Republicans won the fall 1946 congressional elections. Over Truman's veto, the new Congress passed the Taft-Hartley Act outlawing the closed shop and secondary boycotts. Union officers had to swear affidavits that they were not members of the Communist Party.

At the time, total Communist Party membership in the United States was only about 80,000. Nonetheless, the party had acquired a real influence. Its impact was considerable on the labor movement, the entertainment and cultural industries in New York and Hollywood, and the universities to a certain extent. The attack on the Communists in the labor movement in 1946 set the stage for the wave of anticommunist witch hunts that struck many sectors of U.S. life in the late 1940s and early 1950s. These attacks were the internal complement to the emerging Cold War against the Soviet Union and the revolutionary left internationally, the one campaign reinforcing the other.

Anticommunism developed into a populist crusade. This was by no means a spontaneous affair. It was orchestrated by the corporate media and the advertising industry and involved the American Legion, the Catholic Church, the American Federation of Teachers and the National Education Association, the liberal Americans for Democratic Action, and even the leadership of the AFL and CIO. The newspapers, radio networks, and various organs of the U.S. government played a key role in spurring on this anticommunist campaign. A few months after launching the Truman Doctrine to deal with communism abroad, the President announced a Federal Loyalty Program to handle the Communist threat from within. The federal Attorney General was authorized to compile membership lists of subversive organizations, adherence to which warranted dismissal from federal employment. Two thousand federal employees were fired and 212 resigned as a result of this review. J. Edgar Hoover's FBI, meanwhile, was given virtual carte blanche to investigate persons suspected of communist activity. Between 1946 and 1948, the U.S. Congress conducted no less than twenty-six different investigations of communism. The House Un-American Activities Committee organized spectacular hearings into alleged communist influence in Hollywood. Acting under the Smith Act, in 1948 the Justice Department arrested twelve leaders of the Communist Party for subversion and brought them to trial.

Beyond the crippling effects of these witch hunts on the activities of the Communist Party and the U.S. left, in these early Cold War years other deep-seated political and social changes induced a growing conformity in U.S. society. The New Deal had greatly enlarged the role of the federal government in national life. The war confirmed the role of big government while promoting a national security ideology through wartime propaganda. Truman, it is true, demobilized large parts of the armed forces in the immediate aftermath of the war. But the subsequent development of the Cold War abroad and the anticommunist crusade at home in the late 1940s helped to consolidate the national security state that had developed during the war. The creation of the CIA and the National Security Council (1947) and the unification of the armed forces under the Joint Chiefs of Staff (1949) reinforced this process. Big business, which had been in rather bad odor during the New Deal, gradually regained influence over public opinion and politics by spending generously on lobbying, campaign contributions, public relations, and philanthropy. In the meantime, the growing power of the media, public relations, and advertising reinforced the trend toward the emergence of a conformist and increasingly homogenized consumer culture. The political voice, the intellectual potential, and the social autonomy of individual citizens tended to be stifled in the face of such an onslaught. Increasingly, ordinary citizens became spectators rather than participants in political life.

U.S. Foreign Policy

The emergence of a mass consumer market was, in fact, going to become one of the pillars of U.S. economic prosperity in the postwar decades. But Assistant

Secretary of State for Economic Affairs William Clayton, a Texas cotton million-aire, one of the key architects of postwar economic policy, took it as axiomatic that the United States could not operate its economy in isolation from the rest of the world: "So, let us admit right off that our objective has as its background the needs and interests of the people of the United States. ...We need markets—big markets—around the world in which to buy and sell. We ask no special privileges in these markets." Indeed, the immediate problem for the United States was to find trading partners and foreign markets for the vastly expanded manufacturing capacity and agricultural output that had been brought into being by the war. In 1944 exports totaled $14 billion, four times greater than in 1939. How such external markets could be rebuilt, maintained, and enlarged was one of the cen-tral questions of U.S. foreign policy in the immediate postwar period. Equally pressing was the issue of access to raw materials. By the end of the war, the U.S. economy was clearly more and more dependent on imported natural resources. The need for ongoing access to foreign oil—the ultimate strategic commodity—loomed over the horizon. For that reason alone further political isolationism was out of the question. Indeed, oil and other primary products were available prin-cipally in the less developed countries of the Middle East, Latin America, and Asia. Hence, gaining access to them required much deeper U.S. involvement in the politics not simply of Latin America, but of the whole of the third world.

Socialism and state ownership closed off availability to such markets and resources. That was one more reason among many to oppose them. But for the United States the primary motive of its new internationalist foreign policy was not to contain communism. It broader aim was rather to maintain and extend U.S. capitalism based on the principles of economic liberalism. The containment of communism became an important rationale for the postwar internationalism of the United States. The establishment of communist governments threatened to limit the market of U.S. exporters. But so, too, did the protectionist policies, spheres of influence, and colonies of other capitalist states. High tariffs and pro-tectionism had been one of the causes of the Depression. During the 1930s, the Japanese, Germans, Italians, French, and British had created exclusive trading blocs that had crippled U.S. exports. According to this view, these had then trans-lated into political and military blocs and led to war. The United States needed to stabilize the political and economic systems of the other principal powers and restore the international trading order in such a way that would eliminate barriers to trade and finance, exclusive economic trading zones, and restrictive policies of every sort. Other states would have to accept their role as partners of the United States in an open system of global trade.

Most U.S. experts, including Clayton, agreed that massive loans and grants would be necessary to the task. The model for what followed was the British loan of some $3.75 billion negotiated in December 1945. Financially exhausted at the end of the war, Britain received the loan on condition of opening the countries of its Empire to U.S. exports. Since a third of world commerce prior to the war passed through the ports of the British Empire, such a loan was a small price for the the United States to pay for access to such extensive foreign markets. Conditionality, above all, opening up to U.S. exports and capital investment, characterized the terms of offers of financial assistance to other European states. By 1946 the the United States had already advanced loans and grants to the tune of $5.7 billion to the economically beleaguered states of Western Europe. Similar amounts were granted annually over the next three years under the Marshall Plan.

The creation of the International Monetary Fund (IMF) and the International Bank for Reconstruction and Development (World Bank) at Bretton Woods in 1944 provided the framework for these credit arrangements. Headquartered in Washington and dominated by the United States, these institutions dramatically expanded international liquidity by making the U.S. dollar a world currency as good as gold. At the same time, these financial bodies were given the capital to underwrite or guarantee private loans for the reconstruction of the European economy. The liberalization of world trade was the founding principle of a third body, the International Trade Organization, set on foot at the same time. While this organization floundered, a more informal grouping, the General Agreement on Trade and Tariffs (GATT) (1947), helped to complete the architecture of a liberal multilateral economic order dominated by the United States.

The Division of the World

The two great powers shaped global history after 1945. The Cold War that arose between the Soviet Union and the United States tended to force states into one or another camp. Newly independent states that insisted on maintaining neutrality between the United States and the Soviet Union, such as India, Indonesia, or Egypt, were inevitably caught in the middle. Some states in the third world, including Indonesia, Congo, and Egypt, fell victim to these great power rivalries.

On the other hand, India and certain other non-aligned countries were able to play the Cold War rivals off against one another to their benefit. In any case, it proved difficult for states to avoid being implicated in the Cold War.

The influence of the superpowers being acknowledged, it is by no means true that such great power rivalries were the sole determinants of events in the immediate postwar period. The great powers could not do whatever they pleased. The Second World War had mobilized millions of people all over the world into the military or the industrial workforce. The political and social expectations of this multitude having been aroused, these now had to be taken into account. Most Americans, Britons, Canadians, Australians, and New Zealanders expected to be rewarded for their wartime sacrifices. They looked forward to the more peaceful and economically secure futures their wartime leaders had promised. On the European continent, the development of resistance movements in many countries under Axis occupation played an important role in the defeat of fascism. These popular armed insurgencies aroused great expectations for a freer and better life among the European population at large.

The wartime experience of colonized peoples in the Indian subcontinent, East Asia, and Africa proved of great political consequence. For many colonial subjects, military service or work in factories, mines, and transport prepared the way for participation in national liberation struggles and political independence movements in the postwar period. Indeed, the upheaval of war aroused revolutionary expectations among millions of people in the Balkans, Italy, and France, but also in China, Korea, Indochina, Malaya, and the Philippines. Such revolutionary aspirations would have a major historical impact, marking a second and higher crest of the wave of popular revolution initiated in Russia in 1917.

Still, on the European continent, however aroused people were, there is little doubt that in the immediate postwar period the political fate of most was determined in the last instance by the two great powers. Italy, for example, was a country in a state of popular ferment in the wake of fascism's defeat. Led by the Communists, a large and effective partisan movement had developed in the north of the country in the last two years of the conflict. At the end of the military conflict, this grassroots mobilization prepared the ground for a massive surge of unrest among the factory workers in the north, the sharecroppers of Tuscany, and the landless laborers of the south. Membership in the Communist Party rose dramatically to more than two million in 1948 allowing the Communist-led popular front to receive 31 percent of the votes in the national elections of that year. Many on the Italian left at the time believed that this high level of popular mobilization made possible a bid for power by revolutionary means. But the head of the Italian Communist Party, Palmiro Togliatti, in accord with Stalin, had already decided otherwise. The U.S. and British army occupied Italy, and thus the possibility of a successful Communist revolution, even with substantial popular support, was next to nil. Such a non-revolutionary perspective on the Italian situation fit with the view that the Soviet Union above all needed a breathing space within which to reconstruct itself after the war. Even before war's end, Stalin and Togliatti settled on a non-revolutionary strategy of a coalition government of national unity. The Italian Communist Party entered into a postwar government dominated by the Christian Democrats dedicated to reform and reconstruction.

The case of France also demonstrates the capacity of the United States in particular to shape the political order of postwar Western Europe. The United States did not use direct military means to establish control over France. Not that such a military occupation was ruled out. During the war the United States regarded the Vichy regime allied to Germany as an enemy state. Until the last moment before D-Day, it refused to recognize the legitimacy of the leader of the French resistance, General Charles de Gaulle. Indeed, Roosevelt seriously considered putting France under military occupation. The seizure of political power by the French resistance under de Gaulle's direction following the Normandy invasion in 1944 precluded any such move by U.S. forces. But the threat of a U.S. occupation continued in the early Cold War period. Fearing a Communist uprising in France, Truman secretly sanctioned the idea that U.S. troops stationed in Germany would intervene in such an eventuality.

On the face of it, U.S. fears of a possible Communist seizure of power in France were justified. The Communists had played a prominent role in the French resistance. The prestige of the Soviet victory on the Eastern front against Germany benefited them, too. In January 1945 the Communist Party already had 380,000 members and by the end of 1946 it had 800,000. As such, it was the largest party in France and received one of every four votes in the first postwar election. The largest trade union, the Confédération Générale du Travail (CGT), was controlled by it. Twenty to 25 percent of the newspapers bought in France came from the party press. Its mass organizations for women and youth had large postwar memberships.

However France, like Italy, was in the zone of influence not of the Soviet Union, but of the United States. Therefore, as the war drew to a close, the French

Communist Party leader Maurice Thorez and Stalin concluded that, despite the strength of the Communists, France, like Italy, was not in a revolutionary situation. The objective of the Communists became to reinforce national unity around de Gaulle. De Gaulle was a class enemy, but his nationalism made him the best instrument of Communist Party strategy. He would help to create a strong France in the postwar period. This would be the best means of preserving national independence in the face of the hegemonic ambitions of the the United States. Within a government of national unity, the Communists sought nationalizations and social and economic reform. Revolution was not on the agenda.

The immediate problem of France was to restore its infrastructure and productive capacity. Terrible shortages, especially of food, created runaway inflation. As part of the postwar coalition government, the Communist Party and the CGT called on the nation to produce as much as possible in order to overcome inflation. Under such circumstances, they discouraged strikes or confrontations with management. The government, in which the moderate right steadily gained ground, pursued a policy of allowing inflation to run its course as a way of stimulating production, lowering real wages, and wiping out government debt.

The consequent weakness of the value of the franc made it difficult to import U.S. producer goods vital for national economic recovery. Already in December 1945, the French government was forced to seek a $550 million loan from the U.S.-controlled Export and Import Bank. In May of the following year, the Blum-Byrnes Accord provided France with $800 million more in loans. Despite this support, the balance of trade further deteriorated over the next year.

Finally, in the spring of 1947 the United States made known its plans for a European Recovery Program or Marshall Plan which envisioned billions of dollars in grants to France and the other European states. At this point, the Cold War between the United States and the Soviet Union was well under way. Indeed, this program proved to be a major U.S. weapon in the developing conflict. France's coalition government of liberals, centrist radicals, socialists, and Communists became increasingly polarized by these international tensions, specifically by the question as to whether the the United States would provide aid to a government with Communist ministers.

The answer was plainly not. In May 1947 the Communists were ousted from the coalition government. They were by that time more than happy to leave. The Communist Party's policy of national unity had damaged them in the eyes of workers whose livelihood was being crippled by inflation. In addition, the government's uncompromising colonial policies in Madagascar, Algeria, and Indochina had become intolerable. Unlike the Communists in Eastern Europe, the the United States in the end did not have to use directly coercive methods to ensure French adhesion to their camp. Economic inducements sufficed. Communists were similarly expelled from the governments in Italy, Belgium, and Luxembourg. The moderate or social-democratic left and the non-communist trade unions became key popularly based elements of the anticommunist and anti-Soviet Cold War consensus.

The Balkans

As a country that fell into the Soviet sphere of influence, Yugoslavia provides a useful counter-example to Italy and France. As early as October 1944, Churchill had conceded a predominant Soviet influence in the Balkans generally, yet in Yugoslavia he demanded that British influence equal that of the Soviets. Stalin appeared to agree to go along with this demand, but events dictated otherwise. As in most of Eastern Europe, political democracy, literacy, social welfare, national industry, and a strong middle class barely existed in Yugoslavia. At the beginning of the war, the Communist Party was a small and persecuted minority. But the party's policy of national unity and patriotic war proved an effective rallying point in the face of harsh German occupation and vicious ethnic conflict between Croats, Serbs, and Muslims. By 1944 Joseph Broz (Tito), the Communist leader, claimed to lead a partisan army of 150,000 recruited from all components of the ethnically diverse Yugoslav population. As in Italy and France, the Communists rode a wave of popularity; with the retreat of the Germans, the country more and more fell into the hands of Tito's forces. Meanwhile, the Soviet army, rather than Britan or the United States, invaded and briefly occupied a northern section of the country in its drive toward Budapest and Berlin. Limited though the Soviet presence may have been, there was no doubt, in contrast to Italy or France, that Yugoslavia lay in the Soviet rather than in the British and U.S. orbit. Under the aegis of the Soviet Union, then, a genuinely popular revolutionary process led by the Communists was allowed to play itself out.

In assuming power, the Communists also had significant popular support in countries like Albania and Czechoslovakia. The Communist Party and its national liberation movement in Albania emerged as a result of Yugoslav Communist assistance. The ensuing partisan struggle against the Italian fascists and Nazis and their collaborators developed in conjunction with the efforts of Tito. Indeed, in 1944 the Albanian Communist leader Enver Hoxha dispatched forces to clear Albanian nationalist forces out of the Yugoslav province of Kosovo. In today's world of Balkan ethnic divisions such an action is inconceivable. At the end of the war, there was no real obstacle to a Communist consolidation of power in Albania.

Eastern Europe

In Czechoslovakia the propertied class made up of Germans, Jews, and collabo-rationist Czechs had been seriously weakened by the war. At the same time, the Communists had achieved real popularity among the large industrial working class. As elsewhere in Eastern Europe, the Communists at first shared power with other elements of the left and center. In elections in 1948 they obtained 38 per-cent of the vote. In the seizure of power which soon followed, the Czech Communists not only had Soviet backing, but at least the passive support of a plu-rality of the population. As we shall see, the take over in Czechoslovakia marked the real beginning of the division of Europe into two camps.

Elsewhere in Eastern Europe, the transition to Communist rule appears more opportunistic. In Bulgaria, for example, the Communists had not been particularly popular historically, but the cultural, political, and religious ties between Bulgaria and Russia were close. It was noteworthy that, while allying itself with Nazi Germany during the war, Bulgaria refused to declare war on the Soviet Union. The Agrarian Party, the party of the peasant majority, had been politically dominant since the beginning of the twentieth century. The Communist Party during the 1920s was inconsequential with a following composed of a small number of work-ers, peasants, and intellectuals. But in 1931 the Communists made gains in nation-al elections. The next year they won the mayoral election in the capital Sofia, although the courts nullified this election. The Agrarian Party coalition government then expelled the Communists from the parliament and outlawed the party.

By 1934 Bulgaria had become a dictatorship under King Boris and econom-ically and politically allied itself with Germany. Ten years later the Red Army invaded in the midst of the war and quickly occupied the country. Under the auspices of General S.S. Biriuzov, the Soviet representative of the Allied Control Commission, the Communists established a coalition called the Fatherland Front. In the wake of war and Soviet occupation, membership in the Communist Party soared by the hundreds of thousands. Using the Fatherland

Front as its vehicle, the Communists took power in elections in 1946—elections that were boycotted by the Agrarian Party. In the postwar situation, the Communists clearly enjoyed some popularity in Bulgaria. Certainly they had more support there than in states like Poland or Hungary. But it seems that it was Soviet military victory and the presence of the Red Army in occupation that shaped the political outcome.

A country renowned for its hostility to Russians and Communists, Poland is an even better example of the consequences of Soviet occupation. Contrary to common opinion, in 1945 many Poles supported communism. As anticommunist historian Krystyna Kersten has put it: "Nothing could be more incorrect than to characterize society as a whole in 1945–1946 as having an aversion to the USSR, to the Communists, and to their political power. Society was divided, and the dividing line was extremely convoluted." Nonetheless, it is also correct that the Communists in Poland were a minority. Despite major land reform in 1944, the ideological influence of the Catholic Church and the traditional landowning class was still very strong. More significantly, as the Communists were identified with Russia, the historic oppressor of Poland, even many on the left regarded them as an alien element. Their opponents, who had significant popular followings, fought them tenaciously through political channels and even armed resistance. Without the presence of the Red Army and the manipulation of the electoral process in 1947, it is difficult to see how the Communists could have taken power in Poland.

Greece and the Middle East

Greece is the ultimate example of great power politics deciding a country's fate at the beginning of the Cold War. Since 1936 the country had been under the military rule of General John Michael Metaxas. Accepted by the monarchy and the merchant and landlord elite, the government of Metaxas increasingly took on the trappings of Italian and Spanish style fascism. Externally Greece had long been in the sphere of influence of Great Britain, which had historically dominated the Mediterranean. German troops occupied the country in April 1941. The Greek king formed a government-in-exile in London and the remnants of the Greek military were based in Cairo under British command. The Germans, meanwhile, organized a puppet administration. Two-thirds of the country in the remote interior was left unoccupied.

A national resistance movement emerged in the mountains, part of the antifascist resistance movement that arose as well in neighboring Yugoslavia and Albania. The Greek National Liberation Front was composed of a coalition of six parties, including the Communists who tended to dominate the others. It was united not only by its opposition to the Germans, but also to Metaxas and the Greek monarchy. Two other guerrilla groups, liberal and republican, remained independent of the National Liberation Front.

During the war, the British had found it militarily expedient to send increasing amounts of military aid to the National Liberation Front. At the end of the conflict, however, they were not prepared to allow the National Liberation Front to take political power. The postwar British goal was to reassert its traditional influence in the Mediterranean. Blocking the ambitions of the National Liberation Movement was one of the motives behind Churchill's visit to Moscow in October 1944. At that meeting Churchill was able to get Stalin to agree that Greece was part of the British sphere of influence.

The British had already created a Greek government of national unity under the leadership of the social-democrat George Papandreou. In the wake of the Moscow accord between Churchill and Stalin, the National Liberation Front agreed to join Papandreou's government. The German retreat from Greece provoked a crisis. The National Liberation Front controlled most of the country, had a massive popular following, and had 70,000 men under arms. Shortly after the British arrived in Athens in the fall of 1944, the British commander General Ronald Scobie demanded that the National Liberation Front turn in its weapons. On December 1, 1944, the National Liberation Front withdrew from the coalition government. Two days later the police broke up a mass demonstration in downtown Athens, killing fifteen.

For the next six weeks fighting engulfed the country, with attacks on government buildings and police stations. At the end of December 1944, King George II agreed to a plebiscite on the monarchy. A new government assumed office led by the anticommunist resistance leader General Nikolaus Plastiras. The National Liberation Front had not been defeated, but the Soviet Union offered no help. It remained committed to its sphere of influence agreement with the British. The Soviets, accordingly, accredited a new ambassador to the newly reconstituted Greek government. On February 12, 1945 the National Liberation Front accepted the Varkiza agreement, which called for demobilization of the Greek insurgents in return for political amnesty.

Over the next months leading up to the national elections, the British effectively controlled the Greek government. At the same time, they looked the other way
as the police and national guards made up of holdovers from the German occupation carried on a nationwide campaign of repression against suspected
Communists. Economically matters went from bad to worse. During the war,
Greece had suffered half a million deaths out of a population of seven million. In
the postwar period, U.S. food aid provided through the United Nations barely
kept the population from starvation. Production was only 30 percent of prewar levels with run away inflation, low wages, and a balance of payments crisis.

On March 31, 1946, elections took place. The Communists and the rest of the
parties of the National Liberation Front refused to participate in what they considered to be a fraudulent process. The right-wing parties triumphed at the polls,
and in a subsequent plebiscite, the King was restored. Meanwhile, armed clashes
spread through the country. In the ensuing civil war (1946–1949), the government controlled the main towns, communication points, and highways and had
the support of most of the middle class and landlords. The Communists based
themselves on the support of the peasantry. Their tested guerrilla army, although
greatly outnumbered, controlled most of the countryside and held the strategic
initiative. Communist Yugoslavia and Albania supplied substantial aid. The
Soviet Union withheld support, in accord with its reluctance to aid revolutionary
adventures in countries in the Western sphere of influence. Washington, whose
influence in Greece was growing, chose to believe otherwise and denounced
Soviet intervention. By the spring of 1947, British support for the Greek government was clearly faltering owing to British financial weakness. More and more the
Greek regime was forced to turn to the United States for economic help. In
response to these increasingly urgent appeals, in March 1947 Truman committed
the United States to a major intervention in the Greek civil war.

Increasing U.S. involvement in Greece has to be understood in the light of its
growing conflict with the Soviet Union in Eastern Europe and the Middle East.
The Middle East had for centuries been dominated by the Ottoman Empire.
After the First World War, it was largely divided between Great Britain and
France. Maintaining ongoing control of oil resources and the security of the Suez
Canal were the principal preoccupations of the British. Directly or indirectly
Britain dominated Egypt, Iraq, Palestine, Jordan, Iran, and the Persian Gulf
states. France held most of North Africa as well as Syria and Lebanon. To the
north lay Russia, which historically had sought access to the Mediterranean

through the Turkish Straits as well as a sphere of influence along its southern frontiers. Great Britain and Russia had repeatedly clashed over their rival ambitions in the region.

U.S. interest in the Middle East began to emerge in the interwar period. The growing involvement of the United States in the area was, in fact, dictated by the region's oil wealth. In reaction to British domination over world petroleum markets, U.S. oil companies began to prospect for oil in Saudi Arabia during the 1930s. In the course of the Second World War, the Saudi monarchy entered into an exclusive economic and political relationship with the United States as a counter to British control over the surrounding Arab states. By the end of the war, the stakes had become enormous. Half of global oil production was concentrated in the Middle East. State Department planners envisioned postwar expansion of U.S. interests into the oil fields of the Persian Gulf and Iran.

It turned out that Saudi Arabia in particular had the world's largest oil reserves. Indeed, it was from Saudi Arabia and the other oil-producing states of the Middle East that the bulk of new petroleum supplies for the postwar global market would come. In subsequent decades, oil's relative cheapness led to the rapid conversion of the industrialized economies in Europe and Asia from coal to oil. Control of this strategic commodity by the the United States was to prove critical to their dominance over the postwar global economy. Politically, the U.S. goal came to be to reduce or eliminate British and French influence in the Middle East, while increasing its own.

The Russians in the immediate postwar period believed that the inter-imperialist rivalry between the United States and Great Britain would enable them to increase their own influence over the region. They did not take account sufficiently the weakness of the British and their growing dependence on the the United States. The resulting eclipse of British imperialism facilitated the United States assuming a dominant role. An essential element in justifying this expanding U.S. influence involved the pretext of containing Russian or communist influence.

In the first decades of the twentieth century, Iran had been the victim of Czarist Russian and, especially, British imperialism. Following the First world War, the British largely dominated the country, just as they controlled neighboring Iraq. The Anglo-Iranian oil company acquired exclusive rights to Iranian oil. As a counter to British influence in Iran, the Shah Reza Khan Pahlavi more and more assumed a pro-German posture in the 1930s. At the beginning of the Second World War, he refused to allow British military supplies to the Soviets to transit Iranian territory. In August 1941 British and Soviet troops invaded the country. Reza Khan Pahlavi was removed and his young son Mohammed Reza Pahlavi was made Shah. U.S. troops later joined their Soviet and British counterparts in occupation of Iran. Toward the end of the war, Washington was able to acquire oil concessions from the Iranian government. In response, the Soviets, likewise, demanded concessions while backing Kurdish and Azeri separatists in the north of Iran. The U.S. and British governments withdrew their troops at the beginning of March 1946 and demanded the Soviets do likewise. The Red Army was forced out, the separatists quashed, and the Soviet bid for oil concessions refused. U.S. defense of Iranian territorial integrity greatly reinforced their influence in the country at the expense of the USSR and Great Britain. Monarchist politicians looked to the United States to reorganize and equip the Iranian police and army and to plan the development of Iran's oil economy. The United States was well on its way to overshadowing British influence in Iran and elsewhere in the Middle East. Opposition to Russia proved an effective lever in pursuit of this goal.

The new U.S. strategic role was demonstrated in the Turkish crisis, which developed in the immediate wake of the Iranian imbroglio. Here, too, the British had traditionally opposed free Russian access to the Mediterranean through the straits of the Dardanelles. In August 1946 the Soviets sent Turkey a note calling for joint Soviet-Turkish control of the Turkish Straits. The Soviets, in fact, had advanced this idea in one form or another since 1943. The U.S. ambassador cabled Washington that the latest Soviet note was a pretext for full-scale Soviet domination over Turkey. Washington policy makers interpreted the demands of the Soviet Union with regard to Turkey in the light of recently acquired Soviet dominance over Bulgaria and Romania in the Balkans. Washington believed that the Soviet ambition was to control the entire eastern Mediterranean region. The U.S. State, War, and Navy Departments advised Truman to resist the Soviets by force of arms if necessary. On August 15, 1946, Truman ordered all of the destroyers of the U.S. Twelfth Fleet into the Mediterranean. At the end of September the U.S. President committed to creating a permanent fleet in the Mediterranean. Ultimately this became the nucleus of the U.S. Sixth Fleet, which dominates the Mediterranean to this day. The strong U.S. reaction caused the Soviets to back down. Success in Iran and Turkey were part of the process that made the containment of Soviet ambitions the rationale for the emergence of Washington's sphere of influence in the Middle East.

In this overall geopolitical context, U.S. intervention in Greece—stepping stone to the Middle East—was the next logical step. At the beginning of 1947, the British informed Washington that they could no longer meet their responsibilities toward the Greek government in its fight against the Communist insurgents. In March Truman asked the U.S. Congress for $400 million in aid to Greece and Turkey. In his request, which was greeted with appropriate fanfare in the U.S. media, Truman asserted that the existence of the Greek state was threatened by the terrorist activities of several thousand armed men led by Communists. More significantly, he made it clear that the United States in the future would assist free peoples threatened by armed internal minorities or external pressures. The Truman Doctrine was meant to be an essential corollary to the containment policy outlined by Kennan a year earlier. U.S. intervention against revolutions and national liberation movements on a global scale would be based on implementation of this doctrine.

A massive flow of U.S. economic and military aid to the Greek government followed immediately. The Greek army was expanded to more than a quarter million men backed up by U.S. military advisers, at a cost of half a billion dollars. This U.S. effort determined the outcome. Greece became a dependency of the United States, henceforth, providing naval bases for the Sixth Fleet. Soviet aid might have changed the outcome, but Stalin refused to offer such support. In a meeting with the Bulgarians and Yugoslavs in February 1948, Stalin reiterated that Greece lay in the Western sphere of influence control, which the Soviets were unable to challenge. He also ordered the Bulgarians and Yugoslavs to suspend their aid to the insurgents. One of the consequences of Stalin's realpolitik was to be the Yugoslav exit from the Soviet camp.

The Fate of Japan

The influence of the Unites States grew in Western Europe and, increasingly, pervaded the Middle East at the expense of Britain and the Soviet Union. In the Pacific its dominance at the end of the war was already unrivalled. Japan, its only serious competitor in Asia, was now under direct U.S. military occupation. Despite political agreements to the contrary, the Supreme Allied Commander, General Douglas MacArthur, in practice ignored wartime allies like Great Britain, Canada, and Australia in the administration of Japan. U.S. policy makers, accordingly, were free to plan and control the future of the only country in Asia with a modern industrial base. Reformed according to their specifications, Japan along with Germany was seen as key to the establishment of a postwar global trading and political order dominated by the United States.

It was concluded even prior to the end of the war that the traditional social structure of Japan should be reformed not abolished. Japanese imperialism and militarism had been the product of a political and social system dominated by the Emperor, the military establishment, monopolistic corporations, and conservative landlords. Reform but not revolution was necessary. The Emperor, stripped of his divine aura, was to be retained as a symbol of social order. The military was dissolved and thousands of war criminals brought to trial. It was then envisaged that economic monopolies were to be curbed and land reform introduced. Democratic government was to be introduced alongside the protection of civil liberties and trade union rights.

MacArthur exercised control over Japan through the so-called Supreme Command for the Allied Powers (SCAP). Verbally, he was committed to introducing democracy as understood in the United States. But vain and imperious, MacArthur had spent his life as a career army officer with little tolerance for democratic self-expression. He paid lip service to political liberty and trade union freedom, but their actual exercise made him bristle with impatience. His instincts were quite to the contrary of democratic. SCAP itself was divided between New Deal liberals and conservatives. As U.S. policy moved to the right, more and more liberals were forced out or resigned. MacArthur's lieutenant, the Director of SCAP's Public Safety Division, General Charles Andrew Willoughby, not only opposed the liberals, but also kept them and Japanese leftists under close surveillance.

As a result of U.S. bombing and blockade, the Japanese economy was in ruins. Many cities were nearly destroyed and much of their populations remained without a roof over their heads. Millions of Japanese soldiers and civilians had to be repatriated from overseas. Factories were wrecked or otherwise inoperative and many workers left unemployed. Farmers withheld their crops, inflation soared, and the black market flourished. Two years after the end of the war, industrial production had reached only 45 percent, exports only 10 percent, and imports only 30 percent of the 1930–34 level. The possibility of starvation stalked the land. Economic hardship and scarcity continued until at least 1950.

Prior to 1945 the authoritarian nature of Japanese society had limited popular unrest. In the nineteenth century there had been only scattered peasant protest. Disturbed conditions in the wake of the First World War had led to the so-called

Rice Riots of 1919, the first outbreak of major social if not political discontent in modern times. But in 1945 Japan found itself in a political vacuum. It had been defeated in war and was under military occupation. The old political and military elite had been discredited. Indeed, at first the U.S. occupation authorities sanctioned political demonstrations and the notion of trade union rights. Social and political unrest boiled over as Japan experienced major politically inspired protest for the first time. Fuelled by economic hardship, the postwar years were marked by wave after wave of strikes, factory occupations, mass demonstrations, and riots.

The union movement under Communist and Socialist leadership achieved unprecedented influence. Within a year of the end of the war, major strikes and demonstrations had broken out. Recurrent general strikes in succeeding years culminated in a tidal wave of protest in June 1949. On the political front, the left-wing parties in the immediate postwar months had little presence outside the cities. As a result, the first postwar election in 1946 saw only limited gains by the left. But by the next year voting in parliamentary elections gave the Socialists a substantial plurality. Social unrest and left-wing political mobilization unsettled the control of the political elite, landlords, and monopoly business.

Containing the left in Japan became a major preoccupation of the U.S. occupation. House-breaking the unions, as it was called, was considered essential to the overall task of restoring the Japanese economy. By 1947 the goal of rebuilding the Japanese economy came to be perceived not only as urgent in itself, but as part of the more general one of reconstructing the capitalist economy both in Europe and Asia. Japan would have to become a self-supporting part of a global trading structure, if the United States was ever to be freed from spending $300 million annually to make up the Japanese trade deficit. The key to achieving Japan's economic viability was a revival of industry and the restoration of its export potential.

Land reform was itself an important step in that direction. Prior to the Second World War tensions between industrialists and the landlord and military elites had divided the ruling classes. The landlords and military resisted the encroachment of the new industrialists on their traditional prestige and privileges. As in Germany, landlords and military men were particularly attracted to reactionary and anticapitalist ideologies. Capitalist industry remained subordinated within a larger political project of fascism at home and imperialist expansion abroad.

Japan's defeat discredited the traditional classes. SCAP's land reform of 1946 then provided the means for two million peasants, three-quarters of them tenant farmers, to acquire the land they worked. The land reform was bitterly resisted by the ruling Liberal Party and its prime minister, Shigera Yoshida. But they then turned around and took credit for it. Indeed, the popularity of the agrarian reform ironically guaranteed the role of the Liberals as the dominant party in Japanese politics throughout the postwar period. As in Germany, landlord control in the countryside and influence over national political life came to an end. By the close of the 1950s, only 12 percent of arable land in Japan was leased. The dominance of industrial capitalism in postwar Japan was assured.

Agrarian reform still left open the question of the ultimate character of this Japanese form of capitalism. Industry historically was controlled by family monopolies, which themselves were rooted in a section of the landed feudal class. The ten largest of these so-called *zaibatsu,* including Mitsui, Mitsubishi, Yosudo, and Somitomo, directly and indirectly controlled 90 percent of Japanese industry. SCAP's initial view was that these monopolists, alongside the military and landlords, were an integral part of the militarist and imperialist system. Based on U.S. antitrust experience, SCAP called for the break-up of these monopolies and the establishment of a competitive capitalist economy. Such a policy would have required the virtual creation of a new class of middle and small-scale manufacturers.

A review board of interested U.S. business executives, appointed by Assistant Secretary of War William H. Draper, urged a change of course in 1947. The option of industrial deconcentration was abandoned in favor of a speedy revival of the Japanese economy. A task force headed by Draper, a Wall Street investment banker, then recommended an economic package based on spurring export-orientated industry through curbing inflation, reducing imports, keeping wages in check, and stabilizing foreign exchange. At the end of 1948, John Dodge, a conservative Detroit banker, arrived in Japan to implement this SCAP stabilization plan.

Dodge and his superiors dismissed democratic reforms, including trade union rights, as obstacles to rapid economic revival. Such a change, of course, was in part dictated by the deepening of the Cold War worldwide. With the future of the U.S.-backed Nationalist government in China increasingly in doubt, the revival of Japan as the economic bastion of Asia was seen as a priority. Crackdowns on the Japanese unions were initiated in 1947 in parallel to similar repression of organized labor in the countries of Western Europe, the United States, and Latin America. In August 1948 MacArthur ordered the unions to cancel plans for a general strike. Government employees were stripped of the right to strike. To enforce austerity on workers, the United States encouraged the creation of a national police force at the end of 1948. This became the nucleus for the emergence of the Japanese defense forces and later remilitarization.

The austerity program of Dodge, far from stimulating economic growth, dramatically reduced investment, industrial production, and wages. Workers responded with a storm of strikes and mass demonstrations in June 1949. U.S. troops assisted the Japanese police in repressing these protests. SCAP insisted that the Japanese government purge thousands of Communist teachers from the public schools. It sponsored "democratization leagues" in the unions to curb trade union militancy. These became the basis of a new company-dominated union movement that accepted Dodge's austerity program. Purges and unemployment led union membership to fall from 7 million at the end of 1948 to 3.3 million in 1950.

The membership and influence of the Communist Party grew, temporarily, as militants deserted the too compliant Socialists. In the election of January 1949 the Party received 10 percent of the vote. The party's view was that it could take power by democratic means even under the U.S. occupation. MacArthur responded by ordering the purging from public life of 21,000 subversives. The back of Communist influence was broken. The outbreak of the Korean War in June 1950 set off a tremendous boom that continued through the next decade and beyond. Meanwhile the precedent of crushing the unions and the left had created the industrial flexibility that made possible what later came to be called the Japanese economic miracle. The ultimate efficacy of the Dodge economic austerity program was never tested.

The Cold War Deepens: 1947–1950

With the Truman Doctrine, Marshall Plan, and crackdown on Japanese dissent, 1947 proved a watershed in the emerging Cold War. The United States moved decisively to place itself at the center of world events. The announcement of the Truman Doctrine in March committed the U.S. government to global intervention in the name of Soviet containment. The revival of the Japanese economy was made the key to U.S. plans for integrating Asia into the world market. At the same time, the proclamation of the Marshall Plan signaled the U.S. intention to revive the German economy as the pivot of an integrated West European economy. West Germany would serve as the axis of an integrated Western Europe, which would isolate and contain the Soviet Union. In reaction, the Soviet Union proceeded to the full Stalinization of its sphere of influence in Eastern Europe.

The Division of Germany

As early as 1946, there were signs pointing to the future division of Germany. Failure to agree on reparations by the occupying powers soon led to the suspension of reparation payments from the West to the Soviet Union. The French were allowed to consolidate a separate administration of their zone of Germany. In the Russian zone the popular Socialist Party was pressured into a marriage with the Communist Party. But political pluralism in East Germany was still intact in 1946. True, an agrarian reform dispossessed the historic Junker landlord class, but the the United States at that very moment was doing the same to the landlords in Japan. Some industries owned by Nazis in East Germany were seized. Others were abandoned by their owners. The Communist-dominated Free German Trade Union Federation acquired extraordinary powers. But no irrevocable step toward the division of Germany had yet been taken by the Soviets.

At the start of 1947, however, British economic weakness and the continued stagnation of the West German economy led to the merger of the British and U.S. zones of Germany, henceforth known as Bizonia (for bi-zone). Lucius Clay, the U.S. military governor, argued that this act would ultimately force the Russians and French to cooperate in reviving the German economy. In fact, the creation of Bizonia became part of a larger scheme to transform the West German economy into the locomotive of an integrated Western European economy open to U.S. exports and investment.

In West Germany, as in the East, the Socialists were the most popular party. Their leader, Kurt Schumacker, favored a socialist alternative for Germany and the rest of Europe, which would be neither communist nor capitalist. He demanded nationalizations and fundamental political reforms that would purge remaining Nazi influence. The United States felt more comfortable with Konrad Adenauer, head of the middle-class Christian Democratic Party. Prior to the war Adenauer had been mayor of Cologne and a banker with ties to U.S. business. Soviet occupation of East Germany in 1945 led him to the conclusion that Germany would be permanently divided. In response he advocated the integra-

tion of West Germany with the rest of Western Europe. His views accorded with
what by 1947 came to be the dominant opinion of U.S. policy makers.

The the United States initially did carry out anti-Nazi purges that affected
some 300,000 Germans, mainly from the upper and middle class. But they soon
realized that purging so many influential former Nazis was in conflict with the
goal of creating a stable social order. In March 1946 the matter was turned over
to local authorities that subsequently failed to pursue the matter seriously. The
question of deconcentration of industry and banking was settled in a similar fashion. As in Japan, these dominant sectors of the economy were highly monopolistic and had been closely linked to the fascist regime. The original mandate of the
Occupation had been the dismantling of these monopolies. But those who
administered the U.S. zone in Germany, including William Draper, were themselves business leaders or close to them. As a result, the policy of deconcentration
was never carried out.

The Marshall Plan

The integration of West Germany into Western Europe began with the announcement of the European Recovery Program or Marshall Plan in June 1947. From
the U.S. perspective, it was important that the West European economies and,
especially, that of West Germany revive as quickly as possible. But they should do
so as part of a broader international system tied to the United States. In the immediate postwar period, the European states lacked the dollars to buy U.S. goods.
The generous loans made by the United States to the Europeans in the immediate postwar had not solved the problem. The so-called dollar gap was made worse
over time by the compound interest on these loans. In order to reserve precious
foreign exchange for essential imports, the European states closely controlled
external trade and often resorted to bilateral barter arrangements. The danger was
that such arrangements could become permanent. The consequence might be
that the United States might be left commercially isolated with its vast and unsalable surpluses.

As an alternative, the Europeans states would be given, not loans, but grants to
buy U.S. goods. Under joint European and U.S. administration, the Marshall
Plan would disperse some $13 billion over the next four years. States which
received grants under the Plan had to agree to take steps to establish internal fiscal stability, to ensure lower trade barriers, and to join what became the

antecedent of the Organization for European Economic Cooperation (OEEC). As part of this design, the West German economy was given special priority.

It is doubtful that the Marshall Plan by itself led to the European economic revival that began in 1950. In fact, the austerity programs that were part of the Plan deepened a deflation that had begun in 1949 and that was only overcome as a result of the Korean War. It was military spending which ultimately reignited both the West European and Japanese economies at the beginning of the 1950s. Nonetheless, the Marshall Plan must be considered a brilliant success for the United States. Austerity measures, backed up by repression at the national level, beat down inflation and the political and economic expectations of labor and the left, fostered profitability, and bolstered confidence in the future of European capitalism. The framework of business in Western Europe was enlarged beyond each nation-state. The subsequent creation of the European Payments Union (1950) allowed the settlement of credits and debts among the West European states on a multilateral rather than a bilateral basis. Above all, the continent was kept open to the export of U.S. goods and, ultimately, investment capital. West European fears of Germany were calmed, if not resolved, by its economic integration with the rest of Western Europe. The Soviet Union, meanwhile, was left isolated, confined within its Eastern European sphere of influence.

Stalinization

Europe as a whole was effectively split in two by the division of Germany and the Marshall Plan. Indeed, the proclamation of the Truman Doctrine and the implementation of the Marshall Plan had serious repercussions in Eastern Europe. Half-heartedly invited to join the European Recovery Program, the Soviet foreign minister, Vyacheslav Molotov, spurned the offer at the Paris Foreign Ministers Conference in late June 1947. The proposed U.S. supervision of the process of European recovery was completely unacceptable. In addition, the breakdown of inter-allied cooperation over Germany and the prospect of a revival of German power provoked Soviet indignation. By fall 1947 the Soviets were advancing their own plans for the coordination of the economies of the Eastern bloc countries under their control. Simultaneously, they announced the revival of the old Communist International in the form of the so-called Cominform.

Until this point coalitions or so-called popular fronts had been used to build Communist influence in the states of Eastern Europe. Depending on the state, varying degrees of political pluralism had been permitted. But at the first meeting of the Cominform in September 1947, the Yugoslav Communists took the lead in calling for a strengthening of Communist control over these coalitions. In East Germany, the autumn of 1947 saw the introduction of centralized state planning and the emergence of the People's Congress as the predominant political institution. Elsewhere in Eastern Europe, the arrest of opposition leaders, show trials, rigged elections, the nationalization of banks and industries, and the imposition of central planning heralded the arrival of full Stalinization. The virtually simultaneous ouster of Communists from government in Italy, France, Belgium, and Luxembourg—and the breaking of general strikes in Italy and France—prompted the Eastern European Communists to abandon whatever restraints they may have previously felt in implementing this process.

The Communist seizure of power was particularly notable in Czechoslovakia, a developed country with a substantial working class. From 1945 the Communist Party had predominated in a coalition made up of four other parties. As a result of this coalition, a mixed economy with links to both East and West had emerged. While maintaining ties to the West, Czech foreign policy was based on alliance with the Soviet Union. The Soviet Union guaranteed the postwar settlement that had seen the expulsion of millions of Germans from Czech territories. The institution of the Marshall Plan undermined the foundations of coalition rule.

While not committing itself, the Czech government at first sought to take part in procedural discussions regarding the European Recovery Program. Stalin categorically vetoed any such participation. In the fall of 1947, the Soviets introduced measures that tied Czech exports and imports to the Soviet Union. The Communist members of the coalition government called for more nationalizations and the equalization of income. The mounting distrust between members of the coalition was signaled by accusations of treachery and an open struggle to control the police and the ministry of the interior. On February 20, 1948, the centrist members of the coalition resigned in order to create a crisis over the question of control of the internal security apparatus. The Communists armed the representatives of the workers' councils who organized mass rallies. The new government, although nominally a coalition which included Socialists and left-wing National Socialists and Liberals, was effectively under Communist and Soviet control. There seems no doubt that powerful political undercurrents in Czechoslovakia were at work moving toward a Communist takeover. But these forces were finally unleashed by Stalin's veto of deeper Czech contact with the

West. Above all, the fate of Czechoslovakia in early 1948 was the consequence of the final division of Europe into two camps.

By then the development of planned socialist economies in the other states of Eastern Europe was well under way. The sweeping nature of these transformations needs to be emphasized. Socially, Eastern Europe had been dominated by landlords and an established church. Economically, the region had been subordinated to Germany, and other advanced capitalist countries. These countries exploited Eastern Europe as a source of food and other primary products. Such banks and industries that did exist were dominated by Central and West European capital. The economic stagnation of the Depression and the devastation of the Second World War had deeply wounded the still largely peasant population.

In the immediate wake of the war, the idea of radical change and a clean slate appealed to the younger generation and certain elements of the intelligentsia in Eastern Europe. Change came first in the form of massive land reform between 1944 and 1952 in Poland, Hungary, Romania, Czechoslovakia, and East Germany. The seizure initially of large amounts of land from the German ethnic minority in Poland, Czechoslovakia, and Romania had wide appeal among the rural population. The landlords were eventually wiped out. The established church lost its holdings as well. Many landless or poor peasants acquired land. Collectivization of agriculture was a much more prolonged and uneven process continuing into the early 1960s. Mass nationalizations and the institution of central planning began as early as 1946 in revolutionary Yugoslavia and Albania. The process got underway in the following year or so elsewhere. Radical centralization of the economy entailed the breaking of links with the West. The subsistence livelihood of peasants and workers undoubtedly improved and unprecedented educational and employment opportunities for young boys and girls of the underclasses began to open up. Economic activity throughout the region by 1949 was higher than before the war and up to that point compares favorably to the situation in the postwar Western European countries. In the light of the historic dependence of this region on the West and its resultant economic backwardness, these were important initiatives for the better.

As these gains were being registered, the negative effect of Stalinism began to make itself felt. The sweeping nationalization of the whole economy, one party rule, central planning, as well as the beginning of rural collectivization were accompanied by coercion and repression which were at their worst between 1949 and 1953. Harsh political rule was justified in part by the economic need to curtail consumption in favor of massive investment in heavy industry. But fears of nationalist and other deviations clearly were also behind the purges of the Hungarian foreign minister László Rajko, the former head of the Bulgarian Communist Party Traicho Kostov, and Party chiefs Wladslaw Gomulka of Poland and Rudolf Slansky of Czechoslovakia. These were but the tip of the iceberg of a massive crackdown that entailed the arrest, imprisonment, and execution of members of the clergy, bourgeoisie, intellectuals, peasants, and workers in the thousands. In Eastern Europe, terror imposed from the top went hand-in-hand with economic and social transformation.

The Yugoslav Schism

As these events were playing themselves out elsewhere in Eastern Europe, Yugoslavia refused to accept Soviet dictates. Because the Soviet army had briefly passed through the north of Yugoslavia, Western political and military interference had accordingly been excluded after the war. But Yugoslavia had for all practical purposes liberated itself and carried through a revolution. Unlike most of the rest of Eastern Europe, this was not a largely top down affair but a popular revolution. Still, loyalty to the Soviet Union was a fundamental axiom of Tito's regime in the immediate postwar period. The Yugoslavs were given a leading role in the organization of the Soviet dominated Cominform in 1947 and pressed for complete Communist Party control in other Eastern European states. Stalin, nonetheless, was increasingly irritated by Tito's independent course. Yugoslav plans for a Balkan Federation were disturbing. More alarming was Tito's unstinting support for the Greek Communists, which threatened to embroil the Soviet Union in war. Soviet attempts to mesh the Yugoslav economy with its own were increasingly rebuffed. In particular, Tito's planners believed that Yugoslavia would do better to market its important non-ferrous metal deposits in the West rather than in the Soviet Union.

In March 1948 the Soviets withdrew all of their technicians and advisors from the country and attempted to incite pro-Russian elements within the Yugoslav Communist party led by Andrija Hebrang. Mobilizing his supporters, Tito crushed the pro-Stalinist faction, while imprisoning thousands of Hebrang's followers. By June the Cominform expelled the Yugoslav Party from its midst as an instrument of Western imperialism. Tito's response to the psychological pressure, economic boycott, and military threats was two-fold. Professing continued loyalty to Marxist ideology, he collectivized agriculture and bolshevized the structure of the Yugoslav Communist Party. On the other hand, in July 1949 he regretfully signed a trade agreement with the United States and ended his support for the struggling Communist insurgents in Greece. Within two years Washington was shipping military equipment to Yugoslavia to bolster its armed forces. While criticizing Soviet bureaucracy from the left, Yugoslavia began to experiment with so-called workers' control of industry, stepped back from the collectivization of agriculture, and carved out an independent foreign policy based on non-alignment.

The Creation of the Federal Republic of Germany and NATO

The Yugoslav exit from the Soviet camp was greeted as an unexpected boon by the United States. The Communist consolidation of power in Czechoslovakia also served Washington's purposes in the developing Cold War. Marshall Plan aid had already begun to soften Paris's opposition to the reintegration of Germany in Europe. The Czech events heightened anti-Soviet feelings in the French capital. As a result, by May 1948 the French agreed to merge the French zone of Germany with Bizonia and to allow the issuing of a common currency throughout West Germany.

The new currency was conceived as the foundation of a West German state. The introduction of this new currency into the U.S., British, and French occupation zones of Berlin provoked the well-known Soviet blockade of the city. The U.S. response was a gigantic and dramatic airlift (1948–49) to break the Soviet siege of the city. The constitution of the new West German state was signed in Bonn in May 1949 in the wake of this crisis. Four months later the North Atlantic Treaty Organization (NATO) was born. Conceived as the complement to the European Recovery Program, this military alliance was clearly directed against the Soviet Union. But like the European Recovery Program, it was also designed to foster the integration of Western Europe under the aegis of the United States. Indeed, nervous European states like France and Belgium regarded U.S. participation as a guarantee against the revival of German power and militarism. NATO's first General Secretary, British Lord Ismay, noted that NATO was designed to "keep the Americans in, the Russians out, and the Germans down." But the price of this agreement clearly involved acceptance of permanent U.S. protection and the surrender of a certain degree of national independence in foreign affairs. In particular, it would be the United States that would determine the future posture of each member of the NATO alliance toward the Soviet Union.

The Chinese Revolution

The Soviet Union did not stand helplessly by in the face of these U.S. initiatives. The ongoing process of Stalinization ensured the loyalty of most of the Eastern European states to Moscow. In October 1949 the Soviets saw to the creation of the German Democratic Republic as a rival to the West German state. The Soviets meanwhile broke the U.S. monopoly on atomic weapons with the explosion of their own nuclear device in August 1949. The Cold War on the old continent was at a draw. But in Asia an entirely new and unexpected front opened with the triumph of the Chinese Communist revolution—an event whose significance transcends the framework of the Cold War.

At the end of the Second World War, China, potentially the largest market in Asia, appeared to have become a complete dependency of the United States. During the conflict, the United States gave its ally, the Nationalist government, $1.5 billion in economic and military aid. With the help of 50,000 U.S. marines, it helped the Nationalist leader Chiang Kai-shek reestablish control over most of China's cities in the immediate aftermath of the war. Subsequent deliveries of huge amounts of U.S. surplus military equipment and billions of dollars in economic aid were intended to bolster the Nationalist regime further. But such support proved to be of little avail against the insurgent Communist revolutionaries. Militarily and economically, the Nationalist government collapsed under the assaults of the Communist Red Army. In October 1949 the charismatic leader of the Communist movement, Mao Zedong, proclaimed the creation of the Peoples' Republic of China in Beijing. "The Chinese people have stood up," proclaimed the Communist leader.

For centuries Imperial China had been not only the leading state of East Asia, but the focal point of its civilization. In the nineteenth century, landlord oppression, high taxes, and Western imperialism progressively undermined the social and political foundations of the imperial government. The rural masses were impoverished by the oppression of landlords and rich peasants. Beginning with China's defeat in the Opium Wars in the mid-nineteenth century, the European powers occupied portions of Chinese territory. In the cities on the coasts and on the great inland rivers, the foreigners created trading concessions independent of Chinese political authority.

The prolonged and gigantic Taiping Rebellion (1850–1864) was the first major sign of peasant resistance. Displaced peasants then played a major role in the Boxer Rebellion (1900), a traditionalist uprising against the intrusion of Western imperialism. The decadent imperial government was finally overthrown by a revolution in 1911 led by the Nationalist or Kuomintang Party under Sun Yat-sen. Sun Yat-sen attempted to reorganize China according to the principles of liberal democracy. But recalcitrant landlords, rebellious army officers, and intrigues by the imperialists frustrated these somewhat unrealistic political aims. Feuding warlords or Chinese army generals supported by one or another of the imperialist powers divided the country and plunged China into anarchy in the period between 1911 and 1927. Peasant unrest intensified during the so-called warlord era.

In reaction to Japanese attempts to keep control of the important former German concession of Kiaochow, the May 4th Movement of 1919 engendered a modern nationalist ideology, especially among students, the intelligentsia, and an emergent middle class. But still more radical ideas found a receptive audience as well. Inspired by the anti-imperialist ideas of Lenin, the Chinese Communist Party was founded in Beijing in 1921 and allied with the Nationalists two years later. Indeed, Soviet advisers helped the Nationalists to reorganize their army and to launch the Great Northern Expedition (1923–27), which crushed the warlords and reunited China. Growing Communist influence among the peasantry and workers led to a sudden crackdown by Nationalist General Chiang Kai-shek. Allying himself with the secret societies and foreign concession holders in Shanghai, Chiang attacked the Communists in April 1927. Thousands of Communists were exterminated in Shanghai and the other main towns.

In the decade that followed, Chiang Kai-shek consolidated an authoritarian government supported by the landlords and the still small middle class. Landlord oppression and heavy taxation continued, but compared to the anarchy of the warlord period most of the peasantry experienced a decade of relative peace. Industrialization, which had begun in the 1920s, developed further, especially in the coastal cities. The most pressing problem was the Japanese military invasion and occupation of the rich coal and iron province of Manchuria in 1931. Largely helpless, the Nationalists stood by as Japanese military forces and businesses transformed Manchuria into a puppet state serving the economic needs of Japan.

Meanwhile, the persecuted remnants of the Communist Party took refuge in the countryside of south central China. Under the leadership of Mao Tse-tung, the Communists created a number of so-called rural Soviets, the largest of which

lay in the mountainous regions between Kiangsi and Fujian provinces. Their policies of land redistribution, enforced rent reductions, and curbs on usury led to
the growth of rural support and the development of the peasant-based Red Army.
Hemmed in by their Nationalist opponents, the Communists had to abandon
their Kiangsi Soviet in 1934. Fleeing encirclement, they began a yearlong, 6,000-
mile Long March to a new base area at Yenan in Shaanxi province in the remote
northeast. Of the original force of 90,000 that began the legendary Long March,
only 10,000 survived.

In 1936 Chiang Kai-shek was kidnapped and held captive by nationalist-
minded army officers at Sian. They demanded a united front of Nationalists and
Communists to fight the increasingly aggressive Japanese in northeast China.
Chiang was, at least nominally, forced to agree to a truce with the Communists for
the duration of hostilities. None to soon, because in 1937 Japan attacked and
occupied the east coast of mainland China, which included the principal cities.
The Nationalists were driven back deep into the interior, making Chunking on
the upper Yangzte their wartime capital. Holed up there, the Nationalist regime
waited out the war, anticipating a U.S. victory while preparing for an ultimate
showdown with the Communists. Cut off from its middle-class supporters in the
eastern cities, Chiang Kai-shek's wartime government was marked by military
inertia, corruption, and a growing dependence on conservative landlords.

The Communists used the war to carry on an active guerrilla campaign
against the Japanese, sharpening their military skills while establishing their
patriotism by payment in blood. From their base in Shaanxi, they expanded
their influence over much of northern China. Accommodating himself to what
was expedient during the united front with the Nationalists, Mao no longer
redistributed land but emphasized reductions in rent and progressive taxation.
By 1945 Communist Party membership had risen to 1.2 million. By then roughly a quarter of China's population, 120 million out of 500 million, were ruled by
the Communists. Hundreds of thousands of young peasants marched under the
banner of the Red Army.

Wartime mortality in China was particularly horrendous, with losses reaching
almost Soviet proportions. At war's end, the United States did all that it could to
allow the Chiang Kai-shek government to recover control. A U.S. airlift of
Nationalist troops from the interior and the presence of U.S. marines assisted the
reoccupation of coastal China. Japanese occupation troops were also enlisted to
make certain that the Nationalists regained control. Urban manufacturing and

commerce had experienced some damage. Indeed, Shanghai had suffered severe destruction—50 percent of its industry was destroyed. Yet most of the secondary sector survived the war and even expanded overall under Japanese occupation. In the meantime, the armies of the Soviet Union entered Manchuria in the closing days of the war. While recognizing the Nationalist government, the Soviets allowed the Chinese Red Army under Lin Piao to expand its influence by occupying the Manchurian hinterland.

Sensing the strength of the Communists, Washington sent General George Marshall to negotiate a compromise between the two sides. But neither the Communists nor the Nationalists were interested. By November 1946 talks between the two parties had collapsed. Nationalist forces immediately advanced into northern China and Manchuria. The Nationalists focused on controlling the cities and the main lines of communication. The government troops were soon overextended and vulnerable to Communist forces entrenched in the villages and increasingly surrounding and isolating the urban areas.

By late 1947 the Communist forces shifted from guerrilla tactics to positional warfare. They drove the Nationalists from Manchuria and then out of northern China. Nationalist armies refused battle and fled in disorder. Whole divisions abandoned or surrendered their U.S. military equipment, which fell into Red Army hands. As the Communists advanced, they decreed the redistribution of the land, calling the young men to the colors to defend against the return of the landlords. Hyperinflation and corruption destroyed the economic and political bases of Nationalist rule and by April 1949 the Communists had crossed the Yangtze, the great river that was the gateway to the south of China. Shanghai fell in May and Canton in October. Chiang Kai-shek fled to Taiwan with some two million troops and civilian supporters. The First World War had produced the momentous Bolshevik Revolution. The Second World War had now issued in the possibly even more epochal Chinese Revolution.

War in Korea and Its Political and Economic Consequences

The successful Communist revolution in China had an immediate and deep impact on neighboring Korea. The Korean state had emerged as a unified monarchy around the year 1000 A.D. Its mandarin elite reflected the country's ongoing cultural and political dependence on imperial China. As in China, the mandarins were recruited from the landlords who dominated a peasantry crippled by oppressive rents and usury. Following the expulsion of the Japanese in 1590, the regime maintained a policy of deliberate isolation from foreign influence that lasted for four centuries. Toward the end of the nineteenth century, the intrusion of the imperialist powers made isolation untenable. The Japanese made Korea a protectorate following their defeat of first the Chinese (1894–1895) and then the Russians (1904–05). In 1910 Korea was annexed to Japan and governed, henceforth, as a colony. A Japanese bureaucracy, which by the 1940s totaled some 700,000 functionaries, replaced the traditional Korean mandarins.

While imperialism generally led to economic underdevelopment in the European colonies, the Japanese treated Korea differently, if no less cruelly. Under Japanese control the Korean economy expanded impressively in the first part of the twentieth century. The growth of the manufacturing sector in the north of the Korean peninsula was especially noteworthy. At the same time, most landlords remained traditionalists and the peasantry remained among the poorest and most oppressed on earth. Subordinate to the Japanese, a Korean middle class began to emerge, especially in sectors like textiles, banking, and newspaper publishing.

Anticipating the May 4th Movement in China, in March 1919 mass rallies against Japanese imperialism swept Korea. Severely persecuted by the Japanese, the student leaders of the movement went into exile in China and the Soviet Union. It was among these elements that many Communist and Nationalist resistance groups formed. The Korean Communist Party was created in 1925. Among the notable nationalist groups was the Korean Provisional Government, one of whose members was Syngman Rhee, the future President of the southern-based postwar Republic of Korea.

Following the Japanese invasion of Manchuria in 1931, a strong guerrilla movement emerged in the borderlands between Korea and Manchuria. These insurgents included Chinese fighters and as many as 200,000 Korean guerrillas. The modern military elite of the North Korean state traces its roots to this movement. Among its outstanding leaders was Kim Il Sung, the future head of the Democratic People's Republic. Violent Japanese counter-insurgency ultimately suppressed this insurgency.

During the Second World War the Japanese Empire experienced a serious labor shortage. Thousands of Koreans were enlisted as part of the Japanese army, police, and bureaucracy. Millions of others were essentially forced into wage labor in mines and factories in northern Korea, but also in Manchuria and Japan. At the end of the war, many of these uprooted workers sought to return to their towns and villages.

The sudden end of the war in August 1945 set off a popular revolution. In towns and villages across Korea the underground resistance surfaced in the form of a gigantic mass movement of people's committees made up of students, intellectuals, workers, and peasants. Politically left in orientation for the most part, such committees were mainly composed of Socialists, radical Christians, Communists, radical democrats, and left-wing nationalists. Seizing local government from the Japanese and their Korean collaborators, they demanded the restoration of Korean independence and an as yet undefined socialist transformation. In Seoul, the Korean capital, the national leadership of the popular movement proclaimed the establishment of the People's Republic of Korea.

Meanwhile as the war ended the U.S. and Soviet Union agreed to a trusteeship whose terms called for allied military occupation. Korea would be administratively divided with the the United States in control south of the thirty-eighth parallel and the Soviets north of it. When the U.S. occupation forces under General John Reed Hodge arrived in southern Korea in early September 1945, they set about bringing the popular movement to heel. Most Koreans in the south were meanwhile incensed by what they considered to be a reoccupation, the more so as the the United States used the despised Japanese troops and their Korean collaborators to suppress the people's committees. As an alternative to the Korean People's Republic, the U.S. occupiers backed the Korean Democratic Party made up of landlords, business owners, and former collaborators. In October 1945 the right-wing nationalist Syngman Rhee was brought back from exile in the United States by Washington to serve as the leader of conservative forces in the south. Using a hastily formed national police force, the U.S. occupation authorities reestablished conservative control over local government and seized property that had been expropriated by workers and peasants.

Striking parallels exist in the evolution of U.S. policy with respect to Korea and Germany. In both cases the partition of the country was seen to be the preferred solution in dealing with the Communist threat. By 1947, Secretary of State Marshall and Assistant War Secretary Draper looked toward the formation of a separate South Korean state that would link its economy to that of a reviving Japan. In May 1948, a United Nations commission controlled by the United States supervised elections in the south. The left and, indeed, much of the center boycotted the election. As a result, the backers of Rhee and the extreme right won an overwhelming victory. The national assembly then proceeded to elect Syngman Rhee first president of the Republic of Korea.

The Soviet occupiers in the north, meanwhile, at first allowed the thousands of people's committees to establish effective control over local administration. In February 1946 this changed, as Kim Il Sung became head of an Interim People's Committee that became a defacto central government. The next month a comprehensive land reform dispossessed all landlords without compensation. Some 700,000 landlords, bourgeoisie, and wartime collaborators fled southward, reinforcing right-wing elements in South Korea. By August the Communists were in control of political life in the north and by fall an army was being formed. By 1947 industry was nationalized and a two-year central plan instituted. The Democratic People's Republic was proclaimed on September 9, 1948, three weeks after the creation of the Republic of Korea in the south. At the end of 1948 the Soviet army withdrew.

Opposition to the continuing U.S. occupation and the Rhee government was ongoing in the south until the eve of the Korean War. Following the suppression of the Korean People's Republic by the the United States, widespread strikes, mass demonstrations, rebellions, and, finally, large-scale guerilla movements continued at the grassroots. Much of the unrest occurred in the extreme south of the peninsula, well away from the thirty-eighth parallel separating the two states. In 1949 tensions rose along the frontier itself.

It will be recalled that Koreans and Chinese had fought together as guerrillas against the Japanese occupation during the 1930s. The north of Korea then served as a rear area for Chinese Communist troops fighting the Nationalists in Manchuria in the initial phases of the Chinese Civil War. Korean volunteers had then participated in the liberation of China. In the fall of 1949 some 100,000 Koreans who had served as volunteers in the Chinese Red Army in the victorious struggle against the Nationalists returned home to a nationwide heroes welcome. The triumphant Chinese war of national liberation was an important inspiration to these veteran Korean fighters who infused a strongly Maoist tone into the Korean Communist Party and army on their return home. The Chinese Nationalists and their imperialist backers had been defeated through guerrilla and conventional war. Could not the Rhee government and the U.S. imperialists who had divided the country be dealt with similarly? It was this sentiment that played an important part in inspiring the North Korean attack on the south in June 1950.

Kim Il Sung did not recognize the permanent division of the country at the thirty-eighth parallel. Neither did Syngman Rhee. Rhee frequently spoke of

unleashing the South Korean army to liberate t...
1949, there were frequent armed clashes at the bord...
North Korean armies. Indeed, the the United States refus...
planes to Rhee for fear that he would launch an all-out attack...
evidence, likewise, suggests that the Soviets and Chinese tried to re...
itary ambitions of Kim Il-Sung and, while ultimately compelled to pro...
port for the struggle for Korean national liberation, did so reluctantly.

War began on June 25, 1950, with a Communist offensive across the thirty-eighth parallel. The South Korean army proved barely able to resist the steamroller Communist advance. Without U.S. intervention the war would have ended in a matter of weeks with a rapid Communist victory. Why did the the United States intervene to save the South Korean state thereby interpreting the North Korean attack as international aggression? The defense of South Korea, Washington decided, was indispensable to the maintenance of the U.S. position in East Asia. Strategically, the United States had suffered a major setback in losing control of China in 1949 as a result of the Nationalist collapse. With the fall of China, Japan was more than ever seen as critical to the future position of the United States in East Asia. Korea had long been viewed as a military and economic annex to Japan. Holding on to it, accordingly, was seen as imperative to keeping Japan in the U.S. camp. Maintaining a military and economic foothold in South Korea was also now a means of containing Communist China.

While the U.S. intervention in Korea must be considered in the wider context of the Chinese Communist Revolution, it should also be viewed as a riposte to the Soviet explosion of an atomic bomb in August 1949. U.S. foreign policy had assumed as a fundamental premise a continuing U.S. monopoly of atomic weapons. But research in the Soviet Union on nuclear weapons had begun as early as 1943. Wartime spying helped the Soviets solve some of the technical problems involved in producing a nuclear bomb. Especially important was the espionage of physicists Klaus Fuchs and Bruno Pontecorvo who worked in the British atomic weapons program, as well as Theodore Hall who was part of the U.S. Manhattan Project. A stepped-up program of nuclear research then led to the creation of a Soviet atomic weapon within four years of the end of the war. In the summer of 1949 U.S. faith in its continued exclusive monopoly over this decisive military weapon abruptly disappeared.

In the context of the Soviet explosion of an atomic weapon and the Chinese Revolution, the notion of military containment took on greater urgency. The cre-

represented an important first
ınd world communism by mil-
ıon of a Soviet atomic device,
) that the United States would
d despite warnings that such a

was part of a new global military
h was presented to the President in
Nitze, a former investment banker
tate Department, and Robert Lovett,
Secretary of Defense. According to
their ғ⌐ᵖ-   ƞe confronted globally by a long-term
military buildup capable oᵣ ⌐⌐   Soviet Union. In order to carry out this
policy, the two advisors called for a permanent psychological mobilization of the
U.S. population to fight the Cold War.

The apocalyptic and militaristic tone of NSC-68 was too much for some crit-
ics, including George Kennan, a key architect of the original containment policy.
But, in fact, it was a logical product of the development of the postwar national
security state and the increasingly alarmist mood within the United States. The
Red Scare, which had been underway since 1946, reached its climax following
the Soviet explosion of an atomic weapon and the triumph of the Chinese
Communist Revolution. The conviction of Alger Hiss, a senior State
Department official, for denying his contacts with Soviet spies in January 1950,
appeared to confirm allegations that the government was infiltrated with
Communists. The subsequent arrest of Klaus Fuchs in Great Britain and Julius
and Ethel Rosenberg in New York on charges of atomic espionage proved even
more sensational.

The Republicans in Congress seized on these events with a vengeance. Denied
control of the presidency since 1932, their bid to recover control of both the presidency and the Congress had been thwarted by the Truman electoral sweep of 1948. The
frustrated Republican leadership then tolerated, or even encouraged, the anticommunist fulminations of Senator Joe McCarthy of Wisconsin. Initiating his career of dem-
agoguery with a speech on February 9, 1950, at Wheeling, West Virginia, McCarthy
claimed that he had a list of 205 communists employed in the State Department. This
was the beginning of a four-year campaign of wild and unsubstantiated charges of trea-
son and subversion. However false McCarthy's charges were, to many Americans they

he north. From the summer of
er between the South and
d to supply tanks and
on the north. The
train the mil-
ıse sup-

rang true. In their ears they merely echoed the outcries of the anticommunist crusade underway in the United States since 1946. Running scared, influential Democratic politicians in the spring of 1950 informed Truman that something would have to be done to reestablish the image of the Democratic White House as the staunch opponent of communism both at home and abroad.

The resulting U.S. decision to intervene in what was, at root, a Korean civil war led to a three-year conflict that ravaged the peninsula. The Red Scare made it very difficult for people in the United States to question the motives behind Truman's decision to intervene. From a geopolitical perspective, the major feature of the war was the military confrontation between China and the United States. The the United States prevented the army of the Democratic Peoples Republic from overrunning the entire Korean peninsula by establishing a defense perimeter around Pusan in the extreme south in the summer of 1950. They then launched an amphibious invasion at Inchon near Seoul in October. Cut off, the Korean Communists forces were forced to melt into the countryside or retreat north of the thirty-eighth parallel. General MacArthur, the U.S. commander, convinced the White House to allow U.S. forces to reunify the peninsula by advancing to the Chinese border. In December 1950, 300,000 Chinese Red Army volunteers attacked the Americans, driving them back to a line below Seoul. The succeeding years saw a stalemate in which U.S. and South Korean forces were able to reestablish a position close to the original line of demarcation between North and South Korea at the thirty-eight parallel. Only 54,000 Americans died during the conflict, but three million Korean civilians and soldiers, mainly from the north, lost their lives. One million Chinese combatants also perished. The war confirmed and extended the U.S. policy of containing China. Not only would the United States commit itself to defend South Korea, but also Taiwan and Indochina further to the south.

Korea was devastated and permanently divided. What is surprising is that following the war both the North and South Korean states rapidly recovered. Indeed, the land reform introduced by the Communists during their short occupation of the South broke the back of landlord power and prepared the way for the rapid development of industrial capitalism in South Korea. Protective tariffs and monopoly at home and privileged access to the U.S. market abroad facilitated capital accumulation and rapid modernization in the South. Highly centralized and based on state planning, the North Korean economy also made rapid strides until the mid-1970s when it began to falter compared to its South Korean rival.

The Korean War also had the benefit of ending the economic doldrums of postwar Japan. The wartime U.S. military buildup in East Asia appears to have galvanized the Japanese economy, the war serving as an Asian Marshall Plan. The flexible and low-paid Japanese work force created by the postwar crushing of the unions was an indispensable precondition to its international economic success during the next three decades. Japan was favored as well by its just-in-time, quality control, and outsourcing production techniques; close cooperation between government, banks, and industry; protectionism at home; and privileged access to the U.S. markets.

The Korean War proved a tonic to the U.S. economy as well. Although perhaps not a deliberate policy, expenditure on the war helped end the recession that had begun in 1948 and initiated a period of exuberant expansion. Truman had drastically cut military spending at the end of the Second World War. He had relied on pent up consumer demand to sustain the economy. But neither consumer demand nor the European Recovery Program proved sufficient to avoid recession in 1948–49. Truman used the outbreak of the Korean War to bring about the permanent expansion of military expenditure that national security and economic managers had been urging on him for two years. At the height of the Korean conflict, more than 17 percent of U.S. GNP was generated through military spending. The average over the remaining years of the 1950s was around 10 percent. The other members of NATO followed Washington's lead. A kind of military Keynesianism took hold, which saw expenditure on the military as an acceptable way not only of stimulating the economy, but also of spurring scientific and technological innovation and even carrying on certain social programs. Indeed, U.S. military aid to foreign countries, direct U.S. military spending abroad, and the military expenditure of allied states provided the liquidity necessary for initiating global economic expansion in a way that the Marshall Plan did not.

2

Decolonization

By the early 1950s a new global architecture had emerged based on the Cold War. At the center of the capitalist world lay the United States with its powerful economy and armed forces. Across the oceans to the east and west were its two principal extensions, Western Europe and Japan. Meanwhile, standing opposed to the United States, the Soviet Union was completing its postwar reconstruction and consolidating its hold on the states of Eastern Europe. Further east on the mainland of Asia, revolutionary communism had sprouted in China and in the neighboring Democratic People's Republic of Korea. Based on this division between East and West, a Cold War settled in between the two camps in the course of the 1950s. Permanent political antagonism punctuated by localized military conflicts as in Greece and Korea characterized relations between the two sides. Both sought to avoid the outbreak of general war.

In between the two camps, major upheavals erupted in the third world. Rejecting the legacy of colonialism and imperialism, nationalists in Asia, the Near East, and Africa sought political independence from the European powers. In quest of national liberation, more radical third world leaders took things still further. They struggled to free their countries not only from political but also economic dependence on the West. Imperialism had sought access to the primary materials of the third world at the lowest possible cost, while looking for profitable market and investment opportunities. Radical nationalists in the newly independent states sought to raise the price of primary products, to use these products in state-directed economic development programs, and to restrict foreign imports and investments. This demand for economic autonomy threatened the United States, which needed access to foreign raw materials, markets, and investment opportunities. As a result, the United States became increasing entangled in the politics of Southeast Asia, the Middle East, and Africa. U.S involvement was spurred on by the Soviet Union's growing support of national liberation movements in these third world regions.

Postwar decolonization began in Asia and the Middle East. The Philippines (1946), India and Pakistan (1947), North and South Korea (1948), Burma (1948), Ceylon (1948), and Indonesia (1949) became politically sovereign in the immediate aftermath of the war. The 1950s saw the states of Indochina (Vietnam, Laos, and Cambodia) free themselves from French control. In the Middle East, the movement for independence began with the expulsion of the French from Syria in 1946. In North Africa, Libya (1951), Sudan (1956), and the French colonies of Morocco and Tunisia (1956) gained their political freedom. Meanwhile, national revolutions shook Egypt (1952) and Iraq (1958). In sub-Saharan Africa, the independence of Ghana (1957) and Guinea (1958) initiated the movement for political self-determination of the whole region. Most of the other states of Africa were decolonized in the early 1960s.

But such a bare chronicle of the dates marking the formal political independence of ex-colonies risks masking more deep-seated realities. Egypt, for example, supposedly was a politically independent nation already in 1922. But the fact is that it remained a British protectorate until the overthrow of the monarchy (1952) and the proclamation of a republic (1953). Iraq, likewise, was officially an independent kingdom since 1932. But only with the ouster of King Faisal II in a nationalist revolution (1958) did Iraq really free itself from British control. Likewise, certain struggles for political independence that were bitterly contested in the 1950s only reached fruition in the 1960s. Algeria and Kenya, for example, formally acceded to independence in 1962 and 1963 respectively, alongside a host of other French and British colonies. But these dates conceal the fact that throughout the previous decade insurgents in Algeria and Kenya fought bloody wars of national liberation against their colonial masters. The main obstacle to the independence of these two states was not so much the opposition of the colonial powers, but stubbornly resistant white settler populations who were determined to retain their privileged positions. The above examples suggest that formal independence, although not without its importance, was not the crux of the matter. Rather, it was the economic and political realities that underlay the granting of such independence that were determinative.

Imperialism

In the course of the eighteenth and nineteenth centuries, the merchants, bankers, and navies of the leading European states had come to dominate the upper reaches of the markets and commercial life of Asia, the Near East, and Latin America. The British controlled India and Latin America, while Britain and France together dominated the Ottoman Empire. From the 1880s, imperialist states like Britain, France, Belgium, Japan, and Germany took the further step of reducing many parts of the third world to colonies and spheres of influence in which they enjoyed exclusive access. Virtually all of Africa was conquered by the Europeans and placed under colonial administration. China was divided into foreign concessions and spheres of influence. From 1890 and on the United States participated directly in this movement by conquering the Hawaiian islands as well as the Philippines, Guam, Puerto Rico, and Cuba. But rather than continuing along the European path of establishing direct political control, the United States came to prefer financial penetration and timely military interventions in extending its domination over the states of Central and South America.

Despite protestations to the contrary on the part of apologists for imperialism, the net effect on the undeveloped countries was decidedly negative. Linked to the developed economies of the capitalist world, countries in the third world experienced the destruction of local manufactures, an excessive and unbalanced focus on resource extraction, and the development of agricultural monoculture. Communal forms of land ownership and subsistence farming were undermined. Accompanied by rapid population growth, these social and economic tendencies led to a deterioration in living standards. By the opening decades of the twentieth century, many countries in Africa, the Near East, Asia, and Latin America were worse off than they had been in 1800.

Decolonization

Third world resistance to European domination was manifest as early as the end of the eighteenth century. The Tupac Amaru revolt in Bolivia and Peru, the Pontiac rebellion in North America, and the great slave revolt in Haiti deeply threatened the Spanish, British, and French colonial empires. The subsequent Indian Mutiny, the Save the Emperor Movement in Vietnam, the Boxer Rebellion in China, the Islamic Mahdiya in Sudan, the successful rebuff of an Italian invasion by the Ethiopian Emperor Meneluk, and the tribally or religiously based resistance in sub-Saharan Africa against German, British, and French occupation represented traditionalist responses to growing European incursion in the nineteenth and early twentieth century. More modern forms of resistance by third world peoples appeared in the years prior to the First World War with the rise of the Young Turks, the Bengali nationalist movement, the Cuban and Filipino independence movements, and the Mexican revolution.

Nationalist movements in the third world further matured between 1914 and 1945. Led by a more knowledgeable and sophisticated leadership, the popular basis of their support grew larger. True Abdu'l Karim inspired a tribal revolt against colonial rule in Spanish Morocco between 1921–26, while Omar Mukhtar headed a similar uprising in Libya (1912–31). But traditionalist leaders like chiefs, sultans, mullahs, or royal princes were increasingly replaced by nationalist or communist leaders imbued with Western education and ideology. These modern third world leaders were more aware of other nationalist movements and were not infrequently in contact with one another. Many of these newer political leaders came to admire the economic and social achievements of the Soviet Union, which was freeing itself from the shackles of underdevelopment.

The Second World War helped to awaken the political consciousness of millions of colonized peoples in the third world. Large numbers of Africans and Asians served in Allied or Japanese armies or labor battalions, acquiring new skills and political consciousness. The rapid progress of third world manufacturing, mining, and transport stirred nationalist feelings and economic expectations among trade union militants and additional multitudes. In the countryside, peasants proved increasingly restless in the face of landlord exploitation and colonial fiscal exploitation.

In Asia the Japanese conquerors put themselves forward, at least initially, as champions of the colonized peoples and in opposition to Western exploitation. Indians, Indonesians, Burmese, Malayans, Filipinos, and Koreans served with the Japanese military or collaborated with them. Many of these nationalists found attempts by the Western countries to re-impose colonial rule after the war intolerable. Indeed, the weakening of the colonial powers during the war proved important to the success of the subsequent anticolonial struggle. Great Britain, France, and Holland had been defeated in Asia by Japan. On the European continent, France, Belgium, and Holland had been conquered and lived under German military occupation. Britain had resisted on its island fortress, but was weakened and exhausted.

Whatever Western elites may have wished, in the period after 1945 many ordinary Europeans were no longer much interested in holding on to colonies. They were reluctant to make further significant sacrifices to maintain empire overseas. What they wanted, above all, was postwar reconstruction and a better way of life at home. Eventually, West European economic integration tended to liberalize trade globally, lessening the need for exclusive control over third world colonies.

As great powers, the Soviet Union and the United States in principle both opposed colonialism. That made it additionally difficult for the old imperialist powers to hold onto their colonial possessions. From the viewpoint of the Soviet leadership, anticolonial and national liberation movements should be supported even when led by petty bourgeois leaders. Such struggles for national independence and democracy in the third world were progressive by definition. In the Soviet perspective, not only did they entail fighting against feudal landlords, they also constricted the field of operation of imperialism and monopoly capitalism.

The United States also supported decolonization movements, at least in theory. Despite its previous seizure of Puerto Rico and the Philippines as colonies, it opposed colonialism in the name of democracy and the right of self-determination. In 1941 Roosevelt had virtually forced the beleaguered Churchill to sign the Atlantic Charter granting the right of all peoples to democracy and self-rule. Colonies were part of the trading blocs that hampered the progress of U.S. trade and investment. Independence for the British, French, Belgian, and Dutch colonies would open these countries to U.S business. In the post-1945 period such more or less principled U.S positions were tempered by having to deal with the ongoing economic weakness of their European allies, the growing worldwide struggle against communism, and threats to U.S economic interests.

Anticolonialism was one thing, but opposition to economic imperialism by third world leaders was quite another matter so far as Washington was concerned. Free access to markets and investment opportunities worldwide had been the bedrock of U.S foreign policy since 1899 when Secretary of State William Hay proclaimed the Open Door Policy. The growing postwar dependence of the United States on overseas markets and raw materials made access to these markets and resources vitally essential. Accordingly, U.S foreign policy with respect to the third world tended to be anticolonialist. But the United States came to oppose national liberation movements—communist or radical nationalist—that imperiled U.S economic interests in the third world.

Asia

The decolonization process in postwar Asia helps to illuminate these contradic-
tory elements of U.S policy. East Asia was under Japanese control during the war.
The European powers—Great Britain, France, and Holland—were most anxious
to recover their Asian possessions following the defeat of Japan. At the end of the
war, the British quickly moved to recover Malaya. For good measure they assisted France and Holland to take back Indochina and Indonesia on the basis of solidarity between the European colonial powers. In the eyes of some historians, the
actual economic value of Indochina to France is questionable. But there is no
doubt that powerful political and economic interests in France believed it to be
so. Moreover, in the context of recent wartime defeat and occupation, holding on
to empire was a fundamental doctrine across the spectrum of the French political
elite from Gaullist to socialist.

Indonesia

However deluded French economic attachment to Indochina may have been, the
Dutch stake in Indonesia was undeniably important. The petroleum, rubber, and
other tropical products of the vast Indonesian archipelago were important to the
Dutch economy prior to the war. Hopes for economic recovery in postwar
Holland were based in part on reclaiming control of these resources. But within
weeks of the Japanese surrender, the Indonesian nationalists led by Achmed
Sukarno proclaimed the independence of this immensely large nation of 140 million people. British and Australian forces suppressed the nationalists and allowed
Dutch troops to return to Eastern Indonesia. Feigning a compromise with the
nationalists, the Dutch then attacked the rich western islands of Sumatra and Java
at the end of July 1947. Having gained their immediate objectives, the Dutch
broke off their offensive under British and U.S pressure.

In September 1948 the increasingly strong Communist Party organized a
coup d'etat against Sukarno's nationalist government, which was based on the
peasantry and oil workers of Java. Suppression of the coup consolidated the
power of Indonesian nationalists and right-wing politicians while confirming the
importance of the army in Indonesian politics. The Dutch, nonetheless, attempted to destroy the new republic with an all-out attack in December 1948. To this
point the United States had largely overlooked or attempted to moderate Dutch

aggression. They were above all interested in shoring up Holland as part their effort to revive the economy of Western Europe. But Washington became increasingly concerned about the progress of the Communists owing to the popularity of their fierce resistance to the Dutch. Deciding to bolster Sukarno's nationalists as a barrier to the left, Washington threatened to cut off Marshall Plan aid to Holland, forcing the Dutch to desist. Having been jailed by the Dutch, Sukarno now returned to the Indonesian capital of Jakarta in triumph in July 1949. At the end of December, all Dutch troops withdrew amid much hard feeling and considerable economic loss.

Malaya

The British fared better in neighboring Malaya. Small in comparison to Indonesia, the indigenous population of Malaya clung to subsistence activities well into the twentieth century. Chinese and Indian emigrants, meanwhile, flooded in to work in the British controlled mines and rubber plantations. By 1945 the Chinese composed 40 percent of the population of five million. They constituted the majority of businessmen and professionals as well as wage workers.

During the war, a guerrilla resistance movement against the Japanese emerged. British-led, the force totaled some 7,000 troops who were mainly ethnic Chinese with largely Communist sympathies. Indeed, they had close ties to the communist movement on the Chinese mainland. Following the war, the British granted citizenship to the Chinese and Indian population over the protests of the Malay princes, aristocrats, and populace. Supported by Chinese workers and intellectuals, veterans of the wartime guerrilla resistance led a communist-inspired insurgency against British rule in June 1948. The Malay population as well as the Chinese middle class held aloof.

The rubber and tin of Malaya were critically important to the British effort to recover financial solvency in the postwar period. Determined to hold on to the economically valuable colony, the British responded to the revolt by eventually putting some 300,000 soldiers into the field against the guerrillas. By creating strategic hamlets they resettled some 500,000 Chinese workers behind barbed wire, isolating the guerrillas from their popular base. Employing such measures, they were able to bring the insurgency under control by the early 1950s. Independent Malaysia, created in 1957, was dominated by the Malay traditional elite whose government reinforced the position of British economic interests.

The Philippines

The United States had itself granted political independence to the Philippines on similar terms a decade earlier. The Philippines had fallen into U.S. hands as a result of the latter's 1898 victory over Spain. The anti-U.S insurgency that followed cost 200,000 Filipino lives and took more than a decade to quell. The big landowners sided with the U.S. occupation from the first. The middle class was placated by the creation of a national assembly and the opening of positions in an expanded civil service. U.S colonial government continued until the Second World War, based on the idea that the Philippines was being prepared for independence.

The elite and urban populations became Americanized as a result of the introduction of a U.S educational system. Under free trade agreements, the Philippines imported U.S manufactures, while exporting Filipino sugar, tobacco, hemp, and minerals. As plantation agriculture developed, close to 40 percent of the peasantry were reduced to tenant farming. Strong peasant unions and an underground Communist Party developed prior to the outbreak of the war.

Faced with Japan's attack in December 1941, the Americans held out for five months on the fortress of Corregidor before surrendering. Much of the elite collaborated with Japan during the occupation. The Communists and other democratic elements organized the peasants into the Hukbalahap or People's Army Against Japan. The Huks fought the Japanese mainly in central and southern Luzon. By 1944 the Huk army had grown to 10,000, with a reserve of up to 50,000 peasants.

The Americans were welcomed back as liberators when they returned in 1944. They soon attempted to disarm and repress the Huks and Communists. As promised, the United States granted political independence to the Philippines as of July 4, 1946. In elections the U.S-backed Liberal Party, representing the interests of the landlord elite, triumphed. U.S commercial and property rights in the newly independent state were guaranteed. Long-term lease agreements in 1947 ensured U.S control of more than 20 military bases, including the naval base at Subic Bay and Clark Air Force Base. At the same time, a U.S military advisory group counseled the Filipino government on combating the growing rural insurgency carried on by the Huks. Until 1950, the insurgents, who numbered about 12,000, held the initiative. The reorganization of the Filipino army and intelligence services by the United States made it possible to break the back of the insurgency by 1952. Ramón Magsaysay, a military man, who distinguished himself in this counterinsurgency campaign, was elected president.

Indochina

As we have seen, the Communists played an important role in national liberation struggles in China, Korea, Malaya, Indonesia, and the Philippines. Their role was nowhere more central than in the struggle for the independence of Indochina. France had conquered Indochina in a series of campaigns between 1858 and 1895. Following the crushing of the tradition-based mandarin resistance, the French colonial regime organized itself around a relatively small bureaucracy enhanced by a colonial police and army (1895–1925). The French developed rice plantations in collaboration with local landlords, especially in the Mekong River Valley. Rubber plantations and coal mines also became part of the colonial economy. Heavy rents, usury, colonial taxes, and low wages sparked popular discontent. Resistance in this period took the form of peasant protest and an anticolonial movement based on a nationalist and republican ideology.

A new stage of resistance emerged from 1925 onwards. Over the next five years, there was an upsurge of propaganda, agitation, and terrorism. The first significant economic and political strikes by the small working class formed part of this unrest. A number of nationalist parties took form. One of these was the Revolutionary Youth League created by the Comintern-trained Ho Chi Minh. While other nationalist formations were eventually crushed or tamed by the French colonial police and army, Ho's formation transformed itself into the Indochina Communist Party in 1931 and provided leadership during a revolutionary political and social upsurge of peasants and workers (1930–1931). Forced underground during the rest of the 1930s, it shifted its activities from the towns to the countryside. With the Japanese occupation in 1941, the Communist Party created the Vietminh, a nationalist united front, which stressed the fight against French and Japanese imperialism rather than social revolution.

During the war, the Vietminh developed a mass base among the peasantry while carrying on a guerrilla war. With the Japanese surrender, Ho Chi Minh proclaimed the independence of the Democratic Republic of Vietnam (DRV) on September 2, 1945, amidst popular acclamation. The British, meanwhile, were charged by the wartime allies with disarming the Japanese in southern Vietnam. They used the opportunity to help the French re-install themselves there, just as they helped the Dutch to return to Indonesia. The ensuing war of the Vietminh against French colonialism (1946-1954) was internationalized in 1950 when the United States assumed the economic burden of the French effort to hold onto

Indochina in the wake of the outbreak of the Korean War. Simultaneously, the new Communist government in China began to provide the Vietminh with the training and heavy military equipment that made it possible for them to fight an increasingly successful positional war against the French. The ultimate defeat of the France arrived at the celebrated Battle of Dien Bien Phu in May 1954.

The DRV it seemed had defeated French colonialism and recovered the independence of Vietnam. At the Geneva Conference in the summer of 1954, Laos and Cambodia, the two other states of French Indochina, received their independence. But the United States succeeded in dividing Vietnam at the seventeenth parallel, leaving the Communist DRV in immediate control only of the north. In the south, there emerged a U.S backed Republic of Vietnam under the conservative mandarin Ngo Dinh Diem. Diem and the U.S government ignored the provisions of the Geneva Conference that promoted the organization of national elections throughout Vietnam. For good measure immediately following the Geneva Conference, the United States created the Southeast Asia Treaty Organization (SEATO). The alliance included Australia, France, Great Britain, New Zealand, Pakistan, the Philippines, Thailand, and the United States. SEATO was designed to buttress the Republic of Vietnam while blocking the further expansion of Communist China in southeast Asia. The establishment of SEATO as an instrument of containment in Asia paralleled the creation of NATO in Europe five years earlier.

In fact, the DRV had been restrained from pushing to unite the country by force mainly by its communist allies, the People's Republic of China and the Soviet Union. Its sovereignty confined to North Vietnam following the refusal of the Republic of Vietnam and the United States to permit nationwide elections, the DRV in the ensuing years set about a comprehensive agrarian reform, the establishment of a modern educational system, and the construction of hundreds of manufacturing plants. In the south, Diem created a personal regime that rejected any notion of land reform, based its economy on continuous infusions of U.S economic aid, and increasingly resorted to military and political repression against communist, liberal, and Buddhist opposition. The stage was being set for the eventual renewal of the Vietnamese conflict down the road.

The success of the Communists in Korea and Vietnam in contrast to Malaya, Indonesia, and the Philippines, appears to have been, in part, a function of their direct proximity to China and the Soviet Union. On the islands, peninsulas, and archipelagos of the Pacific, remoteness from the Eurasian mainland made it difficult to obtain needed supplies and to create the strategic rear areas necessary to carry through successful struggles against U.S- or British-backed regimes.

India

If Communists played an important role in the national liberation struggles of East Asia, this was less true in South Asia. As in the rest of Asia, the agrarian question was central to the twentieth-century history of the Indian subcontinent. A traditional elite of native princes and landlord-moneylenders dominated the rural areas. They had cooperated with the British in maintaining order in the countryside from the beginning of British rule in the first part of the nineteenth century. There were some well-to-do peasants in the Indian countryside. But most of the rural population was crushed by high rents, usury, and heavy land taxes. A fourth of the rural population was landless laborers, many of whom belonged to the so-called outcasts.

In the cities an Indian capitalist class with interests in commerce, banking, and a still modest manufacturing sector began to appear. Below them was an elite of partially Anglicized Indian professionals and administrators who helped a mere 4,000 British civil servants and several thousand more military officers administer this enormously large country. Merchants, petty bourgeoisie, skilled and unskilled workers, and a huge lumpenproletariat composed the bulk of the urban population.

Increasing through the nineteenth century, the population rose dramatically after 1920 while food production per capita stagnated. By the eve of the Second World War the population had grown to almost 450 million. Light industry, especially cotton manufacturing, grew prodigiously. An iron and steel industry also emerged. The greater part of the national budget administered by the British was committed to defense and justice, with an insignificant amount devoted to economic development.

The Communist Party, which was formed in 1925, played a significant role in the strikes and peasant agitation that marked the anticolonial struggle up to the outbreak of the Second World War. But its subordination to the Soviet-controlled Comintern was to compromise it politically in the struggle for independence. It was the Indian Congress Party that took the lead in the growing anticolonial struggle. The Congress was created in 1885 by a small group of professionals and intellectuals interested in reform and self-government within the British Empire.

Thoroughly middle class in its orientation, it began to reach out to the peasant masses in the wake of the Amritsar massacre perpetrated by the British military against unarmed Indian demonstrators in 1919. A British-educated lawyer, Mohandas K. Gandhi, became the Congress Party's instrument for politically mobilizing the peasants. Abandoning the lifestyle of the Anglicized Indian elite, Gandhi's austere simplicity and charismatic personality helped to gain the support of millions of peasants. His goal was the overthrow of British colonial rule and the creation of a united and democratic India that would include both Hindus and Muslims. The means to the achievement of this objective was mass struggle using the weapons of passive resistance rather than violence. Boycott of British manufactures and the revival of rural cottage industries were key aspects of Gandhi's campaign. While the abolition of untouchability won him the support of the underclasses, his eschewing of class conflict reassured the professionals and business leaders who controlled the Congress Party.

As a result of widespread peasant unrest and strikes (1930–1934), the British decided to offer the Indians self-rule at the level of provincial government. In the elections of 1937, the Congress won nearly half the seats in the various provincial legislative assemblies. But the fact that it won only a small number of the nearly 500 legislative seats reserved for Muslims made this electoral victory a disappointment for the leaders of the Congress committed to the ideal of an independent and secular India. Against Congress demands for a unified secular India, the Muslim League, a party dominated by Muslim landlords and led by M.A. Jinnah, called for the establishment of a separate Muslim state. Based on a policy of divide and conquer, the British deliberately encouraged Jinnah and the League. While Muslim merchants, petty bourgeoisie, artisans, and peasants came to support the League, its critics insisted, with some justification, that the League was dominated by landlords who were determined to hold onto their power.

During the Second World War, London offered self-government to India with the right of succession from the Commonwealth following victory in the war. The Congress responded on August 7, 1942, with the Quit India Resolution demanding immediate Indian freedom. It threatened massive resistance along non-violent lines on British refusal. A wave of British repression followed with the arrest of 60,000 Indians including the leaders of the Congress. The result was a major uprising across northern India in which at least 1,000 died and many thousands were wounded. Students and peasants took the lead. But workers under Communist Party influence refrained from participating in the upheaval owing to the common fight of the Soviet Union and Britain against Nazi Germany. To this point the influence of the Communist Party India had been considerable. Its leadership had been an integral feature, for example, of the agrarian protests of the early 1930s. Indian Communist Party deference to the wartime Soviet alliance with Britain at this juncture, however, cost the party dearly. Its leading role in the independence struggle was compromised.

Meanwhile, a former leader of the Congress, Subhas Bose, sought to push the British out of India with Japanese assistance. By 1943 Bose had organized the 40,000-strong Indian National Army, a force based in Malaya and commanded by the Japanese. Within India itself the situation was dramatically transformed during the war by a huge military mobilization and substantial industrial expansion. The Indian army under British command grew to more than two million men, while the Indian navy added scores of warships to its fleet. India became a supply center for allied forces in the Middle East. Heavy manufacturing in steel, aluminum, and cement grew rapidly as did the manufacture of light arms, uniforms, and blankets. New opportunities opened for technicians and administrators.

The end of the war brought matters to a head. The demands of Congress and the Muslim League were unalterably opposed to one another. The new Labour government in London found that it had other priorities than stubbornly trying to hold onto India. Moreover, given the gigantic size attained by the Indian military during the war, keeping British control of the subcontinent in the postwar seemed daunting. Furthermore, the war had dramatically reversed the balance of payments deficit that had historically benefited Britain. Postwar mutinies in the Indian navy and the outbreak of communal rioting between Muslims and Hindus determined the British to leave. The terms of independence were worked out in the midst of these religious riots, which left one million dead and fourteen million as refugees. On August 15, 1948, India and Pakistan became independent republics.

The Middle East

National liberation struggles in the Middle East had begun in the aftermath of the First World War. That conflict saw the dissolution of the Ottoman Empire, which had ruled the region for centuries. The collapse of Ottoman rule had been, in part, precipitated by an Arab revolt in 1917 led by the Emir Hussein of Mecca. Hussein had raised the banner of revolt partly as a result of the incitement of the British who promised Arab independence in the aftermath of victory. Britain along with France had developed financial and commercial interests throughout the Ottoman Empire during the nineteenth century. Its seizure of Egypt and control of the Suez Canal confirmed its growing political and economic hegemony over the Middle East. Britain was further wedded to the region by the oil that was discovered in Iran and Iraq at the beginning of the twentieth century. In 1907 Britain and Russia partitioned Iran into respective spheres of influence. Prior to the First World War, then, Britain already held sway over Egypt, part of Iran, and the Persian Gulf, while France controlled Morocco, Tunisia, and Algeria as well as exercising political and economic influence in Syria-Lebanon.

In the wake of the First World War, the British and French expanded their influence through League of Nations mandates. Britain took control of Iraq, Palestine, and Jordan. It consolidated its paramount role in Iran, as well, at the expense of Russia. France was given mandates over Syria and Lebanon. The Arab revolt led by Emir Hussein had stirred enormous hopes throughout the Middle East. Subsequent British and French refusal to grant Arab independence following the war produced bitter disappointment. Arab anger was intensified by the Balfour Declaration (1917) in which the British promised Zionists a Jewish homeland in Palestine. Reassurances that the rights of the existing population in Palestine would be protected did nothing to placate Arab mistrust. Revolts in Egypt (1919–20), Palestine (1921–22), Iraq (1921–22), and Syria (1925) marked the beginning of modern Arab nationalism.

The emergence of Arab nationalism based on the struggle against European imperialism had a separate trajectory in each Arab country. It was galvanized by the rise, however modest, in the number of high school and university graduates and the strengthening of the still small middle class in the Middle East in the interwar period. But it was the immigration of increasing numbers of European Jews to Palestine in the 1930s and the creation of the state of Israel (1948) that had the most dramatic influence on its development.

Palestine

For centuries millions of Jews had lived as a subaltern population in Central and Eastern Europe and throughout the Ottoman Empire. Their position in Europe became precarious with the rise of extremist nationalism and political anti-Semitism in the late nineteenth century. In reaction to anti-Jewish feeling, mass migration of Eastern European Jews mainly to North America took place between

1880 and 1920. Opportunities for emigration to the United States were largely closed off in the 1920s as a result of a xenophobic reaction against immigrants. Consequently, the flow of Jewish migration was diverted to Palestine. The number of Jews in Palestine rose to 500,000 after the Nazis took power in Germany in the 1930s.

Made up largely of a European educated Jewish middle and working class, the growing colonial-settler population began to create the foundations of a modern economy. The so-called Jewish Agency was able to constitute a kind of para-state in Palestine under the British mandate, while the Supreme Muslim Council, a largely religious body led by a nationalist Haij Amin al-Husayni, represented Arab political interests. Arabs had also organized trade unions, schools, Muslim-Christian associations, boy scout troops, and an Arab bank. The traditional elite was comprised of landlords, clergy, and other notables. Of the one million Arabs, the majority were unskilled workers and peasants. Created as a reaction to vehement European nationalism, the Zionist movement was exclusionist with respect to the Palestinian Arab population. With some notable exceptions, even left-wing Zionists were at best ambiguous with respect to the equality of Jewish and Arab labor. Access to wage employment became critical as agricultural depression took hold in Palestine in the 1930s. Tensions over these matters as well as increased Jewish immigration and growing dispossession of Arab peasants provoked an uprising between 1936 and 1939. Some 26,000 British troops, the Royal Air Force, and a Jewish auxiliary army of 15,000 were deployed to contain the poorly coordinated, mainly peasant resistance, which had rejected the leadership of the Arab notables and landlords. The repression of the uprising demoralized the Palestinians, undermining their capacity to organize and wage a future struggle. The Palestinian cause attracted wide sympathy in neighboring countries, fuelling Arab nationalism. The defeat of the revolt, meanwhile, strengthened the Zionist movement politically and militarily.

The definitive showdown between Jews and Arabs in Palestine followed the Second World War. The European Holocaust prompted a further flood of Jewish emigration into Palestine. By 1948 the Jewish population totaled 700,000; just three years later, it numbered more than one million. The rising tide of Jewish emigration and the United Nations decision to divide Palestine into Jewish and Arab states (November, 1947) led to the outbreak of war. Postwar sympathy for the plight of the Jews and Zionist pressure led the United States to support the creation of the state of Israel (May 1948). The Soviet Union also recognized the inde-

pendent Jewish state as part of its policy to undermine British influence in the
Middle East. Buoyed by great power support, a growing influx of new immigrants,
and support from the worldwide Jewish diaspora, the new Israeli state and its well-
organized army were able to defeat the disorganized Palestinian Arabs as well as
the invading armies of the neighboring Arab states. Some 600,000 of 1.2 million
Palestinian Arabs were in one way or another forced to flee, taking refuge in surrounding Arab lands. The West Bank territories of the Palestinians were annexed
by King Abdullah of Jordan with the secret agreement of the Israelis. An attempt
to create a Palestinian state in Gaza was frustrated by Egyptian intervention.

Egypt

The defeat of Arab armies and the mass exodus of Palestinians from Israeli-con-
trolled territory had profound repercussions in neighboring countries. Egypt had
long been recognized as the cultural and religious capital of the Arab world. The
nationalist revolution of 1952, which followed the defeat of the Egyptian army in
Palestine, made it the focal point of Arab political aspirations as well. Following the
riots in 1919–20, the British conceded a limited form of independence to the
Egyptian monarchy of King Fuad I. The King ruled through the support of the
Egyptian landlords as well as the merchants of Cairo and Alexandria, many of
whom were foreigners. Britain widened the terms of Egyptian self-government in
1936 but retained control of the Suez Canal. The Egyptian economy, based on the
export of cotton, remained tied to Great Britain. The sharp decline in agricultural
exports during the Depression accelerated peasant proletarianization and migration
into urban slums. The slump in foreign trade was offset in part by the development
of local consumer industries and the emergence of an Egyptian bourgeoisie.

The Second World War brought a crisis in Anglo-Egyptian relations. Like Iraq
and Iran, which also were dominated by British imperialism, the Egyptian government led by the young King Farouk took an increasingly pro-German line.
The crisis deepened as the British military situation in North Africa deteriorated
in the face of the advance of Field Marshal Erwin Rommel's Afrika Korps. On
February 4, 1942, British tanks surrounded the royal palace in Cairo. The British
ambassador then demanded that King Farouk dismiss his pro-German prime
minister and appoint Mustafa Nahhas, a politician friendly to Britain, in his stead.
The Egyptian public concluded that the British concession of political autonomy
to Egypt had been a sham.

In rivalry to the power of the landlords and big merchants, urban-based nationalist parties based on the petty bourgeoisie and workers appeared in the 1930s. Notable was the emergence of Young Egypt led by Ahmed Hussein. At first this party maintained a strictly nationalist orientation, assuming a slightly socialist tinge in response to the shifting mood of public opinion after the Second World War. More popular was the Muslim Brotherhood, which became the prototype for religious parties all over the Islamic world. It sought to combine Islam with nationalism. Eventually, it espoused a religious form of republicanism and a certain kind of socialism. It attracted elements which had been uprooted from traditional, often rural environments, and which had difficulty finding a niche in the secular and modern sectors of urban society. Unlike Young Egypt, the Muslim Brotherhood was more prone to direct action, including terrorism. There also existed a small Egyptian left, the most important element of which was the Communist Party. Although unable to develop a mass base of support, the anti-imperialist analysis put forward by the Communists had a great influence on Egyptian nationalism. It is notable that the young army officers who would lead the revolution in 1952 were greatly influenced by the anti-imperialism that derived from Lenin.

In 1946 the Muslim Brotherhood initiated a campaign of terrorism and mass demonstrations to drive the British out of Egypt. Faced with this rising tide of nationalist resistance, the British withdrew their military forces to the Suez Canal Zone in the course of 1947. That year the Brotherhood sent armed combatants to support the Palestinian struggle against Zionism. The following year the Egyptian army entered the battle in Palestine. The Egyptian army and the military of most of the other Arab states suffered a humiliating defeat at the hands of the fledgling Israeli army. In the wake of this debacle, a secret conspiracy of so-called Free Army Officers came into being. Most of the military officers who joined the conspiracy came from the prosperous layers of the Egyptian peasantry.

In 1951 the Egyptian government unilaterally abrogated its 1936 agreement with Great Britain. Egyptian sabotage operations against the British in the Canal Zone intensified. Alcoholic and dissolute, King Farouk was unable to control his court made up of native and foreign hangers-on who spent their time intriguing and deal making. The courtiers, merchants, and landlords, meanwhile, faced growing political opposition from the middle class, university students, intellectuals, peasants, and workers. On so-called Black Saturday at the beginning of

1952, a massive riot was marked by attacks on downtown merchants and the burning down of parts of the center of Cairo.

Under such circumstances, it was relatively easy for the Free Army Officers to seize power on July 23, 1952. After a power struggle, one of them, Gamal Abdal Nasser, emerged as leader. During the next few years, he consolidated his rule by suppressing both the Communists and the Muslim Brotherhood. In 1954 he negotiated a final evacuation of the British from Egyptian territory. Between 1954 and 1956 he instituted a moderate land reform that favored the more prosperous peasants. At the same time, this enlightened despot began to assume leadership of the Arab nationalist movement throughout the Middle East. At the first meeting of non-aligned states at Bandung in April 1955, Nasser succeeded in getting the participating states to support the Arab position on Palestine.

Having been forced out of Egypt and the Canal Zone, Great Britain became more and more alarmed at the rising influence of Nasser in the rest of the Arab world. The British government's first response was to organize the Baghdad Pact in 1955. Outwardly directed against the Soviet Union, this regional alliance, which included the conservative governments of Iraq, Jordan, Turkey, Iran, and Pakistan, was designed to contain Nasser's radical nationalist appeal to the Arab world. Britain's next step was much bolder. Acting in concert with France and Israel, Britain launched an armed attack on Egypt to recover control of the Suez Canal.

The opportunity for such an adventure followed Nasser's refusal to join the Baghdad Pact and the conclusion of a Soviet-Egyptian arms agreement in the fall of 1955. Tensions between Egypt and Israel had escalated sharply as a result of raids by Palestinian guerrillas from Egyptian-controlled Gaza as well as counterattacks by Israel. The Egyptians kept the Suez Canal closed to Israeli shipping, while blocking Israeli maritime access to the Red Sea by control of the straits of Sharm el-Sheik at the mouth of the Gulf of Aquaba. The Israelis decided to go to war against Egypt at the first opportunity. At the beginning of 1956, they were able to conclude a secret arms deal with the French countering the Egyptian-Soviet pact. The French were furious at Nasser's open support for the national liberation movement in French controlled Algeria. They believed that the destruction of Nasser would demolish the strategic rear area of the Algerian revolt.

Despite his arms deal with the Soviets, Nasser was far from throwing in his lot with them. Based on the principle of non-alignment, he sought to offset Soviet influence with assistance from the United States. Washington had not been upset by the decline of British influence in Egypt. In the years since Nasser took power, their political and economic presence in Egypt had been growing. The lynchpin of U.S. plans was the proposal for the construction of the giant hydroelectric dam at Aswan, which would lay the basis for future Egyptian economic development. But the U.S. Secretary of State John Foster Dulles was upset by the sudden announcement of the Soviet arms deal. In July 1956 he cancelled further U.S. aid for the Aswan project.

Stunned by the U.S. move, Nasser countered within a few days by the announcement of the nationalization of the Suez Canal Company, a private enterprise controlled by British and French investors. The nationalized revenues of the Suez Company would now be used to finance the giant dam project. In reaction, the British Prime Minister Anthony Eden became determined to throw in his lot with the French and Israelis in attacking Egypt. By prearrangement on October 29, 1956, the Israelis attacked the Egyptian army in the Sinai and marched on the Suez Canal. This provided the pretext for Anglo-French intervention. The ostensible goal of the Anglo-French military operation was to separate the belligerents. Its real goal was reoccupation of the Canal Zone. The Egyptians responded to the British and French attack by sinking ships and blocking the channel of the Canal.

The Israelis proved to be the main beneficiaries of the war. As a result of their successful assault on the Egyptians, they forced open the Gulf of Aquaba to their ships and impelled the installation of United Nations peacekeeping forces between their forces and the Egyptians along the Gaza strip. In the meantime, Dulles, whose refusal of aid to Egypt had precipitated the crisis, denounced the Anglo-French attempt to reoccupy the Canal Zone. The United States threatened to cut off supplies of petroleum to its two major allies. Access to oil from Venezuela had become indispensable to them as a result of the blocking of the Canal. Ongoing pressure from Washington forced the British and French to withdraw. Over the long term, the crisis signified the growing dominance of Washington over the Middle East and the further decline of the old imperialist powers.

Despite military defeat, Nasser emerged from the crisis with his prestige among Arabs throughout the Middle East at its highest point. He had succeeded in nationalizing Egypt's greatest single economic asset. For good measure, he nationalized an additional 360 foreign companies, initiating what was referred to as Arab socialism. The state for the first time came to dominate Egyptian economic life. Such was the appeal of Nasser that in 1958 the Syrian regime agreed to merge its government with that of Egypt forming the United Arab Republic.

Inspired by Nasser, on July 14, 1958, Free Army Officers in Baghdad overthrew the Iraqi monarchy. The ensuing Iraqi national revolution destroyed the British-inspired Baghdad Pact.

Iraq

British occupation of Iraq at the end of the First World War provoked a powerful nationalist uprising in 1920, which was supported by religious and tribal leaders. Brutally crushing the movement, the British imposed Faisal, the son of their Arabian ally Hussein, Emir of Mecca, as the Iraqi king. In the mid-1920s, the British mandatory government and the Iraqi monarchy granted the great landowners and tribal chiefs extensive authority over their landed properties, including fiscal and police powers. The new water and irrigation rights of this elite made them very rich at the expense of the rural population.

By the 1950s more than 55 percent of all private agricultural lands was held by less than one percent of landowners. Seventy-three percent of landowners held only 6.8 percent of the agricultural land, divided in small plots of fifteen acres or less. In a rural population totaling 3.8 million, approximately 600,000 heads of households were landless. Massive rural migration made Baghdad a city of 500,000 composed mainly of the poor. British control of petroleum resources was assured by the annexation of the Mosul region in 1925. Oil production grew in subsequent decades. In 1946 annual production already stood at 4.6 million tons. The subsequent expansion of the oil industry's output was prodigious. By 1958 it had reached 35.8 million tons. Oil-inspired economic growth furthered the expansion of the Iraqi middle and working class.

Following the pattern familiar in Egypt, in 1932 Britain accorded the Iraqi monarchy formal independence while keeping control of foreign and military affairs. As in Egypt, the limits of such rule were demonstrated in 1941 when the pro-German prime minister Rashid Ali al-Kilani was deposed by British military intervention. The year 1948 saw the so-called "Leap," the largest mass protest in Iraq's history. Students and workers took the lead in the development of the nationalist cause, which gained momentum in further popular upsurges in 1952 and 1956. Following the revolution in 1958, the highly popular Communist Party emerged as the single most important part of the government organized by the Free Officers led by Abdul Karim Qasim. A sweeping land reform, legal equality of the sexes, and recognition of the equality of Sunnis, Shiites, Kurds, and even

Christians and Jews were among the singular achievements of the new regime. Such was the level of Middle East turbulence in the wake of the Suez crisis, the creation of the United Arab Republic, and the Iraqi revolution that the Britain and the United States felt called upon to intervene militarily in Jordan and Lebanon in 1958 to save the conservative regimes in these two small states.

Iran

British political and economic supremacy was also threatened by nationalist revolution in Iran in the 1950s. In the immediate postwar years, Iranian nationalism had been aroused by Soviet demands for oil concessions and support for Kurdish and Azeri separatists in the north of the country. In the ensuing crisis, Washington was able to get a foot in the door in what had been a British sphere of interest. Nationalist opposition to continued British control of Iran's oil industry was led by an aristocratic reformer, Mohammed Mossadegh, who headed a coalition of the traditional and modern middle classes organized in the National Front. It was backed up by the Communist or Tudeh Party, which was very influential among the emergent working class as well as with students and intellectuals.

In March 1951 the Iranian parliament nationalized the oil industry. Popular acclamation forced the Shah Reza Pahlavi to appoint Mossadegh Prime Minister. By the spring of 1953 Mossadegh appeared to threaten the remaining power of the royal court, the landlords, tribal chieftains, and military officers. Meanwhile, the National Front began to split as traditionalists attempted to block nationalization of the telephones, transportation, and bakeries, as well as legislative measures to emancipate women. Mossadegh himself distrusted the Tudeh Party, which was responsible for organizing many of the mass demonstrations against the British and the royal court. These political splits were made worse by the increasingly serious economic crisis. British and U.S oil companies boycotted Iranian oil on the international petroleum market and gradually undermined the Iranian economy. A group of cashiered military officers loyal to the Shah led by General Fazallah Zahedi began to plot the overthrow of Mossadegh. The coup was backed by Washington, which dispatched Kermit Roosevelt of the CIA to organize and finance it. After a botched first attempt, Mossadegh was finally overthrown in August 1953. The Anglo-Iranian Oil Company was denationalized.

As a consequence of the crisis, a grateful Shah allotted the exploitation of the major part of Iran's petroleum resources to the United States, reducing the British to the role of second fiddle. If British control of the Suez Canal had been lost and Western access to Iraqi oil put in doubt by the upheavals of the 1950s, the petroleum of Iran was once more in secure hands. For now the nationalist revolution in Iran had been thwarted. But the U.S-backed coup of 1953 in Iran would come back to haunt the United States 25 years later.

Algeria

Nationalist revolution, meanwhile, drove the French from Algeria. The French had little problem conceding political independence to neighboring Morocco and Tunisia (1956). Likewise, it would prove relatively easy for them to abandon colonial rule in West Africa in the early 1960s. Most of the ex-colonies remained economic dependencies of France. But Algeria was legally a *département* of the French state. Out of the estimated ten million Algerians, nearly a million were citizens of France. Reeling from defeat in Indochina, France would not easily surrender Algeria to Arab nationalists.

The French conquest of Algeria began in the 1830s and was nearly completed by the end of the 1840s. The last great act of resistance by the Arab population took place during the insurrection of 1871 coinciding with the Paris Commune. By 1930 the French settler population had grown to 900,000. The colonists took over the best land, producing wheat and wine for export to continental France. Meanwhile, many Algerian peasants were dispossessed, while traditional artisans found it difficult to compete with French manufactures.

The French pursued a policy of assimilation, which in practice was domination. Arab law and custom, especially the seclusion of women, were despised and considered proof of Arab inferiority. In agriculture, the Depression of the 1930s led to economic concentration. French colonial society came to be dominated by a small minority of wealthy landowners, newspaper proprietors, and politicians. Many less affluent French colonists abandoned the land and moved to the cities. Ongoing domination over the Arab population became an obsession for these economically marginal colonial settlers. The largely rural Arab population grew rapidly, while becoming more impoverished by the further partition of meager land holdings, indebtedness, and dispossession. The growing mechanization of French agriculture diminished the possibilities for wage labor.

Modern Algerian nationalism was born in the 1920s with the appearance of a party calling itself Young Algeria. This was the creation of Ferhat Abbas, a pharmacist, who emerged as leader of a small group of French-educated, middle-class Arab intellectuals. Admirers of French culture and republicanism, Abbas and his followers sought to integrate the Muslim community into the French political system. They demanded equal rights for Arabs alongside the European colonists as part of the French nation. The appeal of Young Algeria remained limited to the assimilated relatively well-off Arabs. To a greater or lesser degree integrated into the modern sector of the economy, these elements constituted a fifth of the total Arab population.

At the beginning of the 1930s, there appeared the Movement of the Oulémas, which based its nationalism on integral and traditional Islam. The party founded schools, published journals, and preached adherence to a conservative Islamic faith. Their influence remained essentially moral rather than political. In 1937 Messali Hadj created an authentically modern nationalist party. By the end of the war, his Movement for the Triumph of Democratic Liberties (MTLD) had 25,000 militants committed to the idea of total independence from France.

During the Second World War, many French settlers became attracted to the anti-Semitism and authoritarianism of the Vichy government. No sooner did the war end than violence erupted. An Arab insurrection broke out in May 1945. In retaliation for the deaths of 100 French, 15,000 Arabs were slaughtered. Subsequent efforts to provide the assimilated Arabs a political role were frustrated by the French colonists and the governor-general. Militants who originally belonged to the MTLD created the National Liberation Front in the fall of 1954. They were inspired by the example of Nasser and the fall of Dien Bien Phu in Vietnam. On the night of October 31, the Algerian War began with terrorist attacks launched against some 70 French targets across Algeria.

The Algerian insurgents totaling about 25,000 combatants carried on a classic guerrilla campaign. In response, the French ultimately deployed nearly 500,000 troops. Without being able to crush the rebels entirely, the French progressively reestablished control from 1957 onwards, first in the cities, then along the frontiers and, finally, across much of the countryside. Closing the frontiers between Algeria and neighboring Morocco and Tunisia with thick barbed wire and electrified fences, they deprived the insurgents of access to rear bases. Using resettlement camps into which they herded the rural Arab population, the French cut the guerrillas off from popular support in the countryside. In the midst of this struggle, a revolt of French colonists and army units in Algeria in the spring of 1958 led to the overthrow of the Fourth Republic and the accession

of de Gaulle as president of the new Fifth Republic. By 1959 the French had
mastered the revolt.

But public opinion in France had turned against the war. Its sons conscripted,
increasingly an international pariah, and economically drained, France under de
Gaulle sought a way out. By the terms of the Evian Accords (March 18, 1962),
Algeria achieved its political independence, while allowing France access to
newly discovered oil fields in the Sahara. Between 300,000 and 400,000 Arabs
and some 30,000 Frenchmen had lost their lives. Most of the European settlers,
totaling almost a million, were repatriated to France.

Sub-Saharan Africa

The conflict in Algeria had been as lengthy and bloody as it was because of the
French settlers who refused all compromise. In sub-Saharan Africa white colonial
settlers were to prove equally obdurate. The Second World War in Africa led to a
new emphasis on economic development on the part of British and French colonial authorities that had authority over most of the landmass of the continent.
Hitherto, they had tried to perpetuate their control by encouraging so-called tribal authority and the maintenance of traditional culture. But the war brought a new
stress on economic growth based on the surging demand for African primary
products. In contrast with the years of Depression, African minerals, raw materials, and foodstuffs found a ready market. So much so that forced labor was reim-
posed in many regions, justified as a wartime measure.

The boom in the African economy continued in the aftermath of the war. What
has been called a second colonial occupation took place as the continent was
opened to further economic development controlled by Europeans. Highways,
mines, and light industry oriented toward local markets appeared. Notable
increases in urbanization took place in Salisbury, Nairobi, Dakar, Leopoldville,
Accra, Lagos, Asmara, and Addis Ababa. Imports focused on machinery, capital
goods, trucks, and automobiles. European farmers and rich African peasants cap-
italized their lands by the increased use of tractors, mechanical seeders, har-
vesters, and chemical fertilizers. Production surged, spawning soil depletion and
growing social differentiation.

Economic expansion coincided with a postwar influx of white settlers seeking
escape from continued austerity at home in Europe. The late 1940s and early
1950s saw a wave of British emigration into east and central Africa. The high-

lands of Kenya experienced the further development of an intensive capitalist agriculture by British settlers and better off peasants at the expense of subsistence farmers. Worldwide demand for tobacco spurred the growth of tobacco farming in Southern Rhodesia by white farmers on land that had once belonged to local peasants. Between 1945 and 1960 the European population of the Portuguese colonies of Angola and Mozambique as well as the Belgian Congo tripled. There was significant British immigration toward South Africa as well. As in Algeria, the postwar settler-colonists adopted a rigidly racist ideology that was prepared to make few concessions to the African population.

Tanzania

The growth of modern education, service in the armed forces, the displacement of rural peasants, the spread of wage labor, and urbanization began to produce their effects on the East African population. Conflict between peasants and settlers was manifest in Tanganyika by the early 1950s. Attempts by the colonial authorities to include Europeans in organs of local government were rejected by the indigenous population. There was a growing reluctance to pay taxes to the colonial government. The black population increasingly ignored agricultural laws to the benefit of white farmers. A schoolteacher, Julius Nyrere, created the Tanganyika African National Union, which organized a successful struggle against racial discrimination and land dispossession. Britain conceded independence to Tanzania under Nyrere in 1961.

Kenya

In Kenya conflict between an entrenched colonial settler population and incipient African nationalism burst into open war. The Kikuyu, the principal ethnic group, jealously guarded their own customs against the British and by the 1930s were creating their own schools and independent churches. Faced with modernizing European colonial settlers in the postwar period, social unrest developed among the dispossessed Kikuyu squatters of the agriculturally rich Rift Valley. By the early 1950s, the movement was more and more inspired by nationalist and radical ideas picked up from the increasingly restless working class and radical labor leaders of the capital, Nairobi. In 1952 a Mau Mau guerrilla movement based in the forest areas of central Kenya took root. In the course of the revolt, 95

Europeans and 2,000 so-called loyal Africans were killed. The Mau Mau lost with 11,503 dead. White settlers saw the rebellion as proof that Africans could only be kept down by force. Indeed, some 30,000 Africans were interned by the time the insurgency was brought under control in 1956. The more long-term strategy of the British was to foster an African middle class that would protect British economic interests. On this basis, the British gave Kenya its political independence in 1963.

In West Africa, the absence of white settlers helped facilitate the process of decolonization. In Ghana and Guinea the first real challenges were mounted to the perpetuation of post-independence European economic control. Under the visionary leadership of Kwame Nkrumah, Ghana temporarily assumed leadership of the entire decolonization movement on the African continent.

Like the rest of Africa, West Africa saw rapid economic growth during the Second World War. Military service, educational advance, the emigration of young men and women to the towns, and, above all, the strength of organized labor all increased. Rapid inflation and consumer shortages spurred mass protests and strikes by unionized workers on the railways and in the civil service as the war came to an end. Low prices for agricultural goods and the scarcity of imported consumer manufactures sparked discontent among peasants. The fact that half the earnings of the lucrative gold, diamonds, and manganese mines were remitted to Britain created indignation.

Ghana

The beneficiary of a Christian missionary education, Kwame Nkrumah received his university training in the United States and England. There he absorbed the ideas of the Marxist intelligentsia of the Black diaspora including W.E.B. Du Bois and C.L.R. James. Based on his experience in United States, he also conceived the visionary idea of a United States of Africa, which would unite the whole African continent. Returning to the Gold Coast in 1947, his People's Convention Party based itself on the emergent working class and petty bourgeoisie. The party demanded independence from the British, while marking its distance from the old African elite of merchants, lawyers, and tribal chiefs.

Having achieved political independence in 1957, Ghana under Nkrumah built an impressive educational and health infrastructure. Attempting to escape the straitjacket of economic dependence on Britain, the Volta Dam project was meant to provide electricity to the aluminum as well as other nascent industries. In 1958 Nkrumah organized the founding conference of what five years later would become the Organization of African Unity promoting the ideal of the unification of the continent.

Fundamental to the problems that ultimately undermined Nkrumah was the plight of the economically and politically important cocoa farmers. The British had used the so-called Cocoa Marketing Board to keep prices to farmers low, while accumulating cash reserves in London to help with Britain's balance of payments. Nkrumah continued the practice of centralizing resources, albeit using financial reserves from cocoa sales to invest in social and economic infrastructure projects in Ghana. As the primary source of foreign exchange, cocoa farmers were encouraged to produce as much as possible, while prices of cocoa tumbled on the world market in the late 1950s and early 1960s. As a result, Nkrumah lost his rural base of support, the more so as he harshly repressed the tribal chiefs and leaders of regional opposition movements. But he remained a prisoner of international economic forces he could not control. Ghana's export and import sectors, banks, and insurance companies continued to lie in the hands of mainly British capital.

Faced with this reality, Nkrumah built up a cult of personality, centralized decision making in himself, and turned the People's Convention Party into a patronage machine. Growing economic difficulties led him to impose austerity on the urban working class and the poor. Having alienated the mass base of his support, he was overthrown in a 1966 army coup supported by British and local merchants as well as the tribal chiefs. Ghana reverted to a typical neocolonial state marked by economic failure, successive military coups, and dictatorship.

Despite these setbacks, Ghana at least had the honor of leading the way to the political independence of scores of other states of the former British and French African empires. In the early 1960s most of these states, including the regional giant Nigeria, became politically independent. Black rulers and administrators replaced the white colonial elites. As in Ghana, centralized bureaucratic rule over the rural peasantry tended to replace the decentralized tribal model preferred by the colonial governments. Relatively high prices for raw materials and foodstuffs made possible a certain amount of economic growth and social development. Some states like Tanzania under Nyrere became sites of important economic and social experiments. But economic mismanagement, bureaucracies that often were incompetent and sometimes corrupt, and, above all, the inability to gain leverage in the world market led to instability in the 1970s and subsequent economic regression.

Guinea

The contradiction between the aspiration for national liberation and ongoing economic dependence was nowhere better demonstrated than in Guinea. Under the leadership of the militant trade unionist, Sekou Touré, Guinea opted for complete independence from France in 1958. In doing so, Guinea boldly rejected the neocolonial project of France's de Gaulle. Advanced by de Gaulle in the midst of the Algerian War, it provided for independence for most of France's West African colonies within the French Union. Under these new and less than fair arrangements, Senegal, Côte d'Ivoire, Gabon, and the rest of French West Africa were to remain economic dependencies of France while trade unionists and civil servants were deprived of the social and economic benefits of French citizenship. Striking out on its own, the desperately poor country of Guinea quickly became a one-party state basing itself on Marxism-Leninism. Even with close ties to the Soviet Bloc and China, the reality was that throughout the next twenty-six years of Touré's government, Guinea, like many other African states, depended on U.S, French, and other Western companies to exploit its rich iron and bauxite mines. Despite his rhetoric, Touré was conspicuously unable to develop an autonomous process of economic accumulation.

Congo

The aborted national liberation movement in Congo is perhaps the saddest case in the history of decolonization in Africa or elsewhere. Indeed, this is not a case of post-independence economic failure, but of the blatant reimposition of Western imperialist control. Leaving aside its immense forest and hydroelectric potential, Congo possesses extraordinary mineral resources including gold, silver, diamonds, copper, uranium, cobalt, tin, zinc, and iron ore. Such a prize could not easily be surrendered by the Belgians. By the mid-1950s, 24 percent of Congo's GDP came from mining and industry. By then more than one million of the country's twelve million people were wage workers. Heavily engaged in mining, such skilled and unskilled workers were to be found also in manufacturing, construction, transportation, services, and agriculture. By the early 1950s, these workers as well as an increasingly politicized peasantry, constituted the base of an emerging democratic movement led by the radical nationalist Patrice Lumumba.

Rioting in the capital, Leopoldville, in 1959 forced the Belgians to allow national legislative elections in May 1960. Lumumba's Mouvement National Congolais (MNC) was able to command a slim majority of seats in both chambers of the Congolese parliament. Lumumba, consequently, became the country's first prime minister. The presidency fell to Joseph Kasavubu, the leader of the Abako Party, which represented the Western-educated and urban element of the Bakongo ethnic group. Lumumba's MNC was the only party with a national base of support. It gained the backing of workers, peasants, and the educated petty bourgeoisie from all parts of the country. Inspired by Nkrumah, Lumumba was committed to the ideals of national unity, economic independence, and pan-African unity.

No sooner was Congolese independence declared (1960) than the country descended into anarchy. Moise Tshombe's Conakat Party, based in the rich mining province of Katanga and thus committed to keeping close ties with Belgian mining interests, declared the secession of Katanga in concert with the Belgians. With the United Nations forces looking the other way, the Belgians organized the detention and murder of Lumumba by elements of the Congolese army. The *eminence gris* behind the assassination, Colonel Mobutu Sese Seko, emerged as a military dictator largely through the support of the United States.

Decolonization in Africa turned out to be only a partial success at best. Local elites from what may be described as the propertyless but educated middle class, replaced the European colonialists and that was at least an advance over white rule. Corrupt and incompetent as they often were, they at least governed from the point of view of the local population rather than Europe. More significantly, during the 1950s and 1960s, the newly independent African states were able to participate in the global economic progress of those decades to a greater or lesser extent. Indeed, it needs to be underlined that the economic growth and social progress of Africa in these decades was greater than during the previous period of European imperialism.

Growth of per capita GNP in less developed countries, including those in Africa, averaged three percent per annum between 1950 and 1975, only slightly below the increase in the countries of the developed world. Moreover, modern health and educational institutions were put into place in many decolonized states. Tanzania and Zambia became real models of social development. Life expectancies rose, often, in spectacular manner. State-supported manufacturing made significant progress in countries such as Egypt and Turkey.

Perhaps the most spectacular success among non-communist third world states was registered by the geographically and demographically vast country of India. Its economic performance post-independence was far superior to its record under British imperialism. Food security and a stable representative democracy were notable achievements from the perspective of the mass of the population. In order to maintain popular support, successive Congress Party governments instituted essential social programs in health and education and provided subsidies for fertilizers, basic grains, and other necessary commodities. India's most important economic success was its program of industrialization. Strongly protecting its nascent industries against intrusion from outside, the first two decades after independence saw an impressive advance of Indian manufacturing in textiles as well as in heavy industry. Its accomplishments duly noted, it has to be said that India's development programs largely benefited an emergent rural and urban middle class, leaving most of the population in poverty.

Indeed, the gap between the first and third world did not close during this period. The percentage of industrial production in third world countries compared to the developed world only marginally increased. Per capita industrial production scarcely progressed. Third world exports increased dramatically, but remained largely confined to raw materials and primary products. Ongoing export competition between third world countries reduced returns. Leaving aside Brazil, Chile, Argentina, Turkey, Egypt, India, and Mexico, it was only in Asian countries with special relationships with Britain or the United States, such as South Korea, Singapore, Hong Kong, and Taiwan, that significant industrial progress was evident. Whatever endowments they may have had that favored economic growth, these countries were a counterpart of the military bases that ringed the developing giant of Communist China. They were given special access to Western markets in order to bolster their economies. Indeed, U.S wars in Korea and Vietnam, which were really wars of containment against this East Asian Communist colossus, stimulated their growth. However significant the movement toward decolonization in Asia, the Middle East, and Africa, most of the newly independent states were not able to break out of continued economic dependence on the advanced capitalist countries.

3

The Postwar Boom and De-Stalinization

Decolonization reflected the political weakness of colonial powers after the Second World War. Mustering whatever grace they could, and in cases like the abandonment of Indonesia or Algeria there was little grace, the old imperialist states, including Britain, France, Belgium, and Holland, departed their colonial possessions. They were too weak to do otherwise. But the process was made less painful for them by the new liberal global trading order created by the United States after 1945. Rising levels of growth at home and open markets abroad compensated for the loss of political empire. Indeed, as the 1950s continued, the accelerating pace of decolonization came to signify the newfound confidence of the leading capitalist states. In the advanced capitalist countries in the boom years between 1950 and 1973, industry expanded by 5.5 percent on average and trade by 7.7 percent per annum. These historically unprecedented levels of growth created the foundations of a new mass consumer culture that emerged in North America and Western Europe. Whatever were the challenges from the third world or from the seemingly monolithic Communist bloc, they were offset by the economic strength of the capitalist West and Japan. In retrospect these prosperous decades came to be known as the golden years. For the privileged minority of the earth's population that inhabited the advanced capitalist countries this period provided a previously unimagined affluence. Strong economic growth, the dream of social mobility, and consumerism became the ideological shibboleths of the West in the Cold War.

The catalyst of World War had already put an end to the economic paralysis of the Depression. High levels of industrial output between 1938 and 1948 offset the destructiveness of the war. Growth nearly equaled the record economic performances of earlier decades in the twentieth century. Such wartime achievements were based on the extraordinary mobilization of workers for war production, new methods of industrial production, and gains in productivity. After a period of adjustment following the end of the conflict, successive waves of growth after 1950 based on Keynesian principles carried the world economy forward to an entirely new level of output, exchange, and consumption.

Economic Expansion in the Western World

The blueprint for this expansion was largely created by the United States in the immediate postwar period. The basic framework became the restoration of the European and Japanese wings of global capitalism under U.S. direction. Deliberately rejecting the protectionism of the past, the United States created the institutional cornerstones of a new worldwide liberal economic order. The IMF, the World Bank, and GATT became the pillars of this new economic structure. Five successive rounds of GATT tariff reductions based on the principle of most favored nation removed many of the barriers to world commerce between 1947 and 1963. The role of the dollar—its value as good as gold—as global reserve currency enormously increased world financial liquidity.

The Marshall Plan represented a major economic step toward trans-Atlantic multilateralism. U.S. and European rearmament then provided further financial liquidity to the trans-Atlantic and Asian economies. The European states themselves reinforced moves in the direction of multilateralism with the creation of the European Payments Union (1950). The next year, the six-nation European Iron and Steel Community took form based on an exchange of German coal, machines, and machine tools for French, Dutch, Belgian, and Luxembourg foodstuffs and steel. Indeed, German economic advance became the engine fueling the growth of its new partners. The German Federal Republic assumed leadership in moving France and the other Western European states toward the conclusion of the Treaty of Rome (1958) creating the European Common Market (European Economic Community).

Relatively high profits and low labor costs were a major factor behind the economic expansion. The repression or containment of labor's demands had been a major aim of the belligerents on both sides in the Second World War. The end of the war brought a major upsurge in working-class militancy in the United States, Canada, France, Belgium, Italy, and Japan. Militant unions demanded higher wages as well as greater economic and political equality. An apparently coordinated campaign of repression by governments and businesses broke the back of the global labor upsurge by 1948. Meanwhile, emigration from the German Democratic Republic as well as an influx of German refugees from Poland, Czechoslovakia, and elsewhere in Eastern Europe, helped to drive the already low expectations of West German workers still lower.

Migration from the impoverished south to the northern industrial cities in Italy and a continuing rural exodus toward the towns in France helped to keep industrial labor costs in these two states down as well. Some six million further migrants from Greece, Italy, Portugal, Spain, Turkey, Yugoslavia, Ireland, and Finland provided a pool of low cost labor to the core industrial countries of the Common Market. Several million more migrants arrived from North Africa, the Middle East, and Central and West Africa. Hundreds of thousands of migrants from central and southern Africa fuelled the expanding mining and manufacturing industries of the Republic of South Africa. Millions of Mexicans, likewise, migrated to the United States in search of work. Most of this migration from the undeveloped world was made up of unskilled workers. But there was a serious hemorrhage of physicians and engineers from third world countries as well. In the 1950s and 1960s the international migration of workers totaled approximately thirty million. The entry of these workers into the labor pool of the advanced capitalist countries helped to keep labor costs down and to sustain profits.

Productivity

But another major source of profits and, therefore, growth was gains in productivity. The assembly line, mass production, and the business techniques of the modern corporation had, of course, been invented decades earlier. But it was only in the postwar period that they came to operate as leading factors across the whole of the industrial economy. New equipment, technology, and automation played a major part in such advances. The introduction of robots, nuclear power, lasers, new strains of grains, insecticides, herbicides, preservatives, synthetic fabrics and plastics, jet aircraft, rockets, super tankers, transistors, and computers transformed the production and distribution of food and industrial goods.

Gains in productivity were not only the result of the spread of new mass production techniques and inventions. They also came about through the more widespread use of shift work as well as subcontracting. Farmers, small business owners, and truckers were forced to raise productivity as they were squeezed by debt and higher costs. Increased pressure on workers was offset by higher wages and greater purchasing power. Wage increases, in turn, spurred further investments in labor-saving technology. The purchase, consumption, and enjoyment of commodities as central to a good life—consumerism—became deeply embedded in the mentality of North Americans, first of all, and then of Western Europeans. Consumerism proved to be about half of what was required for a fully satisfying life. It proved no substitute for participation in a democratic and egalitarian social order. Unfortunately it was put forward as an alternative to it.

Keynesianism

It was capital that ruled politically as well as economically and its rule was reinforced by consistently high rates of profit. But in this period the expansion of capital based itself on the so-called Fordist model of accumulation, which linked growing consumer demand to the mass production of medium-priced durable goods. Wherever consumerism dominated it reinforced the rule of capital by tending to undercut the significance of mass politics based on organized labor. The golden years saw a visible ebbing away of the political strength of organized labor, especially in the United States. One of the ways that the militancy of labor was tamed was by including it as a junior partner in the management of economic affairs. In the advanced capitalist countries, big capital and big unions together with government constituted a troika, or tripartite partnership, which dominated and regulated the heights of the economy. The management of demand through government fiscal and monetary policy as well as massive state investment in infrastructure, health, and education came to be taken for granted. In economic circles, the notion of managed capitalism based on the teachings of John Maynard Keynes became the new orthodoxy replacing classic free market doctrines. Military spending constituted a significant proportion of overall government expenditure. We have already noted the importance of such spending to the take-off of the world capitalist economy in the early 1950s. Such outlays continued to provide an important economic stimulus throughout the next two decades and beyond.

Relatively slow in Britain, appreciable in the United States, economic growth was particularly fast in Germany, Italy, France, and, especially, Japan. Urbanization worldwide increased dramatically as a result of rural and foreign migration to the towns. In 1950, there were seventy cities with populations of more than one million. Twenty years later, there were 180 such cities. Mexico City grew from three to nine million, while Sao Paolo increased from 2.5 to ten million. Postwar reconstruction and urban expansion led to a vast increase in housing construction. The exodus of the lower middle and well-paid working class into U.S. suburbia created a new culture of mass consumption, while stimulating enormous demand for prefabricated housing as well as cars, consumer durables, and furniture. By the 1960s, the West Germans, the Dutch, and the French were beginning to enjoy comparable levels of affluence. For some, at least, the end of scarcity seemed at hand. Contrariwise, urban downtowns and public transport systems in the United States went into a sharp decline. Millions of urban newcomers—blacks and Chicanos in the United States and third world emigrants in Europe—were excluded from the new affluence.

Consumerism

Advertising agencies, otherwise known as Madison Avenue, became indispensable to stimulating and shaping demand in the United States. Such was their influence that by the 1950s they were running U.S. electoral campaigns, converting politics into a managed spectacle. Soon publicity agencies crossed the Atlantic and invaded Europe. By 1960, some thirty-six U.S. advertising agencies had opened in Western Europe with more than 180 branch offices in the main cities. U.S. advertising, films from Hollywood, popular music, and other forms of mass media and culture played a major role in spreading U.S. mass culture and consumerism to Europe and beyond.

Cars became essential as transport, their use facilitated by massive road and superhighway construction on both the North American and European continents. In Western Europe, automobile production rose from half a million cars in 1947 to more than nine million 20 years later. In the United States and Europe, weekend outing and annual vacation trips by automobile became a norm. In the 1960s travel abroad to Europe by Americans, and to the Mediterranean by Europeans became a mass phenomenon. Leisure and vacation expenditure were made necessary by a more intensive rhythm of life and work. Consumption on this scale was facilitated by a vast expansion of personal credit. The previous resistance to taking on debt by farmers and workers gradually dissolved. The reality of social inequality remained, but was softened by access to consumer goods and the apparent prospect of upward social mobility for the younger generation. Older working-class and ethnic identities declined, if they did not completely disappear. The spread of individualism eroded family, working-class, ethnic, and peasant solidarities. The combination of individualism and consumerism fostered what has been memorably described as a culture of indifference.

Over the period, the drive toward industrial and financial concentration accelerated. U.S.-based transnational corporations dominated the world economy. A third of industrial production came from the United States. Facilitated by the fact that the U.S. dollar was the world's reserve currency, U.S. investment expanded dramatically in Canada, Europe, and the third world. Multinational corporations, U.S. and otherwise, produced a sixth of all of the world's goods and services in the 1960s. The U.S. and British share of world commerce declined relative to Germany, Japan, and other advanced capitalist countries. Trade between these advanced economies tended to be the core of global trade. An increasing fraction of what they produced was traded between them, and manufactures constituted an increasing fraction of such trade. Indeed, a growing percentage of international trade was, in fact, intercorporate.

Employment

The rural work force declined dramatically. In 1950, 30 percent of the work force in Western Europe was still rural. By the mid-1970s, the number of those working on farms had dwindled to 12 percent. In the United States, the number of those living on the land had already declined to 12 percent in 1950 and was to fall to as low as 4.1 percent by 1973. Employment in manufacturing in the advanced capitalist countries peaked in the 1950s and, then, shifted gradually toward the service sector. Hours worked declined across most economic sectors. Public bureaucracies, and also the bureaucracies of private corporations, expanded enormously during the period. The employment of women grew steadily, although they were largely confined to lower paid and less skilled work.

The need for skilled white collar and supervisory personnel led to an explosion of higher education. In France, the number of students in universities grew by ten percent a year in the 1960s. Expansion of university enrollment in the United States and Japan averaged 7.5 percent over the same decade. In Great Britain and West Germany, such enrollments increased on average five percent per annum. The role of the state in upgrading the labor force through expenditure on health, education, housing, and welfare notably increased. Overall state expenditure as a percentage of GDP approximated 50 percent in countries like Sweden, Great Britain, and France. State-financed research and development spending orientated toward the military provided the United States economy a distinct competitive edge.

The U.S. Economy and Society

The expansion of the already large U.S. economy continued at an impressive pace. In the 1950s its GNP increased by no less than 37 percent. Median family income grew by almost as much. Unemployment for the most part was low, while prices increased only slowly. Sparked by expenditure on war, tariff reductions, and increased social spending, the economy under Presidents Kennedy and Johnson expanded even more rapidly in the 1960s. Defense contracts fueled economic growth in the U.S. south and west. Millions of people migrated to this so-called Sunbelt from New England and the Midwest, where industry tended to languish.

As the memory of the New Deal faded, the grip of big business over U.S. society tightened. By 1960, a third of economic output was produced by the 500 largest corporations. The ten largest of these corporations earned as much profit as all the others combined. Indeed, about 150 banks, insurance companies, and manufacturing companies dominated the whole U.S. economy. Despite this monopolistic control of the economic heights, one million intermediate-sized and ten million small businesses made up a vital part of the substantial business class of the United States.

In spite of growing corporate power, unions were apparently at the height of their power at the beginning of the 1950s. Organized labor's strength was symbolized by the merger of the AFL and CIO in 1955. At that time, some 35 percent of the U.S. workforce belonged to unions. Union leaders focused on bread-and-butter gains such as higher pay or shorter hours for the rank and file. In the face of increasingly formidable right-wing political opposition, they largely abandoned attempts to achieve national social programs like public health care. The purge of Communists from the ranks of the labor movement continued through the 1950s, strengthening the trend toward business unionism. Indeed, in certain unions, such as the Teamsters and the East Coast Longshoreman, corruption and racketeering became a problem. Craft, and even some industrial, unions, tended to neglect or exclude the unskilled, especially women and blacks. Union members who moved to the suburbs often lost contact with their old working-class neighborhoods and began to consider themselves middle class. The sense of working-class identity was diluted, despite the fact that real upward social mobility seems to have been at best limited. In the period 1958–63, management carried out a major offensive against labor, weakening unions further. Fleeing the heavily unionized Midwest and Northeast, many companies moved to the South or Southwest where they escaped union influence. The long decline of the U.S. union movement began.

The Eisenhower Presidency

A Republican president, Dwight Eisenhower, dominated U.S. politics during the 1950s. Not the least of General Eisenhower's appeal was his promise to bring an end to the Korean War during the election campaign of 1952. After a generation of upheaval and war under Democratic administrations, peace and consumerism, presided over by an unassuming and plain-spoken Republican president, seemed attractive. It appeared as the preferred alternative to continuous war mobilization offered by the Democrats, who persisted in rhetorically invoking the New Deal electoral promises of the past.

The turn to the right in the United States was paralleled by developments elsewhere. Labour had already lost its majority in Australia and New Zealand in 1949. The Social Christians took power in Belgium in 1950. The Conservatives returned to power in Britain in 1951. By 1958, Canada, too, was ruled by its Conservative Party. Christian Democrat rule would continue in West Germany until the 1960s, and, in Italy, would carry on almost indefinitely.

The return of the Republicans to government signified the end of the dominance of New Deal liberalism in the United States. Eisenhower believed that big government, rather than big business, was the issue. The possibility that both big business and bureaucratic government might be problematic was not discussed. While avoiding frontal attacks on the major programs and regulatory framework of the New Deal, Eisenhower attempted to limit government intrusion into economic life. Republican dominance meant the return of control over national politics to Wall Street and Main Street—big and small business recovered political influence.

The first two years of the Eisenhower administration were dominated by McCarthyism, which continued at high tide. Refusing pleas for executive clemency, Eisenhower presided over the execution of Julius and Ethel Rosenberg on June 19, 1953. The next year saw passage of the Communist Control Act legislatively attacking the Communist Party and its members as well as Communist-dominated unions. Another 6,000 politically and sexually suspect individuals were purged from the federal government under Eisenhower. McCarthy recklessly launched an assault on Communist influence in the military, arousing the ire of Eisenhower, the old soldier. The latter demanded a congressional hearing. The resulting nationally televised proceedings exposed and discredited the Senator who was censured by the Senate on December 2, 1954, putting an official end to the Red Scare.

A paternal and reassuring figure, Eisenhower's tenure in office as president for the duration of the decade was secure. But the Republican Party lost control of Congress in the elections of 1954. Eisenhower, then, worked with conservative Democrats in Congress led by two Texans, Lyndon Johnson, the Senate majority leader, and Sam Rayburn, speaker of the lower house. This was a new version of the old alliance between southern Democrats and Republicans that had narrowed the New Deal domestic political agenda since the late 1930s. With such support, Eisenhower was able to pass the not very controversial Interstate Highways Act. The subsequent construction of a national grid of superhighways confirmed the dominance of automobiles and trucks as the major means of transportation in the United States. Support for urban public transit and the railways withered. A federal aid to education measure passed only due to U.S. consternation at the Russian launch of Sputnik, the first space satellite, in 1957.

Eisenhower, like many white people in the United States, was mildly racist, taking for granted what he saw as the natural inferiority of blacks. Moreover, as a political conservative, he instinctively sympathized with the Southern segregationist shibboleth of states rights against the encroachment of federal power. He was taken aback, then, in 1954 when the Supreme Court ruled that separate schools for black children were unconstitutional. He was even more dismayed when southern white resistance forced him to use federal troops to desegregate Arkansas' Little Rock Central High School in 1957.

The Age of Conformity

While the beginnings of the civil rights movement bespoke a growing restlessness on the part of blacks, Cold War conservatism, echoes of the Red Scare, and the intensification of a homogenizing consumerism undoubtedly intensified social and political conformity among the majority of the U.S. population during the 1950s. More and more people in the United States got their news and entertainment from the new medium of television. Controlled by private corporations and advertisers, the information and mass entertainment made available through television was strictly limited and constrained. The homogenization of thought and taste that such control produced was astonishing. To a remarkable degree people in the United States increasingly took on a new consumer identity engendered by the media.

The Revolt of Youth

Perhaps the conformity of the 1950s has been exaggerated. But a panoramic chronicle of the decline of the U.S. left, Clancy Sigal's forgotten epic *Going Away* (1961), bears witness to the narrowing of political choices and growing social conformity experienced by millions of people in the United States during that decade. J.D. Salinger's novel *Catcher in the Rye* or James Dean's film *Rebel Without A Cause* suggest that the sense of constraint and pressure was deeply felt, especially by the impressionable young. Indeed, frustrated adolescence was a theme of the age much developed in Paul Goodman's essay *Growing Up Absurd*. Alienated, occasionally even rebellious, youth was a new and potent social identity created paradoxically in the midst of this apparently conformist decade.

Massive economic transformation, consumer affluence, and political repression made the young, rather than the downtrodden worker, into a symbol embodying both change and protest. The estranged condition of the young that the old New York intellectual Goodman philosophized about, the Beat Movement, turned into a literary movement and personal lifestyle. From a perspective of deliberately chosen marginality, these young writers and drifters led by Allen Ginsberg and Jack Kerouac rejected literary formalism and social conformity. They attacked consumerism, bureaucracy, militarism, and racism from the point of view of unlimited personal freedom. Legally enforced heterosexual and monogamous sex was strongly challenged by these so-called Beats. Rejection of the sexual restraints and the conformity of the nuclear family, especially in the poems of Ginsberg, represented a direct threat to the heart of middle-class and suburban consumerism. Almost as remarkable as what the Beats were asserting was the notoriety and fame they achieved as a result of the attention they received from a sensation-hungry media.

Indeed, because sex sold, it was featured in the films of Marilyn Monroe, the photos of Hugh Hefner's *Playboy Magazine*, and the steamy novels of the suburban novelist Grace Metalious. The barriers of censorship were broken down and sexuality in entertainment and advertising became more overt. More direct and potentially explosive in its appeal was the sexual and generational defiance embodied in the powerful musical beat and explicit lyrics of artists like Jerry Lee Lewis, Little Richard, and, above all, Elvis Presley. Rooted in the rhythm and blues music of the black underclass, rock and roll would become the musical accompaniment of the protests of youth during the sixties. Exported, differently received, and transformed by the young in virtually every country, U.S. rock and roll would become the take-off point of a new, often highly creative, global popular music.

Women's Role

Along with disgruntled blacks and youth, women, or some women, chaffed at the domestic role they had been confined to in suburbia. Employment gains that women had made during the war had been eroded in the aftermath. Birth rates and the rate of family formation dramatically increased after 1945. The dominant media insisted that women's role lay in the domestic sphere. To be sure, equality between men and women in marriage was advanced as an ideal, but the number of divorces increased. In the course of the 1950s, more and more women, both single and married, reentered the lower end of the labor market. Greater numbers of women enrolled in colleges and universities. The invention of the contraceptive pill (1957) began to give women greater control over their sexual lives.

U.S. Modernism

Popular culture in the United States flourished, but so, too, did high culture. Flush with money, universities expanded prodigiously during the 1950s, producing path-breaking research in both the sciences and humanities. Many of the best universities were graced by a generation of German and Jewish refugees from Nazism who set new standards in scholarship and learning. In the musical work of Gian Carlo Menotti, Charles Ives, and Aaron Copeland, the United States began to produce composers of international quality. This was even more true in literature in which authors such as William Faulkner and Ernest Hemingway emerged as writers of the first order. The United States had already, prior to the war, spawned a great architect in the person of Frank Lloyd Wright. In the 1950s, the power and money of New York provided the setting for some of the great buildings of the so-called modernist international style of Walter Gropius, Le Corbusier, and Mies van der Rohe.

Indeed, it was in the United States that the modernist style seemed to reach its most perfect expression. The origins of modernism can be dated to the epoch of the First World War and the appearance of Cubist, Surrealist, and German Expressionist art. A similar avant-garde rupture with realism can be seen in the strong rhythms and atonalities of the music of Igor Stravinsky, Arnold Schoenberg, and Alban Berg or in the stream of consciousness prose of James Joyce and the austere and formal poetry of T.S. Eliot. Aside from their rejection of realism, the hallmarks of such work were the conscious repudiation of tradition, stress on the laying bare of the techniques and materials of art, rather than on their concealment, and emphasis on the creative freedom of the individual artist. With the exception of German Expressionism of the 1920s, modern art tended to eschew direct political involvement choosing to remain distant from the public sphere.

Many of these modernist trends reached their pinnacle in the New York Abstract Expressionist school, which crystallized in the years after the Second World War. In contrast to German Expressionism, but in keeping with the main trend in modernism, it avoided politics as a subject. Its leading lights—Arshile Gorky, Willem de Kooning, Jackson Pollock, and Mark Rothko—instead created a style of pure form and color of the highest imagination. There were of course other tendencies in U.S. art. Moreover, many found the work of these artists incomprehensible and even subversive. But the New York critics and very rich U.S. patrons and collectors—the Rockefellers, Whitneys, and Guggenheims— who took up the work of these artists, rightly saw in their productions an art of great stature. The canvases of Rothko and Pollock were, indeed, landscapes of the imagination on a grand scale. Moreover, in the context of the Cold War, they seemed to exemplify, at the most creative level, the U.S. notion of individual freedom and self-expression as the highest human values.

The Abstract Expressionist school sought to create an art that rose above vulgar consumer values and the capitalist market place. In fact, its uncompromising individualism, relentless search for innovation, rejection of the particular in favor of what was abstract and universal, and sensitivity to the art market made it the ultimate expression of an increasingly cosmopolitan U.S. enterprise culture. With

Abstract Expressionism, the avant-garde and high capitalism came together in perfect balance. Despite the political conformity of the 1950s, U.S. popular and high culture reflected remarkable creativity. Indeed, culture was to prove one of the most important and enduring U.S. export to Europe and the rest of the world. In part, the appeal of U.S. culture was based on its association with consumer affluence and economic power as much as with the global reach of U.S. media and advertising. But its appeal also lay in the fact that U.S. culture's openness to change and rejection of restraint intuitively responded to the incessant economic and social transformations of the period.

Massive Retaliation and Third World Intervention

Meanwhile, in the realm of foreign affairs the Eisenhower Presidency began auspiciously with the signing of a truce agreement ending the Korean conflict (1953). The ongoing U.S. military presence on the Korean peninsula made it possible to continue with the containment policy against the People's Republic of China. Support for the nationalists on Taiwan and the creation of the U.S.-backed Republic of Vietnam (1955) in the aftermath of the French collapse in Indo-China bolstered that effort. In both the Korean and Vietnam conflicts, Washington had threatened the use of nuclear weapons. Indeed, the threat to use nuclear weapons became an important feature of U.S. foreign policy in the Eisenhower years. Fiscally conservative, Eisenhower sought ways to reduce military expenditure and to staunch the incipient U.S. trade imbalance that had emerged during the Korean War. Following the end of the conflict, the Eisenhower administration pruned the military budget, attempting, especially, to reduce overseas financial outlays. In place of strengthening conventional military forces overseas, it invoked the threat of U.S. nuclear retaliation against Soviet aggression.

The doctrine of massive retaliation, as it came to be called, involved more than the mere threat of a resort to nuclear weapons in case of war. It embraced the option of deliberately triggering such a nuclear war. The Soviet Union exploded a thermonuclear device in 1953 only one year after the United States had done so. Its launch of Sputnik in 1957 then signified Soviet acquisition of an enhanced delivery system for such nuclear weapons. But the reality was that the Soviet Union's nuclear strike capacity was still limited with respect to the United States. It was to remain so until the mid-1960s. Taking advantage of this ongoing strategic advantage, Eisenhower and his war planners advocated preemptive nuclear war. In a political crisis, a first strike would be launched to incapacitate as much as possible of Soviet military capacity, while limiting damage to the United States. On this basis, NATO allies, including West Germany, were in practice permitted access to tactical nuclear weapons.

There was something inherently insane about the logic of destruction embodied in the doctrine of massive retaliation. Eisenhower, in his rare moments of personal reflection, pointed this out himself. Matching talk of massive retaliation, Eisenhower's redoubtable Secretary of State John Foster Dulles threatened to role back the Iron Curtain. That this was illusory rhetoric was clearly demonstrated during the workers' uprising in the German Democratic Republic (1953) and the Hungarian Revolution (1956), when the United States dismissed thoughts of intervening on behalf of the insurgents. By doing so, it conceded defacto that Eastern Europe was a Soviet sphere of influence.

Rather than directly challenging the Soviets in Europe, the the United States covertly or directly intervened against the threat of third world radical nationalism and communism in Iran (1953), Guatemala (1954), Lebanon (1958), and Congo (1960–61). U.S. intervention in Lebanon and Iran and the reining in of its French and British allies during the Suez crisis (1956), marked the active engagement of the United States in Middle East politics for the first time. By 1957 the Eisenhower Doctrine promised to intervene to guarantee the security of Middle Eastern states threatened by Communist subversion. From now on it was Washington, not London, which would endeavor to rein in Nasserism and protect Western access to oil in the Middle East.

During the 1950s, the Marshall Plan and the Common Market fostered a tide of U.S. direct investment in Western Europe. Ford, IBM, Pepsi-Cola, General Electric, and other U.S. companies set up European production facilities during that decade. An important slice of the key economy of West Germany, for example, passed into U.S. hands as a result. Supported by the U.S. government and bolstered by Madison Avenue, such enterprises promoted U.S. production techniques, consumer goods, and mass entertainment.

U.S. policy makers saw European integration and mass consumption as the solution to traditional European conflicts based on national rivalries and class differences. Both the left and the right denounced this Americanization of European life. Consumerism was rightly seen as a threat both to working-class political consciousness and the survival of local traditions. But the unease among the cultural and intellectual elites was not shared by much of the European population, which was attracted to U.S. consumer goods and popular entertainment. To many Europeans from the underclasses, this new lifestyle seemed to undercut the rigidity and snobbery of the traditional European culture that hemmed them in.

West Germany

West German politics in the 1950s were dominated by the dignified figure of the conservative Konrad Adenauer (1949–63). His tenure as chancellor was based on loyalty to the U.S. alliance and the integration of West Germany with the rest of Western Europe. German inclusion in NATO (1955) and the signing of the Treaty of Rome (1958), which created the Common Market, were regarded as crucial steps in the process of European integration. The German army and Prussian landed class having been eliminated as factors, Adenauer's political support was founded on a partnership of industrialists and bankers. Through the Christian Democratic Union, these interests were harmonized with those of the German lesser bourgeoisie, civil servants, professionals, farmers, and Catholics.

The currency reform and economic liberalization instituted by Adenauer's economics minister, Ludwig Erhard, sparked strong economic growth within an increasingly integrated Europe. Steady wage increases and pension guarantees during the 1950s further enhanced the legitimacy of the West German regime in the eyes of its citizens. Industrial militancy was blunted by the so-called co-determination policy, which gave organized labor a partial veto over management decisions in industry. In any case, the influx of millions of East German refugees and foreign guest workers helped to moderate wage claims. Enhanced profitability and investment in new capital equipment helped to restore the supremacy of the German economy in Western Europe. Despite the state's verbal commitment to economic liberalism, the dominance of the big banks and industrial combines and state regulation of labor relations, transport, energy, and agriculture limited the ups and downs of the market.

Italy

Like Germany, the Christian Democratic Party dominated Italy in the postwar period. But the Christian Democrats proved divided. After 1953 they were unable to pull together a stable majority government. The result was a series of unstable minorities. Between 1948 and 1963, there were a total of fourteen different Italian governments. Yet the apparent instability at the top of government was an illusion, as the political class and its business and clerical friends resolutely defended themselves against the threat from the left. Despite the decision of the Communists to pursue a non-revolutionary path, Italy in the late 1940s was shaken by wave upon wave of peasant and worker unrest, both in the industrialized north as well as the south. A third of the electorate voted for the Communists—an impressive result, but not enough to bring them even in sight of power. In the key election of 1948, for example, the sizable vote for the left was dwarfed by that for the Christian Democrats, led by Alciade de Gasperi, who won a decisive victory in parliamentary elections. Closely tied to the Catholic Church and the United States, the Christian Democrats continued to fend off the left through patronage, welfare, bureaucratic control, and political repression.

State-run manufacturing and energy companies as well as heavy public investment in infrastructure helped private industry in Italy lay the basis for economic renewal. Between 1950 and 1960, GNP multiplied 2.5 times, per capita income rose by two-thirds, and industry grew by 7.5 percent per annum, the best performance in Europe. Southern Italian migration to the north provided cheap and abundant sources of labor, enabling highly competitive Italian products to easily penetrate markets in northern Europe and elsewhere from the late 1950s onward.

France

France under the Fourth Republic, like postwar Italy, suffered from apparent political instability. Governments came and went, made up of unstable coalitions of the moderate left and right. Fear of the Communists and of the return of the authoritarian de Gaulle drove successive coalitions of the socialists, radicals, and liberal Catholics (Mouvement Républicaine Populaire) together. But socialist demands for greater government intervention in the economy and for an end to state support for religious education periodically pulled such political alliances apart. Only inaction and inertia could provide stability.

But the German question and the legacy of colonialism provoked political crisis and, finally, the demise of the Fourth Republic. The Korean War had prompted the the United States to press for the rearmament of the new West German state. French unease at the prospect of the reappearance of an independent

German military led the French prime minister René Pleven to advance the idea of an integrated European Defense Community (1951). The idea that the West German army would become part of an integrated European army was greeted with enthusiasm by France's NATO allies. But the combined opposition of the Communists and Gaullists in the French Chamber of Deputies and riots in the streets by the left led to the legislative defeat of the proposal (August 30, 1954). The next year West Germany became a full partner of NATO, and the Soviet Union in response created the Warsaw Pact.

The new prime minister, Pierre Mendès-France, was able to extricate France from the collapse of its colonial empire in Indo-China at the Geneva Conference (July 1954). But miracle-worker that he was, Mendès-France's failure to put an end to the Algerian War led to his resignation 232 days after taking office. Growing exasperation over Algeria then led to French participation in the Suez adventure, which ended in a fiasco. By the beginning of 1958, the French economy was in disarray and the coalition of socialists and the moderate right was hopelessly divided over the future of Algeria. On April 26, a revolt of the settler colonists and army units in Algeria threatened to turn into a military coup in France itself. In order to avoid an army takeover, senior parliamentary leaders invited de Gaulle to assume full powers. This marked the end of the Fourth Republic. De Gaulle would grant political independence to Algeria and other African colonies, while maintaining advantageous economic relationships with them.

Instability at the top of French politics ought not to obscure the stability of France's institutions and the surprising strength of its economy in the 1950s. Whatever happened politically, the civil service of one million, directed by 6,000 to 8,000 highly trained functionaries, continued to superintend every aspect of French society. The economy, important aspects of which were under state control, was carefully managed. The population at large was provided with a great range of social services, including old age pensions, unemployment and maternity benefits, family allowances, and medical care. State management, including investment in infrastructure, fostered the interests of private business above all. Public and private investment, the development of the Common Market, as well as an influx of rural workers into industry, made possible a 40 percent increase in GNP between 1949 and 1958. The purchasing power of workers increased by 50 percent, initiating a consumer boom in houses, automobiles, televisions, washing machines, and refrigerators, which was to fully blossom in the 1960s.

Britain

The Conservative Party dominated British politics in the 1950s. The previous Labour government of Clement Atlee (1945-51), the most notable in the twentieth-century history of Britain, had seen a tide of nationalization and social reform to the benefit of the working class. But the Labour Party was too divided between left and right to win election in the next decade. Following the resignation of the by now doddering Churchill (1955), Anthony Eden, his loyal lieutenant, succeeded him as prime minister. Eden was disgraced by the Suez Crisis and was replaced by Harold MacMillan (1957-63). The Commonwealth and the old trans-Atlantic connection to the United States blocked Britain's full commitment to Europe. Haunted by past glory, MacMillan refused to take Britain into the Common Market. Instead, he repaired relations with the the United States and set in motion the decolonization of the African colonies, which for the most part remained loyal to the Commonwealth following independence. Industrial conflict, poor management, antiquated technology, competition from abroad, and the loss of Empire impeded Britain's economic growth compared to the rest of Western Europe.

Japan

While Britain was relatively stagnant, Japan experienced an extraordinary economic boom during the 1950s under the auspices of the various factions of business leaders, bureaucrats, and politicians that made up the Liberal Democratic party. Successive conflicts in Korea and Vietnam helped to fuel unprecedented economic growth. But so, too, did the close relationship between the government, banks, and manufacturers. Likewise important to the success of Japanese manufacturing was the widespread adoption of the quality control techniques pioneered by the U.S. expert W. Edwards Deming.

Relations with the United States dominated the agenda of Japanese foreign policy. The United States considered Japan its major ally and most important military base in East Asia. U.S. engagement in Korea and Vietnam was justified by its need to protect Japan and its Asian markets. In addition, Japan was given privileged access to the U.S. domestic market. Formal U.S. military occupation came to an end with the signing of a peace treaty and security pact (1952). But scores of U.S. naval and air bases remained on Japanese soil. At the prompting of the

United States, the rearming of Japan took another step forward in 1954 with the creation of the Japanese Defense Force. This measure provoked widespread protest, as did the renewal of the security pact with the United States in 1960. While making these concessions to the United States, the Japanese authorities stubbornly rejected the penetration of U.S. investment into the Japanese economy. Moreover, over U.S. objections, Japan began to open trading relations with Communist China.

The Soviet Union and Its Satellites

The death of Stalin on March 5, 1953, was the decisive event in the communist world in the 1950s. It brought an end to the cult of personality and the reign of terror of the Stalinist period. Under Nikita Khrushchev, the communist system attempted to reform itself. The administrative command system was liberalized in response to the demands of the Soviet and Eastern European population for a better life. Improvements in living standards—modest by Western standards, but important in East European experience—occurred. Within limits, the Soviet Union and other East European governments allowed a certain liberalization of cultural and political life to develop.

Malenkov's Ascendancy

Stalin's death at first took the Soviet people aback. He had ruled almost as a demigod for so long and so absolutely that many felt lost without him. In the immediate aftermath of his death, Stalin's subordinate Georgi Malenkov emerged as head of the Central Committee of the party. Khrushchev, likewise part of Stalin's inner circle, was named to the strategic position of Secretary of the Party. Together with Lavrenti Beria, the head of the secret police, the three ruled as a troika.

The war and the postwar period of economic reconstruction had created new political and cultural forces in Soviet life. The continued repression ordered by Stalin had kept these currents under control. But it was clear that the brutally authoritarian methods of Stalin could not continue, even if there were those of the older generation such as Vyacheslav Molotov and Lazar Kaganovich who wished they could. Accordingly, a cautious de-Stalinization from above set in.

Beria, who was the most compromised by the Terror, took the lead in denouncing violations of socialist legality. Tens of thousands of functionaries were fired or demoted for abuses of power or Great Russian chauvinism against ethnic minorities. In 1954–55 up to 400,000 political prisoners were amnestied. By 1957 two-thirds of the Siberian labor camps were closed and only two percent of prison inmates were political prisoners.

Despite Beria's attempt to exculpate himself, his past as Stalin's executioner had thoroughly compromised him. Abandoned by Malenkov, he was arrested in June 1953 and summarily executed. As a result, the secret police (KGB) were brought back under the control of the party. As it had been the chief instrument of the Terror, the restoration of control over the KGB signified the virtual end of a form of brutal political rule that had dominated Soviet life for more than 20 years. In cultural matters there was a perceptible thaw. Criticism of the foundations of the system was forbidden, but writers were allowed to discuss careerism, bureaucracy, and corruption. The aridity of social realism was remarked and there were calls for greater sincerity in literary expression.

As in the West, economic growth soared during the 1950s. Industry by then had more than recovered from the ravages of war, but agriculture was still in a deplorable state. Since the 1930s, it had been the milch cow of Soviet industrialization. Investment was negligible, wages and prices low, taxes heavy, and illegal flight of labor from the rural collectives serious. On taking power, Malenkov called for improvements in agriculture as the foundation for raising Soviet living standards. Shortly afterwards, wages were raised, delivery quotas to the state reduced, and production from private plots attached to the collectives encouraged. To help rejuvenate the agricultural economy, 150,000 agronomists and party activists were sent into the countryside. From the beginning of 1954, a campaign to open the so-called virgin lands of Siberia and Kazakhstan was initiated. Hundreds of thousands of young people were attracted to this campaign by a combination of idealism and the material incentive of high wages. By 1956 agricultural output had dramatically increased, with peasant income 50 percent higher than in 1950. Alongside these improvements in agriculture, Malenkov put a new priority on housing and light industry to the benefit of urban workers.

Khrushchev's Coup

Khrushchev opportunistically criticized Malenkov's new economic course, as well as his peace and disarmament initiatives, as deviations from Stalinist norms. At the same time, he attacked Malenkov for his role in the Stalinist purges. Backed by the party apparatus and the army, Khrushchev engineered the condemnation of Malenkov's policies by a plenum of the Central Committee in January 1955. Once in power, Khrushchev proceeded to make Malenkov's policies of détente and the raising of living standards his own. Indeed, having seized power, Khrushchev aspired to be a genuinely popular leader. The aspirations of the people were to be met by the more effective management of the country by the Communist Party.

Soviet Foreign Policy

Important steps had already been taken by Malenkov to ease tensions with the West through the settlement of the Korean and Indo-Chinese conflicts. In 1955 Khrushchev patched up relations with Tito and signed a peace treaty with Austria. In order to forestall West Germany's entry into NATO, he proposed to the Western powers the neutralization of a united Germany. Rejection of this offer by the West led to the creation of the Warsaw Pact. In 1956 diplomatic relations were established with Japan.

The Twentieth Communist Party Congress of February 1956 was a political triumph for Khrushchev. At the Congress, he insisted that continuing détente with the West was to be based on peaceful coexistence or the competition between socialism and capitalism that would avoid all-out war. He further asserted that each socialist state should construct socialism according to its own lights. While this declaration was initially made as a gesture in the direction of Tito, it would soon be tested with respect to Poland, Hungary, and China. At the Congress Khrushchev also reported on the economic successes of the previous five-year plan. Emphasizing a 44 percent gain in productivity, he nonetheless underlined the need to further improve methods of work as well as to introduce new techniques. A new five-year plan was announced featuring the goal of increasing wages and meeting the housing needs of workers.

De-Stalinization and Revolt

On February 24, Khrushchev delivered his celebrated secret speech to the Congress on the cult of personality, the purges, and political illegalities of the Stalin period. In the aftermath of the speech, new liberal measures including attempts to revive soviets and trade unions and to democratize the operations of the Communist Party were announced. A partial decentralization of the economy was introduced. In 1957 the last Stalinist holdovers on the Central Committee, Molotov and Kaganovitch, were expelled from the party as a result of their plotting against Khrushchev. Meanwhile, Khrushchev was forced to deal with an increasingly serious crisis in the communist world. A popular upheaval in Poland in 1956 brought the return to power of the nationalist Communist Gomulka. Khrushchev was required to concede a Polish route to socialism in conformity with his own announced view at the Twentieth Party Congress. But the limits of this doctrine were revealed in the neighboring state of Hungary. A much more serious uprising there led to what the Soviets regarded as a counterrevolution. Soviet tanks crushed the Hungarian Revolution.

Cold War Tensions and the Sino-Soviet Split

Khrushchev, like Eisenhower, sought to buildup Soviet nuclear rocket capacity as a way of limiting overall military expenditure. And like Eisenhower, he was not above casually threatening the use of such weapons. The launching of Sputnik in 1957 especially delighted Khrushchev and alarmed the United States. In fact, the Soviet leadership was increasingly worried over the West German military's growing access to U.S. tactical nuclear weapons. Partly as a countermeasure, Khrushchev began to threaten to sign a separate peace with the German Democratic Republic, which would unilaterally deprive the Western allies of their rights in West Berlin. Relations with Washington appeared to improve during Khrushchev's extended visit to the United States in 1959. But the downing of a U.S. U-2 spy flight over the Soviet Union led to the cancellation of the summit conference between Khrushchev and Eisenhower the next year. Instead, Khrushchev attended the fall session of the United Nations General Assembly where he raucously denounced U.S. imperialism in the Congo and consorted with Fidel Castro, the charismatic leader of the recent Cuban Revolution.

The Soviet Union's pursuit of peaceful coexistence with the the United States failed. It contributed to a break in relations between Russia and China (1960) as well. The latter accused the Soviets of weakness in the face of imperialism. In order to prove his revolutionary credentials in the face of this rupture, Khrushchev began to take a harder line with the the United States. East Germany was in crisis due to the flight through Berlin of hundreds of thousands of its citizens to the prosperous West. After a tense confrontation at a summit in Vienna with John Kennedy, the new U.S. president, Khrushchev once again threatened to conclude a separate peace with the German Democratic Republic, unilaterally ending allied occupation rights in Berlin. At the last minute, Khruschev contented himself with building the Berlin Wall (1961), effectively blocking the exit of East German refugees. Taking things a step further, he secretly agreed to send nuclear-equipped short- and medium-range nuclear weapons to defend the Cuban Revolution against the threat of a U.S. invasion. The ensuing October 1962 missile crisis was the most dangerous moment of the Cold War, threatening a nuclear Armageddon. Although he was able to wring important concessions from the the United States, Khrushchev's withdrawal of Soviet nuclear forces from Cuba was regarded as a defeat.

Khrushchev's Fall

The liberal atmosphere in the Soviet Union persisted as 1962 saw the publication of Alexander Solzhenitsyn's *One Day in the Life of Ivan Denisovitch*, which described life in the Siberian labor camps. The economy, or at least the industrial economy, appeared to being doing well. There was a notable improvement in the availability of consumer goods and housing in the last years of the Khrushchev era. But the end of 1962 saw Khrushchev launch an intemperate attack on modern, or as he called it, degenerate art at a Moscow art exhibit. The next year, the poet Joseph Brodsky was denounced for decadence and modernism. In 1964 Brodsky was put on trial and imprisoned for five years for social parasitism. New attacks on religion and the music of the great Soviet composer Dimitri Shostakovitch signaled growing reaction.

While these cultural developments darkened the horizon, it was the state of agriculture that constituted Khrushchev's ultimate domestic failure. His reforms were marked first by his attempt to vastly extend the output of corn and increase livestock production east of the Urals and in the south of Russia, areas that had traditionally been left fallow. He attempted to do this by utilizing the top-down Soviet command system to the fullest. Until the early 1960s, it seemed that he might succeed in making a breakthrough. But long-term under-investment in Soviet infrastructure in the form of roads, storage and supply facilities, farm machinery, and herbicides and pesticides caught up with Khrushchev's overly ambitious plans. They led to declines in output, culminating in a disastrous harvest in 1963.

Prior to this domestic reversal, Khrushchev's failures with regard to China and the Cuba missile crisis had disappointed various sectors of the Soviet leadership. Indeed, his arrogance, voluntarism, and endless rounds of administrative reforms appeared to be leading to confusion, while alienating all sectors of the Soviet elite. Khrushchev's agricultural failure seems to have been the final straw. A restoration of order was demanded by many elements of the elite, including those whose tenures were threatened by his constant reorganizations. Khruschev was removed as First Secretary of the Communist Party by the presidium of the party in October 1964. The leader of the opposition to Khrushchev, Leonid Brezhnev, replaced him.

Khrushchev's nine years in power liberalized the politics of the Soviet Union and visibly improved the standard of living of both the peasantry and workers. His constant reorganization of the administrative apparatus may in part have been a reflection of his impetuous temperament and intellectual confusion. But it also represented an attempt to get the bureaucratic structure of the Communist Party and state apparatus to function more effectively. The future would reveal that Khrushchev's political demise was rooted in a structural problem of the overly centralized regime rather than in personal failure.

East German Revolt

The death of Stalin had its most dramatic and immediate impact in the German Democratic Republic. In May 1953, two months after Stalin's death, Walter Ulbricht, the hard-line leader of the Socialist Unity Party, raised economic output targets by ten percent. The Soviets urged restraint and, at the beginning of June, Ulbricht relented. He promised the East Germans that he would immediately take measures to improve the standard of living. But it was too late. On June 16, workers demonstrated in the Stalinallee, the main street of East Berlin. The next day Berlin and other East German cities exploded in revolt. Soviet tanks and troops suppressed the uprising at a cost of 300 dead and 2,000 wounded. Thousands were arrested, of whom 1,000 were sent to jail and 40 executed.

The death of Stalin precipitated the rebellion by emboldening a resistance that had previously been cowered by repression. But the fundamental causes of the upheaval, of course, were years of heavy pressure on the working population of East Germany. All over Eastern Europe, the period 1949–53 was one of deep economic deprivation. While unions acted entirely as management spokesmen, real wages fell, absenteeism or lateness at work were harshly punished, and piece and voluntary work were demanded. Consumer goods were hard to come by or unavailable. Authoritarian control in the work place was one important aspect of the severe political repression that marked the last years of Stalin. Consumption was deliberately curbed and work intensified in order to dramatically increase economic growth, especially the output of producer or capital goods. In East Germany the situation was made worse by the continuation of reparation payments to the Soviet Union. But however lopsided the economy became as a result, it must be noted that a breakthrough toward industrialization occurred throughout Eastern Europe during this period of high Stalinism.

In the wake of the East German revolt, Malenkov's new economic course in the Soviet Union was introduced in most of the other Eastern European communist states. Investment in producer goods remained a priority for the rest of the 1950s, but not at the same high rates as in the previous years. More attention was now given to an improvement in living standards. Light industry and agriculture saw renewed investment. Real incomes rose accordingly between 1953–56. Curbs were put on the political police and there were fewer arbitrary arrests and condemnations.

Poland's Springtime

In two countries, Poland and Hungary, discontent and impatience led to major crises with differing outcomes. In Poland the death of the Stalinist leader Boleslaw Bierut in 1956 led to concessions by his successor Edward Ochab. Ochab released 30,000 political prisoners, rehabilitated many who had been condemned in the purges, and dismissed certain high-handed officials. Political censorship was reduced, but the Polish intelligentsia and journalists pressed for greater freedom. While workers began to demand a reorganization of factories based on Yugoslav principles of worker self-management, in the industrial city of Poznan the management demanded that workers at the giant agriculture machinery plant of ZISPO raise productivity targets by 25 percent. A revolt in Poznan at the end of June 1956 led to 50 deaths and some 3,000 other casualties.

The resulting political crisis inspired the recall of Gomulka to the Central Committee of the Polish Communist Party on October 19, 1956. The return of Gomulka, who had been purged in 1948 as a nationalist, immediately set off alarm bells in Moscow. Khrushchev first attempted to cower the Polish Communist leadership by flying to Warsaw and threatening direct military intervention. Faced with Soviet threats of Red Army intervention, Ochab and Gomulka presented a united front. The Polish Communist leadership distributed arms to workers in the factories. In many plants, the workers took it upon themselves to form councils on the Yugoslav model. Khrushchev was faced with a nationalist revolt that embraced both the population and the Communist Party. From Belgrade and Beijing, the newly reconciled Tito and the increasingly independently minded Mao urged moderation. Khruschev, then, accepted "a Polish path to socialism." On October 20, Gomulka denounced the Stalinist administration of the past. The next day, he was named First Secretary of the Communist Party.

The Polish population turned out in the streets en masse to celebrate what was called "springtime in October." In the aftermath, the Soviets lost direct control of the Polish military, the process of rural collectivization was suspended, and the special place of the Catholic Church in Polish life affirmed. But as an orthodox Communist, Gomulka quickly scuttled the workers councils in the factories. Without returning to the scale of repression under Stalinism, censorship and the persecution of political dissidents returned.

The Hungarian Revolution

The dramatic events in Poland were closely watched in the adjacent state of Hungary. The unrest there precipitated the outbreak of a much more serious upheaval in Budapest. On October 22, university students in Budapest called for an end to Communist Party dictatorship and of Soviet control over Hungary. A demonstration the next day turned into a national uprising whose character was both anticommunist and anti-Soviet. The revolt was the consequence of a failed effort at reform that had been initiated three years earlier. Like other Eastern European states, Hungary had adopted Malenkov's new course in 1953. But unlike in other states, the reform in Hungary embodied not only economic change, but also political democratization. The Stalinist General Secretary of the Communist Party, Mátyás Rákosi, was forced to share power with the veteran Communist Imre Nagy who became prime minister. Nagy moved to give new priority to consumer needs. At the same time, he created a Patriotic People's Front which would include elements outside of Communist control and which was endowed with real political power. Nagy's goal was to restore the postwar Hungarian Peoples Democracy that had existed before the imposition of

Stalinism. In the new context of an industrializing Hungary, the restoration of Peoples Democracy would open the way to democratic socialism. Not only did Rákosi sabotage this program, he ultimately was able to oust Nagy from the premiership and, indeed, expel him from the ranks of the Communist Party.

But Rákosi failed to suppress the opposition, which continued to adhere to Nagy's program from within and without the party. Following Khrushchev's secret speech of February 1956, the focal point of opposition became a literary society, the so-called Petöfi Circle. In the course of the next months, its meetings turned into mass demonstrations and a nationwide opposition movement. Spurred by events in Poland, the student-inspired demonstration of October 22 transformed the movement into a revolution.

The demonstration in Budapest turned into a full-scale insurrection all over Hungary the following day. By October 26 Nagy had been reinstalled as Prime Minister. The Soviets agreed to this measure in an effort to calm the situation. But the national insurrection left the possibility of further compromise behind. The authority of the Communist Party and the political police collapsed. The revolt was strongly nationalist and hostile to the Soviets. Many antisocialist elements— the old middle class, fascists, and even Western agents—took part. The unreconstructed reactionary Cardinal József Mindszenty, a proponent of clericalism and landlord feudalism, led the clerical component of the revolt. But among the insurgents such elements were only a minority and not particularly well organized at that. Thousands of Communists and tens of thousands of workers joined the insurrection. Indeed, throughout Hungary the latter organized workers' councils. By October 27, Nagy had formed a coalition government made up of the parties of Communists, social democrats, small holders, and peasants. While rejecting the idea of a Communist monopoly on power, the coalition did not call for the abolition of socialism, urging instead the establishment of a parliamentary government and democratic socialism. Likely the direction of things was toward social democracy and a market economy as had emerged in neighboring Austria.

Responding to popular pressure, the Nagy government took a dangerous step. On November 1, it announced Hungary's withdrawal from the Warsaw Pact, declaring its neutrality. In response, Soviet troops in large numbers poured across the frontier. On November 4, the Soviets launched a massive attack on Budapest. As a result of the fighting, 3,000 died, 15,000 were wounded, 20,000 were made prisoners, and more than 200,000 fled the country. Nagy was arrested and later executed. Mindszenty took refuge in the U.S. embassy where he remained until 1971.

The new head of government, János Kádár, recovered control through harsh repression and massive purges. But soon he announced amnesties and closed the internment centers. Emphasis from now on was given to raising living standards as against building up heavy industry. Trade and even cultural relations with the West were widened. Collectivization of agriculture was continued, but it was carried out with a certain finesse. By 1962 Kádár could assert, "Whoever is not against us is with us."

Eastern European Nationalism

Upheaval in Poland and Hungary had in part been the result of nationalism that had been stifled under Stalinism and now came to the fore. The force of Eastern European nationalism in the late 1950s is illustrated by the case of Romania under Georgi Dej. At the latter's insistence, Soviet troops were withdrawn from the country in 1958. Spurning Soviet suggestions that Romania specialize in the production of agricultural commodities within COMECON, Romania redoubled its efforts to develop its heavy industry, while opening trading relations with Western countries. The Romanian government's nationalism was offset by its apparently staunch Marxist orthodoxy, which brooked no internal opposition. Even more ferociously orthodox was the smallest and poorest state of the Eastern bloc, Albania, led by Enver Hoxha. Like the Romanians, the Albanians were offended by Khrushchev's attempts to assign Albania the role of producer of raw materials and agricultural goods within the Communist bloc. More alarming to Hoxha was Khrushchev's rapprochement with Tito's Yugoslavia, which was not only heterodox doctrinally, but also threatened to throttle the independence of Albania. Albania began to strike out on its own, looking increasingly to China instead of the Soviet Union.

China

The 1950s, therefore, brought great changes to the states of the communist world—the ebbing of Stalinism, some improvement in living standards, and popular revolt. Nationalism appears to have been the predominant trend leading to a dilution of direct Soviet control over its sphere of influence. The autonomous character of the economic development of each of these states reinforced this trend. But the most significant and dramatic example of the increasing centrifugal tendencies within the communist world was the break in relations between the Soviet Union and China at the end of the decade.

The Chinese Revolution of 1949 marked the high tide of revolution in the twentieth century. Brought on by the cataclysm of the Second World War, the founding of the People's Republic of China meant that the most populous country in the world had joined the communist camp. Indeed, in the immediate wake of the Communist seizure of power in China, the Soviet Union and People's Republic signed a trade agreement (April 1950). More importantly, close political and military collaboration was established between Stalin and Mao, the latter consistently deferring to the Soviet leader. China's effort in the Korean conflict was largely made possible by deliveries of large amounts of Soviet arms and military equipment.

While fighting continued in Korea, the new Communist government of China proceeded to consolidate power (1949–53). The rampant inflation of the last years of Nationalist power was checked. Per capita economic growth rose 20 percent above 1933 levels with the expansion of the industrial sector and increases in wages leading the way. The key sectors of the economy including industry, banking, and insurance were all nationalized, with the former owners for the most part remaining in place as managers.

Manufacturing was, of course, still limited with almost 85 percent of the population still on the land. The completion of land reform during these years was, therefore, a momentous event. The landlord class, which had taken up to half of output in rent from the peasantry, was swept away by the revolution. Historically, the Chinese state bureaucracy had played a negative role, repressing the mass of the population politically and economically. The new Communist state contented itself with appropriating 17 percent of the harvest as a tax. Under the Communist regime the bureaucracy was now made up of holdovers from the old order as well as new Communist functionaries.

First Five-Year Plan (1953–57)

China instituted its first five-year plan between 1953 and 1957. Gross national product advanced by eight to nine percent per annum with emphasis on the expansion of heavy industry. Accordingly, steel production rose by nearly 300 percent, coal by 96 percent, and electricity output by 166 percent. The number of industrial workers increased by 8.7 million with wages 30 percent higher than in 1953. These accomplishments faithfully reproduced the Soviet approach to economic development with stress on the producer goods sector. Indeed, Soviet influence was directly felt through the presence of some 10,000 Soviet technicians, scientists, and experts and the provision of some ten billion dollars in economic assistance.

Bourgeois property had been nationalized, but the influence of the former middle class or national bourgeoisie as managers, experts, and professionals throughout the bureaucracy and economy was still evident. Agricultural production had risen by a fifth, but, as the population had increased under peacetime conditions, per capita output of food lagged behind industrial growth. Agricultural collectivization began in 1955, but the family plot, making up seven percent of arable, and continued to be a significant factor.

The Great Leap Forward

It was under these circumstances that Mao cancelled the second five-year plan and initiated the Great Leap Forward (1957–59). This ambitious, indeed, utopian scheme was designed not only to speed up economic development, but also to move swiftly from the stage of socialism to communism. Poor in fixed capital, China would mobilize the collective labor of its millions of peasants and unemployed urban dwellers to rapidly modernize. The revolutionary transformation of social relations and the consciousness of the masses would release their latent productive potential. Decentralization of the economy would undermine the authority of bureaucrats and experts who, far from advancing socialism, threatened to restore capitalism.

Khrushchev's attack on Stalin at the Twentieth Party Congress and the ensuing Hungarian Revolution had deeply shocked Mao. The unilateral and unqualified Soviet repudiation of Stalin did not square with his understanding of Communist internationalism. Doctrinally and politically Mao decided to strike out on his own. Mao's first response was the short-lived Hundred Flowers Campaign (1956–57), which allowed intellectuals to criticize Communist rule with a view to a rectification of mistakes.

The Great Leap Forward followed the Hundred Flowers Campaign and entailed a rejection of Soviet-style development. In lieu of the traditional Soviet priority on the development of heavy industry, Mao committed China to the simultaneous enlargement of agriculture and light and heavy industry. The development of the economy would be taken out of the hands of bureaucrats and experts and placed in the hands of the people who would be both red and expert. Social transformation and mass political consciousness would liberate the untapped productive capacity of the population, especially the peasantry.

Starting in the spring of 1958, China's 750,000 rural collective farms were amalgamated into 24,000 people's communes with the intent of achieving economies of scale. The labor of masses of peasants was mobilized for collective agricultural production as well as large-scale water control, irrigation, and hydro-electric projects. The industrialization of the countryside could also begin through the creation of a myriad of rural industries like iron and steel production, tool fabrication, crop processing, simple consumer goods manufacture, and small chemical and fertilizer plants.

The rural communes were seen as not only economic units, but also the basis for a vast decentralization of government, education, culture, and defense. Various measures were taken against bureaucratic centralization. Most spectacularly, hundreds of thousands of party cadres and urban and educated young people were sent down into the countryside to assist the peasantry.

Evoking enormous enthusiasm from the rural population at first, the Great Leap Forward appeared to be an extraordinary success. Dramatic gains were registered in agricultural and industrial production as reported by the leaders of the campaign. But the enthusiasm of the peasantry waned in the face of unending work. The so-called backyard furnaces where iron and steel were produced, in fact, produced an inferior and often useless product. Meanwhile, urban industry was disrupted through the diversion of manpower and supplies to rural enterprises. Agriculture was hard hit by flood and drought in 1959 and 1960. Hundreds of thousands, perhaps millions, died. Indeed, 1960 saw the further disruption of the economy through the abrupt departure of thousands of economists, technicians, and scientists as the Soviet Union broke off relations with China.

As early as August 1959, the Lushan Conference sounded a retreat from the Great Leap Forward. In the following months Mao withdrew from direct control of the Communist Party and affairs of state. He regarded himself as retreating, but not defeated by those in the party who were now taking the capitalist road. He remained Chairman of the Party, but real control devolved to the more cautious and orthodox Liu Shao-sh'i. The authority of the Communist Party and centralized planning authorities was restored. The communes, if not the collective farms, were dissolved, the backyard furnaces abandoned. The economy did not recover fully until 1963. On the other hand, many of the rural industries and new infrastructure remained as a positive legacy of the Great Leap.

The Sino-Soviet Schism

The Great Leap Forward was Mao's attempt to break away from what he regarded as Soviet revisionism or a return to the capitalist road. The Soviets, in turn, charged Mao with idealist and voluntarist deviations for attempting to build socialism in the absence of a proper economic foundation. But this dispute was only part of a much wider conflict that now divided the two giant communist powers. Coincident with the Great Leap Forward, Mao had mobilized his armed forces to confront the the United States over control of Taiwan, shelling the nearby Nationalist-held island of Quemoy in 1958. The Soviets complained that they had not been consulted and, consequently, refused to help the Chinese further with their nuclear program. The Soviets asked for communications and submarine bases on Chinese territory, requests which were rejected. The Soviets insisted on pursuing peaceful coexistence, while Mao stressed the need to support international revolution despite the threat of nuclear conflict. Soviet neutrality in China's growing territorial conflict with India outraged Beijing. China questioned continued Soviet control of disputed border areas in Siberia and Central Asia. Soviet failure to face down the the United States during the Cuban missile crisis proved that the Soviets had taken the path of revisionism. Mao concluded that China would, henceforth, have to assume the leadership of the third world struggling against imperialism.

4

Latin America: From Populism to Revolution

By the 1950s the United States had consolidated its hegemony over Western Europe, Japan, and much of the third world. Its creation of the NATO and SEATO pacts attested to its resolve to contain the Soviet Union and Communist China. Its willingness to directly intervene had been demonstrated by its involvement in the Greek Civil War in Europe, in the Korean and Vietnamese conflicts in East Asia, in the overthrow of Iranian Prime Minister Mossadegh, and in the invasion of Lebanon in the Middle East. Its involvement in the distant Congo crisis reflected the global nature of its commitment to combating radical nationalism in the third world. The worldwide scope of its interventions in defense of its interests was remarkable. But its involvement abroad was most evident in Latin America, its so-called backyard.

As elsewhere in the underdeveloped world, poverty and exploitation in Latin America generated support for radical nationalism and communism. Indeed, it should be stressed that from the end of the Second World War to the present, Latin Americans have demonstrated a remarkable capacity for resistance to oppression and imperialist domination. It was in Latin America that the United States would meet its Cold War nemesis in the form of the Cuban Revolution. Revolution on that small island would turn out to have global implications for the United States, breaking the equilibrium of the early Cold War.

Origins of U.S. Imperialism in Latin America

The Spanish American War (1895–98) marked the start of the U.S. effort to control Latin America. Occupation of Puerto Rico and Cuba signified an initial determination to bring the whole of the Caribbean basin under U.S. control. Over the next four decades (1898–1934), the United States used armed intervention at least 25 times in the Caribbean and Central America to ensure its dominance. Safeguarding the Panama Canal and its approaches was an important aspect of this overtly imperialist policy. But so, too, was growing U.S. economic investment in the region, which by the eve of the First World War already totaled $1.7 billion, mainly concentrated in the states of the Caribbean basin. Between 1914 and 1929, U.S. investment doubled, making it the leading foreign investor and economic force throughout Latin America. During the economic boom of the 1920s, U.S. investment in the petroleum industries of Peru, Columbia, Ecuador, and Venezuela was especially remarkable. Under the regime of the U.S.-backed dictator Juan Vicente Gómez (1908-35), the Venezuelan oil industry, largely controlled by U.S. and British companies, produced ten percent of the world's petroleum.

Latin American Populism

The first challenge to U.S. hegemony arose in the wake of the Depression of the 1930s. The economy of the Latin American continent was still overwhelmingly dependent on the export of primary products. These included sugar, bananas, coffee, cocoa, tobacco, rice, indigo, cotton, and livestock produced on plantations and ranches as well as petroleum, ores, and minerals extracted and mined by largely foreign-controlled companies. While the initial stages of industrialization were evident in Argentina, Brazil, Chile, and Mexico, monoculture, unbalanced economic development, and dependence on imports characterized the economies of most Latin American states. Foreign capital dominated important sectors such as banking, railways, mining, and petroleum, even the sugar and banana industries in some countries.

The Depression hit Latin America hard. Exports of primary products declined by 11 percent, while the terms of trade between imported manufactures and exported Latin American primary goods fell by 31 percent. As elsewhere in the third world, local manufacturing benefited somewhat from the decline in the capacity to finance imports. Economic hardship produced political turmoil with 11 of the 20 Latin American republics experiencing upheavals. In El Salvador (1932), Cuba (1934), and Nicaragua (1927-34) there was revolutionary violence. Peru, Ecuador, Venezuela, Mexico, and Brazil installed populist regimes based on a coalition of bourgeois nationalists, organized workers, and peasants. These regimes fostered state-directed national economic development, while trying to alleviate the conditions of workers and peasants. At the same time, populist regimes in Latin America tried to mute or suppress class conflict through an emphasis on national solidarity. Their attempt to restrict the operation of U.S. corporations, while fostering local business and manufacturing, was especially noteworthy. Latin American populists of the 1930s thus anticipated important aspects of the economic and political programs of many postcolonial governments of the 1950s in Asia, the Middle East, and Africa.

Mexico

Outstanding among the populist leaders was Lázaro Cárdenas of Mexico (1934–40). Mexico had gone through a popular and bourgeois revolution (1910–20) with land reform as its greatest achievement. By the 1930s, the ruling Institutional Revolutionary Party appeared to have lost its appetite for change. But Cárdenas, the son of Indian peasants, surprised the party leadership by resuming the revolutionary process when he assumed the presidency. He broke the grip of the military by arming workers and peasants. Renewing the agrarian reform of the revolutionary period, he redistributed the land of the great ranches on a massive scale. Through his political support, he made the Confederation of Mexican Workers a powerful national union.

Efforts to control manufacturing and the resource sector led to conflict with the United States. The Mexican Revolution of the early twentieth century had caused widespread damage to U.S. enterprises. But the middle-class revolutionaries who consolidated the revolution in the 1920s proved eager to attract fresh U.S. investment. From their perspective, Mexico's future development ought to be largely based on the entrepreneurial initiatives of an expanding Mexican middle class. But development also required carefully controlled U.S. investment. These policies were widely resisted by workers, government functionaries, and radical nationalist elements of the middle class under Cardenas. In 1937 a strike by 17,000 oil workers paralyzed the British and U.S. oil companies in Mexico. When the companies refused to negotiate, Cárdenas responded by nationalizing the oil industry. A temporary U.S. embargo on Mexican silver and a suspension of normal diplomatic relations followed.

Washington's reaction to such populist measures in Mexico was mild compared to its direct military invasion in the midst of the revolution (1916). Indeed, its response was tame compared to its unstinting support for the emerging Somoza military dictatorship in Nicaragua in the wake of the assassination of the liberal insurgent Augusto César Sandino (1933). Likewise, it was moderate in comparison to its machinations in Cuba, which led to the overthrow of the democratic government of Ramón Grau San Martín (1934). In the case of Mexico, at least, it lived up to its newly professed Good Neighbor Policy (1934), which renounced the policy of direct military intervention. True to this Good Neighbor approach, the Roosevelt administration, despite its short-term interruption in relations, pursued a conciliatory line toward Mexican populism. The nationalization of the oil industry allowed Cardénas to defuse more radical demands on the part of workers and to prepare the ground for renewed arrangements with U.S. economic interests. The outbreak of the Second World War made possible a renewal of close ties between U.S. and Mexican business.

Brazil

The political and economic stakes for the United States were not as immediately apparent in Brazil, the other major site of Latin American populism during the 1930s. The largest country in Latin America, the three main parts of Brazil—the northeast, southeast, and Amazon—embodied almost all the aspects of Latin American social and economic development. The northeast had been the focal point of the Brazilian economy under Portuguese rule. Hundreds of thousands of black slaves provided the labor force for the sugar plantations, gold mines, and cattle ranches of the region.

In 1822 Brazil became an independent state, although in the form of a monarchy not a republic. As was the case with most of the politically independent Latin American states, Brazil in the nineteenth century was tied to British finance capital. In 1888 the Brazilian monarchy belatedly abolished slavery. The next year, disgruntled landowners, who had not been compensated for the loss of their slaves, organized the overthrow of the monarchy and the proclamation of a republic dominated by landowners and manufacturers.

Under the oligarchic republic, the feverish economic development of the previous period accelerated. The new focal point of the economy was São Paulo to the southeast, where a coffee boom developed. Here accumulated agrarian capital and further European migration provided the basis for growing industrialization. In the remote Amazon basin, aboriginal, mestizo, mulatto, and black peoples subsisted through farming and hunting and fishing. But this gigantic region, too, began to be slowly integrated with the rest of Brazil through the development of rubber plantations, gold prospecting, cattle ranching, and the migration of tenant farmers and sharecroppers from the impoverished northeast.

Until 1930 the republic was entirely dominated by an oligarchy reflecting the interests of the coffee growers and industrialists of São Paulo and the cattle ranchers of Minas Gervais in the northeast. The Brazilian population was made up of a complex racial hierarchy composed of a largely white upper and middle class with the popular classes divided into mulattos, mestizos, aboriginals, and blacks. One year after the onset of the Depression (1930), Getúlio Dornelles Vargas ran for the presidency backed by liberal reformers. He lost the election, but attracted the support of a group of idealistic young army officers known as the Tenentes. They had attempted three coup d'etats in the previous decade. Following the election of 1930, they leagued with the liberal supporters of Vargas and overthrew the old oligarchic order. Over the course of the next fifteen years, Vargas's populist dictatorship transformed Brazil into a modern state. In order to foster national industry, Vargas raised tariffs and controlled foreign exchange and imports. He built an infrastructure of roads, highways, and bridges; created a national steel industry; and began a search for petroleum.

While repressing the left, Vargas boosted wages and provided workers with housing, medical care, schools, social security, and the right to form unions. He strengthened the hand of the central government as against state governors and local political machines. In 1932 the oligarchs of São Paolo unsuccessfully attempted a rebellion. Three years later, the left, including the Communists, mounted a challenge. In 1937 Vargas called into being his "New State" modeled after Mussolini's corporate state.

United States corporations during the 1930s were involved to a limited extent in Brazilian banking, railways, electrical utilities, rubber plantations, and the growing consumer and mass entertainment market. The United States significantly strengthened its ties to Brazil and the rest of Latin America during the Second World War. Already in 1940, Roosevelt urged a program of U.S. investment in Latin America to assure access to important raw materials and to eliminate German influence. In order to facilitate the process, Roosevelt increased the loan limits of the Export-Import Bank to $700 million. Almost immediately, the Bank approved a U.S. loan of $20 million toward the creation of the Brazilian controlled Volta Redondo steel works after the United States Steel Corporation refused to participate in the project.

The U.S. and Brazilian military developed strong relations in the course of the war. The Brazilian armed forces received a significant share of the quarter billion dollars in U.S. Lend-Lease aid provided during the conflict. Vargas was finally ousted in 1945 by a military coup backed by the Brazilian oligarchy. Formal democracy returned, but very quickly so too did worsening living conditions for workers and the poor. In the meantime, Brazil, along with most of the other Latin American republics, signed the Rio Pact (1947) sponsored by the United States. Paying lip service to multilateralism, the Pact used the Cold War to justify U.S. intervention into the affairs of other states. Most Latin American governments signed the Pact in return for the promise of U.S. military assistance.

In 1950, Vargas won election to the presidency as the candidate of the Brazilian Labor Party, a coalition of nationalists, populists, and leftists. The army and the wealthy were deeply hostile to the return of Vargas, as was the United States. Vargas's program of economic nationalism ran counter to a surge of postwar U.S. investment in Latin America. The future of the burgeoning Brazilian oil industry was of particular interest to the United States, prompting an offer of a half billion dollars in development aid. When Vargas created a state oil corporation, the flow of U.S. aid was cut off. And when he began to outline a land reform program and announced plans to double the minimum wage in 1954, the oligarchy prompted the military to present Vargas with an ultimatum. He committed suicide.

Argentina

The last major holdout against U.S. hegemony in Latin America was the populist regime of Juan Domingo Perón in Argentina (1946–55). Argentina was dominated by grain and cattle barons, export merchants, and bankers. British economic investments were three times the size of those of the United States; together they constituted four-fifths of Argentina's foreign investment. In 1943 a coup ousted a conservative oligarchic government and installed General Pedro Ramírez. Ramírez took power on a wave of pro-Nazi, anti-British, and anti-U.S. sentiment.

The ringleader of the coup was Colonel Juan Perón at the head of a group of nationalist army officers. Perón assumed control of the Department of Labor, through which he gained popular influence and built up trade union support. In return for a no-strike pledge from unions, he raised wages, imposed a minimum wage and eight-hour day, encouraged the unionization of the meat packing industry and the sugar plantations, and passed social security and labor legislation. Opposition to Perón, who had become vice-president, emerged among elements in the army and oligarchy. On October 9, 1945, they attempted a coup. Perón's wife, Evita, and union leaders rallied tens of thousands of trade unionists, who seized control of Buenos Aires. Perón was released from imprisonment and returned in triumph.

At the beginning of 1946, Perón won overwhelmingly in elections for the presidency. A sweeping series of measures dealing with health, education, welfare, and social security were then enacted. External trade and foreign exchange were brought under government control. With the proceeds Perón nationalized the British and U.S. companies that controlled transport and communication. Iron, steel, and hydroelectric plants as well as automobile and airplane factories were built. The merchant marine was greatly expanded.

But Perón refused to confront head on the power of the landlords and merchants, despite having the support of the army and the trade unions. At the beginning of the 1950s, the economic situation deteriorated. Exports fell, as did the price of agricultural commodities. Budgetary deficits mounted. Cutbacks were made, the wage demands of workers sternly rejected, and foreign capital invited back in. U.S. influence rose through the extension of a loan of $150 million and an ensuing flow of direct investment. The United States replaced Great Britain as Argentina's leading trade and investment partner. In the end, Perón was unable to keep control of the military; he was deposed in a 1955 coup.

The economic nationalism of populist governments such as those of Mexico, Brazil, and Argentina during the 1940s and 1950s represented an irksome restriction on U.S. trade and investment initiatives in Latin America. At the same time, the opposition of these populist regimes to class conflict helped to restrain the U.S. compulsion to intervene. Populism was a means of muting and containing working-class and peasant radicalism within a framework dominated by an aspiring middle class. But in the early 1950s working-class and agrarian radicalism simultaneously burst forth into popular revolution in Bolivia and Guatemala. As one might imagine, U.S. reaction to these revolutionary upheavals was immediately negative. But ultimate U.S. policy toward the two revolutionary governments, although equally negative, evolved in quite different ways.

Revolution in Bolivia

The majority of Bolivians belonged to the indigenous Andean nations. Mestizos and cholos, or racially mixed elements, made up a quarter of the population. But it was the minority white population that ruled the country during the long-lived Spanish Empire. In 1825 Bolivia seceded from Spain and became an independent republic named for the Latin American liberator Simón Bolívar. The long dominant silver economy, centered around Potosi, declined toward the end of the nineteenth century, giving way to tin mining. A tin mining oligarchy dominated by the Patiño, Aramayo, and Hochshild dynasties dominated the economy after 1900, in concert with British, French, and, above all, U.S. interests. They leagued with politicians, generals, landlords, and cattle ranchers to assure control over the rest of the population.

The late nineteenth and early twentieth century saw widespread dispossession of the indigenous population. Large landowners controlled most of the land. In the Chaco War against Paraguay (1932–35), Bolivia lost a large part of its known petroleum resources. But indian recruits during the war learned how to use guns and to organize militarily. They also came into contact with the increasingly politicized working class. Defeat in war led to the radicalization of these elements as well as part of the middle class and army. The more extreme leftists formed the Party of the Revolutionary Left as well as the Trotskyist Revolutionary Workers Party. The more moderate and middle-class left constituted the National Revolutionary Movement (MNR). Militant peasant leagues and working-class unions buttressed these parties, especially in the mining industry. After repeated revolts and a 1951 electoral victory that was not honored, the MNR led a popular revolution in 1952. Three days of fighting spearheaded by the miners ended with the rout of the army. The military and the traditional parties were destroyed. The revolutionary government of the MNR led by Victor Paz Estenssoro nationalized the tin mines, carried out agrarian reform, and proclaimed universal suffrage. Workers' and peasant militias were organized. Together with the Bolivian Workers' Confederation (COB), they formed a coalition with the MNR.

These developments alarmed the Eisenhower administration, but no U.S. economic interests were directly threatened by the revolutionary regime. Moreover, despite the fact that the new government came to power through revolution, the MNR was dominated by what, after all, was a middle-class leadership. Washington, accordingly, decided that rather than confront the revolution directly, it would try to disarm it by indirect means. By providing substantial food aid, development assistance, and subsidies to the beleaguered tin industry, the U.S. government secured influence with moderate elements within the ruling MNR. Gaining the upper hand within the MNR, these moderates toned down the anti-U.S. rhetoric of the party and began to distance themselves from the labor radicals and communists. The hand of the moderates was further strengthened by virtue of the land reform. The redistribution of some of the land to the peasantry made them increasingly conservative. With the support of the United States, the MNR government then reconstituted the army as a counter to the militias of the miners. The revitalized army under General René Barrientos was consequently able to overthrow the MNR with the acquiescence of the peasantry in 1964, imposing a long period of military rule and enabling the oligarchy to regain control of the land.

Guatemala's Revolution

Perónist government in Argentina and the Bolivian Revolution were part of a wave of populism that swept Latin America immediately following the Second World War. In Guatemala such reformism deepened into a social revolution. Moreover, the Guatemalan revolution, in contrast to that of Bolivia, was inspired by the Communist Party and directly threatened U.S. economic interests. In Guatemala there were no significant middle-class elements with which the United States could work. The revolutionary regime, unlike that in Bolivia, furthermore refused to recognize U.S. hegemony. The CIA, therefore, directly intervened and overthrew the revolutionary government in 1954.

Most of Guatemala's population of three million lived at bare subsistence. Two-thirds of its people were aboriginals who combined subsistence farming with wage work. Socially superior to them, the ladinos (mestizos) constituted a partly assimilated stratum and were often rural schoolteachers, soldiers, and policemen. They were an intermediate element, dominating the aboriginals while serving as go-betweens for the creole elite and the state administration. A small racially conscious creole elite, which controlled three-quarters of the land, had created a coffee industry in the late nineteenth century. In addition, at the beginning of the twentieth century, the U.S.-owned United Fruit Company had established large banana plantations. The hundreds of thousands of workers on these estates and plantations were paid less than a dollar a day in wages. Much of the aboriginal population was forced to work as many as 150 days per year for land-lords in lieu of tax payments. The literacy rate was 25 percent and life expectan-cy 40 years for aboriginals and 50 for ladinos. Much of the aboriginal population lived in communal villages.

In 1944 popular unrest led to the overthrow of the dictatorship of General Jorge Ubico. Ubico was one of a long line of military strongmen who for decades had governed Guatemala on behalf of the landowning elite. The Second World War had stimulated the development of an urban middle and working class. Workers, shopkeepers, students, and teachers were attracted by the reforms of the populist Cárdenas regime in neighboring Mexico. A popular demonstration against Ubico in Guatemala City on June 29, 1944, ended with 200 demonstra-tors killed or wounded.

As protests continued, Ubico could muster little support in Washington. Ubico had loyally served U.S. interests. Like other rulers in Latin America, the outbreak of war led him dutifully to declare war on the axis powers in solidarity with the Untied States, despite his pro-Nazi sympathies. German properties in Guatemala were seized, the process superintended by the FBI. Despite this sub-servience, the United States concluded that Ubico had outlived his usefulness and offered no help.

On July 1, Ubico resigned in the face of popular protest, handing power to General Federico Ponce. Ponce's ambition was simply to replace Ubico as strong-man. While introducing certain concessions such as raising teachers' salaries, Ponce stepped up political repression. The subsequent murder of a journalist prompted a renewal of popular unrest. Ponce was forced to call an election, naming himself as presidential candidate. He was taken aback when the teachers and other opponents of the regime selected Juan Arévalo as a rival candidate. Arévalo was a university professor who had spent the last eight years of the Ubico dictatorship teaching phi-losophy in an Argentinean university. Arévalo brought with him hopes for the installation of a populist government along the lines of the Cárdenas regime in Mexico. His arrival in the country provoked massive demonstrations in his favor.

Ponce responded by ordering the arrest of Arévalo, who was forced to go into hiding. But the would-be strongman's plans were suddenly interrupted by a mil-itary coup. On October 20, two army officers, Major Francisco Arana and Captain Jacobo Arbenz, staged a mutiny. Ponce was forced to resign and the new junta threw their support to Arévalo. A new liberal and democratic constitution was put into place. In December 1945, Arévalo was elected president with 85 percent of the vote. Following his election, Arévalo introduced a sweeping program of social reforms that included social security and labor rights for urban workers. In 1948 he brought in a limited agrarian reform that gave peasants access to credit, guaranteed their legal title to land they worked, and allowed them to rent soil not being cultivated by landlords.

By this point, three years after Arévalo had assumed power, Guatemala was seething with unrest. Labor unions had sprung up not merely in the towns, but among the rural workers. Labor strife and land occupations multiplied, especially on the plantations of the United Fruit Company. Fights between right- and left-wing political parties intensified. Elements on the right unsuccessfully attempted a coup. Arana, as army chief of staff, became a power unto himself on the model of Ubico and Ponce. He had presidential ambitions and rallied to himself all those opposed to Arévalo's reforms, including landlords, the United Fruit Company, some army officers, and the ladino petty bourgeoisie. The peasants and workers who made up the left looked to Arbenz, the minister of defense, who, alongside Arana, had initially brought Arévalo to power.

Arana prepared a military takeover. On July 18, 1949, Arana was gunned down while resisting Arévalo's and Arbenz's order for his arrest. His death set off an uprising by his right-wing followers. Arévalo distributed weapons to several unions and their armed intervention as well as a general strike brought the coup to an end. In the 1950 presidential campaign, Arbenz ran with the support of the labor unions, peasant associations, left-wing parties, and younger army officers, winning the election with 65 percent of the vote.

The son of a pharmacist, Arbenz's intellectual prowess, equestrian skill, and charismatic leadership made for a brilliant career at the military academy dominated by the sons of the landed elite. His wife, Maria Christiana Vilanova, was the daughter of a wealthy Salvadoran coffee growing family. In defiance of her gender and class, she became a sympathizer of the tiny Guatemalan Communist Party. Arbenz, too, came under its influence.

Arbenz proceeded to radicalize the moderate reform program of Arévalo. In the first place, he challenged United Fruit's dominant influence over the Guatemalan economy. The banana company controlled Puerto Barrios, the only harbor on the Atlantic coast. Arbenz announced plans for a publicly owned port that would compete with Puerto Barrios. Likewise, a new public highway would compete with United Fruit's railway to the coast. A public hydroelectric company would be created alongside the monopoly held by a U.S.-controlled company.

The agrarian law of June 1952 allowed the government to confiscate uncultivated portions of large plantations. All land expropriated was to be paid for in 25-
year bonds bearing three percent interest. The valuation of the land was to be
based on its declared taxable worth as of May 1952. During the 18 months of the
law's implementation, 16 percent of all arable land was redistributed to some
100,000 families. Meanwhile, peasants led by militants of the Communist Party
initiated land occupations outside the law.

Communist parties had come into being all over Latin America after the
Russian Revolution. Unable to constitute a mass base in any Latin American
country, they nevertheless played an influential role in the politics of countries
such as Chile, Brazil, Mexico, Cuba, and El Salvador. It was from El Salvador that
the impulse toward a revitalized Guatemalan Communist Party came in the late
1940s. With a membership at first of no more than several hundred members, the
Communists during Arbenz's government were able, nonetheless, to gain considerable influence in the trade unions, peasant associations, and in the government
bureaucracy itself.

The United Fruit Company took the lead in opposing radical change. The
Arbenz government had initially challenged its control of national commerce and
transportation. The regime's expropriation of land subsequently threatened its status as the largest landowner and employer in the country. In March 1953 the government seized more than 200,000 hectares of uncultivated land controlled by the
company. Almost as galling was Arbenz' compensation offer of $627,000, a figure
based on the understated tax assessment that had been submitted by the company
in May 1952. Disregarding complaints from the United States State Department,
the Guatemalan government proceeded to further expropriations in October 1953
and February 1954. By then half of United Fruit's holdings had been confiscated.

In reaction, United Fruit began to raise the cry of communism and Soviet
takeover in Guatemala. It put its subsequent public relations campaign in the
capable hands of Edward Bernays, a nephew of Sigmund Freud, and one of the
creators of the public relations industry in the United States. Bernays had first
achieved prominence during the Wilson administration. He served in the propaganda campaign that mobilized public opinion behind U.S. entry into the First
World War under the banner of making the world safe for democracy. Convinced
that the majority of people had only limited intellectual capacity, Bernays believed
that an enlightened elite necessarily had to manipulate them by playing on their
emotions. Working for the manufacturers of Lucky Strike cigarettes in the 1920s,

for example, he convinced women's rights marchers in New York City to hold up Lucky Strike cigarettes as symbolic "torches of freedom." For United Fruit, he created Chiquita, the dancing Freudian banana, who mesmerized U.S. television audiences in the 1950s. In order to protect United Fruit's interests in Guatemala, Bernays whipped up a public relations campaign against the communist threat there.

United Fruit had other influential friends. Among its major stockholders were the prominent Cabot and Lodge families of Massachusetts. The Secretary of State John Foster Dulles had been a senior partner in the law firm that represented United Fruit. The Under-Secretary of State, Walter Bedell, was thinking of taking a job with United Fruit and did so in 1955. President Eisenhower's personal secretary was the wife of United Fruit's director of public relations.

Eisenhower instructed the head of the CIA, Allen Dulles, who also had connections with United Fruit, to overthrow the Arbenz government. The CIA had shown its capacity to carry out such an operation through its role in the overthrow of the Mossadegh regime in Iran a year earlier. The chosen instrument for this operation was Carlos Castillo Armas, a military officer, who had been a fervent supporter of the assassinated Arana. A secret army was organized in the neighboring states of Nicaragua and Honduras. Economic pressure and psychological warfare were used to destabilize the Arbenz government. Fearing an attack, Arbenz arranged for the purchase of arms in Czechoslovakia. The arrival of a shipload of Czech arms in Guatemala in May 1954 sent a shock wave through Washington. In mid-June Castillo Armas led a force of several hundred armed men into Guatemala from neighboring Honduras. At first the invaders were repelled. But CIA planes bombed Guatemala City and other urban centers, sowing panic. Critical to the outcome was the attitude of the Guatemalan army. Many of the strongly nationalistic and younger military officers had initially followed the charismatic Arbenz. But fear of reprisal and the threat of a direct U.S. intervention made them think twice. They refused to allow the Czech arms to be distributed to the workers. In the end, they withdrew their support from Arbenz. He and his wife were forced to flee the country.

Castillo Armas was installed as head of government. The entire agrarian reform program was cancelled and the peasantry expelled from the land they had occupied. Castillo Armas was assassinated in 1957. Despite substantial infusions of U.S. aid, the economic condition of most of the population declined. Marxist guerrilla activity began in Guatemala in 1960 when two survivors from an abortive army uprising formed the November 13 Revolutionary Movement. The various rural guerrilla groups were united in the Communist-backed Rebel Armed Forces (FAR), which attracted widespread support among the peasantry in the early 1960s. Strongly supported by the United States, the Guatemalan army increasingly took control of the country. The Communist Party eventually abandoned the rural insurgency, backing the populist presidential candidate Julio César Méndez Montenegro. By 1967 counterinsurgency and death squads had reduced the guerrillas to a fugitive remnant—or so it appeared.

The case of Guatemala, like that of Iran, seemed to demonstrate the CIA's mastery of events in the third world. As the 1950s drew to a close, it seemed that the United States had reconfirmed its control over Latin American affairs. The threats from Brazilian and Argentinean populism had been liquidated. Revolutionary movements in Bolivia and Guatemala had been contained or quashed.

Despite these successes a sense of unease overtook Washington with respect to the situation in Latin America. In 1958 the visit of U.S. Vice-President Richard Nixon to Venezuela was disrupted by a violent assault on his motorcade by an angry crowd in Caracas. The attack was prompted by bitterness over past U.S. support for the recently ousted military regime of General Pérez Jiménez (1952–58) as well as ongoing U.S. control over the economically all-important Venezuelan petroleum industry. It mirrored resentment throughout Latin America toward United States economic domination as well as its close links with dictatorial and military regimes. It was a resentment compounded by the grinding poverty of three-quarters of the peasants and workers of the continent.

The Cuban Revolution

The Cuban Revolution (1959) broke through this logjam. It raised hopes of similar revolutions throughout Latin America among intellectuals, students, workers, and peasants. Socialist and anti-imperialist in inspiration, such revolutionary aspirations posed a serious threat to the dominant classes in Latin America as well as to U.S. hegemony over the region. Indeed, the success of the Cuban Revolution led the United States to intensify its efforts to suppress communist and radical nationalist movements throughout the third world. As events transpired Washington chose to make its ultimate stand against third world revolutionary change not in Latin America, but in Vietnam. The consequences globally would be dramatic.

Cuba developed as the most important naval and military base of the Spanish Empire in the Americas. Unlike most of the rest of Latin America, the island remained a Spanish colony until the end of the nineteenth century. Fearing a revolt by Cuba's millions of black slaves, the Cuban elite, unlike most of the merchants and ranchers of Latin America, foreswore demands for political independence from Spain for decades. Its sugar economy was strengthened by the Haitian Revolution, which ruined the slave-based sugar plantations on that island. The subsequent decline of the sugar-slave economy in the British Caribbean in the first part of the nineteenth century, likewise, increased the value of Cuban sugar. Sugar as well as tobacco and coffee remained the base of the Cuban economy.

The first war for independence against Spanish rule (1868-78) saw the creole elite finally make common cause with peasants and slaves. But racism and slavery divided the insurgents and helped the Spaniards to defeat the revolt. The issue of slavery disappeared when the practice was finally abolished in Cuba in 1886. The second war for independence (1895-98) based itself on a coalition of the landed elite with peasants, ex-slaves, urban craftsmen, shopkeepers, and merchants. The notion of a racial democracy played a large part in galvanizing support for the revolt at the grassroots. Most of the countryside fell into the hands of the insurgents with the Spanish troops retreating to the towns.

At this point, the United States entered the conflict, ostensibly taking sides with the rebels. The United States had been interested in Cuba since the presidency of Thomas Jefferson at the beginning of the nineteenth century. In the antebellum period many politicians from the Southern slave states advocated annexation of the island as a way of strengthening the cause of slavery in the United States. Toward the end of the nineteenth century, significant amounts of U.S. capital began to be invested in the Cuban sugar industry. The prospect of the building of the Panama Canal sparked further U.S. interest, as Cuba guarded the strategic Atlantic approaches to the waterway.

Led by Teddy Roosevelt's Rough Riders, the the United States invaded the island and imposed a military occupation (1899–1902). They only left after they had imposed an amendment to the new Cuban constitution. The so-called Platt Amendment allowed the United States to intervene in Cuba when U.S. lives or property were deemed threatened. The Cubans were also forced to cede Guantánamo Bay as a base for the U.S. navy (1903). Cuban aspirations for genuine national independence were thwarted. From being a colony of Spain, Cuba had become a protectorate of the United States.

In succeeding years the United States repeatedly sent military expeditions into Cuba based on the Platt Amendment. It strongly backed the dictatorship of President Gerardo Machado (1925-34). By 1929, U.S. economic interests had invested $1.5 billion in the Cuban economy, dominating the sugar industry and controlling the heights of the rest of the Cuban economy.

In 1929 Cuba produced 45 percent of the world's sugar. The bottom dropped out of the Cuban economy with the crash of the New York stock market in that year. The price of sugar collapsed, paralyzing economic life and leaving hundreds of thousands of Cubans unemployed. A popular revolution in 1933 ousted Machado and ultimately installed Ramon Grau San Martin as provisional president. Millions of Cubans participated in the revolution of 1933, developing a sense of mass politics for the first time. Grau proclaimed measures that favored the working class, while alienating local business interests and the United States. In the midst of this crisis, Franklin Roosevelt appointed Assistant Secretary of State Sumner Welles ambassador extraordinary and plenipotentiary. He befriended Fulgencio Batista, a non-commissioned officer who had been one of the military leaders of the revolution. In January 1934 Batista ousted Grau San Martin in a military coup with the blessing of the U.S. plenipotentiary Welles. The revolution was quashed.

In the wake of the proclamation of Roosevelt's Good Neighbor Policy, the Platt Amendment was rescinded. A U.S. sugar quota helped to stabilize the Cuban economy and to quiet social unrest. With U.S. support, Batista carried on as dictator through the 1930s. During the Second World War, he dutifully allied with the United States in the war against fascism. Under U.S. pressure, he even allowed clean elections in 1944. Much to Batista's surprise, his old nemesis Grau San Martin was elected president. But corruption, factionalism, and cronyism dominated political life under Grau. Many who believed in political and social reform soon turned against him. In the elections of 1948, Grau's candidate Carlos Prío Socarrás managed to eke out an election victory. But popular disillusionment made it possible for Batista to carry through a second coup in 1952. As the U.S. ambassador later admitted, democracy in Cuba was a sham in that the important political decisions were made in Washington rather than Havana.

Political instability and recurrent dictatorship were symptoms of an underlying malaise whose roots lay in U.S. political and economic domination over the island. Cuba did produce some tobacco, coffee, and nickel. But its economy was more than ever overwhelmingly dependent on the production and export of sugar. The greater part of the good arable land was given over to sugar cane.

Moreover, 40 percent of this output was controlled by U.S. companies that marketed the crop in the United States. The largest part of the profits was remitted back to the United States. In the aftermath of the revolution of 1933, the amount exported and its price was based on an annual U.S. sugar quota. In the postwar period, the limited market based on the quota inhibited new investment in the sugar industry and left large amounts of the land fallow.

U.S. influence over the rest of the Cuban economy was enormous. U.S. interests owned 90 percent of its utilities and all of its railways. The possibilities of creating a more diversified and balanced economy were quite limited. Monoculture and the restricted internal market limited the possibilities for the diversification of capital into other sectors. Indeed, except for some light industries, most manufactured goods were imported from the United States.

The most serious effects of this underdevelopment and U.S. domination were felt by the mass of the Cuban people. Four million of its 5.5 million people lived in the countryside. Of these, perhaps 125,000 made a tolerable living working in the sugar mills. But approximately three million rural Cubans were seasonal sugar workers living in great penury. They worked only part of the year for low wages, depending on credit from the company stores to tide them over the long slack seasons. Access to fallow land was denied to them by the companies in order to keep labor costs down. In addition to these sugar workers, there were approximately one million tenant farmers in the eastern part of the island subsisting with little or no access to credit or other means of improving their condition. Monoculture and dependency on the United States, consequently, led to a tragic under-utilization of land and labor.

The lives of the urban middle class were substantially better. But U.S. domination of the heights of the economy and the limited nature of the internal market restricted the economic opportunities of the middle class and weakened it politically. Many eked out a livelihood as public school teachers, policemen, soldiers, or government clerks. The weakness of the middle class reflected itself in the overwhelming strength of U.S. cultural influence. Meanwhile, the Catholic Church, dominated by expatriate Spanish priests, largely ignored the impoverished rural population. Nepotism, corruption, and dictatorship shaped political life. During the 1950s the Cuban economy largely stagnated.

It was in this context that Fidel Castro came to lead the Cuban Revolution. He was born into the family of a Spanish emigrant who became a successful cattle rancher in the Sierra Maestre of eastern Cuba. Physically and intellectually well endowed, Castro was sent to the elite Jesuit high school in Havana where he excelled as an athlete and student. At the University of Havana law school, he became a student leader of the Orthodox Party, a liberal democratic formation. Yet, as a student, he had begun to read Marx's and Lenin's writings. Raul, Fidel's brother, had already identified himself with the Communist Party.

From the beginning, Castro saw the problems of Cuba from the perspective of Latin America as a whole. In 1947 he joined an unsuccessful conspiracy to invade the Dominican Republic and overthrow Rafael Trujillo, its dictator. A year later, he attended an international meeting of radical Latin American students in Bogota, Colombia, and became a heroic participant in the uprising that shook the city in the wake of the assassination of the liberal populist leader Jorge Eliécer Gaitán. On graduation from Law School, he practiced poverty law in the slums of Havana.

Batista's coup in 1952 led Castro to initiate a counter-coup by raiding the Moncada army barracks in Santiago de Cuba at the head of a group of 120 students and workers on July 26, 1953. Put on trial following the failure of the attack, Castro delivered an impassioned address in defense of democratic ideas. It made him a national figure. Released after a relatively short imprisonment, he went into exile and proceeded to organize the July 26 Movement among exile supporters in Mexico and the United States as well as underground in Cuba. In 1956 he sailed back to Cuba with less than a hundred armed followers on the fishing boat *Granma*. Included among the insurgents was the young Argentinean doctor and revolutionary Ernesto Che Guevera. Setting up a guerrilla base in the mountainous Oriente Province, Castro created military foci among the sympathetic poor tenant farmers of the region. His increasing success against the regular forces of the Cuban army brought more and more recruits. His growing cadre included peasants and trade unionists as well as liberal, Communist, and socialist opponents of the Batista dictatorship. By late 1958, Castro had routed the Cuban army and the whole island was in upheaval as the guerrillas advanced toward Havana. The economy was paralyzed by revolutionary general strikes. The United States searched vainly for a third force between Castro and Batista. At the beginning of January 1959, Batista fled after looting the national treasury. Castro entered Havana in triumph.

An internal struggle then began for control of the revolution. The weakness of the middle class made it relatively easy for more radical elements led by Castro to seize the initiative. The land reform of May 1959 was the decisive act of the revolution, dispossessing the Cuban landed elite as well as the U.S. sugar companies. Some 1.7 million acres of U.S. property were seized. This measure, followed by steps to seize U.S. mining facilities and the oil refineries of Texaco, Shell, and Esso, led President Eisenhower to suspend the Cuban sugar quota in July 1960. All large U.S. enterprises were then nationalized and seized by the Cuban government. In the fall, diplomatic relations between the United States and Cuba were suspended and a U.S. economic embargo instituted. By then, hundreds of thousands of middle-class Cubans had abandoned the island in the face of the growing radicalization of the revolution.

As early as December 1959, Eisenhower ordered the CIA to prepare an invasion of Cuba in the wake of its success in Guatemala. In order to soften up the island's defenses and economy, a systematic campaign of sabotage was carried out by the CIA. Using bases in friendly Nicaragua and Guatemala, a force of 1,500 exiles was prepared. It was the new president, John F. Kennedy, who launched the invasion at the Bay of Pigs on the southwest coast of Cuba in April 1961. The local militia and the Cuban regular army easily defeated the invasion force, as Kennedy declined to directly involve U.S. naval or air forces.

Castro had learned from the mistakes of the Arbenz regime in Guatemala. In contrast to Guatemala, the army of the Batista dictatorship was entirely dismantled by the new regime. It was replaced by a revolutionary army whose nucleus was the guerrilla forces. Indeed, trustworthy elements of the guerrilla army were installed at the top of all the key ministries of the Cuban government. Backing up the new Cuban army were armed militia forces based on local committees for the defense of the revolution. These neighborhood bodies served as community and political centers as well the eyes and ears of the revolution at the local level. At the time of the Bay of Pigs invasion, some 100,000 dissidents who might have aided the insurgents were incarcerated. The expected mass uprising in favor of the invasion failed to materialize.

The Bay of Pigs invasion was defeated in the first instance because new institutions had been created to defend the revolution. But the invasion aborted as well because it had little popular backing. On the contrary, the revolutionary government was riding a crest of enthusiastic support. Between 1959 and 1961 a vast redistribution of landed wealth had occurred in favor of peasants and landless proletarians. These changes had been reinforced by major gains in the provision of health care, child care, and educational services to the mass of impoverished Cubans. Unprecedented employment opportunities had opened up to a chronically underemployed labor force. Laws enforcing racial segregation, which discriminated against half the Cuban population, had been swept away.

In the aftermath of the failure of the Bay of Pigs invasion, Castro declared Cuba to be a socialist country. The Kennedy administration refused to accept this defeat. The president's brother Robert Kennedy was put in charge of Operation Mongoose, a program designed to destabilize and overthrow the Cuban government. In the next year, some 4,000 acts of sabotage were committed, including repeated attempts on the life of Castro. Plans and training exercises for a second invasion were set in motion. The response on the part of the revolutionary government was to turn to the Soviet Union.

The Soviet Union and its allies had already agreed to purchase most of Cuba's vital sugar exports at advantageous prices. It now agreed to shield Cuba from an expected second invasion by the the United States by installing short and medium range nuclear missiles on the island. An additional motive for the installation of such weapons in Cuba by the Soviet Union was the goal of rapidly reversing the strategic nuclear imbalance that favored the United States. As well the Soviets sought to prove their revolutionary credentials faced with the growing rift with Mao's China.

The clandestine installation of Soviet missiles precipitated the Cuban missile crisis of October 1962. Most participants in the crisis and historians of the episode agree that this confrontation was the Cold War period's most dangerous moment. Without last minute restraint on the part of Khrushchev and Kennedy, it seems clear that an all-out nuclear confrontation between the superpowers would have occurred. Kennedy's decision to impose a naval quarantine of Cuba, rather than launch an immediate attack, allowed Khrushchev to withdraw the Soviet missiles and nuclear weapons. In return, the the United States promised to refrain from attacking Cuba and agreed, eventually, to dismount U.S. intermediate nuclear missiles in Turkey and northern Italy.

U.S. agreement to not attack Cuba did not end its hostility toward the revolution. The Cuban Revolution was perceived to be a serious threat to U.S. political and economic interests throughout Latin America. Having entered the Soviet camp, Cuba was regarded as a cat's paw for Soviet penetration of the whole continent. Sabotage operations and clandestine support for anti-Castro guerrillas on the island continued. The strict U.S. embargo on the Cuban economy was maintained, crippling or slowing economic development.

The most serious threat of the Cuban revolution in U.S. eyes was as an example of socialist revolution and national sovereignty. The U.S. fear was that other states in Latin America and beyond might follow the Cuban example of opting for socialism as a way of asserting political independence. Many in Latin American chaffed under what they considered U.S. imperialism. The conditions in Cuba that had precipitated revolution were not that far removed from the situation of other Latin American or third world states. The subsistence or below subsistence living conditions for workers and peasants in most of Latin America fueled the flames of economic and political radicalism.

In the countryside, where about half of the population of Latin America still lived, 70 to 90 percent of the population had no land. Monoculture, unbalanced economic development, and dependence on imports and foreign capital characterized the economies of most Latin American states. Foreign, especially U.S., capital dominated key sectors such as banking, mining, and petroleum. United States companies were increasingly involved in new consumer industries such as automobiles and pharmaceuticals. The $8 billion in direct U.S. investment in Latin America represented a substantial percentage of total U.S. foreign investment. It was now, increasingly, threatened by bitter nationalist and popular resentment.

Guerrilla Warfare and Counterinsurgency

In the wake of the Cuban revolution guerrilla movements inspired by the achievements of Fidel Castro and Che Guevera rapidly sprang into being in many Latin American states. Their objective was to create a nucleus (foco) of guerrillas that could depend on the peasantry and inspire a national revolution. Shortly after the Cuban revolution, attempts were made to establish such foci in Panama, Nicaragua, the Dominican Republic, and Haiti. A second wave of armed foci appeared in Columbia, Venezuela, and Guatemala. Increasing tension appeared between insurgents committed to the notion of guerrilla war and orthodox Communist parties prone to legal forms of struggle and mass organizing. By the mid-1960s, the revolutionary movement had evolved toward a concept of a continent-wide Latin American strategy inspired by the nineteenth-century revolutionary Simón Bolívar. Bolivia was to be the base of an upsurge of guerrilla war in Peru, Argentina, Chile, Uruguay, and Brazil. By 1967 Che Guevera was at large in the countryside of Bolivia in pursuit of this goal. Guevera hoped guerrilla war in Bolivia would be the spark, not of an immediate national revolution, but of an international Latin American people's war that the United States would not be able to control. He was captured and killed, and the insurrectionary movements in different Latin American states were each suppressed. The last phase of guerrilla war saw an upsurge of urban foci in Uruguay and Argentina that continued into the 1970s without positive result.

The foco concept that entailed initiating armed conflict by small guerrilla units as a catalyst to mass mobilization proved a dead end. It was killed off by the police and military of the states threatened by it. But these forces were trained, armed, and guided by U.S. counterinsurgency experts. The army units that hunted down Che Guevera in rural Bolivia are a noteworthy case in point. Indeed, one of the key U.S. responses to the Cuban Revolution was the rapid development of a counterinsurgency capacity with which to fight third world revolution. During the 1960s, an annual average of 3,500 Latin American military men attended special U.S. military schools in Panama and North Carolina where counterinsurgency techniques were taught. In the mid-1960s, U.S. military assistance to Latin America totaled more than $100 million annually. Half that amount again was spent per year beefing up Latin American police forces. Stress was placed on establishing close relations between the United States military and security forces and those of Latin America. Moreover, the Latin American military was increasingly encouraged to become involved in local civic action campaigns that, among other things, increased government control over rural populations.

The Alliance for Progress

Coercion was only one arm of the Kennedy strategy for suppressing revolutionary change. While three-quarters of the Latin American population were living at or near the level of subsistence, there was a substantial middle class of farmers, merchants, bankers, industrialists, and professionals. Kennedy's Alliance for Progress was designed to strengthen this class and enable them to generate faster economic growth. Such growth would raise the whole of the population of Latin America out of poverty, inoculating it from Cuban- and Soviet-inspired revolution. Announcing the Alliance for Progress in a stirring speech delivered a month prior to the Bay of Pigs invasion, Kennedy promised a Latin American Marshall Plan ending poverty and fostering democracy. Some $20 billion in public and private aid would be forthcoming from the United States in the next decade. Together with a prospective $80 billion of local capital available for investment, Latin America could expect a growth rate of 2.5 percent annually, double the rate of the late 1950s.

The theoretical underpinnings of the Alliance were to be found in recent U.S. social science. Political scientists and economists in U.S. universities, such as Gabriel A. Almond, Seymour Martin Lipset, and Walter Rostow, had elaborated theories of economic and political development that were advanced as alternatives to the Marxist theory of history. They claimed a universal and quantitatively measurable movement of all societies from a traditional condition toward a single ideal form of modernized society. Traditional societies had authoritarian political structures, rural and backward economies, and a lack of faith in scientific progress and entrepreneurship. A modern society was one characterized by a commercialized and technologically advanced economy, mass consumption, multi-party democracy, and an educated and geographically and socially mobile population. Such a modern society looked remarkably like that of the United States. According to these modernization theorists, nonetheless, what counted was to move third world states from tradition to modernity. Changing the class structure or the redistribution of wealth was irrelevant and, perhaps, harmful.

The Alliance for Progress failed to achieve its ostensible goals. Rather than $20 billion, total U.S. public and private investment amounted to $14 billion. Latin American finance for development barely materialized. Over the decade, Latin American annual growth averaged two percent rather than the 2.5 percent called for by the Alliance. Half of the investment that did take place occurred in the rapidly expanding manufacturing sector. Agricultural output per capita actually declined, while the number of unemployed increased. Social indicators such as education, infant mortality, and life expectancy barely improved. As the decade of the 1960s ended, more than half the population continued to live on an annual per capita income of $120. The political goal of fostering democracy fell by the wayside as the Kennedy and then Johnson administrations gave more and more priority to fighting communism. In the short period of the Kennedy presidency, the Latin American military overthrew six popularly elected governments. Washington rationalized rule by military dictatorship as strong government that would suppress the communist threat, while forcing through necessary modernization.

Guyana

The United States itself became directly involved in the overthrow of democratically elected governments in Latin America. In 1963 CIA destabilization efforts led to the overthrow of the People's Progressive Party (PPP) government of Guyana headed by the avowed Marxist prime minister Cheddi Jagan. Guyana's population of more than half a million blacks and indians depended on exports of sugar and bauxite. Per capita income of $384 per annum provided the populace a standard of living above the Latin American average. Britain, who along with Canada and the United States controlled the heights of the economy, granted internal self-government in 1953. Elected premier, the radical Jagan was deposed by the British after six months as a result of complaints from propertied interests and the U.S. government. This move, it is worth noting, coincided with the removal of the Arbenz regime in Guatemala.

As independence for Guyana neared in the early 1960s, politics in the small country became divided along racial lines. Forbes Burnham, a black leader in the PPP, broke from Jagan and founded his own racially based political party, the People's National Congress. As a result, the politics of Guyana was transformed from one based on class struggle to one predicated on the racial division between indians and blacks. In elections in 1961, Jagan won a narrow plurality of the popular vote and once again became prime minister. On election, Jagan praised Fidel Castro and initiated commercial relations with Cuba. In February 1962 the United States Secretary of State Dean Rusk informed the British government "it is not possible for us to put up with an independent British Guiana under Jagan." In mid-February a general strike, demonstrations, riots, and looting disrupted life in Georgetown, the capital of Guyana. The CIA, working through U.S. labor unions and foundations, had financed the protests and violence. A year later in April 1963, a second general strike that lasted eighty days shook the country. The CIA helped organize and finance the strike and, perhaps, supplied arms to the supporters of Burnham. At the behest of Washington, the British government changed the electoral system to favor the opposition to Jagan. In the subsequent elections of 1964, Burnham and his conservative allies defeated Jagan. It was Burnham who led Guyana to a nominal political independence.

Brazil

Guyana was among the smallest of the Latin American states. Brazil, the largest country on the continent, likewise experienced the heavy hand of U.S. intervention (1964). This time it came in the form of a U.S.-backed military coup. The populist and nationalist Vargas government that ended with the suicide of the president in 1954 was followed by that of Juscelino Kubitschek (1956-61). Kubitschek went out of his way to maintain friendly relations with the United States. This interlude saw explosive growth as well as social and economic instability. The presidency of João Goulart (1961–64) represented an abrupt return to the nationalist populism of Vargas. Goulart had served as vice-president under Kubitschek as well as a minister of labor. A fiery speaker and populist, Goulart rhetorically identified with the millions of Brazilian poor. He had ties with various left-wing groups including the Brazilian Communist Party. Goulart stoutly refused to accede to U.S. demands that Brazil break diplomatic relations with Cuba. His friendly relations with Cuba were no more acceptable to Washington than Jagan's were. Taking things a step further, Goulart nationalized U.S. properties including those of the International Telephone and Telegraph Company. Although Brazil under Goulart received $700 million in Alliance for Progress aid, Goulart insisted that higher prices for primary products would help Latin American countries more than U.S. aid.

The U.S. government decided that Brazil under Goulart was moving inexorably toward the Communist camp. It duly reinforced its relationships with the Brazilian military and conservative political leaders. The American Federation of Labor and the CIA clandestinely organized strikes against the Goulart government. On April 2, 1964, Goulart was overthrown by an army coup. The U.S. government approved the plans of the conspiracy and pre-positioned war materiel and a naval task force to support the coup in case it encountered serious resistance from Goulart's left-wing supporters. No such intervention proved necessary. Brazil was to live under military dictatorship for the next two decades.

Dominican Republic

Guyana experienced political destabilization, while Brazil underwent a military coup as a result of the behind-the-scenes intrigues of the U.S. government. The Dominican Republic was to live through an outright U.S. invasion. Once again, fear of the contagion of the Cuban Revolution proved decisive in determining U.S. policy. Kennedy had given the green light to the invasion of Cuba at the Bay of Pigs in April 1961. But his behavior with regard to Latin America over all was more even handed at that early point in his administration. In 1930 Rafael Trujillo, an officer of the National Guard, had seized power in the Dominican Republic. The National Guard had itself been organized by the United States in

order to maintain order and protect U.S. interests on the island. For the next thirty years Trujillo maintained one of the most hated dictatorships in Latin America.
At the same time, he fostered U.S. investment and maintained good relations with
Washington. On assuming office, Kennedy decided that both Castro and Trujillo
ought to be overthrown to prove U.S. commitment to democracy. Accordingly, he
nurtured plans for the invasion of Cuba and the overthrow of Trujillo simultaneously. The CIA supplied arms to the Dominican plotters planning to assassinate
the dictator.

While the Bay of Pigs invasion aborted in April, the Dominican action group
went ahead and ambushed and killed Trujillo at the end of May 1961. In the elections that followed, a moderate populist, Juan Bosch, won a resounding victory.
Almost from the first, Bosch was under pressure from holdovers from the old
regime, as well as the U.S. ambassador, because of his tolerance toward left-wing
activists. Bosch refused to crackdown on them because of his democratic political beliefs as well as his need for allies against Dominican right-wing elements.
Bosch was consequently overthrown by a coup organized by the Dominican military and police on September 25, 1963. In April 1965 a popular uprising
attempted to restore Bosch to power. Fearing another Cuban Revolution,
President Lyndon Johnson sent 20,000 U.S. marines to invade the island.
Johnson's action amounted to a repudiation of Roosevelt's Good Neighbor
Policy of 1933, which renounced such armed intervention into the affairs of other
U.S. states. For good measure, the U.S. President issued the Johnson Doctrine,
which promised future U.S. military intervention if a Communist takeover of any
other Latin American state threatened.

The Alliance for Progress failed to deliver political democracy or economic
development to Latin America. But if the U.S. aim was to quarantine Latin
America from socialist revolution it succeeded in the short run. Economic aid in
combination with military and political repression did block or rather postpone
the conquest of political power by Latin American leftists whose programs called
for radical change. But so far as the United States government was concerned, the
threat posed by the example of the Cuban Revolution extended far beyond the
Americas to the rest of the third world. Its efforts to suppress revolutionary
change would be tested not in Latin America but in far-off Vietnam.

5

The Vietnam War
and the Upheavals of the 1960s

The United States was able to keep the specter of revolutionary change in Latin America at bay during the 1960s. But the menace of the Cuban Revolution heightened U.S. resolve to combat the forces of revolutionary change elsewhere. In particular, Washington was determined to confront revolutionary nationalism and communism in the third world. During the presidency of John Kennedy (1961–63), such determination reached a high point. The Cold War in Europe having reached an impasse, the activist Kennedy believed that the decisive theatre of conflict now lay in the third world. It was critical that the United States demonstrate its capacity to prevail over communist and radical nationalist forces, not only in Latin America, but in Asia, Africa, and the Middle East as well.

Mastery over the underdeveloped world would demonstrate U.S. determination to contain communism worldwide. At the same time, the United States would offer the world the liberal alternative that had proved so successful at home and in Western Europe. The will to intervene in the third world was heightened by the strength of the U.S. economy and by its growing need in the 1960s for investment opportunities beyond the industrialized countries. Political and military intervention by the United States overseas in East Asia, therefore, has to be understood as much as a new imperialist venture as a response to perceived threats. Entanglement abroad by the United States must, likewise, be comprehended in the light of the internal evolution of U.S. society. By the early 1960s, the pressure of social discontent was clearly building from within. Consciously or not, carrying the torch of liberal ideology into the third world was perceived as a way of deflecting dissatisfaction at home.

Latin America was a major testing ground during the 1960s of U.S. political and military counterinsurgency. But, in the final analysis, Vietnam proved to be the ultimate proving ground for these policies. Quite unexpectedly, massive U.S. involvement in the Indochina conflict backfired, unleashing a wave of protest that shook the United States from within. France, Italy, and many other capitalist states around the world were also rocked by political and social upheavals. Revolutionary movements in Africa, the Middle East, and Central America also took example from insurgency in Vietnam. Unrest exploded even in the communist world, where challenges to bureaucratic socialism developed in Czechoslovakia and China.

The Diem Regime

The United States decided to create a South Vietnamese state in the wake of the French defeat in Indochina (1954). In setting up a separate state in the south, the U.S. government disregarded the terms of the recently concluded Geneva Accords calling for national elections in Vietnam. Despite these agreements, the puppet monarchy of the Emperor Bao Dai installed by the French came to an end and was replaced in the south by the Republic of Vietnam (RVN). It was presided over by Ngo Dinh Diem, a conservative mandarin supported by the United States. Ho Chi Minh's Democratic Republic of Vietnam (DRV) in control in the North would accordingly be countered by a U.S.-sponsored regime equipped with an up-to-date army and police force able to counter internal subversion or foreign aggression. The containment of China was the primary motivation behind this U.S. commitment. From its perspective, a divided Vietnam, like a divided Korea or Germany, was a better option than conceding the country entirely to the communists. Like South Korea and Taiwan, the Republic of Vietnam would serve to contain China and protect the approaches to Japan and southeast Asia. The growing Sino-Soviet split meanwhile emboldened U.S. policy-makers toward further intervention.

Diem's authoritarianism, aloofness, and Roman Catholicism made him a less than ideal ruler in this overwhelmingly Buddhist country. Diem, nonetheless, had the support of some influential U.S. Catholic leaders including New York's Cardinal Spellman and Senators Mike Mansfield and John Kennedy. They were seconded by a bi-partisan lobby group known as the American Friends of Vietnam made up of Washington liberals and conservatives. Secretary of State Dulles assigned Edward Landsdale to head a CIA mission to organize a viable South Vietnamese state. Modernization of the South Vietnamese state administration and police forces was contracted out to Wesley Fishel of the political science department of Michigan State University. In the succeeding years, U.S. economic, political, and military help enabled Diem to create an authoritarian state based on the support of the Catholic minority, the landlords, the Chinese and Vietnamese middle class, and the army.

A national assembly was selected on the basis of elections. But real power lay in the hands of Diem and his family, especially his brother Ngo Dinh Nhu and Ngo's wife Madame Nhu. They ruled through their party, the Can Lao, and the National Revolutionary Movement. Arrest and imprisonment of thousands of ex-Vietminh as well as others opposed to the Diem government was a major feature of the political life of South Vietnam in the late 1950s. Landsdale himself referred to the Can Lao as the sinews of a fascist state. As early as 1956, Diem abolished elections for village councils, which had been maintained even by the French. The provincial governors, who were directly responsible to Diem, appointed all local officials.

The control of the land on which the great majority of the South Vietnamese lived was the most critical issue. During the first Indochina war against the French, between 60 and 90 percent of the land in the South came under the control of the Vietminh. Most of the landlords were forced to take refuge in the towns. Under these circumstances, the Vietminh redistributed some 600,000 hectares from the landlords and French colonialists into the hands of the peasantry. At the same time, they significantly reduced rents on the rest of the land.

Under the guise of reform, Diem attempted a repudiation of these changes in the countryside. Military and civil overseers, backed by the expanding bureaucracy and army, reoccupied land in an attempt to collect rent. As a result of these measures by the Diem regime, an insurgency began to emerge among the South Vietnamese peasantry in the course of 1958. To counter growing unrest in the countryside, Diem introduced his agroville program in July 1959. This program of rural resettlement was designed to cut the peasantry off from the growing ranks of the guerrilla resistance. It was modeled on the successful tactics used by the British against the insurgency in Malaya a few years earlier. About 500,000 peasants were forced to move into strategically located compounds organized along military lines. Many peasants refused to move to these fortified villages and joined the resistance. By the end of 1960, the agroville program began to flag as a result of the rural revolution. It was revived in 1962 as the strategic hamlet program and was strongly backed by the the United States.

The Democratic Republic of Vietnam

In the north, meanwhile, the Democratic Republic of Vietnam (DRV) vainly protested the refusal of the Diem government and the United States to allow the organization of national elections according to the terms of the Geneva accords. Even the Democratic Republic's allies, the Soviet Union and the Peoples Republic of China, affected to be preoccupied with other matters. Despite these international setbacks, the growing military potential of the DRV based on its own internal development is noteworthy. The focus of the leadership of the Democratic Republic was initially on the question of land reform. Between 1954 and 1959 an estimated 15,000 landlords in the north were killed and 20,000 imprisoned. In the next few years, the peasantry was organized into coopera-tives, strengthening rural solidarity under the control of the state and Communist Party. The resulting gains in agricultural output and political cohe-sion facilitated the conduct of the war between 1960 and 1975. In addition, between 1954 and 1965, some 200 large and 1,000 smaller industrial plants were constructed with the help of China and the Soviet Union. Run along the orthodox Soviet principle of one-man management, the creation of these indus-tries promoted the emergence of a modern industrial proletariat working on the basis of cooperative labor.

The growing sophistication of the work force was reinforced by the creation of a comprehensive system of education that included scientific and technical train-ing through the university level. The emergence of these modern economic and educational sectors organized on the basis of socialist principles promoted the development of a sense of mass mobilization prior to the outbreak of the U.S. phase of the war in 1965. Indeed, the emergence of a modern educational, tech-nical, and industrial infrastructure facilitated the growth of the People's Army of Vietnam (PAVN) as an up-to-date and highly motivated military force capable of directly confronting not only the South Vietnamese army (ARVN) but, ultimate-ly, the U.S. military.

The National Liberation Front

Ongoing political oppression, the struggle over rents, and the institution of agrovilles had created a widespread resistance to Diem in the south. The Lao Dang or Workers (Communist) Party of the DRV responded in September 1960 by sanctioning full-fledged armed struggle in South Vietnam. Its aim was the overthrow of the Diem government and the unification of Vietnam. In December a coalition of opponents of the regime led by members of the Communist Party created the National Liberation Front (NLF) in a secret meeting in the forests north of Saigon. The leadership of the NLF was subsequently strengthened by an expanding flow of cadres from the north. Thrown on the defensive by the strategic hamlet program and stepped up U.S. military aid in 1962, the NLF forces began to win important engagements against the ARVN in the spring of 1963 amid growing rural political mobilization.

International developments worked in favor of the DRV by the early 1960s. During the 1950s, the Soviet Union and China had turned a blind eye to appeals to support the cause of the national reunification of North and South Vietnam. But with the Sino-Soviet split, both states were increasingly prepared to lend their support as a way to prove their revolutionary commitment. Faced with growing U.S. intervention, both China and the Soviet Union increased their economic and military aid to the DRV. As in the Korean War, China, particularly, feared a U.S. attack close to its own borders.

In the aftermath of the Cuban Revolution, Kennedy had committed the United States to fighting communism in the third world. He responded to the growing insurgency in Vietnam by stepping up U.S. military involvement. By the time of Kennedy's death in November 1963, some 16,000 U.S. advisors had been dispatched to Vietnam. Backing up the ARVN, the U.S. military specialists provided Diem's army with military advice, mobility, and firepower. U.S. initiatives also lay behind the revival of the agroville program in 1962. Renamed strategic hamlets, it was asserted by those in the United States keeping tab that by 1963 two-thirds of the South Vietnamese peasantry were housed within these military enclosures. At the same time, the the United States made efforts to get Diem to broaden and liberalize his government.

In none of these initiatives were the U.S. efforts successful. Despite being reinforced, ARVN was unable to reverse the mounting strength of the rural insurgency. The strategic hamlet program turned out to be little more than the Vietnamese version of a Potemkin village. Fewer than 10 percent of villagers were behind barbed wire and most of the young men were strangely absent. Diem spurned any attempt to liberalize his authoritarian regime. He grew alarmed at increasing U.S. military and political interference. Indeed, President Kennedy, senior advisers such as Defense Secretary Robert McNamara and National Security Council head McGeorge Bundy, as well as U.S. diplomats and military commanders in the field concluded that only direct U.S. control over Vietnamese politics and the conduct of the war could reverse the situation.

The Overthrow of Diem

The Buddhist crisis of spring 1963 forced the hand of the U.S. government. The Diem regime largely operated through the Catholic minority that constituted no more than 10 percent of the population. The repression of Buddhist demonstrations at Hué at the initiative of two brothers of Diem, one being the Catholic Archbishop of the city, set off mass demonstrations by Buddhists. These protests spread to Saigon and culminated in the self-immolation of a Buddhist monk. The ongoing Buddhist protests and suicides and the callous and intransigent response of Diem and his family caused a sensation in the United States. Kennedy used the occasion as a means of ousting Diem and vastly deepening U.S. political and military involvement.

On November 1, Diem was overthrown by a coup organized by eight senior ARVN officers, including one who was a secret member of the NLF and Communist Party. Diem and his brother Ngo Dinh Nhu were assassinated. It is difficult to say how deeply Kennedy himself was implicated in the coup. It appears that he looked the other way, while the U.S. ambassador, Henry Cabot Lodge, and CIA operative Colonel Lucien Conein worked with the plotters. Given Kennedy's involvement in the assassination of Trujillo, successive attempts at killing Castro, the coup against the Kassim government in Iraq, assassination plots against Lumumba in the Congo, and the overthrow of Jagan in Guyana, nothing can be ruled out. In any case, Kennedy himself was assassinated in Dallas, Texas, three weeks after Diem lost his life.

Gulf of Tonkin Resolution

The political chaos, upsurge of NLF attacks, and growth of neutralist sentiment that followed Diem's removal led Kennedy's successor, Lyndon Johnson, to mas-

sively deepen U.S. involvement in order to save the South Vietnamese government. As a result of purported attacks on U.S. naval vessels in the Gulf of Tonkin
by North Vietnamese patrol boats at the beginning of August 1964, Johnson was
able to secure a Senate resolution giving him a blank check to escalate the war.
The first major escalation came with the launching of an air assault against North
Vietnam in early February 1965. In response to this first bombing of the North,
the NLF launched a ground attack on a U.S. airbase at Pleiku. Nine Americans
were killed, 137 wounded, and 22 planes and helicopters damaged or destroyed.
Johnson escalated the bombing campaign, which became known as Rolling
Thunder. In order, ostensibly, to protect U.S. air bases in South Vietnam,
Johnson ordered the landing of U.S. ground troops in March. By the end of 1965,
Johnson had dispatched 180,000 U.S. troops to Vietnam. As a result of incre-
mental escalations in succeeding years, more than 550,000 U.S. ground troops
would be stationed in South Vietnam by 1968. Perhaps as many as two million
more U.S. service members would be acting in support of the Vietnam operation
in neighboring countries or offshore.

Johnson was perhaps emboldened by the quick success of 20,000 U.S.
marines charged with subduing a popular uprising in the Dominican Republic
that same year. Indeed, the U.S.-backed military coup in Indonesia, likewise in
1965, led to the destruction of the radical nationalist Sukarno government. The
highlight of this takeover was the killing of hundreds of thousands of communists
by the Indonesian army in collaboration with the CIA. As in Latin America, the
U.S. involvement in Vietnam was essentially a unilateral one. The United States
received limited support from regional allies such as Australia and South Korea.
But its principal allies, such as Great Britain, France, and Canada, withheld their
support and, at times, were critical. In prosecuting the war, Johnson adopted a
policy of step-by-step escalation of the violence. The policy of escalation was
designed to compel the communist North sooner or later to reduce its support for
the war in South Vietnam where it was faced with the buildup of overwhelming
U.S. force. At the same time, gradual escalation was meant to lower the risk of a
major intervention of the Soviet Union or China on the side of the DRV. Indeed,
such a great power confrontation was avoided, although both the Soviets and
Chinese provided massive economic and military support to Hanoi. Such aid
largely compensated for the destruction of the DRV's modern infrastructure as a
result of U.S. air attacks. Contrary to U.S. expectations, furthermore, the flow of
North Vietnamese troops and supplies to South Vietnam enormously expanded

in the wake of the U.S. escalation. It proved impossible through aerial attack to interdict this traffic along the well camouflaged and rapidly developing Ho Chi Minh trail. Neither did the U.S. bombing offensive affect the agricultural base of the DRV.

The U.S. commander in Vietnam, General William Westmoreland, adopted a policy of attrition with respect to the NLF and PAVN. Such a strategy entailed wearing down the enemy's capacity to make war, using the advantage of modern military technology. The war would be won by invoking superior firepower and mobility, while minimizing U.S. casualties. Westmoreland envisioned a three-phase approach for winning the ground war. It was believed in 1965 that half of the territory of South Vietnam and half its population was in communist hands, with the rest of the country not secure. In the face of this perilous situation, the initial goal of the U.S. escalation would be to stabilize the situation while a military buildup took place. In this opening phase of the buildup, priority would be given to protecting towns and air bases. In phase two, the the United States would take the initiative by carrying out search and destroy missions in the countryside. By probing and then attacking communist staging areas, the enemy would be forced to fight. In successive engagements, the U.S. forces would triumph based on their superior mobility and firepower. Phase three would be a mopping up operation with the enemy scattered or in flight. An expanded ARVN, meanwhile, would carry on guard duties and village pacification, while undergoing training and upgrading. With the NLF neutralized and PAVN forced to retreat back across the seventeenth parallel, the communists would be forced to come to terms. Accompanying this strategy was the establishment of a host of quantitative measures designed to measure the progress of the military campaign as well as the pacification of the countryside. This numbers game in part was one of the constituents of a vast public relations campaign designed to prove to U.S. public opinion that progress was being made and that the war was being won.

Faced with the U.S. strategy, the Communists at first shied away from major confrontations. They avoided pitched battle and prolonged engagements and reverted to guerrilla warfare. In the course of 1967, U.S. search and destroy operations did lead to large-scale battles in the Central Highlands and along the demilitarized zone (DMZ) between North and South Vietnam. Massive air power and artillery bombardment seemed to give the the United States the advantage in these engagements. The Communists took heavy casualties. But so, too, did the the United States.

Moreover, it was the Communist side that determined when or if there would be a battle. Furthermore, the forces of the NLF and the PAVN over time were increasing rather than decreasing in number. Indeed, it seems that the major engagements in the Central Highlands and along the DMZ were part of a Communist strategy designed to lure the U.S. forces away from the towns and cities along the coast and away from the heavily populated south of the country.

General Thieu's Regime

The consequence of the overthrow of Diem at the beginning of November 1963 was growing insurgency and ongoing political chaos in South Vietnam. Over the next two years popular uprisings and land seizures swept the countryside, requiring massive U.S. ground intervention to salvage the regime. Ambitious military officers launched coup after coup in Saigon. The last of these upheavals brought General Nguyen Van Thieu to power in February 1965. With U.S. help, Thieu was able to provide a stable government on the basis of unrelenting hostility to the NLF and the DRV. A veneer of constitutional government was maintained, but real power under Thieu lay with the commanding officers of the ARVN. As field commanders capable of leading their troops in battle, these South Vietnamese career officers left a lot to be desired. Their preoccupations were rather with promotions, patronage, and money. The Thieu regime was able to maintain the loyalty of this military elite by providing a steady stream of such incentives. At the same time, Thieu built close relations with the long established Chinese, and an emerging Vietnamese, business elite. On the basis of such military and business support, he was able to create a reasonably stable political regime.

The spending and investments of the business, government, and military officials connected to Thieu created a boom in urban real estate and consumption, especially in Saigon where an eighth of the population lived. To be sure, the viability of the government and economy completely depended on an uninterrupted stream of economic and military aid from the United States. By 1967, 40 percent of the GDP of the RVN was made up of imports financed by U.S. aid. In 1970, half of the GDP was so composed. In other words, no independent economic foundation for the RVN was created. Thieu's ability to assure ongoing access to U.S. largess was indispensable to the survival of the government of the South.

Failure to create a viable economic base was compounded by the ongoing military incapacity of the Saigon government. The ARVN did have some elite units that fought well. But for the most part ARVN was a mercenary army recruited from the urban poor. Already totaling 800,000 troops in 1967, its numbers reached no less than 1.2 million in 1972. Recruited as a result of economic privation and accompanied by their wives and children, the troops of ARVN were seldom motivated to put up a serious fight against the enemy.

Many of these ARVN recruits had been driven from the countryside by war and U.S. air attacks. Bombing, which was much heavier in South Vietnam than in the DRV, caused millions of peasants to leave the countryside and move to the cities. It is estimated that in 1964 little more than a quarter of the population of South Vietnam was urban. Largely as a result of bombing, 43 percent lived in towns and cities by 1971. U.S. political scientist Samuel Huntington euphemistically described this process as one of "forced modernization." Part of the rationale for driving people out of the countryside by bombing was that it drained the sea of rural people in which the communist insurgents swam. In the early 1960s, it was estimated by the the United States that a third of the peasantry were NLF supporters, a third were opposed, with the remainder sitting on the fence. But, contrary to Huntington's view, those among the peasantry who supported the NLF stubbornly clung to their villages despite the bombing, while those who opposed them fled, increasing rural support for the insurgents. Meanwhile, the peasants who escaped into the towns were socially fragmented and economically marginalized and were consequently unavailable to the Saigon government as a political force which could be mobilized against the NLF.

The Tet Offensive

The Tet offensive represented Hanoi's belated response to the Americanization of the war in 1965. The overwhelming U.S. advantage in firepower made it difficult for the communist side to confront them in large-scale positional combat. Accordingly, they at first reverted to a strategy of protracted conflict based on small-unit operations. Hanoi attempted to keep the tactical initiative, inflict a maximum of casualties, and force the dispersal of enemy forces as much as possible. On the other hand, it was understood by the communist leadership that the revolution would be aborted if there were no decisive response to the U.S.

buildup and offensive military operations. In the spring of 1967, the leadership in Hanoi determined to launch the Tet Offensive. It was designed to take advantage of two perceived weaknesses on the enemy side, i.e., the political and military incapacity of the RVN and the ARVN and the growing weakness of U.S. resolve in prosecuting the war.

On January 30, 1968, Vietnam's New Year's Day, some 84,000 troops of the NLF and PAVN attacked the major towns and cities of South Vietnam. According to the best accounts, the rural population massively supported this assault on the urban centers. Saigon, the six largest cities, 36 of 44 provincial capitals, and 64 of 242 district capitals were attacked. In the meantime, the PAVN had stepped up its offensive against the major U.S. marine base at Khe Sanh close to the DMZ and the Laotian border. There, 6,000 marines were besieged by some 40,000 PAVN troops. Enemy attacks along the DMZ and in the Central Highlands had convinced the U.S. commander Westmoreland that a major communist attack would be aimed there and not the urban centers. Large numbers of U.S. troops had been redeployed from the cities and the south to the north.

Taken aback at first by the widespread assault, the U.S. and ARVN forces ultimately rallied. They drove the insurgents from the towns, while massive U.S. bombing raids helped lift the siege of Khe Sanh, inflicting heavy losses on the communist side. The ARVN fought better than the Communists had expected and there was no substantial urban uprising in support of the Communist attack.

Communist assaults against the towns and in the countryside nonetheless continued into the summer. In order to expel the communists from the cities, the rural areas were virtually abandoned to them. As a consequence, by 1971 the communists were able to reconstitute their guerrilla forces in the countryside. More immediately, the claims of the Johnson administration to be winning the war were shown to be hollow. Indeed, support for the war among the U.S. population sharply plunged in the wake of Tet. With the decline of popular approval and a growing loss of confidence in the U.S. dollar internationally, the Johnson policy of escalation and, indeed, the future of his presidency appeared doubtful. The Tet Offensive forced Washington to come to grips with the fact that it was not winning the war and that its ability to do so on terms that were politically acceptable was doubtful.

The U.S. Antiwar Movement

Hanoi had closely monitored the situation within the United States before launching the Tet Offensive. Indeed, the disintegrating political situation on the U.S. home front was a key factor in reinforcing the political impact of Tet. Protests against U.S. intervention into the war had already had a major impact on public opinion prior to the offensive. By the summer of 1967, opinion polls indicated that most people in the United States believed that the Vietnam War was a mistake. More fundamentally the bi-partisan consensus over the Cold War in U.S. mainstream politics was unraveling.

The emergence of the U.S. New Left had a lot to do with this major political fracture. The creation of this new movement was centered on the Students for a Democratic Society (SDS), which came into being at the University of Michigan in 1960. Its Port Huron Statement of 1962, which marked its debut as a national movement, signaled the tentative revival of left-wing politics on college campuses across the United States. The Port Huron document contains a laundry list of essentially social democratic reforms that, however significant, did not frontally challenge the capitalist order. Indeed, in the context of the Cold War, it pointedly rejected any identification of its politics with those of the Stalinist left. Rather, it called for the creation of a new left based on the idea of "participatory democracy," a term which would become one of the iconic concepts of the 1960s. Campus activism dramatically accelerated at the University of California at Berkeley where the university administration in 1964 attempted to ban campus political activity focused on civil rights and defense of the Cuban Revolution. The Berkeley Free Speech Movement, which emerged in reaction to the attempt to limit political activism, pioneered mass student protests that would shake university campuses during the late 1960s.

During the 1950s, the rapid expansion of California's higher education system into a bureaucratic mega-university generated a politically conscious sense of grievance among Berkeley students. Led by the fiery activist Mario Savio, the Berkeley Free Speech Movement spearheaded an assault on the corporate university. From the perspective of Savio and the other leaders of the movement, the University of California's attempt to ban political discussion from the Berkeley campus was the symptom of a more profound malaise. The bureaucratized higher education system in California and elsewhere in the United States reflected the undemocratic nature of both the government and the business organizations that dominated U.S. society.

Coincident with the U.S. escalation of the war, 3,000 students turned out for a "teach-in" on Vietnam at the University of Michigan in March 1965. The teach-in soon spread to more than a hundred other major college campuses. As early as April 1965, SDS sponsored an antiwar march in Washington that attracted 20,000 participants. Over the next year, SDS grew to a national membership of about 15,000, with chapters in a diversity of institutions of higher learning from prestigious Ivy League university campuses to state colleges. By 1967, the membership of SDS had doubled again and its leadership explicitly identified itself not only with the NLF, but also with the cause of third world revolution. Far removed from elite institutions, schools such as Southern Illinois University eventually saw growing student protest over undemocratic university governance fuse with antiwar protest and a festive culture of partying. Southern Illinois, too, soon had its chapter of SDS. Major antiwar protests would eventually engulf even a conservative campus such as Michigan State University, the home institution of Wesley Fishel, the chief U.S. political consultant to the Republic of Vietnam. Antiwar activity spread from universities into the major metropolitan centers. By 1967, there were large-scale antiwar marches in New York, San Francisco, and Washington based on coalitions of radicals, liberals, and pacifists in what became national resistance to the war.

Civil Rights and Black Liberation

Although it was denied at the time, the Johnson administration was deeply shaken by the antiwar movement. Its anxiety was heightened by the fact that antiwar protest was increasingly linked with what became a mass-based black liberation struggle. During the 1950s, the civil rights movement had focused on school desegregation in the U.S. south. The black boycott of segregated bus transport in Montgomery, Alabama, initiated by the sit-down of Rosa Parks in 1955, made the desegregation of public facilities another focal point of protest. In 1957, Martin Luther King and others involved in the Montgomery campaign organized the Southern Christian Leadership Council (SCLC). At the beginning of February 1960, four students at a black college in Greensboro, North Carolina, inspired by King and Gandhi, sat down at an all-white lunch counter in Woolworth's Department Store and demanded service. By April, lunch counter sit-ins were underway in 54 southern towns. That month black students from throughout the south came together to form the Student Non-

Violent Coordinating Committee (SNCC). Thousands of northern white students joined the civil rights effort in the south. In the spring of 1961, SNCC and the Congress of Racial Equality (CORE) initiated Freedom Rides designed to force the integration of interstate transport. The ensuing racial violence led the Kennedy Administration rather plaintively to plea with SNCC and CORE to call off the rides lest the image of the United States be damaged in the Cold War. In the end, the Attorney General was able to negotiate an end to racial segregation in interstate transport.

The Kennedy administration was, indeed, embarrassed by the gathering storm over civil rights. It was drawn into the civil rights struggle despite its reluctance at the prospective loss to the Democratic Party of the southern white vote. Indeed, under the leadership of King, the SCLC raised the ante. Intensive civil rights activity at Albany, Georgia, in 1962 was followed by a major drive at Birmingham, Alabama, to desegregate local public facilities, hotels, restaurants, and economic life in the spring of 1963. Bloody confrontations made Birmingham the focal point of national attention, leading to the celebrated March on Washington and King's famous "Free at Last" speech in August 1963. The next year, voter registration or desegregation campaigns were carried out in Cambridge, Maryland; Greenwood, Mississippi; and Selma, Alabama. Violent confrontations between civil rights advocates and the police at Selma and the subsequent march on Montgomery in 1965 led to the passage of the Voting Rights Act, which enfranchised millions of southern black voters.

The civil rights campaign by blacks had been massively supported by northern liberals. Indeed, thousands of white activists had gone to the south to work in voter registration drives and so-called freedom schools. The leadership of SDS and the Berkeley Free Speech Movement had been largely formed through this civil rights involvement. But the sudden emergence of black activism in the north in 1964 signaled a growing racial divide between blacks and whites.

Over three million southern blacks had migrated to the north during the 1940s and 1950s. The mechanization of southern agriculture and the lure of higher paying factory jobs in the northern cities spurred the movement. But blacks found that unofficial segregation in housing and education continued to confront them in the north. Job opportunities were limited by the racism of craft unions in the American Federation of Labor and the suburbanization of new factory employment. By the early 1960s, most northern blacks were confined to ghettoes in the decaying inner cities.

The fraying of unity between blacks and northern whites became evident in February 1964 with the boycott of New York City public schools by half a million black students. Parents of black students denounced de facto, rather than legalized, segregation based on discrimination in housing, unemployment, and the ghettoization of the black population. The confrontation between increasing black militancy and white backlash had begun. Sensing the growing unrest, President Johnson and the Democratic Party enacted a battery of legislation including Medicaid, Medicare, and federal aid to education in a so-called War against Poverty.

At the beginning of 1965, the assassination of Malcolm X, the leading advocate of black power and separatism, turned many politically engaged young blacks in the direction of radical nationalism. At a more popular level, black anger welled up in a major riot in the Watts section of Los Angeles in August. Congested, plagued by poor schools, drugs, crime, poverty, and unemployment, police harassment set off the Watts uprising. It took 16,000 police and national guardsmen to quell the upheaval, leaving 34 dead, 1,000 injured and 4,000 in jail. The Watts riot set off a cycle of uprisings in black ghettos across the United States. In the summer of 1966, there were 43 such upheavals, and the next year 55, including large and deadly riots in Detroit and Newark. It was ominous for the Johnson administration that in the throes of such events, SNCC turned to radical black nationalism and a new revolutionary black organization, the Black Panthers, began to attract thousands of supporters.

The radicalization and politicization of young blacks inevitably had its impact on the prosecution of the Vietnam War. Escalation of the war led to a scaling back on Johnson's war against poverty, further fueling discontent. At the same time, both moderate and radical blacks were aware that poor blacks constituted a disproportionately large percentage of the combat soldiers in Vietnam. Indeed, growing direct contacts with radical nationalists and Marxists in Africa led many younger black political activists to develop an anti-imperialist perspective on the Vietnam War and U.S. involvement in the third world. Pressure built on the leadership of the civil rights movement to take an antiwar stand. At the beginning of April 1967, Martin Luther King denounced the Vietnam War, describing the United States as "the greatest purveyor of violence in the world today." Mohammad Ali, the heavyweight boxing champion of the world, refused induction into the U.S. army, asserting that he would not serve in this "white man's war."

The End of the Johnson Presidency

It was in the context of increasingly intense racial and political division within the United States that news of the Tet Offensive fell. As a result, open revolt broke out in the Democratic Party as first Senator Eugene McCarthy of Minnesota and then Robert Kennedy announced their candidacies for the Democratic Presidential nomination as peace candidates in rivalry to Johnson. The problems of military reverses and internal political conflict were made worse by the increasingly diffi-cult financial situation of the United States internationally. Johnson had insisted on maintaining spending on the war against poverty as much as possible while pros-ecuting the war in Vietnam. The deficits and inflation that resulted threatened to undermine the value of the U.S. dollar in global financial markets. The threat to the dollar was aggravated by the fact that the United States had been running a trade deficit with the rest of the world since the early 1950s. The United States was over-extended and over-committed in terms of its worldwide interests. As a result of these financial problems abroad and growing instability and dissent at home, Johnson was forced to abandon plans to send more troops to Vietnam. At the end of March 1968, he called for the suspension of bombing of the North and the opening of peace negotiations. He further announced that he would not be a can-didate for a second term of office as president. It would be left to the next U.S. president, Richard Nixon, to extract the United States from the Vietnam quag-mire. He would do so through his policy of Vietnamization and by seeking a rap-prochement with the People's Republic of China.

The Counterculture

The internal upheaval in the United States was not confined to the antiwar and black power movement. It manifested itself also in the upsurge of the so-called counterculture, which intersected at various points with antiwar and black protest. The most explicitly political aspect of this counterculture was the folk music revival pioneered by Pete Seeger and the Weavers in the 1950s. In the 1960s, singers such as Joan Baez and Bob Dylan used this music to inspire the civil rights and antiwar movements. The less overtly political counterculture of the hippies, rock festivals, and communes found inspiration in the rock-and-roll music, beat protest, and growing sexual freedom of the 1950s. The use of marijuana, LSD, and other drugs increased, and monogamous sexuality and traditional dress and decorum were generally rejected. The 1960s saw the creation of thousands of rural and urban communes across the face of the United States. Millions of young people were swept up in the movement to a greater or lesser degree.

It is difficult to say to what extent this cultural revolution was a creation of the media, as some conservatives have claimed. Others have insisted that the counter-culture was simply the establishment of a new style of consumerism that would fully reveal itself in subsequent decades. Yet it would be quite wrong retrospectively to dismiss this counterculture as an authentic protest movement. At its best, this culture represented a significant form of revolt against bureaucratized capitalism and big government. Reflected particularly in its music, its creativity sharply challenged the conformist culture of the Cold War. In the name of love and community, it opposed the work ethic, the monogamous family, consumerism, and individualism. As such, it reflected an unprecedented challenge to the established values in U.S. society and the expression of emancipatory ideals that transcended the immediate moment of the 1960s.

In the final analysis, intense as the crisis of the 1960s was, it did not turn into a fundamental or revolutionary challenge to the established order in the United States. That it did not do so has to be credited in the first place to Nixon's Vietnamization program that entailed U.S. withdrawal from direct involvement in the ground war. The resultant decline in U.S. casualties helped to defuse antiwar sentiment. Further obstructing the development of a mass radical consciousness was racism. Conservative and reactionary politicians, including President Nixon, helped to arouse white racism, blocking the emergence of a sense of popular unity by promoting division between whites and blacks. Black nationalists also played their part in dividing the population.

Still more important was the legacy of McCarthyism. The ouster of Communists from the labor unions and the repression of the Communist Party during the 1940s and 1950s undermined the possibility of a sustained and organized radical politics. Certainly revolutionary and anticapitalist ideas were widespread among the young and minority groups in the late 1960s. By 1968, one million U.S. university students identified themselves as part of the left. Moreover, revolutionary ideas were pervasive in the black population as well as increasingly among Chicanos and Native Americans. Even workers were infected by insurrectionary sentiments as the unprecedented number of wildcat strikes during these years attest. Opposition to the Vietnam War was stronger among workers than it was among the middle class. But no mass-based radical or even socialist party emerged. The labor movement, meanwhile, remained firmly under the control of conservative union leaders such as George Meany of the AFL-CIO and Jimmy Hoffa of the Teamsters Union.

Indeed, at the beginning of 1960s much of the new left, including SDS, opposed any organized and centralized Marxist political party as reminiscent of Stalinism. Belatedly, toward the end of the 1960s, the most politically conscious radicals recognized the need for such an organization, but by then the mass movement was ebbing and decomposing. Finally, it should not be forgotten that the upheavals of the 1960s took place during a period of unprecedented economic prosperity. Revolutionary political parties seldom prosper during such periods.

The lack of staying power of the protests of the 1960s in the United States and elsewhere having been acknowledged, the unprecedented extent of the upheavals of the 1960s should be emphasized. Student and worker protest welled up on every continent to an extraordinary degree. Moreover, the infectious quality of these global upheavals is undeniable. Increasing economic and cultural contact inspired worldwide emulation. Upheavals in one country helped to inspire uprisings and protests in other countries in a kind of chain reaction sparked by local conditions.

May 1968 in France

In France as in the United States, the protests of the 1960s proved to be a flash in the pan. But, unlike in the United States, in France protest assumed the form of a genuinely revolutionary crisis. In May 1968, an incontestably revolutionary movement engulfed the country. That this insurrection did not succeed surely was not the fault of the working class, which en masse joined what became a revolutionary general strike. It was, rather, the refusal of the leadership of the Communist Party to take charge of the revolution that ensured its failure.

France had been a liberal democracy since the foundation of the Third Republic (1870). But this republic had been consolidated on the defeat of the revolutionary and socialist Paris Commune in 1871. The Paris Commune was only the last of a succession of popular revolutions that marked the history of nineteenth-century France. In 1936 in the wake of a mass general strike, the first elected socialist government in French history took power. Following the landing of the Allies in Normandy, the French Resistance of 1944 assumed the form of a popular insurrection. As a consequence of this ongoing history of popular strug-

gle, a revolutionary and socialist ideology was deeply entrenched in the mentality of the rural and working-class population. In May 1968, a mass uprising
inspired by this outlook suddenly challenged an apparently inexorable process of
post-war capitalist modernization.

De Gaulle had taken power in 1958 in the midst of an army revolt provoked
by the Algerian War. Contrived according to the new ruler's authoritarian specifications, the constitution of the new Fifth Republic made de Gaulle a president
vested with unprecedented executive power. Based on this enlargement of central
authority, de Gaulle was able to end the Algerian War, proceed with the decolonization of Africa, and preside over an increasingly prosperous nation that
enjoyed the benefits of membership in the European Common Market. In foreign
affairs, de Gaulle challenged U.S. domination over Europe, withdrew French
forces from NATO command, developed an independent nuclear deterrent,
opened a dialogue with Moscow, and attacked the U.S. war in Vietnam.

Since 1945 a rapid concentration of industry and capital had occurred. By the
late 1960s, the growth of French industry had totally overwhelmed the traditional peasant economy. Farm employment, which had occupied 36 percent of the
population at the end of the war, now occupied only 15 percent. There had been
a substantial expansion of employment in the health, educational, technical, and
scientific sectors. These so-called new workers were to take their part in the
events of May 1968 alongside blue-collar workers. Many workers had acquired
cars, washing machines, and televisions, but inequality was still a glaring fact of
French life. Forty percent of wage earners received less than $1,800 per year while
less than a thousand had a declared income of $240,000 or more.
Authoritarianism marked relations between the state and citizens, teachers and
students, as much as between employers and employees. The prominence of
young workers in the upheaval was to be notable.

Only a quarter of all workers belonged to unions. Of these, the majority
adhered to the Communist dominated CGT, while the rest subscribed to the
Catholic Confédération Française Démocratique du Travail (CFDT) and the
smaller business union known as Force Oeuvrière. In practice, all three unions
were reformist. Yet the working class, organized or not, still resisted the idea of
capitalist hegemony over society. The Communist Party, nominally still committed to socialist revolution, continued to receive a quarter of the vote.

As in the United States, the previous two decades had seen a dramatic increase
in the number of university students. But a lack of investment in teachers, build-

ings, and libraries compounded the problems of bureaucracy, institutional rigidi-
ty, and student alienation. Radical minorities of Trotskyists, Maoists, and
Anarchists to the left of the Communist Party roiled the university student body.
In the late winter of 1968, the campus of the suburban Nanterre campus of the
University of Paris was agitated by an administratively enforced sexual segrega-
tion of male and female students.

Many students paid close attention to the Vietnam War. Word of the Tet
Offensive exploded like a firecracker into this milieu. Commandos of youth
attacked U.S. businesses in the center of Paris, leading to several arrests. A protest
meeting at Nanterre ended in the storming of the administration building on
March 22. For the next five weeks, the Nanterre campus was in a state of constant
turmoil. On May 2, the dean closed the campus. The activists transferred their
activities to the campus of the Sorbonne in the heart of the Latin Quarter. A meeting of several hundred students in the courtyard of the Sorbonne led the rector to
call the police. Confrontations between police and students precipitated an all-
out battle on the Left Bank during the night of May 5. A nationwide strike of high
school and university students broke out in solidarity. On May 11 the prime minister, Georges Pompidou, announced the release of all prisoners and the reopen-
ing of the Sorbonne.

But organized labor had already entered the struggle. The CGT and CFDT
called for national mass demonstrations in support of the students. As many as a
million turned out in Paris on May 13, and there were parallel popular demonstrations in other French towns. The next day, workers in Nantes occupied a factory and initiated a nationwide wave of strikes and factory occupations. By May
22, ten million blue- and white-collar workers, constituting virtually the whole of
the French workforce, were on strike. On the weekend of May 25–27, round table
talks between the unions and employers organized by Pompidou produced a
compromise based on economic improvements known as the Grenelle
Agreements. The Communist Party and the CGT, which rejected the revolutionary path to socialism, supported the Grenelle terms, but were taken aback when
union stewards from all over the country reported the rejection of Grenelle by the
majority of workers. In many places, workers called for "a government of the people." In essence, the rank-and-file workers and students rejected the tyranny of
the capitalist workplace as well as state authoritarianism.

By May 28, both the Communist and Socialist Parties belatedly spoke of forming an alternative government. But this irresolute response was followed by deci-

sive action from the right. De Gaulle rallied the leaders of the French military and a massive right-wing demonstration in the heart of Paris helped to restore the confidence of conservatives. The army and paramilitary police began to challenge worker control over essential services. The unions now announced that they were ready for negotiations. By mid-June, the strikes had petered out. The Grenelle Agreements became the basis of settlements concluded by the unions in the workplace. May 1968 ended with a whimper rather than a bang.

Ongoing Struggle in Italy

The student-led upheaval in France was echoed worldwide in countries as diverse as Great Britain, West Germany, Mexico, South Korea, Burma, Japan, Philippines, Ethiopia, South Africa, and Turkey. Nowhere was mass protest more prolonged or stronger than in Italy. Indeed, student and popular protest began earlier and was more prolonged than in France. The aches and pains of rapid capitalist development were felt more strongly in Italy than in France. By the early 1960s, the system of mass higher education had many of the same or even worse problems than in France. Student protests swept the country starting as early as the fall of 1967 and reached a climax in February 1968 with bitter clashes between students and police in Rome. Meanwhile, a grassroots protest movement emerged in the factories of northern and central Italy. Rank-and-file committees inspired by revolutionary politics seized the initiative from Communist Party-controlled trade unions. Workers demanded an end to wage differentials and the tying of wage increases to gains in productivity. Mass assemblies and wildcat strikes occurred frequently during 1968–69. Workers would down tools and undertake organizing and agitation within the factories during normal work time. The objective came to be to change the relations of production in the workplace. In the summer of 1969, major confrontations occurred between the police and thousands of students and workers in the highly industrialized northern Italian city of Turin. In the fall, the trade unions sought to recover their influence by organizing large-scale walkouts in the metal trades. In the course of 1970 and 1971, strikes spread throughout the Italian economy to a degree not seen since the early post-war period. Outside of work, attempts were made to create red nurseries, supermarkets, restaurants, and schools. Economic crisis and serious inflation in the early 1970s brought the Italian worker offensive to an end.

Polycentrism in Eastern Europe

The Communist world was by no means spared the upheavals of the 1960s. Here, too, students took the lead in attacking bureaucratic rule and the domination of elites over the labor process and political life. In the so-called Prague Spring of 1968, a bold attempt was made to dismantle the Stalinist bureaucratic order and to introduce a democratic socialism in its place.

More than a decade had passed since the uprising in Hungary. During that period, the communist bloc had evolved in the direction of political diversity. As the Sino-Soviet rift deepened, the conflict deteriorated into armed clashes and preparations for all-out war in the late 1960s. Taking advantage of this schism, the Albanian Communist leader Enver Hoxha chose to side with China against what he denounced as Soviet revisionism. In this way, Hoxha was able to affirm Albania's independence from both the Soviet Union as well as Yugoslavia.

Romania, which earlier had negotiated a withdrawal of Soviet troops from its territory, ceased to participate in Warsaw Pact military training exercises after 1960. While continuing to insist on its ideological orthodoxy, it progressively distanced itself from Soviet influence. By the mid-1960s, its trade with West Germany was greater than with all of the countries of the Eastern bloc. It maintained good relations with Israel as well as with China and Albania, despite Soviet disapproval. An economically backward country even among East European states, Romania continued to insist on giving absolute priority to the development of heavy industry. Rigid ideological and social control was used to maintain labor discipline amid ongoing consumer scarcity. While most states of the region suffered some leveling off in economic growth as compared to the postwar years, rates of accumulation in Romania remained at a very high level.

Hungary presents a complete contrast with the situation in Romania and Albania. Following the events of 1956, Hungary made raising living standards rather than the development of heavy industry its priority. At the beginning of 1968, the introduction of the New Economic Mechanism saw two cornerstones of the Stalinist system—centralized planning in quantitative units and centralized allocation of resources—abandoned. Enterprises were enjoined to make profits based on the operations of the market. The state withdrew from controlling the short-term operation of the economy, while continuing its role of long-term economic management by planning the overall allocation of investment. Emphasis on consumer needs was matched by a relaxation of ideological constraints.

Romania and Albania remained the most orthodox of Communist states, Hungary the most relaxed, while the situation was more mixed in East Germany, Poland, and Bulgaria. In these states repression alternated with some relaxation of censorship. Following the 1956 crises in Hungary and Poland, the Soviet Union had accepted or had been forced to accept the increasingly polycentric nature of the Eastern bloc. But the 1968 reform movement in Czechoslovakia, which aimed at creating a democratic socialism, crossed the line of what was acceptable to the Soviet leadership.

The Prague Spring

The Prague Spring originated as a response to economic crisis and the legacy of Stalinism. Citing the Hungarian Revolution as a dangerous example, the Czech Communist leader Anton Novotny stonewalled attempts to liberalize the regime during the late 1950s. But ongoing political pressure from within the Communist Party and from the intelligentsia forced Novotny to appoint a commission in 1962 to review the purges of the Stalinist period. Many political figures that had been imprisoned or executed, including the former party leader Rudolf Slansky, were exonerated. The next year, the Writers' Union called for the extension of the process of rehabilitation to artists who had been repressed in the Stalinist period. The more liberal mood opened the way for a renewal of Czech culture, reflected, for example, in the successful novels of Milan Kundera and the movies of Milos Forman.

Demands for further political and cultural liberalization were coupled by a struggle between party conservatives and liberals over economic matters. The Czech economy was, along with that of Eastern Germany's, the most sophisticated in the Eastern bloc. Unlike the other Communist states of the region, it suffered a serious economic slowdown between 1961 and 1965. The setback was, in part, caused by the collapse of the Chinese market due to the Sino-Soviet split as well as other exogenous factors. But such difficulties were compounded by the highly centralized and bureaucratized organization of economic activity. Liberals called for economic decentralization and the introduction of market mechanisms.

Adopted in part, the liberalizing reforms produced higher prices, shortages, and fears of unemployment. Always a reluctant reformer, Novotny attempted to control such adverse trends through administrative measures such as price fixing. Ota Sik and other economic liberals called for still more liberalization as the remedy to the adverse effects of the use of market mechanisms. Meanwhile, Novotny was experiencing growing difficulty keeping intellectuals, journalists, and artists under control. The situation was compounded by growing Slovak demands for political and economic autonomy.

In October 1967 police repression of a student protest in Prague set off demands in the media for a public inquiry. Such outcries were coordinated with growing calls for democratic reform by more liberal Communist Party functionaries and intellectuals. At a plenum of the Central Committee at the end of October, the liberal Slovak Party leader Anton Dubcek called for across-the-board democratization. In December Soviet leader Brezhnev visited Prague in order to shore up support for Novotny. But on December 20, a Communist Party plenum voted against Novotny. On January 5, 1968, Dubcek was unanimously chosen First Secretary.

Fully committed to reform and democratization, Dubcek moved decisively toward decentralization, market mechanisms, and democracy in the workplace. Trade unions were allowed to operate independently of the government and party. Small-scale private enterprises were legalized. Independent student unions began to emerge, while the Catholic Church as well as Protestant and Jewish communities and the Hungarian and Ukrainian minorities were given more autonomy and freedom.

The Communist Party was divided between liberal and conservative elements. But the liberal-minded majority committed itself to withdraw from direct control over the state and economic and social life. In the future, the party would have to lead by example and by setting over-all goals. Censorship ceased to exist. Steps were taken to democratize the workings of the party itself. Limitations were placed on terms of office and on the accumulation of offices. Secret ballots in party elections were mandated and greater authority was vested in the party's elected organs. Demands were made to allow rival political parties. On this latter point Dubcek demurred, more for reasons of expediency than out of principle. The republic was federated into a Czech and Slovak state in order to assuage Slovak nationalism. Dubcek moved toward increased and more open contact with the West on the basis of loyalty to its allies in the Warsaw Pact.

From its inception, the leaders of the Soviet Union and East Germany criticized Dubcek's reforms. The Czech reforms were perceived to threaten the foundations of Soviet-style communism. Freedom of expression and association as well as the move toward political pluralism were attacked as incompatible with socialism, which was equated with the dictatorship of the Communist Party.

These criticisms of the Prague Spring must be understood particularly in light of the evolution of the internal situation in the Soviet Union under Brezhnev. The Prague Spring developed only four years after Khrushchev had been removed from power. Under his successor, Leonid Brezhnev, emphasis was placed on the reestablishment of a centralized Communist Party and state authority rather than on political devolution or economic experimentation. There was no question of restoring full Stalinism in the Soviet Union. Limited openness to new tendencies was allowed in order to keep the support of moderate members of the Soviet intelligentsia. On the other hand, radical proposals for democracy in the Soviet Union such as those of Roy Medvedev and Andrei Sakharov were rejected out of hand. The arrest and trial of the writers Andrei Siniaviski and Julii Daniel in 1965–66 was meant to signal that radical dissent would not be tolerated. Even Soviet Prime Minister Leonid Kosygin's limited attempt to introduce the idea of measuring economic success by sales, profitability, and technological innovation rather than quantitative output met with determined obstruction from state bureaucrats, factory managers, and party functionaries. Such was the disposition of the Soviet elite faced with the reform movement in Czechoslovakia in 1968.

Moscow and Berlin charged that the Czech reforms were undermining socialism. Dubcek answered that the reforms were appropriate to an economically and culturally mature socialist society. Czechoslovakia would provide an example for industrially developed countries by combining democracy and socialism. The similarity of this program to that of Mikhail Gorbachev's platform of glasnost and perestroika two decades later is patently evident.

In mid-May 1968, the Warsaw Pact met in Moscow in the absence of the Czechs. It adopted a resolutely negative attitude to the Dubcek reform program. As a result, stepped up attacks were launched in the Soviet and Warsaw Pact media against the Czech reforms. They were denounced as a threat to the leading role of the Communist Party and as antisocialist. Dubcek responded by insisting on the principle of non-interference in the internal affairs of a socialist state by other socialist states. He denounced the holding of meetings that attacked the policies and activities of a socialist state while its representatives were absent. On July 23, a compromise appeared to have been worked out between Dubcek and Brezhnev. Despite appearances, a secret decision to invade was taken by Brezhnev and his allies in mid-August.

Warsaw Pact forces invaded Czechoslovakia on August 20–21 encountering no armed resistance. In retrospect, what proved decisive in the decision to invade was

the democratic political program and not the economic reforms of the Czech leaders. The continuing dictatorship of the Communist Party proved to be the ultimate
point in question. Soviet troops remained in occupation, while a gradual purge of
liberal Communists including Dubcek was carried out. In the wake of this counterrevolution, the Soviets issued the so-called Brezhnev Doctrine. It declared that
the sovereignty of socialist states was limited if socialism as defined by Moscow
was threatened. The extinction of the Czech experiment in combining socialism
and democracy sealed the ultimate fate of bureaucratic socialism in Europe.

China's Cultural Revolution

The last great upheaval of the 1960s was the Great Proletarian Cultural Revolution
in China. The Cultural Revolution began in 1965, reached its peak in 1968, and,
in name at least, continued until the death of Mao Tse-tung in 1976. Like the
upheavals in the United States, France, Italy, and Czechoslovakia, the convulsions
in China were directed against a ruling bureaucracy and were carried forward by
the young. Like these other upheavals, the objective that inspired the revolutionaries was the prospect of greater democracy. But, in the case of China, the strings of
power remained in the hands of Mao, whose cult became a substitute for the discredited authority of the Communist Party and the state bureaucracy.

In the first half of the 1960s, Mao remained on the sidelines in the aftermath
of the failures of the Great Leap Forward. Control of the party and state were in
the hands of the orthodox Communist Liu Shao-sh'i and his lieutenant Teng
Hsiao-p'ing. They preoccupied themselves with putting right the disorder and
economic losses caused by Mao's reckless policies of the previous decade. Stress
was laid on respect for the hierarchical and bureaucratic norms of the Leninist
party-state. The privileges and status of experts and intellectuals as against those
who did manual labor or were not educated asserted themselves once again. In
the factories, the authority of managers and technical experts was advanced at
the expense of workers. Stress on piece rates and bonuses to spur productivity
widened differences within the working class. Drastic reductions in the number
of state employees increased the chasm between relatively privileged regular factory workers and a constantly increasing semi-proletariat of temporary and contract workers. State economic and fiscal policies, meanwhile, favored urban
inhabitants as against those in the countryside. Rural industries, health care
facilities, and schools were neglected as against those in the cities. The virtual

crippling of the rural communes and de-emphasis of collective labor, coupled with a greater stress on private plots and rural markets, fostered inequality in the countryside.

In semi-retirement, Mao worried about the reassertion of bourgeois, feudal, and revisionist tendencies and the waning of the revolutionary impulse at all levels of Chinese society. The increasingly open dispute with what he regarded as the revisionist Soviet Union increased Mao's concern. Meanwhile, Liu Shao-sh'i and Teng Hsiao-p'ing, who were proponents of Soviet-style bureaucratic socialism, emphasized the significance in Marxist terms of the elimination of the old landlord and bourgeois classes and downplayed new forms of inequality. The principle contradiction in their eyes was between the advanced socialist system and the backward productive forces. Whatever social differences existed were based no longer on class, but merely on a division of labor in the same class. In contrast to this view, Mao by the early 1960s was concerned about the emergence of a new class of privileged party and state bureaucrats that controlled the fruits of social labor as it did in the Soviet Union. Mao's Cultural Revolution attempted to shake up and democratize the leadership of the revolution in the name of equality. It would use the young to undermine those who controlled the party and state apparatus.

In the spring of 1965 media attacks began against certain intellectuals who were under the protection of Liu Shao-sh'i and Teng Hsiao-p'ing, including their protege, the mayor of Beijing, P'eng Chen—who had attacked Mao. Under the command of the Maoist loyalist Lin Piao, the army declared itself the mainstay of the dictatorship of the proletariat and asserted that it would play an important role in the unfolding Cultural Revolution. In the middle of May, a directive drawn up by Mao in the name of the Politburo condemned P'eng Chen and denounced the revisionism that it claimed had infected the party. The Beijing Communist Party as well as the cultural and propaganda apparatus was purged.

The Cultural Revolution Group, headed by Mao's wife, Chiang Ch'ing, and other radical intellectuals, was created to direct the Cultural Revolution. By raising political consciousness and mobilizing the masses, the state and party structure would be refashioned to salvage the socialist ideals of the revolution. By the end of May, students in Beijing began to mobilize in response to Mao's call to rebel against established authorities. Hailed by Mao, their wall posters and protest demonstrations quickly were imitated by students all over China. In the ensuing struggles, young Maoist Red Guards were soon rivaled by other units of Red Guards composed of the offspring of government and party functionaries who tried to deflect attacks on the established educational and party authorities. Intellectuals and those with suspected bourgeois backgrounds were singled out for attack. By August, there were tens of millions of Red Guards marching in cities all over China in obedience to Mao's injunction to destroy "all ghosts and monsters." In July, to great fanfare, the 73-year-old Mao demonstrated his continued physical and political prowess by swimming nine miles in the Yangtze River. In mid-August, Mao appeared emperor-like before a million students in Tiananmen Square to accept an armband as head of the Red Guards. Meanwhile, a Maoist-controlled meeting of the Central Committee approved the purging of the party and society of revisionism by arousing the masses. Liu Shao-sh'i and Teng Hsiao-p'ing as well as their followers were expelled from their posts and placed under arrest.

During the rest of 1966, the Red Guards rampaged through the cities and towns and even ventured into the countryside attacking the symbols of feudalism and western capitalism as well as intellectuals and party and state functionaries. At times, the Red Guards would be confronted by rival worker or peasant militants or fought amongst themselves. On the orders of Mao, Red Guards were given free transport, food, and lodging, and their activities were assisted by Lin Piao's Peoples Liberation Army. By the end of the year, some 12 million Red Guards had visited Beijing to see Chairman Mao.

The leaders of the Cultural Revolution underestimated both the level of disorder inspired by the followers of Mao and the power of local party organizations to resist the movement. In November, revolutionary workers in the largest Chinese city, Shanghai, challenged local municipal and party administration. The radicals in the city organized themselves as the Workers' Second Regiment, composed of some 500,000 young and radical workers; the Workers' Third Army, made up of a comparable number of radical students and workers; and the Red Flag Army, composed of demobilized soldiers. These mass organizations in Shanghai were made up of younger, less skilled, low paid and contract workers as well as the unemployed. They were opposed by the conservative Worker's Scarlet Guards for the Defense of Mao Tse-tung Thought. The 800,000 members of the Scarlet Guards were older, more skilled, and highly paid workers wishing to preserve the established order. In mid-December, Shanghai was paralyzed by pitch battles between the two groups.

At the beginning of January 1967, the radicals overthrew the municipal and party government of Shanghai. One of the leaders of the Cultural Revolution

Group from Beijing, Chang Ch'un-ch'iao, took over, promising direct mass democracy according to the principles of the Paris Commune of 1871. In reality the Shanghai commune depended from the beginning on the authority of Chairman Mao, the People's Liberation Army, and the political police. Indeed, by February Mao called for the establishment of revolutionary committees made up of mass organizations, representatives of the Peoples Liberation Army, and local party cadres to restore order. The pattern of events in Shanghai was echoed in many urban centers in 1967. But outside of Shanghai the mass movements were less strong and organized and the power of local officials greater. In any case, the revolutionary committees now became the model for local government all over China. They signaled a retreat from mass democracy and the eventual return to control by a reconstituted Communist Party. Indeed, the army acted to check the radicalism of the leaders of mass organizations and to support party functionaries.

In the summer of 1967, however, a last gust of radicalism by radical students and workers challenged the movement toward the restoration of order. Despite Mao's orders to the contrary, the radicals were suppressed by a coalition of army commanders, party officials, and conservative workers in the industrial city of Wuhan. The Wuhan military commanders were arrested on the instructions of Mao and returned to the capital in disgrace. Encouraged, radicals in many places now verbally and physically challenged the army and threatened civil war. On September 5, the army was directed to restore order. The crackdown that followed marked the end of radical mass agitation and another step toward a gradual restoration of the authority of the party and state. In the summer of 1968, the Peoples Liberation Army carried out a general repression of Red Guards and other radicals. In 1969 the commander-in-chief of the Peoples Liberation Army, Lin Piao, whose political role had become critically important, was named Mao's successor.

It is estimated that some 400,000 deaths resulted from the upheavals and ultimate suppression of the Cultural Revolution. Millions of Red Guards and educated urban youth were sent to work in the countryside, becoming in retrospect a lost generation, especially in their own eyes. But the real failure of the Cultural Revolution was in its inability to produce enduring democratic political institutions or to allow workers greater control over the means of production. Instead, the monolithic authority of the party was step-by-step restored. The elimination of Lin Piao, Mao's would-be successor, in 1971 marked an important stage of the process of restoration. The finale was the arrest of the leaders of the Cultural

Revolution, the so-called "Gang of Four" which included Mao's wife Chiang Ch'ing. This coup immediately followed the death of Mao in 1976. The reemergence of Liu Shao-Shi's protege Teng Hsiao-p'ing and his subsequent ascent to the Chairmanship of the Communist Party marked the full return to normalcy.

6

From Revolution to Neoliberalism

The Tet offensive and President Johnson's abandonment of his reelection prospects represented grave reversals for the U.S. military effort in Vietnam. By then most people in the United States had lost the stomach for the conflict and considered the continuation of the war counter-productive or immoral. But the Vietnam War did not end. Instead these reverses brought to the fore a new president, Richard M. Nixon, convinced that he, unlike Johnson, could extract a semblance of triumph from the jaws of defeat. Under Nixon, the U.S. government desperately held on for years in southeast Asia, trying to avoid humiliation by invoking one diplomatic or military stratagem after the other. In the end, Nixon's efforts failed and he too, like Johnson, suffered personal humiliation and loss of the presidency. But by then the revolutionary mass movements in North America, Europe, and China that had been galvanized by the Vietnam War had clearly ebbed in the face of military and police repression, resistance from state bureaucracies, and the stubborn opposition of upper-class power. In the wake of the war, third world revolutionary movements continued to gain ground through the 1970s. But a conservative counter-offensive—economic, military, and ideological—emanating from Washington began to turn the tide as the decade unfolded.

The U.S. government was able to compensate itself in part for its eventual defeat in Vietnam by playing one Communist giant off another. In a major diplomatic and ideological revolution, the United States recognized the People's Republic of China. The two erstwhile enemies now informally allied themselves against the Soviet Union. This rapprochement signaled change at a deeper level. The consummation of the Sino-Soviet split did incalculable harm to radical and revolutionary movements worldwide. The venerable international communist movement, which had inspired both China and the Soviet Union as well as successive generations of revolutionaries, seemed politically to have exhausted itself.

The success of U.S. diplomacy rather than U.S. arms was reflected in other areas of the world as well. In the Middle East, the United States committed itself to a close alliance with Israel in the aftermath of the Six Days War (1967). Israel's crushing defeat of Nasser's Egypt in that conflict dissipated the immediate threat of Arab nationalism to U.S. Middle East interests. Israel became the military proxy of the United States in that region. U.S. influence in the region grew following the Yom Kippur War (1973) as Egypt deserted its alliance with the Soviet Union and turned instead toward political and economic dependence on the United States. In Latin America, U.S. interests as well as those of local elites were secured by coups that imposed the Brazilian and Bolivian model of military dictatorship on Uruguay, Chile, and Argentina.

In North America and Europe, popular interest in revolutionary politics was gradually replaced by an immediately less threatening commitment to the ecological movement or to identity politics based on gender, sexuality, or ethnicity. Starting in France some intellectuals turned away from searching for unity based on class in the Marxist tradition. Instead, they put stress on the philosophical importance of difference, on language as a source of misunderstanding rather than effective communication, and on conflict as an inescapable, yet historically meaningless, struggle for power.

But in much of the third world, revolutionaries continued to act as if the 1960s had not ended. Communist success in Vietnam inspired Marxists on three continents. These third world Marxists sought to deepen the anti-imperialism that marked the decolonization wave of the 1950s and 1960s. They endeavored as well to confront and overthrow the landed and mercantile elites that dominated the internal economies of many of these underdeveloped states. Guatemala saw the redevelopment of a low-level, but increasingly well rooted peasant insurgency. In El Salvador, a front of Marxist guerrillas mounted a challenge to the power of the coffee and cotton oligarchy. Meanwhile, in neighboring Nicaragua a popular revolutionary front toppled the long-standing dictatorship of Anastasia Somoza. Defeat in Vietnam made it hard for the United States to intervene directly in these upheavals. Likewise, it proved difficult for it to find an effective response to

Marxist-inspired revolutionary movements in Guinea-Bissau, Angola, Mozambique, Southern Rhodesia, and even backward Ethiopia. Likewise, in Afghanistan the Marxist People's Democratic Party seized power. In Iran, too, Marxist revolutionaries made a serious bid for power following the overthrow of the U.S.-backed Shah, only to be bested by religious revolutionaries who were equally anti-U.S. Indeed, third world anti-imperialism did not remain confined to Marxist-inspired revolutionary movements. Through the Organization of Petroleum Exporting Countries (OPEC), even conservative governments in Nigeria and Indonesia joined with radical nationalist regimes such as Libya and Algeria in raising oil prices at the expense of the United States and its Western allies. Inflation and lower profit margins weakened the foundations of U.S. and world capitalism. The postwar order of liberal capitalism based on Keynesian principles was shaken.

The End of the Indo-China Wars

Peace talks between the United States and the DRV opened in Paris in 1968. Nixon's strategy was to prevent the DRV from gaining a complete victory by bolstering the ARVN, while attempting to induce the Soviets and Chinese to broker a compromise peace. Under pressure from antiwar protesters who had succeeded in undermining popular support for the war, Nixon was forced to begin withdrawing U.S. ground troops piecemeal. To buy time and to attack the supposed nerve center and the supply lines of the Vietnamese Communists, he ordered an invasion of eastern Cambodia at the end of April 1970. Massive antiwar mobilizations followed and were intensified by the killing of protesting students by National Guard and police forces at Kent State University in Ohio and Jackson State College in Mississippi. The DRV, meanwhile, based its hopes on the ultimate withdrawal of U.S. ground forces and the underlying weakness of the ARVN and the RVN. A first test came in February 1971 with an ARVN attack into Laos to cut the Ho Chi Minh trail there. This attempted invasion of Laos ended in the rout of the South Vietnamese army by the PAVN in a ground battle in which the the United States could not intervene. The hollowness of Nixon's Vietnamization plan was plain to see.

With its military power curtailed, U.S. leaders sought a stronger hand through diplomacy. In July 1971, U.S. Secretary of State Henry Kissinger visited China, preparing the way for Nixon's historic journey to Beijing the following February.

The United States gave up its objections to seating the People's Republic of China in place of the Taiwan government at the United Nations. In the face of continuing military confrontations with the Soviet Union, Mao and the Chinese leadership obtained U.S. diplomatic recognition and entered into an informal entente with the United States. Mistrustful of China's intentions, the DRV responded to the latter's political rapprochement with the United States by launching an Easter 1972 offensive that drove the ARVN out of the northernmost provinces of South Vietnam.

In the wake of renewed U.S. bombing of North Vietnam, the U.S. government signed a peace treaty with the DRV in early January 1974. With the conclusion of the treaty, the last U.S. forces were withdrawn from Vietnam and a military standstill agreement between the communist and non-communist sides was concluded pending further negotiations. A massive military reinforcement of the ARVN took place on the eve of the final U.S. withdrawal. But the intrinsic weakness of the ARVN and dramatic cuts in U.S. economic aid undermined the RVN. On March 8, 1975, the PAVN and NLF launched a final military offensive that saw the fall of Saigon on April 30. The decades long struggle by the Vietnamese Communist Party to recover national independence and unity had ended in victory. In neighboring Cambodia, the United States had been heavily bombing suspected Communist bases or supply lines since 1969. These attacks as well as U.S. support of a right-wing military coup against the neutralist government of Prince Sihanouk (1970) enabled the so-called Khmer Rouge to mobilize a large peasant guerrilla army. Despite heavy bombing by the the United States, the Khmer Rouge army overran the capital Phnom Penh (April 16, 1975). The new Communist government of Cambodia (Kampuchea) introduced an ultra-leftist program that called for evacuating the population from the towns and forcing it into rural collectives. This political program was based on long-standing peasant hostility to the relatively privileged urban population and a far-fetched notion of exclusively rural socialist development. The consequence of this plan—a distant reflection of Mao's Great Leap Forward—was the horrendous die-off or murder of hundreds of thousands of urban dwellers.

Vietnamese Communists had tried to moderate and control the Cambodian revolution in order to make use of Cambodian territory as a sanctuary for the NLF and PAVN fighting in South Vietnam. The Cambodian Communists had deeply resented these efforts. Sino-Soviet rivalry exacerbated the division between the Cambodian and Vietnamese revolutionary regimes. The Cambodians feared Vietnamese plans to dominate all of Indo-China. Continual provocations against the DRV by the government of Communist Cambodia (Kampuchea) led to an invasion and rapid occupation of the country by the PAVN in 1979. A Cambodian government friendly to Vietnam was installed. China responded to this Vietnamese attack on Kampuchea, its ally, by launching a short-lived invasion of North Vietnam to teach the Vietnamese a lesson. The lesson did not take. Indeed, the real lesson was that all semblance of unity in the Communist world had long since collapsed in the wake of the Sino-Soviet split.

The Indo-China War was also fought in Laos, a country of about 3.5 million people. While escalating the war in Vietnam, President Kennedy had agreed in 1962 to the neutralization of this remote and underdeveloped country close to the Chinese border. A coalition government of royalist, neutralist, and Communist factions under Prince Souvanna Phouma was formed. But in order to interdict the Ho Chi Minh trail and to maintain its electronic monitoring stations in Laos close to Hanoi, the United States ignored the neutrality agreement, and through the CIA, organized a clandestine war against the Communist Pathet Lao army. Relying on massive and continuous bombing and the support of the mountain-dwelling Hmong minority, the U.S. effort was reasonably successful until the Tet Offensive (1968). With the support of the PAVN, the Pathet Lao were then able to seize the forward electronic listening posts of the the United States in the mountains of northeast Laos and drive the Hmong from their mountain redoubts. Reorganized as the Secret Army, 30,000 Hmong under the mercenary general Vang Pao backed by U.S. air power were able to stave off Pathet Lao offensives until the signing of the Paris Peace Accords in the spring of 1973. A new coalition government under Souvanna Phouma ruled the government until 1975, when the Pathet Lao took power.

The U.S. defeat in southeast Asia was cushioned by its new relationship with China. Although the initial rationale for U.S. intervention had been the containment of Chinese communism, both sides now downplayed their ideological differences. Rapprochement with China was reinforced by an ongoing U.S. alliance with Japan, which continued to look to the United States for protection and markets. In this way the United States secured its long-term position in Asia, while gaining an important new partner against the Soviet Union.

The Six Days War (1967)

The United States had also strengthened its hand in the Middle East during the Six Days War (1967). During the 1960s, Israel's growing economic and military potential was fuelled by foreign aid and continuing immigration. Although ostensibly inferior in personnel and weaponry to the neighboring Arab states, the Israeli armed forces became an efficient and formidable military machine. The 1956 war had opened the Gulf of Aqaba to Israeli shipping and installed a UN peacekeeping force on the border between Israel and Egypt. But Nasser was perceived as a continuing threat to Israel. The plight of the Palestinians remained the key source of conflict between the Zionist state and Arab countries. The Palestine Liberation Organization, created in 1964, and the Arab League demanded the repatriation of Palestinian refugees and the destruction of Israel. The Israelis refused to recognize the problem of the Palestinian refugees or, indeed, the existence of a Palestinian nation.

France had become an Israeli ally prior to the Suez conflict. It remained its close friend and major source of armaments. Meanwhile, the relationship between Israel and the United States grew warmer. President Kennedy gave the Israelis antiaircraft rockets and his successor, Johnson, committed the United States to significant arms deliveries. In the early 1960s, Egypt became involved in a civil war in north Yemen threatening U.S. oil interests in neighboring Saudi Arabia. Israel covertly aided the United States by helping to frustrate Nasser's ambitions in Yemen. Egypt increasingly aligned itself with the Soviet Union politically and militarily, as did Syria and Iraq. Tensions between Israel and Syria were heightened by disputes over land and water rights on their borders.

Responding to an Israeli threat, a new radical Baath government in Damascus signed a defense treaty with Egypt in November 1966. In early April 1967 there were major ground and air clashes between Israeli and Syrian forces in the Galilee. Egypt responded to reports of Israeli troop mobilization against Syria by ordering the Egyptian army into the eastern Sinai. On May 18, Nasser demanded the withdrawal of UN troops along the border. He then once more ordered the closing of the Gulf of Aqaba to Israeli shipping. On May 30, Jordan placed its army under Egyptian command.

Early on June 5, the Israeli airforce launched a preemptive strike that destroyed most of the Egyptian airforce. The Syrian and Jordanian airforces were eliminated the same day. Deprived of air support, the Egyptian army was routed from the Sinai by June 8. By June 10, Israel had taken East Jerusalem and the West Bank from Jordan and seized the Syrian-controlled Golan Heights. As a result of these stunning victories, Israel became the predominant military power in the Middle East. Nasser's prestige in the Arab world suffered an irreversible decline. The United States, reeling from defeat in Vietnam, made Israel its chief ally in the region. The land, water, and cheap Arab labor that Israel acquired on the West Bank further bolstered its economy.

The Yom Kippur War (1973) and the Reversal of Alliances

The Yom Kippur War of October 1973 saw the Egyptians and Syrians attempt to recover their honor. On October 6 (Yom Kippur), the armies of the two Arab states launched sudden coordinated attacks across the Suez Canal and the Golan Heights against the Israelis. The Arab side had been bolstered in the lead up to the war by substantial new deliveries of Soviet arms. Meanwhile, the increasingly massive direct U.S. military aid to Israel was in part justified by the withdrawal of its once reliable British partner from the defense of the oil rich Persian Gulf. During the twenty days of the conflict of October 1973, both the Soviet Union and the United States reinforced their respective partners through large-scale airlifts of more weapons. Having fought well and made initial gains, the Egyptians and the Syrians were ultimately driven back. Israeli moves to surround the Egyptian Third Army were met by Soviet mobilization of seven of its own airborne divisions. Washington put its military forces on precautionary alert. On October 25, hostilities ended with a UN ceasefire resolution accepted by both sides.

Nasser had died in 1970, and his successor, Anwar Sadat, had begun to eliminate leftist sympathizers from his government and to liberalize the largely state-controlled Egyptian economy even prior to the Yom Kippur War. The spread of Saudi Arabian money, its presence expanded by a dramatic surge in oil prices as a result of the Yom Kippur War, subtly influenced the evolution of Egyptian politics, and the Middle East generally, in a direction favorable to the United States over the course of the next decade. Leading politicians and the content of newspaper and journal articles in Egypt and elsewhere increasingly came under Saudi influence. Following the war, Sadat directly turned to the United States to mediate between Egypt and Israel. In 1975 the Egyptian leader asked the Soviet Union to place a moratorium on its ten billion dollar debt. Soviet refusal led to the abrogation of the frayed Soviet-Egyptian alliance. In September 1978 President

Jimmy Carter brokered the Camp David Accords ending the state of war between Israel and Egypt. In order to gain peace with Egypt, the Israelis agreed to withdraw from the Sinai Peninsula. Erstwhile enemies, both states were now allies and economic clients of the United States. In the wake of this rapprochement, Saudi financial and religious influence in Egypt grew.

Military Coups in Latin America

Support from the United States for military coups in Brazil and Bolivia (1964) had muzzled rising levels of class conflict in those nations. In the 1970s the same solution was extended to little Uruguay as well as the important states of Chile and Argentina in the southern cone of Latin America. Uruguay is a small country with a population of largely European descent tucked away between Brazil and Argentina. Emerging from British economic tutelage, it had developed its economy in the first part of the twentieth century on the basis of traditional livestock ranching and state-supported industrialization. By the 1950s, Uruguayans enjoyed the highest per capita income in Latin America with the lowest rates of illiteracy and birth and infant mortality and the highest levels of social security and life expectancy on the continent. Two parties of the privileged classes, the Colorados and Blancos, traditionally dominated its politics. From the mid-1950s, diminishing returns on agricultural exports and the mounting expenses of industrialization engendered prolonged economic stagnation. The result was growing peasant and worker unrest and the upsurge of the Tupamaro urban guerrilla movement in the late 1960s. The election of a right-wing Colorado president in 1971 in a reputedly fraudulent election prepared the way for a direct military takeover in June 1973. The United States supported the authoritarian drift with economic aid and by backing the intervention of right-wing Brazilian military officers into Uruguayan politics.

Chile

The hand of the United States was even more plainly evident in the overthrow of the elected socialist government of Salvador Allende in Chile. Nineteenth-century Chile had been dominated by a coalition of landowners, merchants, and Roman Catholic clergy. By 1929 the United States had replaced Great Britain as the major foreign presence in the country as a result of its half-billion-dollar investment in the increasingly important copper industry. The Second World War and the Korean War saw rapid growth based on the expansion of this industry. Economic slowdown, persistent unemployment, and inflation marked the late 1950s and 1960s, eroding the wages of both the rural and urban working class. Nonetheless, a certain diversification into manufacturing by a growing middle class took place. Agriculture remained technologically backward, with large estates employing the labor of hundreds of thousands of landless peasants.

Both rural and urban workers responded to these conditions with a growing militancy in the 1960s. Some 110,000 rural workers organized themselves into nearly 500 local unions, eventually joining together as the United Popular Action Movement, which based its ideology on Catholic Liberation Theology. Increasingly, they acted in concert with the Marxist-dominated Ranquil peasant confederation. Together they led a historic rural general strike in 1970 that demanded radical land reform. Since the 1950s, urban workers had been organized into the Single Workers Central that fought the erosion of wages through inflation and government-imposed austerity by launching wave upon wave of strikes. Socialists, Communists, and other leftists grouped themselves into the Popular Action Front (FRAP), which vainly backed a Socialist doctor, Salvador Allende, as candidate of the left in the 1958 presidential election.

Electoral politics during the 1960s were dominated by another new political formation, the Christian Democrats, which gained support from both liberal and conservative elements. The Christian Democratic Party espoused a kind of centrist populism that ostensibly rejected both capitalism and socialism. Invoking corporatism, it sought to reorganize political and economic life by channeling social conflict through so-called interest groups, preserving powerful economic interests while modernizing Chile. Warning of the dangers of a socialist takeover, the Christian Democrats led by Eduardo Frei won the presidency in 1964.

The CIA spent $20 million to assure the Christian Democratic electoral victory. The United States' Alliance for Progress of the 1960s considered the Frei government a model of democratic reformism. In subsequent years, U.S. economic aid per capita to Chile was the highest in Latin America. Such aid was coupled with an equally significant boost in support to the Chilean army and national police. Many military officers received training and indoctrination in the United States. The training courses of the American Institute for Free Labor Development enrolled some 10,000 students who would later play an important part in destabilizing the socialist government of Allende.

Under Frei, investment by U.S. multinationals rose to more than one billion dollars. Twenty-four of the top thirty multinationals in the United States invested in Chilean banking, mining, and industry. U.S. investors were also prominent as stakeholders in 18 of Chile's 20 leading corporations. Indeed, a symbiosis developed between U.S. investors and the Chilean business elite. But foreign investment did not end economic stagnation. Per capita economic growth declined between 1967 and 1970. Unemployment fluctuated between 20 and 25 percent. The business elite and the large landowners began to turn away from the Christian Democrats and toward the conservative National Party created in 1966. In 1970 the National Party decided to run its own presidential candidate, splitting the vote of the center and right and allowing the election of the socialist Popular Unity Government led by Allende.

Responding to a direct order from President Nixon, the CIA attempted to organize a coup even prior to Allende's assuming the presidency. As part of this plot on October 22, 1970, René Schneider, the constitutionalist army chief of staff, was assassinated in the streets of Santiago. Public outrage ensured Allende's ascension to the presidency. Over the next year, the new president began to implement the anti-imperialist program of the Popular Unity coalition. Public utilities, banks, and basic industries, including the U.S.-dominated copper industry, were nationalized. A major land reform to the benefit of the rural landless was implemented. The U.S. government and private corporations together with the Chilean business elite responded with an economic and financial embargo as well as a campaign of terror and sabotage. Despite these efforts at undermining the socialist government, economic growth and income redistribution increased in the initial years of Popular Unity. As a result, Popular Unity made further gains in local and congressional elections. Indeed, the right wing's inability to stymie Allende electorally led to a military coup. The military had been steadily gaining influence inside the government as a result of the continuing unrest in the country. Pro-Washington military officers including General Augusto Pinochet came to the fore in the spring of 1973. Acting in close concert with U.S. naval intelligence officers, they staged a coup d'etat on September 11. The elected president died defending the presidential palace in the center of Santiago.

Argentina

The military seized power in Argentina three years later. The coup was preceded by the return of Juan Peron from exile and his reelection as president in

1973. Peron returned to power because class conflict in Argentina had made the country ungovernable. Most workers had remained Peronists after 1955, pining for a return of the prosperity of the 1940s. The military, landowners, industrial-financial oligarchy, and civilian politicians were against Peron's return. During Peron's 20-year exile, Argentina had fully entered the U.S. economic orbit. Investment by U.S. companies totaled $1.2 billion by the late 1960s, concentrated in industries such as cars, pharmaceuticals, chemicals, machinery, and banking. Economic growth continued but only to the benefit of the middle class. Foreign indebtedness dramatically increased as well. In the wake of the Cuban Revolution, urban and rural guerrilla movements had emerged. The military responded by imposing its own regime between 1966 and 1973.

But military dictatorship did not end the challenges from the left. In 1969 workers and students calling for a socialist revolution seized the industrial city of Córdoba. Revolutionaries in three other industrial cities followed suit. While this insurrection was crushed by military intervention, new guerrilla formations appeared in the wake of the uprising. They included the urban desperados known as the Montenoros who resorted to bank robberies and the kidnapping of industrialists and rich foreigners. Peron the populist was brought back in 1973 in order to try to resolve this polarized situation. He died and was succeeded by Isabelita, his third wife. Internal war soon resumed between the Montenoros and the army. Economic conditions deteriorated as a result of the recession of 1973–74, ongoing inflationary pressures, and the flight of capital abroad. In June 1975 an austerity program was introduced, which was followed by a military takeover in March 1976. The so-called dirty war that followed led to the deaths of some 20,000 suspected leftists.

The seizure of power by military dictatorships first in Brazil and Bolivia and then in Uruguay, Chile, and Argentina marked the end of an era. Efforts throughout Latin American to foster income redistribution and industrial growth by policies of state intervention and limited protectionism came to an end. Business operators and bankers turned to the army and police forces to suppress populist opposition. Militancy on the part of labor unions and peasants was suppressed. Multinational and U.S. capital and technology were welcomed. A new phase of U.S. domination over Latin America under the banner of neoliberalism had begun. The United States itself would take the same neoliberal direction by the end of the 1970s.

Rise of Environmental and Identity Politics

The early 1970s in the United States were marked by a complex political evolution. The invasion of Cambodia in the spring of 1970 provoked what was perhaps
the most widespread of all antiwar protests with over five hundred college campuses shut down in May. But the subsequent step-by-step withdrawal of U.S.
troops by Nixon drew the teeth of the antiwar mobilizations and of the New Left.
The Students for a Democratic Society had broken apart in 1969 and its extremist element, calling themselves the Weathermen, was underground. In the next
few years, it carried on a guerrilla war against the U.S. government. Meanwhile,
various sectarian Communist groups vainly tried to establish a mass base among
students and workers.

Interest in a politics based directly on class flagged among those who had been
part of the New Left. In its place came a concern for the environment and political realignments based on questions of identity and ethnicity. Or rather such
movements, which had already begun to emerge in the midst of the black liberation and antiwar struggles of the 1960s, now came to the fore. Despite the fading
of class as an immediate issue, the rise of the environmental, feminist, gay, and
Native American movements deepened the culture of protest in the United States
and, ultimately, worldwide.

Environmentalism

Concern for the environment had existed in the United States since the late
nineteenth century. Preserving wilderness areas was the main preoccupation of
environmental organizations such as the Audubon Society, the Sierra Club,
and the Wilderness Society. Rachel's Carson's *Silent Spring* (1962) signaled
the beginning of contemporary environmentalism. Carson put the focus for
the first time on the effects of industrial pollution on society and human
health. Erstwhile civil rights and antiwar activists in the late 1960s then provided the shock troops that energized older environmental organizations or
created new ones such as the Environmental Defense Fund, which concerned
itself with nuclear, chemical, and petroleum pollution and food adulteration.
Greenpeace, an international organization founded in 1971 largely to protest
nuclear testing, seized the limelight with dramatic interventions on behalf of
seals, whales, dolphins, and other endangered species. In succeeding years,

concern with the treatment and survival of other species would spawn the animal rights movement.

Environmentalism found a particularly favorable reception among the educated middle class. The U.S. Congress had first responded to environmentalist political pressure with the conservation-minded Wilderness Act (1964). But then it took up the concerns of the modern environmental movement by passing a strengthened Clean Air Act, a Water Quality Control Act, and a Resource Recovery Act regulating toxic waste. Whatever his private reservations, Nixon was forced in 1970 to agree to the creation of the Environmental Protection Agency and to sign five major pieces of environmental legislation. But the potential to co-opt environmentalism was reflected by the first Earth Day in April that year, the celebration of which attracted the support of the U.S. Congress and even major private corporations. There was, to be sure, a radical environmentalism in North America that continued as a current within the environmental movement. But from the beginning, the mainstream of environmentalism in North American stressed reform within the existing order. It was far otherwise in West Germany, the other major site of environmental activism. There the connection with the antiwar and antinuclear movements remained close. Moved by a bitter generational conflict over the legacy of Nazism and the Holocaust, the German student and youth movements of the late 1960s marked a critical turning point in post-war German history. Opposition to increasing German reliance on nuclear power became the focal point of the emerging ecological movement. Large-scale and vehement protests developed around proposed or existing nuclear power facilities. The established political parties, including the Social Democrats and the government bureaucracy, turned a blind eye to the concerns raised by the protesters. Such political exclusion fostered a strong oppositional counter culture through the 1970s, which ultimately issued in the creation of the Green Party (1980). The new party was committed to ecology, grassroots democracy, social justice, and non-violence and became the model for such parties around the world.

Feminism

Just as the publication of Rachel Carson's *Silent Spring* initiated the environmental movement, Betty Friedan's *The Feminine Mystique* (1963) sparked second wave or post-1945 feminism. Friedan, a middle-class labor activist prior to the

McCarthy witch hunts, re-emerged in the 1950s decrying the oppression of the suburban housewife. While calling for the entry of women into the paid workforce, she attacked wage discrimination, sexual harassment, and the absence of proper childcare facilities. In 1966 she helped to found the National Organization for Women (NOW) whose aim was to challenge legal discrimination, ensure formal equality, and open educational and employment opportunities for women. During the late 1960s, a younger stratum of women who were veterans of the civil rights and antiwar movements created a more radical feminism. Stung by discrimination at the hands of male activists, they employed their gender-based analysis of society to create the women's liberation movement, echoing third world and black liberation movements.

Between 1968 and 1970 women's liberation groups sprouted rapidly across the United States. Consciousness-raising about the reality of sexual inequality and about the politics underlying personal relationships were important activities of these groups. As early as 1968, women staged the first all-women antiwar march and demonstrated against the Miss America beauty contest in Atlantic City. Across the United States, women challenged existing images of women by invading bridal fairs, sitting down at the offices of mainstream women's magazines, and parading as witches. In August 1970 the Women's Strike for Equality saw tens of thousands of women demonstrate for 24-hour daycare, abortion on demand, and equal employment and educational opportunities.

Kate Millet's *Sexual Politics* as well as other theoretical writings of the early 1970s called for the elimination of sex roles. Theoretical understanding of women's oppression notably advanced through the work of Millet, Germaine Greer (*Female Eunuch,* 1970), Shulamith Firestone (*Dialectics of Sex,* 1970), and Luce Irigaray (*Mirror of the Other Women,* 1974). By the end of the decade, many feminists began to search for women-centered definitions of female experience. Womanly qualities depreciated by men were redefined as positive female attributes. Yet many differences between feminists soon surfaced. Middle-class white women's aspirations clashed with women who were poor, of a different color or culture. Gay/straight conflicts were much in evidence. Middle-class reformists clashed with socialists. Despite these disputes, legislatively mandated opportunities for women, especially middle-class women, grew as a result of ongoing demonstrations and protest. Feminist studies became institutionalized in the universities. Over time a major restructuring of labor markets in favor of women would emerge.

Gay Liberation

Gay liberation was launched in reaction to a police raid on June 27, 1969, on the Stonewall Inn, a Greenwich Village, New York, bar frequented by gays and lesbians. To the astonishment of the police, the normally intimidated bar patrons, joined by sympathizers from throughout the Village, fought back. Bars were one of the few public spaces controlled by gays in a society that fiercely repressed homosexuality. There had been several earlier incidents of homosexual resistance in New York and San Francisco. But the resistance at the Stonewall Inn turned into a full-scale riot.

During the 1950s two organizations, the Mattachine Society and the Daughters of Bilitis, had struggled to defend homosexuals. The homosexuality of the outstanding Beat poet and publicist Allen Ginsberg opened a space for homosexuals on the margins of U.S. society. But the Stonewall riot led to the mass coming out of homosexuals. The Gay Liberation Front organized in the wake of Stonewall identified with the broad anti-imperialist and self-determination goals of the New Left, despite the frequent rejection of homosexuality voiced by numerous New Left figures. Preceding and concurrent to this leftist strain, more conservative gay and lesbian activists, such as the Gay Activist Alliance (1970), focused exclusively on the needs of the gay and lesbian community. The subsequent declaration by the American Psychiatric Association and the American Psychological Association in 1973 that homosexual orientation was not an illness helped to remove the stigma from homosexuality. So, too, did acceptance of homosexuality by some of the more liberal Protestant churches. A veritable homosexual community emerged across the United States made up of bars, nightclubs, athletic teams, choruses, resorts, and political clubs.

The American Indian Movement

Until the 1960s modern resistance to the dominance of white capitalist society in North America by aboriginal populations had been scattered and local. In the first part of the twentieth century, the North American Church had a membership made up of aboriginal spiritual leaders and tradition-minded Indians. They stubbornly clung to the old ways as a form of resistance to the domination of European culture.

The National Indian Youth Council appeared as the first modern pan-Indian movement not under the control of the U.S. federal government. In 1968 aboriginals in Minneapolis who shared a common experience of urban poverty and imprisonment created the American Indian Movement (AIM). The new organization's goals were to combat police brutality and improve opportunities for Indian people. AIM's militant style, willingness to go anywhere to support local struggles, and the harsh reality of life for Indians both on reserves and in the cities engendered support from young aboriginals. In 1969 AIM participated in the occupation of the federal prison of Alcatraz. In 1972 militants of AIM occupied the Bureau of Indian Affairs in Washington. The next year a bloody confrontation between the federal government and AIM militants at Wounded Knee, South Dakota, attracted national attention. Although its ongoing organizational weakness tended to sap AIM's effectiveness, for the rest of the 1970s it remained a major force in Indian communities throughout North America.

AIM also related Indian struggles in the United States to the worldwide struggle against imperialism. The awakening provoked by AIM speedily reflected itself, for example, in the remote Northwest Territories of Canada where the indigenous people in short order formed the Indian Brotherhood of the NWT (later Dene Nation)(1969), the Committee for Original People's Entitlement (COPE)(1970), the Inuit Tapisarat of Canada (1971) and the Metis Association of the NWT (1972). Indeed, the seeds AIM planted in countries such as Canada and New Zealand would flower in the following decades into an international indigenous peoples movement. The claims advanced by these groups conflicted with the hunger of corporations for access to the oil and other resources that lay under aboriginal ancestral lands.

Chicano Resistance

Mexican Americans, likewise, mobilized themselves during the 1960s and 1970s. White landowners had displaced many Mexican farmers in the United States in the first part of the twentieth century. Many consequently worked as seasonal workers in agriculture or on the railways. During the 1930s and 1940s many of these workers became involved in militant trade union activities. Starting in the late 1950s, Reies López Tijerina initiated campaigns in New Mexico and Colorado to reclaim alienated lands. Further migration from Mexico during the 1950s reinforced the strength of the Mexican community. By the 1960s farm workers and youth took the lead in the resurgence of a Mexican challenge to Anglo economic, cultural, and political supremacy. Beginning in 1962, César

Chavez organized the United Farm Workers in the U.S. southwest. Through strikes and nationwide boycotts, Chavez helped to improve the condition of Mexican farm workers. The Crusade for Justice in Colorado, the emergence of La Raza Unida Party in Texas, high school strikes in East Los Angeles, Texas, and Colorado, and the Chicano Student Movement on college campuses reflected the emergence of a new Mexican American nationalism.

All of these movements began in the 1960s and continued into the 1970s. The antiwar and New Left movements meanwhile ebbed away. But in the final analysis, the proliferation of these new groups reflected a deepening of the agenda of human liberation. They made it possible to envision a highly diverse civil society of the future not dependent on the division of labor created by the market. Ultimately, they furnished a more profound sense of the notion of class itself. But as they took their distance from the broad movement of the left, they reflected the ebbing and fracturing of the movement of the sixties. Certainly the government saw them as less of an immediate threat than the antiwar movement and those who called for a class-based movement against capitalism.

Postmodernism

Culturally, too, a sense of fragmentation set in with the growing U.S. prominence of the writings of a postmodernist group of Paris-based intellectuals including Jacques Derrida, Jacques Lyotard, and Michel Foucault. Their questioning of the notions of the integrity of the individual subject, the truths of rational thought, and the idea of human progress, represented a fundamental challenge to Western modernist thought and aesthetics.

The emergence of postmodernism is a complex matter. It can no more be reduced to right-wing politics than can the romantic movement of the early nineteenth century. It certainly was not exclusively reactionary from a class perspective. Among other things, postmodernism attacked some of the intellectual foundations of the bourgeois social order as well as those of Marxism. It challenged the shibboleth of the modern whose unstated premise is constant change— change issuing from unending economic accumulation to the benefit of the few. On the other hand, the postmodern questioning of the certainty of knowledge, of foundational concepts, and of the pretensions of grand philosophical and historical narratives clearly reflects a skepticism toward and, indeed, in some cases a rejection of Marxism. In certain respects, its attack on some varieties of Marxism was well merited. The Soviet Union's quashing of the Prague Spring led many in France and elsewhere to turn their backs once and for all on Marxism. Marxist dogmatism that had little room for feminism and homosexuality or, more generally, questions of desire, pleasure, sex, language, or art, likewise, deservedly inspired postmodernist contempt.

Yet postmodernist assaults on Marxism and even modern scientific rationalism sometimes seemed to verge on irrationalism. Objective knowledge is not the same thing as absolute truth. Most rational thinkers claim no more than that the vessel of knowledge is half full. To complain that there is no knowledge because the vase is not absolutely full is to overstate the case. Moreover, Marx himself always insisted that the content of the container was always changing. Knowledge, including the concepts of science and Marxism, are historically conditioned and must, necessarily, change. Because knowledge is contingent makes it no less knowledge. Postmodern rejection of essences likewise constitutes an attack on the possibility of knowledge, which of necessity entails a process of abstraction from appearances. On the other hand, postmodern stress on signs, textuality, discourse, and culture at the expense of material factors risks lapsing into a new form of idealism. It is one thing to say that historical realities can be read as a text and another to assert that historical reality is merely a text. Indeed, the escapist and schizoid character of postmodernist idealism is mirrored in the otherwise all-pervasive economism of the dominant ideology of neoliberalism that emerged from the 1970s onward. The same people who during the day asserted that reality was only to be understood as a system of signs carefully checked quotations on their stocks in the newspapers at night. Such numbers were considered all too real.

Indeed, there exists a profound homology between the endlessly proliferating signs and differences of postmodernist theory and the increasingly pervasive and inchoate world of fragmented universal commodification in the era of neoliberalism. Michel Foucault's insistence on the ubiquity of struggles over power in societies past and present is no doubt true. Nonetheless, such an insight is meant to undercut and deny the emancipatory character of one particular and historically meaningful form of social conflict, namely, class conflict. Finally, it is one thing to challenge the modern in the name of all those who have been left out or left behind as do subaltern scholars. But it is another to abandon all emancipatory critique by exalting the state of being oppressed and subaltern.

Central America

A world away from the hothouse of Parisian intellectual life or the classrooms of Yale, Marxism and nationalism remained strong in Central America, southern Africa, the Middle East, and throughout the third world. Guerrilla insurgency, which had been contained in the rest of Latin America by the early 1970s, flared up again in the Central American states of Guatemala, El Salvador, and Nicaragua. In the wake of its defeat in southeast Asia, the so-called Vietnam Syndrome inhibited the United States from direct intervention in these conflicts. Any proposal for the United States to intervene directly in a third world conflict met an almost phobic public response in the United States. U.S. casualties in such conflicts were out of the question. As a result, the United States deployed so-called low intensity means of warfare designed to minimize U.S. losses by using indirect ways of combating these third world liberation movements.

Export-orientated agriculture had long been the mainstay of the republics of Central America. The postwar period saw the intensification of sugar, banana, coffee, cotton, and beef production in Honduras, Guatemala, El Salvador, and Nicaragua. The production of livestock expanded, especially in Nicaragua, in order to serve the burgeoning North American market. Beef exports from Central America to the North American fast-food industry multiplied eleven times between 1966 and 1979. The output of cotton based on large farms employing seasonal labor increased prodigiously both in Nicaragua and in El Salvador. In the late 1960s overproduction of cotton led to the conversion of some large farms to sugar and corn production. Guatemala, too, saw an expansion of acreage devoted to the production of sugar.

Part of the extended acreage of these large capital-intensive farms was obtained by opening new land. But much of it came at the expense of peasant families who were dispossessed of their small corn plots either legally or through coercion and fraud. Many of the displaced moved to the cities, eking out a living on the margins of urban society. In Nicaragua, for instance, the urban population increased from 19 percent in 1950 to 54 percent in 1980. Some peasants were forced to subsist in marginal mountainous regions, supplementing their livelihood through seasonal labor on the large farms. Social inequality, historically very high, increased throughout this period. In 1970 one-fifth of the population of the region received 61 percent of the income.

Guatemala

Endemic poverty and violence characterized Guatemala in the wake of the overthrow of the Arbenz regime. By the late 1960s, counter-insurgency and death
squads seemingly had reduced the guerrillas to a fugitive remnant. But rural
insurgency re-emerged in the 1970s. Economic crisis at the beginning of the
1980s intensified discontent. By then the threat from guerrilla movements, radical unions, student organizations, and peasant associations once again grew serious. The oligarchy and military responded by installing a reign of terror under
military strongman General Efrain Rios Mott (1982). While the United States
publicly distanced itself from the military dictatorship, it covertly supported it.
Overall, the army killed perhaps 200,000 peasants, workers, and guerrillas.
Hundreds of thousands fled for refuge to the mountains or into Mexico. In 1986
a facade of political democracy was restored while the popular organizations and
political parties emerged from underground.

Nicaragua

Insurgencies grew from similar conditions in Nicaragua and El Salvador in the
early 1970s. The modern history of Nicaragua begins with the presidency of José
Santos Zelaya (1894-1909). A liberal modernizer, he developed Nicaragua's coffee economy at the expense of the indigenous peasant population whom he saw
as a barrier to progress. His resistance to growing U.S. political and economic
penetration led to an initial U.S. military intervention in 1909. When U.S. control
over the affairs of Nicaragua appeared to be challenged once more in 1927, U.S.
marines occupied the country again. General Augusto César Sandino led a stubborn guerrilla resistance to the U.S. occupation for the next seven years. In 1934
the the United States withdrew, placing their confidence in the U.S.-trained
National Guard led by their protege Anastasio Somoza García. Assassinating
Sandino in an ambush, Somoza made himself president in 1937.

He and his sons, Luis and Anastasio Somoza Debayle, controlled the country's political life for the next four decades. They and their cronies were the main
beneficiaries of the economic boom of the 1950s and 1960s. Economic growth
based on exports was increased by an influx of funds from the Alliance for
Progress and the creation of a Central American Common Market (CACM). By the
1970s the Somozas and their partners controlled 21 percent of the land, nearly all

mining activity, and many other enterprises. Their combined holdings accounted for 41 percent of Nicaragua's gross national product.

An earthquake that leveled the capital Managua in 1972 and the subsequent OPEC oil crisis brought the period of prosperity to a close. Inflation, declining exports, mounting external debts, and higher taxes fuelled discontent. The 1970s saw increasing left-wing political agitation and growing peasant and labor unrest. The ideas of liberation theology became pervasive among the Catholic lower clergy and their parishioners. The left-wing opposition to Somoza was more and more attracted to the Sandino National Liberation Front (FSLN). Founded in 1961 in the wake of the Cuban Revolution, the FSLN was made up of diverse radical tendencies including a proletarian or Marxist element. It was highly nationalistic and anti-U.S., demanding fundamental change in favor of the poor. The moderate opposition consisted of the economically and politically progressive middle class that was frustrated by the domination of the Somozas and their friends over the political and economic life of the country.

Somoza's National Guard, backed by U.S. military aid, defeated a Sandinista guerrilla offensive in the mid-1970s. In 1978, however, the regime ordered the assassination of Pedro Joaquín Chamorro, the editor of *La Prensa*, the major newspaper of the moderate opposition. There followed a national strike and insurrection during which the FSLN and moderate opposition drew together. Under President Jimmy Carter, Washington's policy wavered between sustaining and repudiating the Somoza dictatorship. In the post-Vietnam epoch, the U.S. government had sought to regain international credibility as a champion of human rights against third world dictatorships as well as Communist regimes. Carter's vacillation toward the oppressive Somoza government enabled the Sandinistas to launch a successful final offensive in the summer of 1979. They, rather than the moderate opposition, dominated the new provisional government.

El Salvador

The development of insurgency in El Salvador took a similar if not identical course. The Salvadoran coffee oligarchy had been challenged in 1932 by an unsuccessful popular revolt, the so-called Matanza, led by the fledgling Communist Party. Some 17,000 peasants were killed in the repression that followed. A close alliance between the military and the coffee-growing elite ruled the country during the succeeding decades through a tightly controlled electoral process. The oligarchy continued to dominate the postwar economy based on cotton, beef, and sugar exports. Less than 1 percent of farms controlled nearly 40 percent of the land, while 49 percent of farms were based on less than one hectare. Lack of access to land meant that more than half of the rural population was made up of seasonal or full-time wageworkers.

In 1972 the regime allowed José Napoleon Duarte, the popular Christian Democratic mayor of San Salvador, to run in the presidential elections. His victory was annulled by the military. Political repression and growing economic difficulties sparked increasing dissent. By the mid-1970s covert guerrilla groups, including the Farabundo Marti Popular Liberation Forces (FMPL) and the Revolutionary People's Army (ERP), were operating in the towns and countryside. In January 1979 the largest mass demonstration in El Salvador's history led to the massacre of 20 people and the wounding of 200 others by the army. By 1980 about 1,000 suspected opponents of the government were being killed every month by the military or death squads. El Salvador descended into full-scale civil war following the assassination of the Archbishop of San Salvador Oscar Romero. His death came the day after he called on soldiers to refuse orders to repress the population.

Africa

In Africa, meanwhile, the relatively peaceful decolonization movement of the 1950s and 1960s was followed by an upsurge of bitter national liberation struggles in the Portuguese colonies of Angola, Mozambique, and Guinea as well as in British Southern Rhodesia. Resistance to majority rule and independence was based on the existence of large white settler populations in these colonies. The number of white settlers had swelled through an influx of new European immigrants following the Second World War. The white settlers jealously excluded the black population from civil service or skilled labor opportunities as well as from the land.

The Portuguese Colonies

Indeed, Portugal's authoritarian state tenaciously clung to its so-called African empire. The colonies furnished an important and exclusive market for the home economy's backward textile manufactures and its wine exports, while providing cheap raw materials, diamonds, cocoa, and coffee. In the 1960s oil was discovered in Angola, making that colony a particularly valuable posses-sion. Mozambique, meanwhile, was part of the ambit of the expanding econo-my of the apartheid regime in South Africa. The Portuguese government claimed that its African possessions were an integral part of the mother coun-try. According to the official view, Portugal had a unique capacity to Christianize and assimilate the indigenous populations into a non-racial peo-ple. The reality was completely different. Only one percent of the population qualified for the status of assimilated. Racism characterized every aspect of the colonial administration and labor market.

Organized opposition to Portuguese rule emerged mainly among educated, racially mixed, or assimilated Africans. Expatriates, including Agostinho Neto, Eduardo Mondlane, and Amilcar Cabral, founded the Movimento Anti-Colonista in Paris in 1957. These Marxist-inspired leaders would direct radical national lib-eration movements in Angola, Mozambique, and Guinea-Bissau. Peasant and worker discontent in the colonies was contained until 1961 when, finally, major uprisings broke out.

In Angola an urban educated elite with a nationalist and anti-imperialist per-spective constituted the Popular Movement for the Liberation of Angola (MPLA) led by Neto. Some Africans based in rural and ethnically homogenous areas viewed the cadres of the MPLA as essentially urban mulattos who were remote from the social institutions and networks within which most Angolans lived. In the north of Angola, a rival anticolonial movement, the National Front for the Liberation of Angola (FNLA), led by Holden Roberto, emerged among the Bakonga people who lived both in northern Angola and Zaire (Congo). To the south, Jonas Savimbi organized the National Union for the Total Independence of Angola (UNITA) among the Ovimbundu people. His small circle of lieutenants, mainly from Protestant mission schools, espoused a Maoist ideology that emphasized peasant revolution. The three revolts failed to unify: MPLA relied on support from Cuba and the Soviet Union, FNLA depended on aid from the Zairian dictator Mobutu, and UNITA gained sup-port from Zambia.

Cabral, meanwhile, had taken the field against the Portuguese at the head of the African Party for the Independence of Guinea and Cabo Verde (PAIGC) and Mondlane served at the head of the Mozambique Liberation Front (FRELIMO). Cabral's PAIGC soon controlled two-thirds of the Guinean countryside with the Portuguese holding on to the towns. Mondlane's forces first challenged Portugal by invading the Makonde region of northern Mozambique, aided by the support of neighboring Tanzania. After Mondlane's assassination in 1969, leadership devolved on Samora Machel, a brilliant military tactician. From 1970, when it was allowed to operate from bases in neighboring Zambia, FRELIMO's military position dramatically improved.

By the early 1970s, Portugal was clearly overextended having to fight on three fronts. Some 180,000 conscripts from Portugal were required to hold down the African guerrilla movements. Tens of thousands of young men fled Portugal to work in France and Germany to avoid the draft. Meanwhile, the Portuguese population chaffed at the rule of the right-wing premier, Marcello Caetano, who sought to extend the long dictatorship of Pedro Salazar (1932-1968). On April 24, 1974, a conspiracy of middle-ranking army officers seized power in Lisbon and installed a junta headed by General Antonio de Spinola, initiating a tortuous transition ending in the establishment of a liberal democracy. The new Portuguese regime simultaneously entered into negotiations with the liberation movements in Angola, Mozambique, and Guinea-Bissau, which led to the independence of all three colonies in 1975. Some 800,000 white settlers fled back to Portugal.

War in Angola and Mozambique

After liberation, civil war almost immediately broke out between the rival guerrilla movements in Angola. The MPLA was supported by the Soviet Union and Cuba. The CIA backed Holden Roberto's FNLA and Joseph Savimbi's UNITA. The MPLA held Luanda, the capital, as well as the newly productive oil regions to the north of the city. Bolstered by thousands of troops from South Africa, UNITA and the FNLA launched an offensive from South African-controlled Namibia in the south. Cuba unexpectedly responded with thousands of troops of its own. The Cubans and MPLA were able to rout the advancing South Africans and their UNITA and FNLA allies (1975). This setback would not deter the United States from continuing its support for its allies in Angola. The MPLA, in turn, would use its oil wealth and Cuban military advisers to hold out against repeated attempts to destabilize it. The prolonged war wreaked havoc on the population, towns, and countryside. Meanwhile in Mozambique, the Marxist regime of FRELIMO faced a devastating insurgency sponsored by the South African government.

Southern Rhodesia

The British settler colony of Southern Rhodesia, likewise, was caught up in a liberation struggle. Reinforced by an influx of Britons after the Second World War, the white minority reaped the benefits of the postwar export boom in tobacco, corn, beef, gold, and other commodities. The increasingly arrogant settler population deprived the indigenous peasant majority of land and kept urban and working-class blacks under close control through policies of racial exclusion and police and state surveillance.

Black demands for power sharing were met by stubborn intransigence on the part of the white settlers. In defiance of the British, Ian Smith, the Rhodesian Prime Minister, unilaterally declared independence from the mother country in 1964 on the basis of exclusive white rule. Britain did little to bring the Smith government to heel, while the South African government provided political and economic support to the whites-only regime. Two nationalist organizations, the Zimbabwe African National Union (ZANU) led by Robert Mugabe and the Zimbabwe African People's Union (ZAPU) led by Joshua Nkomo, operating from bases in Mozambique and Zambia, respectively, carried out guerrilla campaigns against the white government throughout the 1970s. As a result of the sacrifice of some 25,000 black lives, the Smith regime was forced to negotiate an end of the conflict on the basis of majority rule. In 1980 Mugabe won a comfortable electoral majority.

Ethiopia

Upheaval in Africa in the 1970s was such that it ultimately embraced even Ethiopia, the least developed state in Africa. With an area approximately twice the size of France, it had a population of roughly 35 million living mainly in the relatively temperate high plateau and mountainous regions. For many years this officially Christian state had been headed by Emperor Haile Selassie, who ruled through an ethnic elite, the so-called Amhara. They dominated other ethnic groups including the Eritreans, Tigreans, and Oromono peoples. Most of the population was subsistence farmers, paying rents to a landlord class that dominated the villages, clans, and tribes. In the post-1945 period, some wealthier farmers began to produce coffee as an export crop, while foreigners invested some $300 million in various businesses, mainly in the capital of Addis Ababa. Like the

Mobutu government of Zaire, another repressive regime governing a large country, the Ethiopian monarchy of Haile Selassie was a close friend of the United States. Between 1951 and 1976 the U.S. government provided Ethiopia more than $600 million in military and economic aid. The the United States used Ethiopia as part of its worldwide military radio communications network.

Eritrea, a Muslim-populated area of Ethiopia on the Red Sea coast, had become an Italian colony in the first part of the twentieth century. During the period of Italian rule, the Eritrean population developed a sense of autonomy from the rest of Ethiopia. In 1961 an insurgency began in Eritrea against the Haile Selassie government. At first led by Muslim religious leaders, the insurgents more and more came under the influence of Marxist ideology. Arab countries lent support to the rebellion, which the Ethiopian government was unable to bring under control.

The bureaucracy and army had expanded in the post-war years to around 150,000, creating new employment opportunities. By the 1970s, there were some 40,000 trade unionists and some 75,000 high school and university students, located mainly in the capital Addis Ababa. It was among these elements that new ideas, especially Marxism, began to circulate.

Chronic famine and landlessness resulted in as many as 400,000 Ethiopians dying in the famine of 1971–72. Inflation, brought on by food shortages and the OPEC oil crisis, damaged the fragile urban economy. The regime tried to ignore or cover up the famine and its consequences. Students in the capital, nonetheless, protested and called for land reform. In Europe and the United States, thousands of expatriate Ethiopian students organized themselves into radical groups. Secret opposition elements also emerged in the middle ranks of the army. An army mutiny at Neghelle in January 1974 set off a revolutionary movement that led to the deposition of Haile Selassie and the establishment of a radical government controlled by the army.

In the long term, this new military regime proved unable to deal with the chronic problems of drought and famine as well as growing ethnic revolt. With Cuban and Soviet help, it was successful in turning back a U.S.-supported invasion of its eastern territories from neighboring Somalia in 1978. But the insurgency in Eritrea only grew in strength. By the 1980s, other ethnic groups, notably the Tigreans, also rose in revolt. Despite these problems, the regime, inspired by third world Marxism, instituted an effective land reform and definitively separated church and state.

Afghanistan

Third world Marxism, likewise, inspired revolution in Afghanistan, the least developed state in Central Asia. Historically a crossroads of trade and conquest, Afghanistan is a landlocked country largely made up of arid plateaus and mountains. Its population of 15 million was mainly composed of peasants tilling the six percent of the land that was arable, while the remainder of the rural population eked out a living as pastoralists. Fervently and conservatively Muslim, the population was largely composed of a Pashtun majority as well as Tajik, Uzbek, and Hasara minorities. These ethnic groupings, as well as family and kinship groups, were the fundamental elements of Afghan society. Tribes, clans, and sub-clans were in a constant state of friction over land, water, and grazing rights. With the exception of a few large traders, khans, and members of the royal family, most of the population lived at a subsistence level.

Historically Russia and Great Britain had struggled for predominance in the Kingdom. Following the Second World War, U.S. influence eclipsed the British presence. In 1953 a relative of the reigning King Zahir Shah, Mohammed Daud, became prime minister. He initiated a ten-year program of modernization based on support from rival U.S. and Soviet aid programs. The fall of Daud in 1963 brought a brief period of constitutional government, followed by a renewal of political conservatism and repression. Daud's modernization efforts had produced hundreds of thousands of high school and university graduates, which the economy and bureaucracy were unable to absorb. Out of such elements was created the Communist or People's Democratic Party (PDP) in the mid-1960s. In alliance with the moderate or Parcham wing of the Communist Party, Daud overthrew the monarchy in 1973 declaring himself royal president. Parcham's goal was to use Daud as the basis of a national democratic program ending tribalism and landlord power, separating church and state, creating a secular educational system, and implementing gender equality. Parcham looked to intellectuals, the urban middle strata, the emergent bourgeoisie, women, and the military as the social basis for such reforms.

In 1975 Daud turned on Parcham, having been assured support from the bourgeoisie, state bureaucracy, landlords and aristocrats, the Iranian monarchy, and the United States, the latter the primary source of economic assistance. However, Soviet influence was especially entrenched in the military, which was trained and equipped by the Russians. Repression of the Communist Party set the stage for a coup led by pro-Communist elements of the army on April 27-28, 1978. The new PDP government at first consolidated its power by moderate policies. But by the spring of the following year, the extremist faction of the party, known as the Khalq and led by Hafilah Amin, ousted the moderate Parcham. Amin moved ahead with a compulsory literacy campaign, abolition of the bride price system, and a radical land reform. There was a growing polarization between progressive urban dwellers and some poor peasants, on the one hand, and mullahs, tribal leaders, and landlords and their followers on the other. In most of the countryside, it was the mullahs, tribal chiefs, and landlords who carried the day as vertical ties between family, clan, tribe, and religion tended to override class antagonisms in this still underdeveloped country.

The Khalq leader Amin responded to growing opposition with harsh repression, even against members of the Parcham. Half of the army deserted, while armed resistance against the regime in the countryside increased. Dismayed by Amin's extremism, Soviet aid expanded in order to try to gain political leverage over the situation. With Soviet support, elements of Parcham carried out a coup in December 1979. Amin was assassinated and the Parcham leader, Babrak Karmal, was named prime minister. In the face of growing U.S. assistance to the rural insurgents, Karmal called for stepped-up Soviet military assistance. A total of 130,000 Soviet troops were sent into Afghanistan.

Iran

As these events were unfolding, a massive revolution erupted in neighboring Iran. Bolstered by the United States, Shah Mohammed Rhez Pahlavi had ruled the country with an iron hand since the fall of Mossadegh in 1953. Rapid economic development was combined with ever increasing levels of political repression. This proved a recipe for a massive popular revolution in 1978–79, which swept aside the Shah and destroyed U.S. influence in the country.

In the wake of Mossadegh's fall, Shah Rheza Pahlavi consolidated power between 1953-63. The dispute over oil with Britain was ended on the basis of an equal division of the profits. But now U.S. oil companies were given equivalent treatment to the British. Henceforth, the Iranian regime became politically and economically dependent on the United States. With U.S. as well as Israeli help, special attention was paid to building up the military and internal security apparatus (SAVAK). The Iranian Parliament was totally controlled by parties obedient to the Shah. The intelligentsia and the left were closely controlled, while the traditional middle class and the Islamic clergy were left alone.

In 1963 the Shah launched the White Revolution. Among other measures, this attempted revolution-from-above nationalized the forests, introduced profit sharing for workers, privatized state industries, and extended the vote to women. Massive increases in government expenditure were fueled by rising oil revenues, especially during the early 1970s. The Shah lavished billions of dollars on the armed forces. But he also spent ten billion dollars on economic development (1963–73). An impressive buildup of infrastructure and industry occurred. In 1966 only 38 percent of the population was urbanized. Ten years later almost half of the population lived in cities. A vast expansion of educational opportunities for both men and women occurred. Improvements in health standards led to a rapid expansion of the population. By the mid-1970s half the population was under 16 and two-thirds were under 30.

The Iranian upper class was made up of some 1,000 individuals who owned 85 percent of major private firms in banking, manufacturing, foreign trade, and insurance. The propertied middle class of about a million included bazaar merchants, shopkeepers, Muslim clergy, and well-to-do entrepreneurs. Among the latter were owners of modern factories and Western-orientated wholesale or retail businesses. But despite the growth of modern industry and commerce, a substantial amount of trade and manufacture remained in the hands of the more numerous traditional bazaar merchants and shopkeepers. It was from the sons of this element that the Muslim Shiite clergy originated. During this period of unprecedented economic growth, prosperous bazaar merchants built mosques in the countryside, helping to extend the influence of the Muslim clergy over the rural population.

The numbers of the middle class increased during this period of economic growth. But the white- and blue-collar salaried or wage-earning class grew even more rapidly. The expansion of women's participation in the labor force as teachers and civil servants was especially notable. In addition to these middle and working classes, there were about 1.2 million urban poor made up largely of impoverished migrants from the countryside. During the White Revolution, major land reforms were instituted, giving hundreds of thousands of peasants' access to land. But many who still had too little land or none at all found their way to the cities, where they became part of a swelling tide of under-employed or unemployed workers.

By the mid-1970s the regime's tentacles had penetrated deeply into the countryside. Its bureaucrats were able to challenge the influence of local landlords and tribal leaders. In 1975 the Shah decided to extend his political control further by creating a one-party state. He dissolved the two royalist parties and established the Resurgence Party as the only legal political party. The level of censorship and repression reached unprecedented levels. All social groups were brought under close surveillance.

Under these new measures, the activities of the bazaar merchants were subject to unprecedented supervision. Their workshops, which employed tens of thousands, were placed under government scrutiny for the first time. Merchants had to register their workers with the labor ministry and pay monthly medical insurance benefits for them. State corporations were established to distribute food, threatening the traditional grocery trade. The clergy came under government supervision as well. To their consternation, religious corporations were forced to submit their accounts to government audits. Changes to the calendar and legislation restricting the power of husbands over wives were enacted. The clergy closed down seminaries and organized demonstrations in protest. The Shah answered with more repression.

Most other arenas of protest having been closed off, it was toward the religious that the public increasingly looked for leadership. It was the Ayotollah Ruhollah Musalvi Khomeini who became the focal point of opposition. From early in his career as a theologian, Khomeini had espoused a religious teaching that combined strict adherence to Islamic doctrine with social activism. During a period of major political unrest in 1963, he took the lead in denouncing corruption and calling for social reform and an Islamic state. From exile in Iraq and France, his recorded sermons broadcast to crowds in Iran attracted more and more popular support. The charitable networks of the Islamic clergy provided a pole of attraction for increasing numbers of the dispossessed and impoverished urban population. From the beginning of 1977, the tempo of strikes and demonstrations accelerated.

The Tudeh Party, which had been forced underground after 1953, emerged to play its part in the upheaval. But it was a pale shadow of what it had been. Indeed, the left was no longer united. To the left of the Tudeh Party was the Fedai Khalq, a Marxist guerrilla organization inspired by the theories of Che Guevera. From 1977 it began a campaign of armed attacks against businesses and government installations. As early as 1971, a similar campaign had been initiated by the

Mujahedin-e Khalq, which sought to combine Shiite religious ideas and Marxism. These left-wing organizations appealed mainly to the white- and blue-collar working classes. But Khomeini's appeal proved much broader and included the traditional middle class, first generation workers who had emigrated from the countryside, the urban poor, and the peasant majority. All of these groups were threatened by Western-style modernization. The followers of Khomeini promised a utopia based on a reactionary return to theocracy and patriarchy.

Mounting political unrest was fueled by an overheated economy induced by the oil boom of the 1970s. The Shah wantonly spent billions on the military. Meanwhile, the regime was forced to import massive amounts of food as a result of the failings of Iranian agriculture. Rapid urbanization had created chaotic conditions in the towns of Iran. Between 1966 and 1976 Tehran grew from a population of 2.7 to 4.5 million. Hundreds of thousands lived without employment, running water, or sanitation facilities. The unrest in the cities, which began in 1977, developed into a revolutionary crisis. The religious and secular opposition united, while the loyalty of the 500,000-man army crumbled. In mid-January 1979 the Shah was forced to flee and Khomeini assumed power. Rejection of the Shah also meant repudiation of Iran's alliance with the United States and the collapse of U.S. influence. Iran was proclaimed an Islamic Republic and the left-wing parties were step-by-step suppressed.

Non-Marxist, the Iranian Revolution, nonetheless, represented a tremendous blow to U.S. influence in the Middle East. Along with Israel and Turkey, Iran was the main ally of the United States in the region. It was a major supplier of oil to the West. Under the Shah it had been one of the keystones of the U.S. Cold War project of containing the Soviet Union on its southern flank. Now it, too, had become a focal point of radicalism. Indeed, its religious fundamentalism was to prove far more contagious throughout the Middle East than communism ever was. Along with the insurgencies in Central America and Africa, the revolutions in Iran and Afghanistan signaled the weakening of U.S. control over the third world in the wake of defeat in Vietnam.

Oil Shocks

Perhaps the most serious blow to the United States from the third world in the aftermath of the Vietnam War was the oil crisis of the 1970s. As late as 1968 the leading British and U.S. oil companies controlled nearly 78 percent of world oil production, about 61 percent of refining and more than 55 percent of marketing facilities. But by then many independent oil companies—U.S. as well as Japanese and Italian—were able to offer better terms to the oil-producing states than the leading companies. This loss of economic control by the major companies coupled with the decline of U.S. political and military influence in the post-Vietnam period changed the situation dramatically. The Organization of Petroleum Exporting Countries (OPEC) had been founded in 1961 but, initially, had little influence. In the early 1970s it suddenly emerged as a major force with which the West had to reckon. Between 1970 and 1975, Libya, Algeria, Iraq, Iran, and Venezuela nationalized their oil industries. Other OPEC countries, meanwhile, gained control of a larger share of their oil industries, while forcing the Western oil companies to accord them much better terms. In reaction to the Yom Kippur War, OPEC member states dramatically raised the price of a barrel of oil from $2.55 to $11.65. The price hikes of 1973–74 increased the revenues of the oil producing companies by $64 billion. The United States, reeling from its approaching defeat in Vietnam, considered and then abandoned plans to invade and occupy Saudi Arabia, choosing to negotiate new mutually beneficial financial arrangements instead.

To offset inflation OPEC raised the price of oil to $14 a barrel over the next five years. As a result of the Iranian Revolution, the price again rose spectacularly in 1978–79 to a high of $28. These dramatic increases during the 1970s proved a windfall for the OPEC countries. Ironically, Iran's economy and political order were destabilized by the wealth flowing from the oil boom, helping to set off its revolution. Saudi Arabia, meanwhile, used its new wealth to strengthen the hand of conservative Sunni Islam over the Middle East in an attempt to dampen the fires of radical Arab nationalism in counties such as Egypt. In Baathist Iraq, a large part of the new oil wealth was employed to expand the military but also to build an impressive modern infrastructure and raise living standards.

The OPEC oil shocks had a devastating impact on most other third world countries. By the 1970s oil had become the indispensable fuel of the economies of most nations, including those of the less developed states. With demand for their exports in decline as a result of global stagnation, the countries of Africa and Latin America had considerable difficulty paying for increasingly expensive oil imports. Only massive borrowing from the banks of the advanced capitalist countries kept these states afloat. Meanwhile, the major capitalist countries, too, had to readjust to rapid increases in energy costs. Rapidly rising oil prices contributed to the dramatic inflation as well as economic slowdown that characterized the decade. Japan coped with these constraints best among the advanced capitalist states. It did so by undertaking a comprehensive program of energy conservation and fuel efficiency. Faced with sharp inflation, Germany instituted austerity, throwing hundreds of thousands out of work and crippling purchasing power. Rather than coping with the situation directly as the Germans did, France, Italy, and Great Britain chose an indirect approach in the face of union militancy. They elected to allow inflation to run its course, undermining real wages and increasing unemployment. The United States had its own difficulties dealing with higher energy costs. But it still obtained a certain competitive advantage over its European competitors. This was possible as a result of the dominant role of its oil companies in the international market place and its privileged access to U.S. and Canadian oil fields. It was helped, too, by new financial accords in which Saudi Arabia and the other OPEC oil states agreed to recycle petrodollars through the New York banks. Nonetheless, its inability to intervene militarily or politically to reverse the situation reflected the deepening threat to its hegemonic role in the wake of defeat in Vietnam.

Stagflation

The sudden oil price hikes of 1973 and 1979 by OPEC were part of a pattern of revolt against the dominance of the West that developed in the third world consequent to the Vietnam War. But these political and economic challenges have to be understood in the context of growing economic problems in the principal capitalist countries themselves. The policy of guns and butter pursued by the Johnson administration unleashed powerful inflationary currents that by 1974 averaged 15 percent per year. A pattern of instability characterized by hyperinflation and sharp and severe recessions became evident throughout the capitalist world. Economists spoke of stagflation as output faltered, unemployment rose, and real wages fell. Growth rates, which had reached unprecedented heights in the previous two decades, fell during the 1970s. Critical to the erosion of growth was the fact that the rate of profit, which was the engine of the global capitalist economy, declined.

Politically conscious workers in countries such as France and Italy as well as politically indifferent workers in the United States united in their demands for constantly increasing wages during the late 1960s. Partly these demands were in response to galloping inflation. Nonetheless, by the opening years of the 1970s real wages on average were increasing one percent faster than in the 1960s. Within the productive process, workers rebelled against fragmented, repetitive work and speed-ups. Absenteeism increased as well as turnover rates as workers increasingly came and went as they chose. Between 1966 and 1972 turnover at the Fiat works in Italy stood at 100 percent, reached 40 percent at Ford in Britain, and was reported to have grown from 40 to 60 percent in eight U.S. processing industries. Lack of interest and carelessness at work became widespread. Profit margins eroded as a result of all of these factors. Higher costs for materials also affected profitability. Under-investment in the raw materials sector during the boom gradually led to price increases. Meanwhile, toward the end of the 1960s existing markets in certain sectors such as consumer goods began to become saturated. The great wave of suburban construction in the United States and reconstruction in Europe petered out. The project of equiping these homes and offices with durable goods was mainly complete. Competition sharpened and profit margins declined.

During the 1950s and early 1960s, whatever problems there had been with maintaining profitability had been offset by the new techniques of business organization and industrial production, the latter accompanied by unprecedented technological innovation. The resulting productivity increases, more rapid turnover of capital, and opening of markets for new products enhanced profitability. This wave of innovation, too, seemed to falter by the late 1960s. Entrepreneurs became reluctant to invest further in technological innovation as the cost of capital investment in innovation began to outweigh potential profitability. Meanwhile, labor shortages made it difficult to intensify or reorganize work as an alternative means of increasing productivity.

The U.S. Dollar in Peril

Amid these difficulties, there arose growing uncertainty over the U.S. dollar —the cornerstone of the international financial system. Throughout the post-war period the dollar had functioned as the standard for all other currencies. The dollar valued at $35 per ounce of gold was regarded as good as gold. Until the mid-1950s, the fundamental problem of the capitalist countries outside the United States was the dollar "famine." In other words other countries lacked the dollars to buy U.S. goods. The reconstruction of Japan and Europe and the relaunch of world trade required an infusion of U.S. dollars. Between 1945 and 1952 U.S.

grants and loans to its trading partners totaled $38 billion. The subsequent economic recovery, modernization, and growing competitiveness of these trading partners were reflected in a strengthening of their currencies and an improvement in their current account balances. The United States share of production in the capitalist world fell from 70 percent in 1950 to less than 50 percent by the beginning of the 1970s. Its share of trade was reduced from 50 to 25 percent. Notable was the growing competition the United States experienced from German and Japanese exports in international markets. By the late 1960s, heavy United States spending and capital investment overseas exacerbated by Vietnam War expenditure led to a chronic balance of payments deficit and a crisis of the dollar. The buildup of dollars held by U.S. trading partners overseas and devaluation of these dollars by accelerating inflation within the United States led to a dumping of the U.S. currency by international investors and the abandonment of the gold standard by President Nixon in 1971. In order to hold on to its global economic hegemony, Washington, in a quite calculated fashion, would make a virtue of the floating of the dollar.

Recession

In the short run, however, loss of confidence in the international reserve currency only added to the sense of mounting difficulties induced by growing inflation, higher labor costs, growing international competition, higher materials costs, and the consequent erosion of profits. The last straw was the OPEC oil price increases. In the summer of 1974 a major crash began. Between July 1974 and April of the following year, industrial output in the advanced capitalist countries fell by 10 percent. International trade in 1975 was 13 percent less than the year before.

The recession of 1974–75 was the steepest since the Depression and definitely brought to a conclusion the so-called golden years of the previous two decades. This slump was followed by a period of stagnation punctuated by bouts of persistent inflation. It ended in another sharp recession in 1981–82. The initial response to the downturn was a resort to Keynesian pump-priming in the advanced capitalist countries. The United States took the lead in resorting to fiscal and monetary stimulus during the downturn of 1974–75. As a result, by 1976 industrial production and the GNP in the United States were significantly higher than during the recession. But by the second half of 1976 the growth rate had slowed, the balance of payments deficit widened, and the dollar continued to decline. Other advanced Western countries had similar disappointing experiences.

Governments began to resort to protectionist measures including quotas on selected imports, subsidies to local industries, and the encouragement of cartels to regulate output and prices. Despite such measures, the economies of the advanced capitalist countries failed to recover the dynamism of earlier decades. Growth was insufficient to significantly lower unemployment. Indeed, in the European Common Market unemployment increased in every year but one between 1973 and 1983. As a result, real incomes for the decade tended to stagnate for the first time since the postwar recovery. Indeed, the second slump of 1981–82 set in under even less propitious conditions than had the slump of 1974.

Recovery in the late 1970s, such as it was, had come from the stimulus of growth in Eastern Europe and the more advanced third world countries, especially on the Pacific Rim. The market for loans in advanced capitalist countries being stagnant, Western banks made massive loans to Eastern European states as well as Brazil, Mexico, and middle-income, less-developed countries in Asia. Less generous but still significant loans were made to poor third world states in Africa and Latin America. In part Western banks advanced their own capital and in part they recycled petrodollars deposited by the newly flush OPEC countries. These loans were used, above all, to sustain imports, notably petroleum. The interest on these loans, as well as exports of machinery and high-tech products to these countries, helped to support the otherwise stagnant economies of the West. Likewise favoring the Western economies, the OPEC countries also increased their imports in the late 1970s.

The Debt Trap

As a result of this borrowing, an immense increase in international indebtedness took place across the decade. In 1970 annual international borrowing was less that ten billion dollars. By 1978 it had reached $100 billion. Accumulated international debt by then had reached $267 billion and more than $500 billion by 1982. This debt was owed by poor third world countries such as Uganda and Kenya, as well as better-off economies such as Brazil and Mexico. Higher oil prices, relatively low commodity prices, and mounting interest payments on outstanding loans compounded the debt problem. Even economies in Eastern Europe such as Poland and Hungary found themselves confronting repayment problems. Between 1973 and 1980 their debt to Western banks rose from five to $44 billion. Control of third world states and leverage even over Eastern European communist states by private Western financial institutions increased as a result.

The Wall Street-Treasury Axis

This happened by design rather than by accident. Despite the decline in the competitiveness of the U.S. economy and the abandonment of the gold standard in 1971, Washington used a combination of financial, political, and military leverage in a remarkably successful strategy to maintain the primacy of the dollar and U.S. hegemony worldwide.

Nixon accompanied the ending of the gold standard by deregulating international financial movements, a step that opened new profit opportunities for the major U.S. banks and multinational corporations. The relative position of the U.S. dollar against other currencies was further strengthened by OPEC oil price increases—the U.S. economy being the least affected. Indeed, the New York banks assumed the main role in recycling the petroleum profits of OPEC states in the form of dollar loans to third world and Eastern European countries. The mounting indebtedness of these countries in turn reinforced the power of this Wall Street-United States Treasury regime. Using the IMF and World Banks as its auxiliaries, U.S. private and public financial institutions were increasingly in a position to make or break weakened foreign economies through international debt management practices and credit manipulations. Indeed, the purveying of essentially unpayable loans seems to have been part of a deliberate strategy pursued by the United States as a way of gaining or regaining political and financial control. Washington's growing financial leverage was to become the primary means by which it re-imposed control over third world countries in the post-Vietnam period.

By the mid-1980s three-quarters of Latin American countries and two-thirds of African countries were under some kind of IMF-World Bank supervision. A fundamental requirement of such regulatory or structural adjustment regimes was the unrestricted opening of these countries to Western capital and exports. At the same time, the deregulation of international financial movements initiated by Nixon and expanded upon by his successors became the major feature of the international economy in the concluding decades of the century. Despite the relative weakening of the U.S. economy, other advanced capitalist countries such as Japan, Britain, and West Germany accepted the continued primacy of Washington and New York because the benefits outweighed the costs. None of the governments separately or together could replace the primary role of the U.S. dollar in international markets. The relatively large size of the U.S. economy, the allure of its financial markets, and the strength and security of its financial institutions continued to make the U.S. currency attractive despite its depreciating economic value. In the context of the continuing Cold War, going it alone was still unthinkable. At the same time, U.S. treasury officials, policy makers, and military officials remained committed to a multilateralism from which the principal allies of the United States continued to benefit. As a result, the U.S. dollar from the 1970s became a kind of global fiat currency.

In retrospect, the 1970s appears as a transitional decade between the regulated Keynesian market economy of the postwar period and the subsequent period of neoliberalism. Faced with slower growth, rampant inflation, and lower rates of profit, governments during this decade were still prepared to use the panoply of interventionist fiscal and monetary mechanisms to try to restore balanced growth. By the end of the decade, these policies came to be seriously questioned, especially in the English-speaking countries.

The Trilateral Commission

The United States economic and political elite—its position weakened by the looming prospect of defeat in Vietnam, growing third world unrest, and international economic instability—attempted to reassert its global leadership as best as possible in the early 1970s. The Nixon administration, in addition to abandoning the gold standard and devaluing the dollar, imposed quotas on manufactures from Japan, South Korea, and Taiwan. Other countries as well began to move toward protectionism, threatening the liberal world trading system of the postwar period. It was in order to address these problems that the head of Chase Manhattan Bank, David Rockefeller, and an influential U.S. academic, Zbigniew Brzezinski, launched the Trilateral Commission in 1973. Made up of key business, political, and academic figures from the leading capitalist counties, the Commission reflected the point of view of international capital. Indeed, the objective of the Commission was to breathe new life into the liberal international economic order. Among its objectives was the encouragement of the governments of the advanced capitalist countries to confront third world economic nationalism and political radicalism, to undertake the recycling of OPEC financial surpluses so as to stabilize the world economy, and to resist protectionism in favor of free trade.

The Trilateral Commission bemoaned what it termed the "excess of democracy" that had developed, especially in third world countries. At the same time, it took pains to foster the protection of human rights, a category defined largely in political and legal, rather than social and economic, terms. This represented a throwback to an anti-Soviet strategy pursued during the 1950s and 1960s by the CIA-backed International Commission of Jurists. It was re-invoked by Brzezinski when he became national security council advisor to President Jimmy Carter in the late 1970s. Deployed against Soviet treatment of dissidents and Jews and selectively against some third world regimes, it served to somewhat rehabilitate the tarnished reputation of the United States in the wake of the Vietnam debacle.

The Conservative Revival in the United States

The Trilateral Commission and the U.S. human rights campaign harked back to the liberal internationalism of the early Cold War. Yet we can already see in the internal evolution of the United States emerging signs of a much more tough-minded approach rooted in political, social, and economic conservatism. The 1960s had seen a dominant liberalism challenged from the left by the antiwar, anti-imperialist, black liberation, feminist, Chicano, aboriginal, environmental, and consumer movements. But on the right, conservatives sought to find a popular base, to redefine themselves ideologically and to organize themselves more effectively. At first sight this seemed a fruitless task. The New Deal and the postwar interventionist state once and for all seemed to eclipse traditional U.S. conservatism. It appeared that the managed economy, the welfare state, strong unions, the idea of racial equality, and coexistence, if not acceptance, of communism internationally, had become axiomatic concepts in U.S. politics. Nonetheless, all of these liberal truisms were to be challenged in succeeding years and with increasing success by the rise of the neoconservatives.

Fundamental to the conservative revival was a recrudescence of popular racism in direct reaction to the civil rights and black power movements. The civil rights movement in the south provoked a resurgence of Ku Klux Klan activity among lower-class southern whites. More respectable whites across the south organized resistance through White Citizens Councils. Politically, white southern resistance manifested itself in an increasing antipathy toward the Democratic Party. During the Kennedy administration, the Democrats, however reluctantly, committed themselves to the cause of civil rights. The result was manifest in the presidential election of 1968, when only 10 percent of southern white voters supported the Democrats. This would become the pattern for the future. White voters in the south on this occasion split their vote between the Republican candidate Nixon and the governor of Alabama, George Wallace, who led the southern-based American Independence Party. Wallace had emerged as the leading opponent of the desegregation of the south during the early 1960s and had become a national figure by 1968. His campaign was based on a not-too-subtle racism evoked through calls for a restoration of law and order mixed with demands for patriotic support of the Vietnam War. It found a loud echo among not only southerners, but also working-class whites of both southern Protestant and European Catholic extraction in the northern and western states. Many of these were hostile to blacks, antiwar protesters, and the so-called counter culture.

In the election of 1968 Nixon voiced similar themes to Wallace and shared about half of the white southern vote. Henceforth, the white south as well as some white working-class voters in the north moved toward the Republicans. In contrast to the social legislation of the New Deal, the programs of the Great Society were seen by the white working class to be catering to blacks, euphemistically referred to as special interests. The working-class vote permanently split on the basis of race to the advantage of the Republican Party. These trends favorable to the Republicans were reinforced by the emergence of a new region-based layer of the middle class. The development of largely defense-related industries in the south and the southwest became the economic foundation of this aspiring body of middle-income suburbanites. Politically, the regions where they were concentrated began to return solid Republican majorities.

Reinforcing these trends was the growth of fundamentalist and evangelical religion among this new middle class. While mainline Protestantism tended to languish, evangelical and fundamentalist church membership grew dramatically from the 1960s onwards in the south and southwest. Denouncing the sexual freedom and permissiveness toward drugs of the counter culture, such churches reasserted family and traditional values.

They were particularly exercised by court decisions prohibiting school prayer (1963) and liberalizing access to abortion (1973). Local ordinances in favor of gay rights also drew their ire. The legislative attempt to add an equal rights amendment for women to the U.S. Constitution (1972) became a focal point of conservative resistance. It was these churches that took the lead in creating thousands of new Christian private schools in order to avoid desegregation. Fundamentalist schools, colleges, and universities, and radio and television networks proliferated in the 1970s. By 1979 the Reverend Jerry Falwell, a leading fundamentalist preacher, organized many of these elements into an explicitly political movement known as the Moral Majority.

The conservative revival was also based on ultra-patriotism and anticommunism. These, of course, had been the themes played upon by Senator Joseph McCarthy and his followers in the early years of the Cold War. This patriotic and xenophobic faith was kept alive by the John Birch Society, founded by a conservative New England businessman, Robert Welch, in 1958. By 1967 the Birch Society had perhaps 80,000 members organized in 4,000 chapters mainly located in Texas, Florida, and California. Members of the Birch Society were able to gain election to municipal offices, state legislatures, and the U.S. Congress. They routinely called for a crusade against international communism. But they went so far as to claim that secret communists, including President Eisenhower, controlled the U.S. government.

The Birch Society and other groups like it prepared the ground for the 1964 presidential campaign of Senator Barry Goldwater of Arizona against Lyndon Johnson, the assassinated Kennedy's successor. Goldwater, of course, was crushingly defeated in the general election. Reeling from the Kennedy assassination, the United States was not prepared for a Goldwater platform of economic and political libertarianism, virulent anticommunism, and resistance to civil rights. Yet his conservative followers—Birchites, Young Americans for Freedom, the Young Republicans, William F. Buckley, and the *National Review*—were able to capture control of the political machinery of the Republican Party from the Eastern establishment. In the process, they transformed conservatism into a mass political movement.

The multimillionaire William Buckley's *National Review* played a key role in this takeover of the Republican Party. The journal's fervent anticommunism and defense both of traditional Christian values and the free market attracted both conservative intellectuals and activists. Generally opposed to the civil rights movement on the basis of states rights, it occasionally invoked the cultural supremacy of the white race against demands for black equality or liberation.

While many of the notions in the *National Review* were intellectually dubious, its economic philosophy of laissez-faire gained academic credibility as a result of the crisis of Keynesianism.

As we have seen, the 1970s were marked by a decline of profitability that pervaded the global capitalist economy. The major symptoms of this malaise were sluggish growth as well as serious inflation. Attempts to revive the economy through Keynesian policies proved unsuccessful. Into this void stepped the leading economist at the University of Chicago, Milton Friedman. Friedman's own nostrum for the economy was based on a revival of the previously discredited quantity theory of money. So-called monetarism quickly turned out to be a sham. What proved more lasting was Friedman's commitment to the revival of laissez-faire economics. Basing himself on the libertarianism of his teacher Friedrich von Hayek, Friedman not only attacked the economic failures of Keynesianism, but also its political premises. Government intervention and state economic planning were not only the wrong medicine; they fundamentally undermined the political freedom of the individual, which was the highest achievement of Western Civilization. Friedman's economic arguments were backed up with the philosophical arguments of Leo Strauss, another University of Chicago professor. According to Strauss, a good society was based on virtuous and moral citizens. State attempts to engineer equality or freedom undermined the virtue of citizens by relieving them of the responsibility of facing the consequences of their individual acts. Strauss further believed that religion and nationalism, however counterfeit they might be, promoted the morality of the individual citizen while liberalism and secularism undermined it. Strauss called for a moral and intellectual elite to promote these traditional ideals. Behind this high-minded and self-contradictory rhetoric lay the demand for the liquidation of the interventionist state and the restoration of the free market as the basis for restoring profitability and social discipline. In succeeding decades Friedman's economic view would become the paradigm for professional economics in North America and Europe, as obviously true as the Keynesian paradigm that had preceded it. Strauss's philosophy would at the same time inspire some of the key political advocates of neoconservatism.

By the end of the 1970s, the conservative movement had a popular following, was well organized, and had an intellectual foundation. But it was the support of big business that was decisive in bringing it to power. The latter had been deeply worried by the upheavals of the 1960s and 1970s that had explicitly challenged the actions and, indeed, the legitimacy of corporate capitalism. Part of the legacy of that challenge to capitalist excesses was the so-called public interest movement. Of the 83 public interest organizations in Washington in 1977, nearly two-thirds had been established since 1960 and nearly half since 1968. These citizen lobbies were interested in a variety of issues including the environment, consumer safety, defense and foreign policy, the rights and status of women, the rights of blacks and the poor, as well as the question of ethics in government. Many of the concerns of such public interest groups focused on the power and social impact of the large corporations that dominated U.S. life. Largely as a result of their efforts, between 1966 and 1974 the U.S. Congress had passed 20 major pieces of regulatory legislation. Given the decline in profits that marked the 1970s, the lobbying of these organizations was felt as an intolerable constraint on business.

In response, organized big business dramatically stepped up its own lobbying and politicking. Thousands of lobbyists were mobilized to work for the leading 500 U.S. corporations, the Chamber of Commerce, and the National Federation of Independent Business. Especially influential was the Business Roundtable, founded in 1972 with a membership restricted to the heads of major U.S. corporations. Foundations and think tanks funded by business and dedicated to advancing a right-wing political and economic agenda proliferated. Political action committees acting in behalf of big business began to dramatically increase campaign contributions to the Republican Party, far out-stripping the amounts raised by the Democrats.

The fracturing of the New Deal coalition, the decline in the power of organized labor, the growing strength of conservative ideas, ongoing economic stagnation and inflation, and continuing foreign policy reversals were reflected in the policies of the beleaguered Democratic President Jimmy Carter (1976-80). In his last two years of office, Carter found himself forced to support budget cuts, deregulation of key sectors like transport, corporate tax relief, reduced social spending, and increases in military expenditure. In doing so Carter prepared the ground for the ultimate political triumph of conservatism under President Ronald Reagan in 1980.

Thatcherism in Britain

The Reagan electoral triumph was preceded by that of the conservative Margaret Thatcher in Britain a year earlier. As in the United States, the conservative conquest of power arose directly from the inability of the previous Labour government to solve the problem of stagflation. Complicating this general problem was the continuing relative decline of the British economy in comparison to other advanced capitalist countries. The result was a chronic balance of trade and payments problem reflected in recurrent bouts of government-induced deflation. Through all this economic difficulty, the standard of living of British workers had steadily risen, in part as a result of the militancy of a highly organized union movement. But among the economic and political elite, including elements of the Labour Party, this was increasingly seen as a problem.

The Labour governments of 1974–79 attempted to govern by means of a social contract with labor. During this period of labor accord, the Chancellor of the Exchequer, Denis Healey, dealt with yet another foreign exchange crisis through budget cuts and wage restraint. Like Carter, he was inadvertently opening the way for the neoliberal era that would follow. For a time these policies seemed to work, as pay demands and inflation moderated between 1976–78. The increasing availability of North Sea gas and oil appeared to resolve Britain's energy problems. But by late 1978 the unions had had enough of restraint and rejected the government's call for yet more. The social contract collapsed in a series of major strikes that led to calls for strong measures. The election that ensued (May 1979) saw a Conservative Party victory with 43.9 percent of the vote. Thatcher then proceeded at full speed with massive income tax cuts for the rich, sharp increases in indirect taxes hitting the less well-off, and a enormous and deliberate deflation to kill inflation and discipline labor.

Thatcherism soon became the vogue in other English-speaking counties including the United States, Canada, New Zealand, and Australia. Savage neoliberalism of this type was politically unacceptable on the continent of Europe and in Japan. Nonetheless, in indirect or piecemeal fashion, it became the norm of the global capitalist economy in the concluding two decades of the twentieth century. The disembedding of the market from the political and social institutions that had restrained it since the Depression of the 1930s became a global phenomenon.

In retrospect the turn of the tide between 1970 and 1980 was remarkable. The world moved in ten years from a mood of insurrectionary radicalism to one of neoconservative resignation. It is important in conclusion to consider how this was accomplished. At the beginning of the 1970s the United States—the epicenter of the capitalist world—appeared to be in the throes of a profound crisis. Its adventure in southeast Asia had deeply miscarried, splitting apart U.S. society and unleashing forces of revolutionary change both within the United States and worldwide. At the same time the Keynesian foundations of the postwar global economy appeared to be crumbling. Countries like Germany and Japan were challenging U.S. leadership economically, while France was prepared to contest its political dominance.

By 1980 these problems had been contained if not yet mastered. Disengagement from Vietnam appears to have been the key factor in bringing the crisis under control. War has been the great destabilizing force of the twentieth century. It helped to produce the upheavals of the 1960s as well as the preceding Chinese and Russian Revolutions. On the battlefield and on the home front in all three cases, war swiftly changed lives, mobilized populations, and transformed consciousness in unexpected and radical ways. Reversals in battle translated into protest and revolt at home. Nixon's consequent step-by-step withdrawal of U.S. ground forces from Vietnam was crucial to stabilizing U.S. society and dampening down if not extinguishing unrest abroad.

The Sino-Soviet split proved a boon to the United States and conservative forces throughout the world. The open antagonism between the two leading communist powers weakened communist and radical nationalist forces worldwide. Indeed, U.S. diplomacy was able to range these two states against one another politically and militarily. Such a division speaks volumes about the nature of the leadership in both the People's Republic of China and the Soviet Union. Meanwhile in the West, the power of reformist and bureaucratic communist parties and unions in France and Italy and the lack of discipline among the new left in North America disarmed revolutionary mass movements.

The last major factor in turning back the tide of revolution globally was what may be described as an upper-class counter-offensive organized from the United States. Deep-lying factors were behind the collapse of the Keynesian boom of the 1950s and 1960s. The stagflation of the 1970s was the result of forces that were beyond the control of capital, labor, or government. But it was the Nixon administration and its political and business allies in New York, London, Paris, Bonn, and Frankfort who controlled the heights of political and financial power. It was they, and not organized labor or the disorganized mass of the population, who were in a position to manage the economic crisis to their advantage. Initiatives such as unpegging the dollar based on the Wall Street-Treasury axis, liberalizing global capital movements by recycling petrodollars, facilitating loans to third world and communist countries, creating overseas dollar markets, and organizing the Trilateral Commission helped to foster a new global financial and political order that eventually would bring organized labor in each country to heel and take the wind out of the sails of third world nationalist regimes. Finally, as our discussion of the development of the conservative movement in the United States has suggested, untold millions of dollars were spent by business and right-wing elites to create an institutionally and ideologically powerful conservative movement that gained control of government and gained leverage over culture and the media for its agenda.

7

The United States Wins the Cold War

The prospects of the United States still appeared bleak at the beginning of the 1980s. It was true that neoliberalism was triumphing politically and ideologically in the United States and other English-speaking countries. The United States had been able to widen the breach between the major Communist states, the Soviet Union and China. Growing economic adversity over the previous decade had made the working class in the West and the populations in many underdeveloped countries more cautious. On the other hand, regimes hostile to the United States had recently taken power in Nicaragua, Grenada, Mozambique, Angola, Guinea-Bissau, Zimbabwe, Ethiopia, Afghanistan, and Iran. Further challenges to U.S interests in the third world continued to develop, notably in El Salvador and South Africa. The United States appeared helpless in the face of OPEC control of world energy prices. In the United States and other capitalist states, slow growth and chronic inflation seemed to have entrenched themselves. Moreover, ongoing competition from Japan and Germany appeared to threaten U.S economic primacy. The Soviets and their Eastern European allies had their problems, but the communist order seemed a stable one. Moreover, Soviet arms and economic aid were providing unprecedented levels of support to national liberation movements hostile to U.S interests in the third world.

The United States Resurgent

But these threats to U.S power proved illusory. In the United States, a strong dose of deflation at the beginning of the 1980s brought the high-wage demands and the indiscipline of the working class sharply to heel. Unemployment, massive restructuring, and ongoing job insecurity intimidated labor with only a minimum of resistance. By the middle of President Reagan's first term of office, profits were resurgent in the United States and the conservative ideological reaction victorious.

It was not that the U.S. government and the forces pushing neoliberalism proved to be so strong. Rather, their enemies proved pushovers, surprisingly weak and unable to resist. Organized labor in the United States, long dominated by a business union leadership, put up scarcely any resistance to the Reagan anti-labor onslaught. In Poland in 1981 bureaucratic socialism—supposedly the embodiment of working-class rule—was challenged by a revolt of the whole working class organized as a national trade union known as Solidarity. Driven underground, the Polish revolt prefigured the collapse of the Soviet Union and the whole communist system in Eastern Europe ten years later. Third world revolutionary movements, likewise, fell victim to a combination of U.S counterinsurgency and Western economic pressure.

The increasing weakness of the Soviet Union during the 1980s opened the way for a reassertion of U.S influence over the third world. In Latin America, Africa, and the Middle East, the United States used economic measures, counterrevolutionary surrogates, and sophisticated weapons and technology to minimize its own losses while step-by-step undermining revolutionary movements and governments. Elsewhere, the debt problems of many third world countries opened the way for re-imposing economic and political control through agencies controlled by the United States and its allies. Dependent on imports of foreign oil, expertise, and advanced machinery, many third world countries had no choice but to accept the imposition of the economic dictates of the IMF and World Bank. As for OPEC control of access to oil, the Iran-Iraq War proved a means of dividing the OPEC countries while strengthening U.S influence over the Middle East. Reduced demand and new supplies of North Sea, Alaskan, and Russian oil were also used to undercut the unity of the OPEC monopoly. Western Europe was forced to open its markets to U.S investment in finance, advanced service industries, electronics, and defense industries. These sectors were considered critical to continued U.S economic dominance.

Japan continued to be a formidable economic competitor to the United States despite U.S countermeasures. Having been forced by the Reagan administration to dramatically revalue its currency upward in 1985, Japan used the occasion to tie the developing economies of the rest of Asia to itself while reducing dependence on the United States. But these efforts foundered when the over-heated Japanese economy fell into an indefinitely long economic slump beginning in 1989. During the 1980s Germany was able to continue to prosper and successfully compete against the United States on the basis of its highly productive work force, international competitiveness, and further steps toward European integration. But, like Japan, its economy also succumbed to prolonged slump early in the next decade. At the end of the 1980s, meanwhile, the Soviet Union disintegrated and the communist regimes of Eastern Europe were overthrown in a series of largely bloodless revolutions. The Cold War ended in a breathtaking U.S victory. By the beginning of the 1990s, a new unipolar world dominated by the United States appeared in the offing, symbolized by the grand military coalition organized by the United States to fight the Persian Gulf War (1991).

The Neoliberal Order

Neoliberalism asserted that intervention into the market by government only triggered inflation while it slowed growth and fostered unemployment. On the contrary, markets free of government regulation would create jobs and spark strong economic growth. Based on these principles or ideology, neoliberalism helped to justify a sweeping revival of the economic and political power of the capitalist class in the United States and the rest of the world in the following two decades. Under neoliberal auspices, economic growth and profits recovered in the first world, but to a level well below that of the golden age. More seriously, weaker average growth and the decline of the state's economic role were accompanied by rapidly increasing inequality and declining levels of public welfare. Under the aegis of neoliberalism, the fate of the third world was much worse. Overwhelmed by debt, most of the countries of Latin America and Africa were forced to surrender control of their economies to Western banks and international financial agencies controlled by Western governments. As a condition for loan bailouts, such countries had to raise interest rates, lower tariffs, and open their economies to direct and indirect Western investment. They were forced to deregulate their economies and massively reduce social, health, and education spending in an effort to clean up their financial balance sheets. Such neoliberal prescriptions were designed to restore economic equilibrium and stimulate growth and exports.

In only a few cases did they do so. Rather than growth, most undeveloped countries suffered massive economic regression. Wages fell while unemployment, poverty, and social inequality grew. Major new capital investment was evident in Asia. But in the rest of the developing world, U.S and European capitalists generated profits instead by taking over land or publicly or locally owned manufacturing capacity and through the privatization of financial resources such as pension funds. Accumulation occurred through dispossession rather than investment. Everywhere the wealthy enhanced their position by simply appropriating a greater share of existing wealth at the expense of the rest of society.

Deeper Trends

At a deeper level of change, a certain hollowing out of old and, in some cases, ancient social structures became evident from the 1980s onward. Reflecting trends evident since the 1960s, if not earlier, ties of family, religion, birthplace, work, and class that had helped give moral and social meaning to human existence for centuries appeared to give way to the forces of the capitalist market. The erosion of family was most apparent in countries such as the United States, Germany, and France. It was less true in Italy where two- and three-generation families proved to be an effective means of adapting to the exigencies of the neoliberal marketplace. But, increasingly, the trend was toward that of the atomized individual obliged to confront the overwhelming power of capital and state bureaucracy. The alternative, if there was one, to an emergent disconnected individualism appeared to be the politics of identity. Feminism and gay liberation were more benign or positive forms of this new kind of politics; more pernicious examples were a murderous ethnic or religious antagonism.

Among the most dramatic of social transformations was the urbanization of the third world, a process that began seriously after 1945. Induced in part by the pressure of a developing rural capitalism, the flight to the towns by the 1980s reduced the peasant population of the world to a minority for the first time in recorded history. Well more than half of the new urban majority in the third world was entirely unemployed or unable to earn a living wage. In part this was due to a lack of skills or education, or because of their immigration status or gender. But it was also the result of the inability or unwillingness of the globalized capitalist economy to provide sufficient or decently paid work. Indeed, the movement of industry from high-wage advanced capitalist countries toward low-wage undeveloped regions accelerated dramatically. By the end of the 1980s, for the first time, the majority of industrial workers lay in the third world. As a result, the percentage of urban dwellers in the advanced capitalist countries who were unemployed or under-employed also increased.

The global pool of cheap labor available to capital for wage work was enlarged. It was increased, too, by the massive entry of women into the labor market both in the developed and undeveloped world. While most such women found themselves working in low paying or less well paid jobs, wage work gave women at all levels an unprecedented independence from male and traditional family control. Birthrates worldwide visibly declined. Rural migration to the cities and the industrialization of the third world held out the prospect of a better life for some. But it seemed doubtful that the global economy at current growth rates could provide work for the billions of peasants still left on the land. Those that remained on the land meanwhile were ever more closely tied to the market and more and more politically and even ecologically conscious. They nonetheless faced the uninviting prospect of rural immiseration or a future life in urban shantytowns as unemployed paupers. In the meantime, the last great territories of indigenous peoples living in a subsistence economy in Central and Latin America, Central Africa, the Australian outback, the Canadian North, eastern Asia, the highlands of Papua New Guinea, and southeast Asia were forced open to modernization, resource extraction, and ecological degradation. Partly in response to these trends, international migration from lower- to higher-wage economies, which had started in the 1950s, passed the 100 million mark by 1985. By 2000 it stood at 175 million. Like the movement from country to city, migration overseas was accelerated by the growing influence of agricultural capitalism and global agribusiness, driving peasants off the land. Migration has been augmented by escalating ethnic wars that have arisen through the breakup of old empires or by problems within states whose borders were defined by colonialism. While totaling only a small percentage of the world's population, immigrants from the underdeveloped countries began to change the society and culture of host countries such as Canada, the United States, England, and France. There were problems, no doubt, especially xenophobia and economic exclusion, but the societies of such countries became more interesting and less rigid as a result of this influx. The cultural if not the economic divide between the Western capitalist countries and those of the third world weakened. Moreover, remittances from immigrants back to the

Philippines, Egypt, and the countries of Latin America and Africa played an increasingly significant economic role. In the case of China, India, and Israel, the overseas diaspora provided important connections and proved an important source of foreign direct investment.

The collapse of the Soviet bloc and the establishment of liberal democracy in Eastern Europe at the close of the 1980s was part of a wider trend echoed by the end of military dictatorships in Brazil, Chile, and Argentina, as well as the collapse of apartheid in South Africa and the fall of the Marcos dictatorship in the Philippines. For the first time, liberal democracy incontestably became the preferred form of government worldwide. Yet citizenries all over the world were increasingly aware of a growing lack of substance to these democratic and parliamentary regimes. Such governments were more and more perceived as being unable to control national economic life or protect social programs in the face of the demands of powerful corporate interests, international financial agencies, and the overwhelming military and political power of the United States. Indeed, this sense of estrangement from government was nowhere felt more strongly than in the United States itself.

Political alienation within the United States reflected a society that was increasingly polarized between rich and poor. The United States continued to be in the forefront in important new areas such as computers, the Internet, and biotechnology. But there were negative economic and social trends. Failing infrastructure, decaying cities, increasing rates of incarceration, and under-investment in public education and health care were undermining the quality of the workforce and eroding the competitiveness of the U.S economy. The United States' relative share of world manufacturing, communications, trade, and services continued to decline, reflected in chronic balance of trade and payments deficits. East Asian countries such as Malaysia, Singapore, Hong Kong, Taiwan, South Korea, and, above all, China, meanwhile, made notable gains. Indeed, East Asia took form as a new global growth pole in contrast to the faltering economies of North America, Europe, and, indeed, most of the rest of the third world.

Poland's Solidarity

The death knell of Eastern European communism was sounded first in Poland. For 12 years after the suppression of the Prague Spring, Eastern Europe was politically quiescent. Western recognition of the Eastern European states holding to so-called actually existing socialism was confirmed by the signing of the so-called Helsinki Accords by the United States and its European allies in 1975. Moreover, the Soviet Union continued to supply petroleum at stable prices to the by now industrialized economies of Eastern Europe. As a result, in contrast with the West, these economies continued to perform well until the mid-1970s. But matters deteriorated sharply thereafter.

The Polish economy generally conformed to this pattern. In 1956 the communist system in Poland had been stabilized by the installation of a more nationalist regime under Gomulka. Despite his nationalism, Gomulka proved to be an orthodox communist leader in other respects. An attempt by students and intellectuals to widen the bounds of cultural and intellectual freedom in 1968, for example, was suppressed. On the other hand, Gomulka avoided falling back to the level of repression of the Stalinist period. His rule ended as a result of a violent workers uprising in the northern port cities in 1970. Government-imposed price hikes, especially on food, provoked the revolt. Several score deaths and several hundred wounded proved the price for the restoration of order by the regime. The new leader, Edward Gierek, de-emphasized ideology and stressed political pragmatism. Above all, he put the priority for the first time on meeting consumer demands. The primary means of increasing personal consumption were to be loans from Western banks. The loans would be used to build light or consumer industries. Debts would be repaid by exporting a portion of the new consumer products back into Western markets. As in the past, financing the development of heavy industry would continue to be based on the surpluses generated by the Polish economy.

By the late 1970s, Polish society had been almost completely transformed from what it had been in 1950. Whereas the country had once been overwhelmingly peasant, now two-thirds of the population was white- or blue-collar workers employed in state enterprises. At the top of the social hierarchy were the functionaries of the Communist Party. Next in line came the humanistic and technical intelligentsia who managed society. Below them were the white-collar or clerical workers, generally with a high school education or less, who staffed the state and industrial bureaucracies. Then came the blue-collar proletariat, many of whom were well trained in technical schools. At the bottom of the social hierarchy lay the peasantry.

By the end of the 1970s the peasantry made up less than 23 percent of the population. Collectivization having been abandoned in 1956, most peasants owned their own plots and were quite inefficient as producers. Underproduction of foodstuffs restricted agricultural exports on which the state relied to import new technologies. Indeed, a lack of agricultural productivity forced the authorities to subsidize the cost of food to keep prices down. Attempts to correct the situation by raising food prices, as in 1970, were resisted by the working class. During the 1970s, largely unsuccessful attempts were made to increase agricultural output by increasing the efficiency of private farms.

Population in postwar Poland had increased rapidly, but the fast growing economy created a chronic shortage of labor. In postwar Poland there had been the typical communist over-investment in heavy industry at the expense of agriculture, light industry, and infrastructure. High wages and the continued stress on heavy industry and food exports produced a persistent shortage of food, housing, and quality consumer goods. Nonetheless, between 1950 and 1978 national income had increased seven times and industrial output multiplied 16 times. Everyone had a job, lived better than their parents had, and enjoyed the benefits of a comprehensive health, education, and welfare system.

As we have seen, Gierek's program called for continuing investment in heavy industry while resolving the problem of consumer scarcity by developing light industries financed by borrowing from the West. A decline in borrowing owing to recession as well as the need to recycle petrodollars made banks in the West more than willing lenders to communist Eastern Europe. Indeed, other Eastern European countries such as Hungary, Romania, and Yugoslavia were also taking out substantial loans from the West. Ultimately, such borrowing facilitated the penetration and control of the Eastern European economies by Western financial institutions. By 1975 Poland had already borrowed some $7.4 billion from Western banks. Nonetheless, Gierek's policies produced unprecedented consumer affluence through the early 1970s. But five years later Poland's debt to the West had accumulated to $21 billion. The rapidly accumulating debt reflected the failure of Gierek's program of increasing industrial exports. Gierek had proposed to pay off bank loans by exporting consumer manufactures from Poland to the West. But economic stagnation in the Western countries and strong competition from Asian manufacturers selling into Western markets frustrated Poland's efforts. The consequence was that Poland could only pay what it owed by exporting coal and food to the West at the expense of internal consumption.

In Poland, meanwhile, the groundwork for a challenge to the regime was developing. Within the Polish Communist Party itself, the old, idealistic leadership gave way to an openly managerial elite obsessed with power and privilege. Party membership increased, but the percentage of blue-collar members declined. The armed forces were loyal to the Polish state, but their loyalty to the regime against rebellious workers could not be guaranteed. Accordingly, in the wake of the unrest of 1970, Gierek created a special militarized police corps (ZOMOS) to protect the regime. A force approximately a third the size of the Polish army, ZOMOS members were recruited in large part from the dregs of society and despised by the population.

The most venerable opposition to the regime came from the clergy of the Roman Catholic Church. Poles overwhelmingly identified with the Church, which had championed the cause of Polish national independence for 120 years. During the Second World War, it had stood with the population in the face of Soviet and Nazi occupation. Under attack from the Communists up to 1956, it thereafter became the only legitimate opposition, led by the politically astute Cardinal Wyzinski. The original communist ideal of separation of church and state went by the boards. The Polish state found itself obliged to support the 14,000 churches and 20,000 clergy of the Catholic Church. Such was the Church's influence that it was able to insist on religious instruction in state schools and the provision of Catholic chaplains in the armed forces. The goal of the Church was ostensibly propagation of the faith and an avoidance of social upheaval. In fact, it cooperated with the regime, while seeking an opportunity to undermine it.

Another focal point of opposition was the secular intellectuals of largely middle-class and noble origin. They despised the Russians and strongly identified with the West. Many greatly resented the power of communist functionaries of lower-class origins whom they considered crude upstarts. A minority, nonetheless, who were attracted to the idea of social justice, threw in their lot with the Communists.

But it was the blue-collar workers who, to the surprise and delight of anticommunists, would become the real gravediggers of the regime. Among the working class the leadership came from the skilled industrial workers whose numbers rose from 600,000 in the 1950s to 2.4 million at the end of the 1970s. Technically educated in vocational schools, they were proud of their role at the heart of the industrial sector of the economy. Indeed, the official Marxist ideology of the state reinforced this proletarian *esprit de corps*. Better paid than intellectuals, they nevertheless could not buy sufficient consumer goods and were extremely sensitive

to price increases on foodstuffs. But they were also troubled by the regime's neglect of issues such as job safety and working conditions. Given a good general
knowledge of Polish history and literature as part of their education, they strongly identified with the country's nationalist tradition. Many were of peasant origin
and remained deeply Catholic.

The crisis of the regime began in 1976. Responding to fiscal pressures, the
regime once again announced major increases in food prices. The working class
once more responded with violent protests, especially at Radom and Ursus, two
major industrial centers. At these two sites, workers took to the streets and
attacked party headquarters. Five people were killed and hundreds injured in the
course of the repression carried out by the ZOMOS. Some of the leaders of the
protests were put on trial. Fourteen prominent intellectuals organized themselves
into a committee known as the Committee for the Defense of Workers (KOR).
The regime hesitated to move against KOR as it had wide support among the
intelligentsia and even in the liberal wing of the party. More significantly, as a
result of the initiatives of KOR, ties were established between the dissident intelligentsia and the working class. The election of the determinedly anticommunist
Cardinal Karol Wojtila as Pope John Paul II (1978) represented another blow to
the regime. The Polish Pope's subsequent visit to his homeland caused a sensation. Wojtila began to discretely concert his moves with those of the Reagan
administration in Washington from 1980 onwards.

As a result of the failure of the export drive and problems attendant on mounting debts, the standard of living in Poland had fallen precipitously from its height
in 1975. At the beginning of the summer of 1980, the government was compelled
once more to raise food prices. Factory occupations began at once all over
Poland. Strike committees immediately established contact with one another
nationwide. The workers at the Lenin Shipyard in Gdansk assumed leadership of
the movement. There Lech Walesa, a dissident worker, emerged as a charismatic
leader of what became a new national union known as Solidarity. Walesa and
other working-class leaders united with the leading elements of the dissident
intelligentsia at the head of the organization.

Faced with an all-out social revolution led by the working class—the ultimate
nightmare of bureaucratic socialism—the Communist Party was obliged to negotiate. At the end of August, the party was forced to recognize the legality of
Solidarity. The party's monopoly of power—the keystone of bureaucratic socialism—had collapsed. By fall 1980 membership in Solidarity totaled nine million

out of a workforce of 16.5 million. Many grassroots communists joined Solidarity. In the following months, the party and Solidarity jockeyed for position. In a context of growing political and economic chaos, the military emerged as another focal point of authority. The military's rise in influence was reflected in the growing authority of the communist general and commander-in-chief Wojciech Jaruszelski.

Jaruszelski presented himself not only as an arbiter of order, but also as a patriotic defender of Polish sovereignty against the threat of a Soviet invasion. In February 1981 he was named prime minister and first secretary of the Communist Party. In December he imposed martial law on the country. The military assumed power, suspending the activities of the Communist Party, Solidarity, the state bureaucracy, and all other social organizations. The new government based itself on the armed forces and a team of technocrats. A new government-sponsored union was created as a rival to Solidarity. Solidarity went underground, aided by the Church, and continued to operate in defiance of the government. No effective censorship was reestablished. The economy recovered in the late 1980s, but only to the level of 1978. Meanwhile, the foreign debt based on accrued interest had risen to $42 billion.

Bureaucratic Communism at an Impasse

The situation in the other Eastern European states was not as dramatic as in Poland. But symptoms of economic stagnation and a loss of political will abounded. The centralized bureaucratic economic mechanism had produced substantial growth and significant improvement in living standards from the 1950s to the 1970s. But by the 1980s this economic model appeared to be exhausted as growth slowed in comparison with previous decades. The Hungarian regime responded with what amounted to a program of market socialism and growing political liberalization accompanied by increased loans from Western banks. Like Hungary, the German Democratic Republic was by the 1980s heavily indebted to the West. Indeed, its economy was more and more linked to that of West Germany. Living standards were the highest in Eastern Europe. But the economy there, too, showed signs of flagging. Like other Eastern European states, Romania had also acquired a heavy burden of Western debt. The authoritarian Stalinist leader Nicolae Ceausescu responded in a radically different way than the Hungarian and East German leadership. Determined to continue on the path of rapid accumulation through industrialization and to pay off the external debt as quickly as possible, he imposed a program of extreme austerity on an already deprived and long-suffering population.

Bureaucratic socialism had lifted Eastern Europe out of economic backwardness. Growth undoubtedly had slowed down by the 1980s but, as a matter of fact, no more so than in Western Europe. But whatever the past benefits of bureaucratic socialism, further advance required the democratization of political life and a greater degree of integration into the world economy. As events transpired, it seemed that much of the elite and the public at large had drawn the same conclusion. Did that require a turn toward capitalism? Too much water had passed under the bridge for it to be otherwise. The legacy of Stalinism and the encroachment of the West ensured that that would be the outcome.

But it is worth noting that a different outcome was possible. The dismantling or withering of state and party dictatorship could have issued in the actual rule of the working class. This would have entailed worker's control in the workplace, political democracy, and a proletarian rather than bourgeois civil society based on a wide gamut of feminist, ecological, gay, ethnic, religious, cultural, and other groups. It is not inconceivable that global capitalism could end in this way.

In any case it was from further east that exit from a politically and economically outmoded system finally arrived. The Soviet Union had crushed the Prague Spring in 1968. The Czech liberalization had been sparked, in part, by the political blockage of a fully industrialized and developed economy. But the Soviet leadership saw the implementation of market socialism and political democracy at that time as a threat to the Communist Party's control of political and economic life. As a result, Brezhnev ordered that an end be put to such experiments. But by 1982 the Soviet Union had reached nearly the same impasse as Czechoslovakia in 1968, reflected in declining growth rates and falling productivity.

The Brezhnev Years

The problems of the Soviet Union were in part a reflection of its success. Under Brezhnev, the broad coalition of elites that had ousted Khruschev remained united. As a result, Brezhnev brought the Soviet Union a prolonged period of internal political and social stability and a modest prosperity. In external affairs the Soviet leader projected an image of the Soviet Union as a stable, pragmatic, and responsible global power.

Khrushchev had fallen from power largely because the various Soviet elites resented his frequent political reorganizations and threats to bureaucratic tenure. On the contrary, stability of cadres became a byword of Brezhnev's administration. His administration was a kind of reformed Stalinism. The basic institutions of the Stalinist state were retained without heavy or widespread police terror or much of a cult of personality. In foreign affairs, Brezhnev pursued a more prudent and patient line than Khrushchev, although one which was no less ambitious. He aimed at strategic military parity with the United States, while preserving peaceful coexistence. Faced with ongoing rivalry with China, he sought to reassert Soviet predominance in the communist sphere of influence. In Europe his goal was Western official recognition of the postwar political settlement. At the same time, he sought to extend as much as possible Soviet influence in the developing world.

A major buildup of Soviet delivery systems led to the achievement of parity in long-range nuclear forces with the United States by the end of the 1960s. Permanent Soviet naval fleets were put on station in the Mediterranean and Indian Oceans as the Soviet Union became a global naval power. In Europe Brezhnev was able to pursue rapprochement with de Gaulle's France, which was eager to distance itself from the United States. Likewise, the Soviets benefited from West Germany's Ostpolitik or policy of reconciliation between East and West initiated in 1966 when the Social Democrat Willy Brandt became foreign minister. Growing détente with the United States was reflected in the conclusion of the ABM and SALT I Treaties (1972) and by the SALT II Treaty and Helsinki Accords (1975). But at the same time, direct aid or aid through its proxy Cuba extended Soviet influence to national liberation and revolutionary movements in Nicaragua, South Africa, Ethiopia, Angola, and Afghanistan. The Soviet Union, like the United States, had its setbacks. China's rapprochement with the United States as well as post-Nasser Egypt's abandonment of its alliance with the Soviets represented diplomatic reversals during the 1970s. Nonetheless, toward the close of the Carter presidency, the opinion grew in Washington that the United States was losing ground in the post-Vietnam world and should pursue a tougher line with the Soviets. It was this U.S perception that led to a new chill in relations between Washington and Moscow at the end of the 1970s.

Détente with Washington had in part been the payoff for a Soviet arms buildup during the 1960s, but the buildup proved very expensive. Increasing Soviet commitments in the third world during the 1970s added to the burden at a time when Soviet economic growth conspicuously slowed. Western and Soviet estimates of economic performance vary. Western estimates put Soviet growth at less than 2 percent during the 1980s. But experts from both sides concur that growth declined from the mid-1970s onward.

It is generally agreed that the fundamental problem of the Soviet economy was that the phase of earlier and successful extensive growth based on the centralized marshaling of surpluses of labor and resources had ended. Future growth would have to depend on a more intensive use of these factors based on technological improvements, a more efficient organization of production, and more effective allocation of resources between economic sectors. The central planning mechanism's inability to deal with the requirements of an increasingly complex economy, it is generally agreed, explains Soviet failure. The central plan's incapacity to allocate goods efficiently, obsession with quantitative growth, especially of heavy industry at the expense of other sectors, incapacity to acquire and to respond to economic feedback, reluctance to reorganize production, and failure to foster more efficient production in existing industries weighed down the economy.

The growing problems of the Brezhnev period were masked by the modest affluence that emerged during his tenure in office. The Soviet population was increasingly well educated and urbanized. Increasing stocks of new low-rent apartments were furnished with televisions, refrigerators, washing machines, and other consumer durables. The state continued to provide job security, relative income equality, free medical care, education, and generous social welfare. Available survey research from the 1980s suggests that the great majority of Soviet citizens, while not uncritical of the government, were nonetheless broadly satisfied with their lives and accepted the regime's claims of the superiority of the Soviet to the Western way of life. Higher levels of material consumption in the West were acknowledged, but stress was laid on the greater degree of equality and economic and personal security in the Soviet Union. Generally, Soviet citizens believed that their way of life, although materially poorer, was morally and culturally superior to that found in the West.

That being said it seems apparent that the existing bureaucratic party apparatus, which controlled all aspects of Soviet political, economic, and social life under the aegis of the Communist Party, atrophied under Brezhnev. Access to major positions and privileges within the system were more and more controlled by networks of clientage and influence manipulated by the communist elite. Corruption, complacency, and intellectual stultification crippled political and technological innovation. By the early 1980s these problems reflected themselves in economic stagnation in the official economy and the rise of an unofficial and subterranean market economy. The attempt to impose socialism from on high rather than from below had reached a dead end.

The Rise of Gorbachev

Yuri Andropov succeeded Brezhnev as general secretary of the Communist Party in 1982. Head of the KGB under Brezhnev, Andropov had carried out the repression of political and intellectual dissidents in his time. But unusually he was also acutely aware of the urgent need for the reform of Soviet society. During his short tenure in office, Andropov began to promote reform-minded technocrats and administrators to senior positions in the party and state. Among these was the young and reform-minded Mikhail Gorbachev.

Andropov died of kidney failure in early February 1984. He was replaced by a reliable follower of Brezhnev, the elderly Konstantin Chernenko. Gorbachev emerged as leader of a reform faction in the Politburo, and at the age of 54 was named general secretary on Chernenko's death in March 1985. Vested with enormous power as general secretary, Gorbachev was in a position to introduce thoroughgoing change. Nonetheless, the new general secretary started from the assumption that the Soviet system was essentially sound. It needed modernization, streamlining, and discipline to revitalize economic growth. This policy of reform or so-called acceleration governed Gorbachev's outlook during his first two years in office.

Gorbachev made sweeping changes in personnel, purging Brezhnev holdovers at the top levels of the party, state, and economy. By February 1986, 40 percent of key posts had new incumbents. The five-year plan announced that year set dramatically higher production targets. Quality controls were increased and new levels of performance and discipline demanded from the bureaucracy and working population. A nationwide antialcohol campaign was the most dramatic aspect of these reform initiatives.

This program of modernization assumed that the problem of the inertia of the Soviet state and party could be dealt with by personnel changes and initiatives from on high. But in the face of ongoing resistance by the *nomenklatura* or Communist elite, Gorbachev concluded in 1986 that the conservative attitude of the nomenklatura was a systemic barrier to change. Accordingly, he decided that the Communist elite had to be impelled to change by mobilizing public opinion as a counterpower. Greater openness in public life, freer access to information by ordinary Soviet citizens, intellectual criticism, and an aroused public opinion could become levers to push the bureaucracy toward reform. Gorbachev's program of openness or so-called *glasnost* led toward the rapid development of a free press, a proliferation of other media, and cultural freedom. Toward the end of 1986, Gorbachev took the critical step of sanctioning the so-called informal movement or the creation of organizations outside Communist Party control. By the end of 1987 there were some 30,000 such informal organizations. Most of these thousands of groups had no political agenda, but a significant number of environmental, liberal, and nationalist groupings appeared. The new liberal and nationalist bodies were to play a significant part in the undermining of the Soviet Union.

Gorbachev believed that he could allow political freedom in the midst of wholesale economic transformation. Indeed, the second part of Gorbachev's program entailed economic restructuring or *perestroika*. The Soviet economy was to move away from central planning and state-directed management toward market socialism. Managerial and worker autonomy was introduced in 1987. The following year the regime allowed the formation of cooperatives, including small private businesses, as well as the leasing of land by families or individuals.

While these internal changes unfolded, Gorbachev also took dramatic new steps in Soviet foreign relations. Under President Reagan the United States had launched a massive arms buildup in response to the Soviet invasion of Afghanistan and the extension of its influence in the third world. Reagan's belligerent rhetoric and plans for a missile defense system or Strategic Defense Initiative (Star Wars Program) heightened the risk of nuclear confrontation. Gorbachev concluded that a Soviet attempt to match the expansion of U.S military power would doom the planned renewal of the Soviet economy. Accordingly, Gorbachev responded to U.S belligerence with diplomatic retrenchment. Taking the position that the challenges of growing global interdependence demanded an end to the Cold War, the Soviet leader called for the humanization of international relations.

In April 1985 Gorbachev announced a moratorium on the deployment of SS-20 intercontinental ballistic missiles. This was followed five months later by the unilateral suspension of underground nuclear testing. In November a first meeting between Gorbachev and Reagan led to an initial thaw in Soviet-U.S relations. Impasse at the Reykjavik Summit between the two leaders in October 1986 represented a temporary setback. The next year saw Gorbachev renounce the arms

race by proclaiming a new military doctrine calling for so-called reasonable suffi-
ciency instead of parity in means of defense vis-à-vis the United States. In
December Moscow and Washington mutually agreed to eliminate intermediate
range nuclear missiles. In 1988 Gorbachev announced the withdrawal of Soviet
forces from Afghanistan while abandoning the Brezhnev doctrine. In 1989 the
Soviet premier ordered substantial unilateral cuts in Soviet military expenditures
and troop levels. Soviet foreign policy statements no longer spoke of supporting
national liberation movements, but of comprehensive systems of international
security. States such as Angola and Nicaragua were left to their own devices.

By 1988 Gorbachev's reforms began to create growing confusion in the Soviet
economy. The central planning and administrative apparatus started to break
down, but market mechanisms to replace them were not in place. At every level of
the economy, hoarding, scarcity, and inflation began to become serious.
Economic growth, which had spurted to 4 percent in 1986, fell to less than two
in the next three years. The members of the central political and economic apparatus were unable to resist Gorbachev's commands directly, but some were determined to obstruct him indirectly.

In an effort to broaden support for his reforms, Gorbachev organized democratic elections in 1988. The ensuing Congress of People's Deputies of 1989
elected a Supreme Soviet. Designed to provide Gorbachev an independent power
base, the democratically elected Supreme Soviet proved to be a cockpit for rivalries between so-called conservatives and emergent liberal and nationalist factions.
Indeed, increasing economic difficulties sharpened political conflicts, weakening
Gorbachev further as a result.

The Velvet Revolution in Eastern Europe

Increasingly vulnerable at home, Gorbachev was hardly in a position to intervene
against the popular revolutions that swept through the other communist states in
Eastern Europe in 1989. The political or strategic rationale for holding on to
these states as a sphere of Soviet influence was evaporating. Indeed, these Eastern
European upheavals were themselves inspired by Gorbachev's own initiatives. At
the end of the 1980s, these states were divided into three categories. In the first
lay Poland still under martial law and facing continuing economic problems. With
the emergence of Gorbachev, the government of General Jaruszelski decided to
move toward political pluralism. Similarly, Hungary was inching toward liberal-

ization as a way of addressing its economic difficulties. The German Democratic Republic and Czechoslovakia made up the second category of Eastern European countries. These two states rejected the liberalizing tendencies in Poland and Hungary, preferring to bolster popular support through the provision of more consumer goods from their still growing economies. Romania in the third category remained a relentlessly Stalinist dictatorship. Bulgaria was situated somewhere between categories two and three.

Poland

In the years following the declaration of martial law, Polish Solidarity lived on as an underground organization sustained by the Catholic Church. Its influence was reduced by a new government-sponsored union as well as the impatience of younger workers. At the end of the 1980s, the Polish economy had barely recovered from the upheaval of 1981. Attempts by the government to institute reforms at the expense of workers were met by new strikes. The only way to make such measures palatable, it seemed, was to move toward political pluralism. A citizens' committee led by Lech Walesa entered into roundtable negotiations at the invitation of the communist government at the beginning of 1989. At the end of two months, an agreement legalizing Solidarity and establishing a timetable toward free elections was announced. The subsequent election saw the victory of the first non-communist government in Eastern Europe led by Solidarity's Tadeusz Mazowiecki, a Catholic intellectual.

Hungary

In response to the need for economic reform and the pressure of public opinion, Hungary followed Poland's example. In June 1989 the reburial of Imre Nagy, the martyred leader of the Hungarian Revolution, attracted the presence of hundreds of thousands of the citizens of Budapest. As in Poland, roundtable discussions led to the legalization of liberal and nationalist parties and the scheduling of free elections.

East Germany

While change in Poland and Hungary was the result of negotiation, in the German Democratic Republic transformation occurred under the pressure of dramatic popular mobilizations. During the summer of 1989, tens of thousands of East Germans suddenly fled to the consumer freedoms of West Germany. Lutheran pastors in Leipzig had been organizing peace vigils through most of the 1980s. In the wake of this sudden wholesale exodus to the West, the Leipzig assemblies turned into mass demonstrations demanding political democracy. On November 7 the entire political leadership of the GDR resigned. Two days later the Berlin Wall was opened. Elections in March 1990 brought the Christian Democrats to power in East Germany. With the agreement of the government of West Germany, the Christian Democrats proceeded to German unification on October 3, 1990. East German hopes were bolstered by the promise of massive economic and financial assistance.

Czechoslovakia

In November 1989 mass demonstrations developed in Prague. Led by the liberal author and intellectual Vaclav Havel, a new opposition movement, Civic Forum, emerged. Backed by overwhelming public support, it forced the resignation of the communist government and installed Havel as interim president. In elections organized the following June, Civic Forum won a landslide victory. The almost effortless surrender of these communist regimes in part was the result of their loss of self-confidence in the face of the liberalizing trends underway in the Soviet Union. In the case of Hungary and Poland, growing skepticism about the viability of the existing socialist economic model played a part. In East Germany, Poland, and Czechoslovakia, the previous dismissal of democratic institutions came back to haunt the regimes in the form of irresistible mass movements of opposition.

Romania

To this point the collapse of the communist governments of Eastern Europe had proceeded virtually without the shedding of blood. But in Romania, the overthrow of the Ceausescu regime was marked by violence. In Transylvania the impoverished Hungarian ethnic minority looked toward an outspoken pastor, Laszlo Tokes. His removal from the pulpit by the Romanian authorities set off large-scale demonstrations in the regional capital Timisoara. Police and security forces fired on the crowds, killing many demonstrators. When Ceausescu appeared in front of large crowds at a pro-government rally in Bucharest on

December 21, he was taken aback by unprecedented antigovernment outbursts from the large assembly. Dissidents within the Communist Party, military, and security forces then carried out a coup supported by the population. The new government, calling itself the National Salvation Front, ordered the execution of Ceausescu and his wife four days later. As many as 1,000 died in the upheaval. In Bulgaria the flight of almost 350,000 Turks as a result of growing xenophobia connived at by the communist regime led to the emergence of an organized opposition and the dissolution of the communist monopoly on power.

The Emergence of Yeltsin

In the midst of these Eastern European upheavals, the newly elected Congress of Peoples Deputies met in the Soviet Union. Eighty-seven percent of the elected delegates were members of the Communist Party. But the party itself was now divided between liberals, nationalists, and conservatives, the latter still committed to bureaucratic socialism. The leader of the Russian liberals and nationalists was Boris Yeltsin. Yeltsin had been appointed to the Central Committee in 1985 as part of the new wave of appointees brought in by Gorbachev. The confidence that he initially inspired was further reflected in his appointment to the Politburo and as party secretary of Moscow. But by 1987 he fell out with Gorbachev and resigned his positions. In 1988 he was dropped from the Central Committee and emerged as leader of the anticommunist Russian liberals and nationalists. Under Yelstin there coalesced a block of party leaders, intelligentsia, and elements of the underground economy who championed a rapid capitalist transformation based on liberal ideology.

The Nationalist Threat

Nationalist fractures were an even more serious threat to the continued existence of the Soviet Union. Using the informal groups allowed by Gorbachev as an initial organizational base, nationalist movements emerged as a strong force in the Baltic states. They swept local elections as well as the election of delegates to the Congress of Peoples Deputies in 1989. Local Communist Party elites were even prepared to seize the nationalist bandwagon to resist Gorbachev. In Lithuania, for example, Party First Secretary Algirdas Brazauskas responded to the rise of a Lithuanian nationalist popular front by taking a hard line against Moscow. By December 1989 the Lithuanian Communist Party broke from the Communist Party of the Soviet Union and established itself as a separate social democratic party. Although it failed to stem the immediate nationalist electoral tide, it stormed back to power in 1992 as the elected Labor Party in an independent Lithuania.

In Georgia the rise of nationalist sentiment forced the authorities to hold multi-party elections in August 1989. The result was the first non-communist republican parliament in the Soviet Union dominated by the militant nationalist Zviad Gamsakhurdia. He would declare Georgian independence in 1991. By 1990 nationalist feeling had reached the point that the neighboring Soviet republics of Armenia and Azerbijan were effectively at war over the disputed territory of Nagorno-Karabakh. Party leaders in the two republics jumped on the nationalist bandwagon and declared independence from the Soviet Union.

But it was the rise of anticommunist nationalism within Russia that finally undid the Soviet Union. In May 1990 Yelstin was elected to the newly created office of president of the Russian Federation. He began to usurp Soviet powers and property claiming them for the Russian republic. In reaction to these centrifugal forces, through the winter of 1990–91 Gorbachev flirted with conservatives in the Communist Party, Soviet army, and KGB. But finding this uncongenial, by spring he was approaching elected republican leaders, including Yeltsin, to try to find a new basis for the Soviet Union. For conservatives this was the last straw. In August 1991 they attempted a coup while Gorbachev vacationed in the Crimea. In the face of KGB and military inertia and resistance on the part of the most politically active part of the population, the coup failed. In the wake of this failure, Yeltsin usurped full state power in Russia, Gorbachev resigned, and the Soviet Union dissolved (December 1991). Liberalism became the order of the day throughout Eastern Europe.

Tiananmen Square in China

The year 1989 would see a liberal challenge to state socialism even in China. But there the communist regime survived largely as a result of the economic reforms of the previous decade. The largely negative results of the Cultural Revolution had helped discredit the ideology of Marxist-Leninism as a basis for legitimizing the continued hegemony of the Chinese Communist Party. Under Teng Hsiao-p'ing a development program calling itself socialist modernization would become the rationale for the continued existence of the party-state. Banks and key manu-facturing industries remained in state hands. But rural communes were disman-tled and the peasantry given long-term leases to family plots. Rural industries ori-entated toward supplying the needs of both internal and export markets were encouraged. Private retail trade and small businesses were authorized. More autonomy was given to managers of state industries. Coastal development zones appeared, which attracted foreign investment, especially from Hong Kong, Taiwan, and Singapore. During the Maoist period, China had made remarkable economic progress. Under the new, more liberal conditions, growth accelerated, expressing itself for the first time in the form of feverish market activity and an unprecedented consumer boom.

Inflation, corruption, and oppressive government then provoked a rising tide of complaint from all sectors of the population. As was customary in China, stu-dents took the lead in voicing such grievances. Emboldened by new influences from the West and from Eastern Europe, students organized mass demonstrations in Tiananmen Square in the spring of 1989. The tenor of such demands was unmistakably in the direction of liberal democracy. Some entrepreneurs and workers supported the students. Teng Hsiao-p'ing, backed by most of the com-munist leadership, coolly ordered the crushing of counterrevolution by the Peoples Liberation Army. He then proceeded in schizoid manner to accelerate market reform under party guidance.

The Reagan Revolution

Neoliberalism, in the meantime, was utterly triumphant in the West. Led by the English-speaking states, the principal capitalist countries marched in step toward disarming the state and unleashing the market. With the election of Reagan in 1980, the United States took the lead in implementing the neoliberal agenda. The new president, like his purported idol Franklin Delano Roosevelt, was determined to implement a new deal, but only in reverse. Like Roosevelt, he would save U.S capitalism, but unlike his hero, he would do so through deregu-lating the economy, dramatically reducing the welfare state, curbing labor, and lowering taxes.

Chronic inflation had plagued the U.S economy during the 1970s. Reagan responded with interest rates hikes in the high double digits and with cutbacks in the money supply. The result was a deep recession in 1981–82, which boosted the unemployment rate to 9.5 percent and left tens of millions jobless. This assault on workers was reinforced by Reagan's draconian response to the strike of air controllers in August 1981. Firing these 10,000 government employees, Reagan proceeded to decertify the union. Totally disarmed by years of business unionism, organized labor put up no resistance. Reagan was able to serve notice that a new and harsher deal for labor had arrived. Wage rates fell, and strikes dwindled to next to none. Inflation declined sharply from 10.4 percent in 1980–81 to 3.2 percent in 1983. By curbing inflation and the demands of labor, a new and more stable environment for the accumulation of capital had been created.

Business confidence was further bolstered by passage of the Economic Recovery Tax Act of 1981, which dramatically cut taxes, especially for corporations and the well-to-do. The resultant huge deficits were then used as a device justifying cuts of 10 percent to government social spending. A key element in the burgeoning deficit was the military buildup ordered by Reagan. Total military spending over the eight years of Reagan's tenure totaled more than $2 trillion. By the end of the 1980s, the national debt had risen from $1.5 to $4 trillion, of which half a trillion was held abroad.

Increased military spending, a decline in interest rates, and an increase in the money supply fueled an economic recovery by 1983. High-tech computer companies, military firms, and deregulated financial institutions created new focal points of capital accumulation, notably in the south and far west. A new mood of entrepreneurship and ostentatious consumption pervaded an emerging new financial and high-tech stratum composed of fast moving young men and women of power, wealth, and connections. The incomes of the wealthiest Americans increased dramatically, while the average U.S family saw a decline in personal income of between 4 and 6.5 percent. Parallel cuts in social spending reduced what may be called the social wage. In the name of shareholder value, stress was placed on immediate financial returns to institutional investors rather than the long-term strength of industrial enterprises. This partly accounted for the fact that real growth rates and gains in productivity did not return to the levels of the 1950s and 1960s. As a result, trade deficits continued to mount. Under Reagan the relative economic decline of the United States with respect to the rest of the world continued.

While Reagan faced serious resistance in Congress against his moves to deregulate controls on pollution, the regulation of banks and investment firms was largely abandoned. In 1982 the savings and loans industry was given the right to make commercial loans. Speculators soon tapped into billions of savings and loans dollars to finance dubious real estate ventures. The ultimate collapse of this sector (1987) required a half trillion dollar government bail-out. At the same time, junk bonds, leveraged buy-outs, hostile takeovers, and corporate restructuring unleashed enormous speculative activity generating fortunes for high-flyers such as Michael Milken, T. Boone Pickens, and Ivan Boesky. Ballooning credit and deficits carried the stock market dizzily upward until the crash of October 19, 1987, when Wall Street suffered the largest loss to that point in its history. The growing disproportionalities between the financial economy and the real economy were the most notable feature of the period. Coupled with the increasingly unregulated and accelerated movement of dollars internationally, the stage was set for the unprecedented dominance of global finance capital that marked the closing years of the twentieth century.

Thatcherism in Great Britain

The Thatcher government in England proceeded along much the same path. Advancing with a savage audacity, Thatcher pushed ahead with massive income tax cuts for the rich, sharp increases on indirect taxes hitting the poor, and a deliberate deflation to kill inflation and discipline labor. The defeat of the national coal miners' strike in 1984–85 marked the high water mark of her government. Thatcher privatized state-owned industries and utilities; cut income taxes, especially on the wealthy; and introduced more market-orientated mechanisms into health and education. Starting with telecommunications in 1984, virtually all public utilities including gas, electricity, water, and the railways were privatized. In addition, the private financing initiative entailed the market financing of schools and hospitals, as well as the contracting out of public services. Nine labor acts crippled the trade unions and created the most unregulated labor market in any of the OECD countries. The government also introduced an unpopular poll tax that provoked rioting and defiance. The poor and unemployed were harshly attacked by cuts in welfare spending and increased bureaucratic control. The ostensible justification of these policies was to reduce the role of the government and to make people more self-reliant, putting an end to a so-called culture of dependency. In fact, government intrusiveness and taxes on ordinary people increased during the 1980s and 1990s. It became a characteristic of the neoliberal regime in Britain and elsewhere that regulations on business were reduced while bureaucratic and police control of the rest of the population dramatically increased. At the same time, social polarization between rich and poor grew rapidly. Economic growth was a paltry 1.9 percent during the decade, doing nothing to halt the economic decline of Great Britain relative to other advanced capitalist countries. At the same time, it must be conceded that Thatcher succeeded in making material success and competitiveness the dominant values of British society as never before.

France and the Neoliberal Turn

The strength of the neoliberal tide is nowhere better illustrated than by the case of France. There the 1980s began with the election of François Mitterand as the head of a socialist-communist government. The new president's commitment to a so-called social growth economy appeared to be the realization of some of the long-held aspirations of both old and new left. It stood at 180 degrees from the neoliberal program of Thatcher's Britain or Reagan's America. Economic growth was to flow from domestic demand generated by higher wages and social transfers. Twelve main industrial groups, 39 banks, and two financial holding companies were nationalized in accord with socialist principles. At the same time, an ambitious industrial policy aimed at strengthening national industry was initiated in order to reconquer the internal market. The Auroux Law gave workers a somewhat expanded role within businesses.

Within two years, Mitterand had abandoned this Keynesian project. Rather than strengthening French industry, the expansion of internal demand led to a flood of German and other foreign imports. Growing demand occasioned inflation without curbing rising unemployment. Increasing government deficits and the deterioration of the trade balance threatened the stability of the franc. The failure of these policies demonstrated that the integration of the French economy into the European Economic Community had passed the point of no return. A national economic policy independent of Germany and the rest of the European Community was no longer tenable. In March 1983 Mitterand executed a U-turn. Curbing inflation and reducing the public deficit became the new priorities. Social transfers were put into the back seat. By 1984 the restructuring of deficit-making industrial sectors was announced as an additional goal. Prudent deregulation and liberalization, especially of the financial sector followed. With the election of the neo-Gaullist government of Prime Minister Jacques Chirac (1986-88), the nationalization of industries and banks of the early 1980s was dramatically reversed. Mitterand presided over this process as president, devoting himself to adorning Paris with a new modernist architecture.

Germany

France had to knuckle under to the reality of growing integration and competition from within the European Community. Its interdependence with Germany could not easily be ignored. Paradoxically, it was Germany which best withstood the demands of neoliberalism during the 1980s. Its comprehensive welfare state, its labor-management productivity pacts, and its commitment to state investment in research and development made it highly competitive internationally, enabling it to churn out a respectable average growth rate of 2 percent during the 1980s. It had a problem with chronic unemployment, as did the other Western European states. But such structural unemployment was directly related to continued high levels of investment in the mechanization of the economy in marked contrast to the stagnation of such outlays in the United States.

Despite this advantage, German business executives, as well those of the other states of Western Europe, complained of economic stagnation, especially compared to the performance of the United States. For this increasingly unified European elite, the way forward appeared to be toward creating a politically and financially integrated European Union under the auspices of the neoliberal ideology. Economic and labor regulations, as well as social transfers embedded at the national level, could be superseded at the level of European-wide integration. At the same time, reinforcing the European Economic Community institutionally could foster a strengthened home market, while making European businesses more competitive internationally. Liberal ideology being unsalable to the European populace, liberalizing measures could nonetheless be implemented under the guise of European integration. An important group spurring this project was the European Round Table of Industrialists created in 1983. Composed of prominent European industrialists, it lobbied for European-wide infrastructure and research and development projects, while promoting further pro-business integration. While the resultant Maastricht Treaty (1992) did lay down some social preconditions for further European integration, the heart of it consisted of monetary union based on the liberal economic concepts of fiscal stability, deficit control, low inflation, low interest rates, and economic convergence. Moreover, the political structures of the European Union remained profoundly undemocratic.

Reagan and the Second Cold War

The Reagan administration nostalgically sought a restoration of U.S economic power through the free market. Indeed, the spread of neoliberal ideology to other countries was seen as part of the reassertion of U.S leadership. But in the post-Vietnam era, Reagan was anxious to affirm U.S power internationally by directly political means as well. Détente with the Soviet Union, considered a product of U.S defeat in Vietnam, was shunted aside. While bolstering the economy of the United States, a massive U.S military buildup would slow the Soviet economy if it tried to keep up. The deployment of cruise missiles in Europe and the initiation of the Strategic Defense Initiative (1983) would end nuclear stalemate in favor of the United States. It would put a price on stepped-up Soviet support to national liberation movements in the Middle East, Africa, and Latin America.

Reagan thus reverted to the old Cold War policy of military containment with respect to the Soviet Union. But with regard to national liberation movements in the third world, Reagan was prepared to take things a step further. Subsequently baptized the Reagan Doctrine, the new policy in the third world called for active U.S military and political intervention to challenge communist-inspired movements and governments. It was a version of the 1950s program of rollback, which had been invoked in Korea and Eastern Europe, now applied to the third world.

Under the Reagan Doctrine, the United States would challenge third world radical regimes while avoiding a major entanglement that might be costly in U.S lives. In this context, so-called low intensity warfare came into its own. In order to counter enemies in the third world, economic blockade, support for counter-revolutionary armies, death squads and guerrillas, covert psychological and high-technology warfare, and even lightening strikes by U.S troops might be used. What was to be avoided was a large-scale and long-term commitment of U.S ground troops.

Counterinsurgency in Central America

Reagan's first target was the Marxist government that had taken power in 1979 on the little Caribbean island of Grenada. A lightening attack by elite U.S forces was able to bring a quick and easy victory in 1983. But the ouster of the Marxist government of Grenada was only a prelude to Reagan's main priority in Latin America: reversing the course of the Sandinista Revolution in Nicaragua. The Sandinistas had been able to install themselves in power during the Carter administration. By confiscating the extensive properties of Somoza and his associates, the Sandinista government had been able at a stroke to nationalize fully a quarter of the economy. The revolutionary government also attempted to achieve food self-sufficiency, cautiously initiate income redistribution in favor of the less well-off, cut luxury imports, and diversify its trade partners. As a result of the latter policy, only a quarter of Nicaragua's exports still went to the United States by the mid-1980s. The rest went to Western Europe, the socialist countries, and the third world.

A mass literacy campaign reminiscent of the Cuban Revolution sharply reduced the level of popular illiteracy. By 1985, 80 percent of the population had access to medical care reducing infant mortality by half. Women were accorded equal pay for equal work. A land reform provided two million acres to 60,000 landless rural families. In addition, land titles to some 4.6 million acres of land were provided to other families already working the land. Elections in 1984 gave the Sandinistas 67 percent of the vote.

By then the Reagan administration had launched a massive destabilization campaign. Economic blockade was followed by attacks by so-called armed contras, financed by the United States, who invaded Nicaragua from Honduras and Costa Rica. The Sandinista government was forced to raise an army of 100,000 men in an attempt to combat the insurgents. Led by holdovers from Somoza's National Guard, the contras never posed a direct military threat to the existence of the Sandinista regime, but they ultimately killed or wounded tens of thousands of Nicaraguans. At the same time, waging war against the contras drained precious resources from the civilian economy. Coupled with the U.S embargo, this economic attrition led to a decline in GNP of nearly 40 percent in the 1980s. Demoralization based on economic failure and war weariness led to the defeat of the Sandinistas in the elections of February 1990. The parallel collapse of the socialist bloc in Eastern Europe likely added to the political discouragement of the Sandinistas. The revolutionary government was replaced by a 14-party alliance led by Violeta Chamorro, a liberal opponent of the Sandinistas. All the social gains of the revolution were erased.

El Salvador

The decade of Sandinista rule in Nicaragua coincided with a fierce civil war in El Salvador. Following the murder of the leading champion of liberation theology, Archbishop Romero, in 1980, the principal guerrilla organizations, democratic parties, and mass organizations formed the Farabundo Marti Front for National Liberation (FMLN) under a common program of popular revolutionary democracy. At the beginning of 1981, the FMLN launched a general offensive, but was unable to defeat the military in a head-on assault and assume power. The Salvadoran police and military subsequently deployed death squads that killed thousands of known opponents of the regime. Despite this repression, the guerrillas increased their numbers from 2,000 to 10,000, recruited principally from students, workers, and peasants. The FMLN came to control about a third of the country, mainly in the eastern upland region. Its weapons were largely supplied through the Panamanian arms market.

Operating out of their base in the uplands, the FMLN guerrillas attacked economic targets in the rich agricultural lowlands or laid ambushes against the Salvadoran military, which proved ineffectual in battle. The United States provided some one billion dollars in aid to bolster the Salvadoran army whose numbers were expanded to more than 50,000. Some 200 U.S military advisers, pilots, and CIA operatives superintended the counterinsurgency effort. The Salvadoran airforce was expanded to 175 planes that were used to bomb and strafe the guerrillas and their rural supporters in an increasingly devastating air campaign. Unable to crush the insurgents, the United States was nonetheless able to impose a stalemate. In April 1991 the FMLN and the government signed the "Mexico Agreements" excluding the military from politics. Subsequent arrangements reintegrated the members of the FMLN into the political process. The war left 75,000 dead and 8,000 missing with nearly one million in exile. The dislocations of war and subsequent imposition of neoliberal policies exacerbated the misery of those who remained inside the country. Hundreds of thousands of Salvadorans made their way legally or illegally northward into the United States where they formed part of the expanding pool of unskilled labor from the third world. Political consciousness and levels of organization remained quite high among Salvadorans both at home and abroad.

Guatemala

By the mid-1990s even the long-standing guerrilla war against the Guatemalan military dictatorship ended. During the 1970s, the initial insurgent force known as the Rebel Armed Forces (FAR) was joined by the Poor People's Guerrilla Army (1975) and the Organization of the People in Arms (1979). Between 1954 and 1982 some 80,000 peasants and workers were killed by the army in an effort to stamp out resistance. In 1982 the insurgents came together forming the Guatemalan National Revolutionary Unity (URNG). The military dictatorship of General Efrain Rios Mott responded with a campaign of unbridled terror. In his first year of power, 15,000 Guatemalans were killed, 70,000 fled to neighboring countries, especially Mexico, while 500,000 others took refuge in the mountains. Hundreds of villages were destroyed. Peasants were forced to move to closely controlled model hamlets and enrolled in government militias to fight the guerrillas. While the United States officially distanced itself from the excesses of the Guatemalan military, it secretly supported their efforts. Prolonged negotiations between the Guatemalan government and the guerrillas led to an end to the conflict in 1995. In the aftermath of the conflict, political and economic conditions barely improved if at all. As in Nicaragua and El Salvador, drug trafficking, criminality, and youth gangs were rife. The United States meanwhile helped to establish hundreds of textile and garment manufacturing enterprises in Central America to help to keep control of the area while taking advantage of its cheap labor.

Counterinsurgency in Africa

United States intervention was able to block the development of a revolutionary process in Central America. Politically and economically, the region was brought back firmly under Washington's control. Meanwhile, in southern Africa contra wars against Angola and Mozambique raged through the 1980s. The United States had been involved in the initial attempt to block the MPLA from coming to power in Angola in 1974–75. The intervention of Cuba forestalled this intervention. Indeed, the Reagan administration of the 1980s was especially galled by the continued presence of thousands of Cuban troops in Angola. It actively encouraged the apartheid regime in South Africa to escalate both direct and proxy attacks on the Marxist governments of Angola and Mozambique, while continuing to provide clandestine financial support for UNITA.

Angola

In August 1981 the South African army advanced 200 kilometers into Angola's Cunene province. In justification the apartheid government complained that Angola was serving as a rear area for SWAPO (South West African People's Organization), the liberation movement struggling for Namibian independence from South Africa. The actual goal of this military campaign was to establish a liberated political and military zone in southern Angola as a base for UNITA. Effective Angolan and Cuban resistance contained these military intrusions. The expense and destruction of the war, nonetheless, ruined the Angolan economy, which was maintained only by its enormous oil reserves. U.S opposition to the government in Luanda was somewhat moderated by the fact that the U.S oil companies Gulf and Chevron were the main beneficiaries of the Angolan oil concessions. Ongoing access to these important Angolan oil reserves, as well as those of other West African states, including Nigeria, Equatorial Guinea, Gabon, and the Republic of Congo, increasingly became a strategic focal point of Washington's long term Africa policy.

The cost of the war, international pressure, and the growing success of the antiapartheid movement within South Africa obliged the apartheid regime to seek negotiations to put an end to the Angolan conflict. In December 1988, South Africa, Cuba, and Angola signed a Tripartite Accord ending the war between Pretoria and Luanda. It provided for the independence of Namibia and the withdrawal of South African and Cuban troops. In 1991 a peace accord between the Angolan government and UNITA paved the way for elections the next year. The ruling MPLA won with nearly 50 percent of the vote. The head of UNITA, Savimbi, refused to recognize the outcome and carried on fighting in the bush until his death at the hands of government forces in 2002. In the meantime, the MPLA abandoned its Marxist-Leninist ideology and accepted an economic adjustment program imposed by the IMF and the United States. Its leadership increasingly adopted an entrepreneurial outlook.

Mozambique

In the first five years of its 1975 independence, Mozambique's FRELIMO government emphasized the formation of state farms and industrial and agricultural cooperatives, support for the liberation struggle in neighboring Rhodesia and adherence to Marxism-Leninism. In 1981 South African forces invaded while bombing the suburb of Matola in Maputo, the capital. The South African regime organized a contra force known as RENAMO, which spread havoc through the countryside. Led by supporters of the former Portuguese dictator Salazar and a cadre of mercenaries, RENAMO ultimately recruited an army of some 20,000 young soldiers largely through coercion. In 1986 the Mozambiquan President and leader of FRELIMO, Samora Machel, died in a suspicious plane crash and was succeeded by Joaquim Chissano.

The next year the government of Mozambique announced a rethinking of its economic strategy. A more flexible policy toward foreign investment was introduced and individual producers were given more autonomy. By 1989 the regime officially committed itself to the creation of a mixed economy and dropped all references to Marxism-Leninism. In 1992 peace was made with RENAMO, the civil war having cost more than one million lives. The next year national elections were organized which FRELIMO won. That year Mozambique participated in joint military maneuvers with the United States for the first time.

South Africa

South African military intervention in Angola and Mozambique had been provoked by growing support for the antiapartheid struggle stemming from these states, as well as the other so-called front-line states of Tanzania, Zambia, and Zimbabwe. Such external support, as well as growing economic and political isolation internationally, wore away at the apartheid regime. But the increasingly organized popular struggle within South Africa proved decisive in the collapse of the regime in the course of the 1980s.

South Africa had been a self-governing dominion of the British Empire since 1910. In practice this meant the rule of a British minority over a largely rural Afrikaner or Dutch-Calvinist population as well as an overwhelming black majority. Deeply divided between themselves, the British and Boers (Afrikaners) united around the common goals of maintaining the superiority of white labor and procuring black labor at minimum cost. Dispossessed from their tribal lands and legally prohibited from permanent residence in the towns, blacks were consigned to reserves or worked as transient labor or domestics on the farms, mines, factories, and homes of the whites. Despite such impediments, economic expansion during the Second World War led to the consolidation of an urbanized black working class.

A small mission-educated black middle class also developed, made up of teachers, lawyers, traders, clerks, and nurses. The African National Congress (ANC), founded in 1912, reflected the perspective of this latter group. It believed in the superiority of European culture and the notion of gradual economic and social enfranchisement of blacks through education. Limiting its campaigns for equality to protests and pamphlets that appealed to the liberalism of the whites, the ANC foreswore attempts to galvanize the black majority. The small Communist Party advocated a policy of mass mobilization, but went unheeded by the largely middle-class leadership of the ANC.

The Apartheid System

The aftermath of the Second World War brought dramatic change. In 1948, the party of the Afrikaners, the Nationalists, won a convincing electoral victory. For the Afrikaners, electoral success signified their triumph against both the hated British and the black majority. In order to insure future white supremacy over the blacks, the new Nationalist government then instituted its program of apartheid or separate development. Building on previous acts of exclusion, apartheid consisted of a comprehensive system of racial segregation in employment, education, residence, land ownership, marriage, and sexual relations. Enforcement included the right to search without a warrant, detention without trial, and the suspension of habeas corpus. From 1952, it included a comprehensive pass law system that permitted close police control over the movement of blacks throughout the country. In 1959 the Bantu Self-Government Act updated previous laws governing reserves and restricted black rights to own land outside such so-called self-governing homelands.

Black South Africans vehemently opposed these policies of so-called separate development. As far as they were concerned, the establishment of so-called Bantustans was an attempt to retribalize and divide the black population and to deny the role that blacks played in national development. By design, such Bantustans were neither politically nor economically independent.

Emergence of Black Resistance

Faced with intensified repression, the ANC began to abandon its traditional policies of petition and peaceful protest. In 1949, it adopted a so-called action program promising more militant resistance. The Communist Party was banned in 1950. It went underground with many of its members subsequently becoming prominent in the ANC. The growing links between the Communist Party and the ANC reinforced the latter's militancy. ANC ties with the South Indian and colored communities also grew stronger. In response to the pass law, the ANC, together with the Indian Congress, launched a campaign of defiance in 1952. After several months of civil disobedience, rioting broke out in several cities resulting in 40 deaths and major property damage. In 1955 the ANC proclaimed the Freedom Charter calling for political democracy, land redistribution, and the nationalization of certain key industries.

The Sharpeville Massacre

The Sharpeville Massacre polarized the situation more deeply. In 1959 young black militants broke away from the ANC to form the Pan-African Congress. Espousing the cause of black nationalism, they rejected the cautious multiracial approach of the leadership of the ANC. At a mass meeting of the new organization at Sharpeville in 1960, the police shot and killed 67 protesters while wounding several hundred others. The protests and mass arrests which followed led to the banning of the ANC. The ANC and the already underground Communist Party, now closely allied, created Umkhonto we Sizwe (Spear of the Nation) to wage armed struggle against the apartheid regime.

But the next decade saw the enforcement of a kind of social peace based on massive repression and economic opportunities. Indeed, the South African economy boomed during the 1960s as foreign capital poured in, quintupling investment between 1958 and 1968. Four hundred United States corporations located in South Africa to take advantage of the cheap labor. Driven by the poverty in the homelands, rural workers poured into the shantytowns on the outskirts of the principal cities.

Militant Trade Unionism

A general strike in Durban by black workers in 1973 shattered the calm and announced the birth of an increasingly class-conscious black working population. Strikes multiplied in succeeding years. In the gold fields, the years 1975–77 were marked by strikes and disturbances which helped to drive up wages by some 11-

fold over the decade. Black miners broke into white labors' hitherto exclusive control of skilled positions in this industry. After recognition of the mineworkers union in 1982, 60 percent of miners adhered to the union. By 1985 a national union movement, the Congress of South African Trade Unions (COSATU), whose cadres were closely tied to the underground ANC and Communist Party, emerged.

Uprising in Soweto

By then popular resistance against the apartheid system had become endemic. In June 1976 tens of thousands of high school students in the Soweto suburb of Johannesburg initiated what became a national student strike. The government had announced that half of school subjects in the future would have to be taught in Afrikaans, which was seen as the language of the Boer oppressors. Black students en masse abandoned their schoolrooms. Over the next months, more than a thousand black students were killed and many thousands more were wounded and arrested by the police.

The students were inspired by the writings on colonial oppression by Franz Fanon, the works on national liberation of the leader of the national liberation struggle in Guinea-Bissau, Amilcar Cabral, and the words of U.S civil rights and black power leaders such as Martin Luther King and Malcolm X. A young student leader, Steve Biko, assumed leadership until murdered during detention by the South African police in 1977. Many black young people permanently abandoned their studies to join underground resistance groups or to receive guerrilla military training in the nearby frontline states.

Botha's Reforms

In May 1983 Prime Minister P.W. Botha introduced a constitutional amendment providing for a tricameral legislature with separate chambers for whites, Indians, and people of mixed race, the so-called coloreds. No political role was provided for blacks. White control of the office of presidency and the president's council ensured the continuation of white rule. When put to a referendum, the result was an overwhelming rejection of the amendment by the Indian and colored population. Meanwhile, in the black townships the population suffered from unprecedented levels of crime, chronic unemployment, and poor living conditions. The result was a major uprising between 1984 and 1986. Government attempts to repress the upheaval by savage acts of violence, including the use of black and white vigilantes, proved of no avail. In 1986 Botha attempted to replace some of the racially based apartheid laws with purely economic instruments for enforcing ongoing racial segregation. The hated pass law was abolished.

The Collapse of Apartheid

The tightening of the international embargo compounded the difficulties of the regime. Sanctions on South Africa had grown increasingly tough during the 1970s. However, the refusal of Great Britain and the United States to join the international embargo limited its effects. But in response to the ongoing repression, in 1986 the United States Congress passed the Comprehensive Anti-Apartheid Act overriding a veto by President Reagan. Bank loans, access to nuclear or computer technology, airline landing rights, and the sale of Krugerrand gold coins were all cut off. The internal rebellion, economic sanctions, and ongoing conflict with the frontline states had a cumulative impact. The South African economy went into a tailspin.

By 1989 the government was able to maintain a degree of order only by maintaining a continuing state of emergency, banning a number of black political and labor organizations and press censorship. National strikes, boycotts, protest marches, and sabotage were ongoing despite such prohibitions. The South African business community began to urge compromise. Botha stepped aside as President in favor of the more moderate F.W. de Klerk. In 1990 the long imprisoned leader of the ANC, Nelson Mandela, was released and the ANC as well as the Communist Party legalized. The coincident demise of the Soviet Union encouraged the Nationalist party and the white elite to hope for a liberal outcome to the end of apartheid. Prolonged and complicated bargaining ensued between the Nationalist Party and the ANC leadership. De Klerk was able to extract constitutional guarantees of the right to property and minority rights. On this basis, national elections were organized in April 1994 and the ANC, led by Mandela, won an overwhelming victory. A non-racial capitalism began to emerge in which differences based on racial discrimination were replaced by social divisions rooted in class inequality.

South Africa like the rest of Africa increasingly fell into the economic and political orbit of the United States and its Western allies. This was signaled by the acceptance by South Africa's ANC government of a 1994 IMF loan of $850 mil-

lion on condition of lowering its tariffs, cutting the state budget, and making large
cuts in public sector wages.

The United States in the Middle East

Reassertion of U.S control over Latin America and Africa during the 1980s had
occurred at relatively little cost to the United States. But securing the Middle East
with its critical oil reserves demanded a major military and political effort. The
Camp David Accords (1978) between Israel and Egypt had increased U.S influence in the region. On the other hand, the coincident Marxist revolution in
Afghanistan and subsequent Soviet invasion set off alarm bells in Washington.
The simultaneous Iranian Islamic Revolution provoked a still greater sense of
panic. With the fall of the Shah's government in Iran, Washington lost a major
strategic ally and source of oil. Far worse, the Iranian Revolution threatened to
engulf Saudi Arabia, the Persian Gulf states, Lebanon, and, possibly, the rest of
the Middle East.

Securing the Persian Gulf

The Carter administration responded by establishing a joint military task force
called the Rapid Deployment Force in February 1979. Made up initially of 50,000
troops, its purpose was to safeguard the oil supplies of the Persian Gulf. It was to
be reinforced by the presence of the new U.S. Fifth Fleet operating from its principal base of Diego Garcia in the Indian Ocean. Formally or informally the United
States was able to acquire naval or air basing rights in Oman, Kenya, Egypt, and
Saudi Arabia in addition. Carter, meanwhile, declared that an attempt by a foreign
power to gain control of the Persian Gulf would be considered an attack on the
vital interests of the United States. By 1983 the Rapid Deployment Force was
renamed United States Central Command (CENTCOM). Its complement of
220,000 personnel would rise to more than 400,000 by the end of the 1980s.

Lebanese Incursion

U.S troops conducted training exercises in Egypt in 1980 for the first time. The
next year U.S jets shot down Libyan air force planes off the coast of Libya, throwing down the gauntlet against the radical nationalist regime of Colonel Muammar

al-Qaddafi. United States marines made a foray into Lebanon in 1982 as part of a multilateral Western force in the wake of the Israeli invasion of that country. The United States subsequently reinforced this effort with military planes and ships to shore up the Maronite Christian dominated government against the predominantly Shiite opposition. The latter were increasingly inspired by a new political-military movement, Hizbollah, which was linked to the Islamic Revolution in Iran. The U.S intrusion led to the October 1983 truck bombing of the U.S military encampment in Beirut. With 241 marines dead, the Reagan administration quickly evacuated the remaining Americans, abandoning as too dangerous any plans to try to directly control events in Lebanon.

Intifada I

U.S hopes for pacifying the region received a further setback with the onset of the Intifada among the Palestinian Arabs of Gaza and the West Bank. The uprising began in a Palestinian refugee camp in the Gaza strip and soon spread throughout Gaza and the West Bank, including East Jerusalem. Mainly young protestors attacked the Israeli occupation soldiers with stones and Molotov cocktails. The latter responded with tear gas and bullets. The Intifada stemmed from 20 years of Palestinian frustration and humiliation under Israeli occupation. Their rights to land and water were increasingly threatened by the encroaching Israelis who used the Palestinians as a source of cheap labor. A downturn in the Israeli economy, as well as economic difficulties throughout the Middle East, led to growing unemployment and declining wages. The Palestinian capacity to engage in mass struggle, meanwhile, had been strengthened under the Occupation by the development of trade unions, students groups, and women's associations. Young educated Palestinians assumed the lead, taking over leadership from an older generation of notables who had sought accommodation with the Israeli occupation authorities. During its first four years, the Intifada cost more than 1,400 Palestinian lives with 90,000 or a sixth of all Palestinian males arrested.

Unrest in Saudi Arabia

The Islamic Revolution in Iran and the Soviet invasion of Afghanistan threatened no Middle East state more than the conservative Saudi monarchy. The call from Tehran to overthrow corrupt pro-U.S regimes found an echo among the Shiite population of the eastern Saudi provinces. Indeed, it found resonance in the Saudi population at large who were deeply pious, conservative, and anti-Western. In 1979, an armed uprising at Mecca by more than 300 Islamic militants led by a Sunni extremist, Juheiman al Utaiba, had to be quelled by the Saudi army.

But the Saudi monarchy was not without its own means of defense. The unprecedented hike in oil revenues as a result of the OPEC price hikes of the previous decade gave it immense resources. The economies and governments of neighboring Arab states, including Egypt, felt the attraction of Saudi money. Hundreds of thousands of middle- and working-class Arabs from Egypt and the rest of the Arab world found work in Saudi Arabia and were able to remit money from the Kingdom to their needy families.

The Waning of Radical Arab Nationalism

In the meantime, the influence of radical nationalism, which had dominated the Arab world in the 1950s and 1960s, began to wane. In the wake of the Arab defeat in 1967, many intellectuals and other elements of the Arab middle class turned to Islam. The persistence of patriarchal and authoritarian attitudes in many Islamic countries proved fertile ground for such a turn. Not that radical nationalist regimes had not had some success. In Baathist Iraq and Syria, state-directed economic development had eliminated landlord domination, strengthened the independent peasantry, nationalized the oil industry, fostered the development of a certain amount of industry, promoted legal equality between men and women, and created a national education system. But the Baath regimes in these two states were repressive and, along with the other Arab states, were unable to cope with Zionism. In Egypt and Algeria the radical nationalist regimes proved incapable of dealing with the problem of mass poverty among the urban poor and peasantry or creating the basis for sustained economic development. Indeed, leadership in these two countries devolved on a state bureaucracy and a military and economic elite dedicated to preserving their own political power.

Rise of Islamic Fundamentalism

As a result of such disappointments, from the 1970s onward some of the middle class and the poor increasingly put their hopes in religion. The Saudi monarchy did all that it could to foster this reorientation. Whatever Islamic extremists of middle-class origin might think of the Saudi princes, they were deeply committed to the Wahabbi conservative form of Sunni Islam. The Saudi regime began to funnel large amounts of money to conservative Sunni Islamic educational and charitable institutions all over the Islamic and Arab world. A kind of Sunni fundamentalism arose in competition with Shiite radicalism. Some Sunnis were drawn to fundamentalist Islamic groups dedicated to the idea of transforming all of the Arab states into radical Islamic states.

The Saudi regime provided refuge and funding to the Muslim Brotherhood, which had been outlawed in Egypt under Nasser. The Pro-U.S Sadat regime that succeeded Nasser turned a blind eye to the Brotherhood's activities, while the Saudi government supported its charitable and educational activities. The Brotherhood was able to restore its influence at al-Azhar University, considered the official theological center of Islam. The modus vivendi between the Brotherhood and the Sadat government fell apart as a result of the growing disparity between rich and poor in the country, as well as Egypt's conclusion of the Camp David Accords with Israel. Sadat was assassinated in 1981 and many of the thousands arrested in the aftermath were members of the Brotherhood. Nonetheless, Egypt during the 1980s became a hotbed of Sunni fundamentalism and radical Islamic groups, including al Gamaat al Islamiya and al Jihad al Islami.

Mujahidin in Afghanistan

With U.S support, Saudi Arabia and Egypt played important roles in organizing the resistance to the Soviet-backed government in Afghanistan. Various local Afghan religious and ethnic groups had begun to organize resistance against the urban-based Communist regime as early as 1978. A plethora of so-called armed *qaums*, groups reflecting different ethnic, regional, and religious loyalties, emerged in the countryside in opposition to the Marxist centralized state. They were then reinforced by an inflow of mujahidin or jihadi fighters from Saudi Arabia and Egypt. In addition, Saudi Arabia and Egypt supplied arms and money to the developing resistance.

The Role of Pakistan

From the 1970s, Saudi financial support also flowed into the founding of a network of madrasas or religious schools throughout Pakistan. These tuition-free academies inspired by Sunni fundamentalism recruited the sons of poor Afghan or Pakistani peasants many of whom ended up as mujahidin. It was the Pakistan Inter-Services Intelligence (ISI) that organized the training, arming, and combat of the mujahidin in Afghanistan. Since independence Pakistan has fought three disastrous wars against India, its powerful neighbor. The war of 1971 led to the secession of heavily populated East Pakistan region (Bangladesh). Despite its abysmal military record, the Pakistani armed forces remained the most important national institution holding what was left of the country together. In fact, the army had ruled Pakistan during half the period since independence in 1947. Parliamentary politics, such as they were, were a faction-ridden and corrupt game of the political elites. Riven by ethnic conflicts and dominated by corrupt land-lords, the peasants for the most part were abysmally poor. Per capita GDP at about $2,000 was 20 percent lower than that of India's. Save for the progress of cotton manufacture, industrial progress had been almost nil. Economic and military aid from the United States and the increasingly important trade in opium and heroin kept the country going. Water pollution, soil degradation, and desertification threatened its 150 million people with ecological disaster.

In this context, the increasingly successful Mujahidin war against the Afghan government was fully endorsed by the Pakistani army and political elite as a diversion. Overshadowed by India on the subcontinent, Pakistani military men and politicians sought to compensate by developing a sphere of influence in Afghanistan. Through Afghanistan, Pakistani religious fundamentalism, narcotics, and arms made their influence felt in the Central Asian republics and Chechnya in the post-Soviet period.

Contra War in Afghanistan

Pakistan's involvement in Afghanistan was motivated above all by the desire to ingratiate itself with the United States on which it was economically and politically dependent. Indeed, the CIA undertook to coordinate an international campaign against the Marxist-dominated government in Kabul and its Soviet protectors. As well as supplying weapons of U.S manufacture, the CIA purchased or arranged the manufacture of Soviet-style weapons from Egypt, China, Poland, and Israel for use in Afghanistan. CIA agents worked closely with Pakistani intelligence and army officers, training, deploying, and supplying the Mujahidin in Afghanistan. During the decade of the 1980s, the U.S effort cost at least $5 billion dollars. An additional $2 billion came from Saudi Arabia.

The Soviet-backed Afghan regime attempted to save itself by abandoning land reform, building mosques, playing up to Pashtun and Baluchi nationalism, and bribing tribal leaders. As part of Gorbachev's abandonment of Soviet support for wars of national liberation, Gorbachev recalled Soviet troops in 1989. Without Soviet support, the Marxist-led government in Kabul fell to a coalition army of mujahidin fighters in the spring of 1992. More than one million Afghans had died in the fourteen years of war. But the fall of the Marxists did not end the conflict. The seven or eight rival groups of mujahidin began to fight bitterly for power between themselves.

The Iran-Iraq War

While bent on destroying Soviet influence in Afghanistan, the United States also took the lead in bringing the Islamic Revolution in Iran to heel. The Baathist regime in Iraq became its chosen instrument. During the 1970s, the Iraqi government had carried out major economic and social development programs based on windfall profits from its nationalized oil industry. Power in Iraq during that decade gradually devolved on Saddam Hussein, who, in 1979, ousted his rival Ahmad Hassan Bakr as chair of the Revolutionary Command Council.

Iraq and Iran had had ongoing disputes over the treatment of the Kurdish minorities in their respective countries. In addition, control over the right bank of the mouth of the Tigris and Euphrates rivers was disputed. But it was the Islamic Revolution in Iran that brought matters to a head between the two states. Iranian Shiite fundamentalism fundamentally challenged the secular and nationalist basis of Baathist power in Iraq. Sixty percent of Iraqis were of Shiite origin and resented Baathist and Sunni domination. Taking advantage of the struggle for power in Iran between religious and Marxist revolutionaries, Saddam Hussein launched a surprise attack against Iran in September 1980.

The Iraqi army attacked all across the frontier, focusing on the oil-rich province of Khuzistan to the east of the mouth of the Tigris and Euphrates. Some 10,000 square miles of Iranian territory were occupied, Hussein claiming that he had taken back Arab land from the Persian Iranians. The invasion created a surge of patriotism in Iran, unifying the mass of the population around the Khomeini regime. Faced with stiffening resistance, the Iraqis hesitated to push forward for fear of unacceptably heavy losses.

In the long run the patriotic and religious zeal of the Iranians and their three-to-one numerical advantage determined the course of the war. Between November 1981 and May 1982 the Iranians slowly drove the Iraqis back. In order to keep popular support, Saddam Hussein endeavored to pursue a guns-and-butter policy in Iraq. But ongoing military reverses and growing economic difficulties set off Shiite unrest in Iraq in May 1982. The next month Iraq announced a withdrawal of its forces to the internationally recognized frontier.

In the face of persistent Iranian assaults, Iraq then offered a cease-fire. The Iranians, however, were determined to press forward. The Iranians seemed unanimous in their determination to punish the infidel Saddam Hussein for invading Iran. Indeed, the war was helping Khomeini to consolidate his regime at home. Moreover, the dream of spreading the Islamic Revolution abroad to other Muslim countries remained a vivid one. In the meantime, the continuing high international price of oil made the continuation of the conflict possible. Having liberated Iranian territory, the Iranian army crossed the Iraqi border in July 1982.

The Soviet Union had long been the principal backer of the Iraqi regime. Soviet military equipment, training, and advisors were the heart of Iraq's defense. Now fearing that an Iranian triumph would destabilize the whole region, France and West Germany stepped up their military, economic, and intelligence assistance to the Iraqis. The United States, under cover, provided billions of dollars worth of conventional weapons, technology used for the production of chemical weapons, and intelligence and targeting assistance. Financial aid from the Saudis and other Persian Gulf oil states further helped to shore up the Iraqi government. Fearing the Islamic Revolution, these states ultimately provided $55 billion in loans to Iraq.

From July 1982 to 1987 Iran attempted to break through Iraqi defenses. The Iraqis staved off Iranian human wave assaults by building successive heavily fortified trenches, by launching air attacks on Iranian cities, ports, and oil facilities, and by using chemical weapons. In the spring of 1986, Saudi Arabia and Kuwait flooded the oil markets driving the price of oil to ten dollars per barrel. Iran's ability to finance the war was hit hard by the consequent fall in oil prices. Iraq in contrast was cushioned by loans from these same states. Nonetheless, in the first part of 1987, Iranian offensives nearly captured the key Iraqi town of Basra in the south, while taking part of Iraqi Kurdistan in the north. In July, a Kuwaiti oil tanker under U.S protection hit a mine said to have been planted by the Iranians. The subsequent naval buildup by the United States and its allies brought 60 warships into the Persian Gulf region. By fall the U.S navy was launching strikes on Iranian ships, port facilities, and oil installations. At the beginning of 1988, an Iraqi counteroffensive was able to recover lost territories. On July 3, the United States shot down an Iranian air liner carrying 290 passengers on the way to Mecca. In fear of an all-out confrontation with the United States, Khomeini reluctantly decided to bring an end to the hostilities. On August 20, a United Nations truce brought the conflict to an end.

Iraq Invades Kuwait

The material cost of the Iran-Iraq war was estimated at $250 billion. It is believed that as many as 350,000 combatants died in what had been the longest conventional war of the twentieth century. Iranian ambitions had been curbed, but the aspirations of Saddam Hussein had if anything been whetted by this pointless and wasteful conflict. Iraq's military had expanded to about 1.6 million men equipped with some 4500 tanks and 400 combat aircraft. It had held off the Iranian enemy and even won some victories toward the end of the conflict. In his own eyes at least, Saddam Hussein's credentials to become the leader of the Arab world had been enhanced.

The Iraqis, along with many other middle-class and working-class Arabs throughout the region, were generally contemptuous of the oil-rich feudal and tribal monarchies of the Gulf. Iraq's relations with its neighbor Kuwait were particularly tense. Iraq alleged illegal Kuwaiti siphoning of Iraqi oil and chafed at Kuwait's refusal to lease two small Persian Gulf islands to Iraq. As the Kuwaiti monarchy faced mounting democratic agitation from within, Saddam Hussein decided to assert his leadership of the Arab world by launching an attack on Kuwait.

The First Gulf War

The Iraqi invasion of Kuwait of August 2, 1990, could not have been more miscalculated. Based on conversations with the U.S ambassador, Saddam Hussein mistakenly assumed that the United States would grudgingly accept Iraq as regional hegemon. On the contrary, Washington's establishment of CENTCOM and its military buildup during the 1980s were designed for just such an eventuality as the Iraq invasion of Kuwait. Indeed, the United States during the 1980s had begun to put the Vietnam syndrome behind it. Its arms buildup, low intensity warfare campaigns, and structural adjustment programs were in the process of restoring or extending U.S. control over Latin America and Africa. Moreover, at the beginning of the 1990s the Soviet Union, which had long been the military and political patron of Iraq, was in the throes of disintegration. The invasion of Kuwait—and the prospect of defeating Iraq—offered the United States the perfect occasion to establish once and for all its dominance over the oil-rich Middle East. Indeed, it was to become the moment for the assertion by George H. W. Bush of a New World Order based on U.S leadership. As the single world power in the post-Cold War, the United States would assert its dominance by organizing a multilateral military and political coalition to expel Iraq from Kuwait.

On August 2, the UN Security Council unanimously condemned the Iraqi attack and demanded immediate withdrawal. A subsequent UN resolution imposed sanctions on the Iraqi government. In succeeding months, the UN military buildup in the Persian Gulf reached nearly 700,000 service personnel. A total of 28 other states joined the U.S.-led coalition, including 220,000 troops from Muslim and Arab states. Joining the coalition became a test of fealty to the new dominant world power. The decline of the Soviet Union even led to a rapprochement between Washington and Syria, long held to be a terrorist state by the U.S State Department. The United States de facto accepted Syrian hegemony over Lebanon as a way of ending Lebanon's 15-year-long civil war while enlisting Syrian help against Iraq.

Hostilities opened with a month-long air campaign by the United States and its allies against Iraq between January 16 and February 24, 1991. It then took just three days for the ground assault of the U.S.-led coalition to expel Iraq from Kuwait. On February 27, Iraq announced that it had completed its military evacuation of Kuwait, while some 640 Kuwaiti oil wells were set on fire. The estimated financial cost of the coalition effort was some $82 billion, of which the United States had to pay only $18 billion.

Indeed, the gain for the United States was immense. Its dominance over the Middle East and its petroleum resources was now incontestable. Likewise, its post-Cold War role as global hegemon was also confirmed. Iraq, meanwhile, had suffered the loss of an estimated 100,000 soldiers. Damage to Iraq's infrastructure from the bombing was put at $200 billion. United Nations economic sanctions on Iraq were continued, subject to an inspection regime entailing the destruction of weapons of mass destruction and missiles. Iraqi no-fly zones were instituted over the Kurdish and Shiite areas of the north and south. Iraq was to be permanently weakened and kept off-balance. Washington at this point rejected the idea of occupying Iraq and removing Saddam Hussein as too destabilizing. It settled rather for indefinite containment of both Iraq and Iran through a regional balance of power under overall U.S control.

8

Toward Empire

The dominance of neoliberal ideology and policies hardened in the early 1990s into a new global order. Political and social questions receded in importance. Politics were seen as a market constraint that might be made to "wither away." This would be done not through the socialist agenda of Karl Marx and Frederick Engels, but through the liberal prescriptions of Adam Smith and David Ricardo. The problem of poverty would be resolved by the creation of wealth. An economistic discourse exalting liberalism as part of the natural and inescapable order of things formed the framework of both higher learning and popular culture across the globe. In the United States and United Kingdom, of course, but even in France, Italy, and much of Latin America, neoliberalism's economic logic was disseminated by academics, the press, and the so-called talking heads who controlled an increasingly narrow political discussion on television and radio. Where once students at the Sorbonne, the focal point of May 1968, had avidly read *L'Humanité* or *Autogestion*, they now bought the British *Financial Times* as their morning paper. In the states of the underdeveloped world, think tanks, policy networks, university chairs, and non-governmental organizations—all largely paid for by the United States and the World Bank—promoted neoliberalism and the rule of law. In popular culture and society at large, status seeking and vulgar consumerism became the norms of global aspiration as purveyed by television, film, and corporate advertising.

The Clinton Presidency

Despite his Gulf War triumph, George H. W. Bush, the Republican incumbent, was defeated in the 1992 U.S presidential election. His failure to fully revive the

U.S economy from the recession of 1990–91 was to blame for his defeat. But the victorious Democratic candidate, Bill Clinton, proved even more committed to liberal market orthodoxy than Bush. He made only token gestures to the U.S working class. Under Clinton the minimum wage was raised from $4.25 to $5.15 an hour, still 35 percent below the real value of the minimum wage in 1968. Clinton's Democratic administration largely dismantled welfare programs for the poor. Pruning the budgetary deficit, lowering market interest rates, and opening overseas markets to U.S business became the economic goals of the Clinton presidency. The Democratic administration pulled out all the stops in pressing for global free trade in such key sectors as financial services and information and communications technology, as well as in the protection of intellectual property rights. Market-driven growth was considered the key to job creation and the reduction of poverty among the working class.

Neoliberalism in Europe and Asia

In Europe, neoliberal ideas became increasingly important among decision makers, even on the social democratic left. No frontal attack on the Keynesian state or social welfare occurred on the continent, but the European Union's Maastricht Treaty (1993) established a central bank, enabling the implementation of a fiscal and regulatory regime biased in the direction of neoliberalism. The EU's Stability and Growth Pact (SGP), concluded at Dublin at the end of 1997, stipulated that government deficits should not exceed 3 percent of GDP. Accompanied by sanctions, the SGP was an important tool for implementing neoliberal policies, including reducing the role of the state and fiscal restructuring in favor of private enterprise and high-income individuals.

Governments dominated by social democrats proved useful in facilitating the acceptance of such prescriptions at the level of the national state. The socialist Lionel Jospin's coalition government, which came to power in France in 1997, for example, privatized and deregulated the economy to a degree the previous right-wing French government thought politically impossible. That same year in Britain, when the Labour government of Tony Blair took power from the Conservatives, it abolished Labour's commitment to public ownership and committed itself to the so-called third way: social democracy within the limits of neoliberalism.

Even governments in Asia were forced to pay lip service to the neoliberal agenda. Under U.S prodding, many were forced to liberalize rules governing the entry and exit of short-term foreign investments. In India during the 1990s, the economy was for the first time opened to foreign competition and investment. The turning point came during a 1991 debt crisis provoked by an oil price shock and the collapse of remittances from workers in the Persian Gulf. The IMF then provided loans to India subject to neoliberal conditions. These reforms were welcomed by neoliberal economists, expatriate Indian entrepreneurs, and domestic business owners, many of whom were nouveaux riches frustrated by government regulation and attracted by foreign technology and the prospects of international cooperation. But along with private corporations and the financial and business networks of wealthy families, the state's role in the economy still remained important in Asia.

Capitalism in Eastern Europe

In the wake of the collapse of centralized planning in Russia and the rest of Eastern Europe, neoliberalism became the dominant ideology throughout the region. Western economic advisers as well as local policy and opinion makers touted its virtues as a panacea to be swallowed quickly and in the largest possible dose. This so-called crash course toward capitalism led to economic chaos and the looting of wealth on a vast scale in the name of privatization. This was justified as the price to be paid for normalizing the economy in a capitalist sense and integrating with the global market as quickly as possible. It produced a massive regression in economic output in the former Soviet Union and elsewhere in Eastern Europe.

While growth has resumed in some of these former communist states, the initial economic regression has still not been made up. Yet in the midst of chaos and decline in agriculture and industry, an Eastern European middle class has slowly emerged from the ruins. Dependent on the state to a greater or lesser degree and given to shady dealing, its ability to produce solid economic growth based on private capital investment remains in doubt. The apologists of this new ruling class fanatically promote the free market as key to future prosperity, while most of the population has been plunged back to a level of poverty perhaps worse than before the Second World War. The subsidies and public services provided during the communist years have all but disappeared. Insecurity, unemployment, social inequality, and regional disparity have induced a deep malaise.

Global Stagnation and Inequality

The rhetoric of neoliberalism promised that the unfettered market would produce high growth rates worldwide. Removing political and social constraints would unleash rapid economic progress. The free market would be the nostrum that would cure the economic stagnation of the 1970s and 1980s. But in reality, growth rates in the 1990s remained markedly lower than during the golden years of the 1950s and 1960s. Indeed, global growth in the 1990s (2.3 percent) was lower than the already modest increase of the 1980s (3.1 percent). Per capita global growth in fact averaged a pitiful 1 percent over the decade. Inequality grew worldwide between 1980 and 2000, especially between the very top and bottom of the population. Excepting China, inequality grew by 19 percent between the richest and poorest 10 percents of the global population. It increased by 77 percent with respect to the richest and poorest 1 percents of the world's population. In 1980 the income of the advanced capitalist countries, in proportion to their population, was 11 times greater than the rest of the world. By 2000, it was 20 times larger. At the beginning of the new millennium, the richest 20 percent of the globe's population enjoyed 82.7 percent of the world's income with the bottom 60 percent left holding a mere 5.6 percent. Although the lot of the very poor improved in China, even there inequality increased.

Among the advanced countries, the United States and the United Kingdom led in the race toward inequality. Over the period 1977–99, the real income of the poorest 20 percent in the United States decreased by 9 percent. Meanwhile, the top 20 percent over the same period increased their incomes by 43 percent. Indeed, the incomes of the upper 1 percent of Americans grew by 115 percent. In the United Kingdom, matters were as bad or worse. Excluding the value of housing, the bottom 50 percent of the population had 12 percent of the wealth in 1976. In 2005, they enjoyed 1 percent of the wealth. In an era of relative economic stagnation, the wealthy worldwide have maintained and even strengthened themselves by aggregating more and more income from the rest of society, especially from the poor. If these trends induced by neoliberalism are not interrupted, social and economic polarization in these countries as well as elsewhere can only increase.

The Woes of the German and Japanese Economies

It is true that, among developed countries, the United States and Great Britain enjoyed markedly higher growth than other countries. The relative success of the

English-speaking countries is accounted for by higher rates of investment resulting from sweeping economic deregulation in accord with neoliberal notions. As
part of this agenda, the 1990s saw further attacks on the wages and social benefits
of the working class and growing inequality in these two countries. Indeed,
Germany's growth lagged precisely because it did not deregulate or attack workers and the poor to the same extent. This workhorse of the European Union also
had to bear the welfare burden of the working class of East Germany whose manufacturing sector for all practical purposes collapsed as a result of reunification.

Japan had been an economic powerhouse since the 1950s. It weathered the
economic turbulence of the 1970s better than all other developed countries. In
the 1980s, it enjoyed an unprecedented financial and real estate expansion. The
rest of Asia looked to it as a market as well as a source of investment capital. But
following the collapse of this boom at the end of the 1980s, Japan fell into the
economic doldrums from which it has barely emerged. The impulse toward
Japanese economic recovery, such as it was, lay not in the U.S market, for the
first time, but in Asia. It was there that significant growth in the world economy
occurred during the 1990s. In that decade, India's growth rate was close to 6
percent per annum, while China's hovered around 12 percent. Other countries
in Asia, such as Vietnam, Cambodia, South Korea, Indonesia, Thailand, and
Malaysia, also performed well. Led by China, the countries of Asia were likely
to emerge as the most dynamic region of the global economy in the next century. But this growth is unlikely to continue without further political and economic upheaval.

Deregulation and Economic Instability

The economic model of countries such as Thailand and Indonesia was orientated mainly to foreign exports, real estate investments, and stock market speculation. Currency flight led to the 1998 financial collapse and economic deflation in
these two states, as well as in South Korea. The crisis was made worse by tight
money policies imposed by the IMF. The financial crisis spread and took on new
forms in Russia and Turkey, as well as Brazil and Argentina. When the crisis
reached the United States, the Clinton administration did all it could to try to sustain the speculative bubble. Indeed, it felt compelled to bail out Long Term
Capital Management, the single most important venture capital firm on Wall
Street, for fear of a dramatic financial panic. But this intervention only added fuel

to the speculative fires on Wall Street, which burned more and more fiercely as the century approached its end.

The financial panic of 1998 was only the latest and largest of a series of financial shocks, including, notably, the 1982 third world debt crisis, the 1987 stock market and savings and loan crises in the United States, and the subsequent Mexican default (1994–95). Deregulations of financial flows at the international and national level were largely responsible for these panics, as investors were able to move massive amounts of money with great speed from one economy or market to the next. The ongoing unregulated flow of capital around the globe, which sparked this instability, produced an alternating sense of euphoria and dread as the 1990s ended.

Globalization

The increasingly unrestricted movement of global finance and investment, the more extensive and rapid flow of information and goods, the growing availability of vast pools of cheap and educated labor in China, India, and Eastern Europe, and the deepening of the international division of labor helped to give birth to the new ideology of globalization that crystallized in the 1990s. Reflecting the perspective of the heads of some 37,000 transnational corporations, as well as internationally orientated bankers, wealthy investors, exporters of goods and services, state functionaries, and high flying, well paid media publicists and academics, this ideology based itself on the assumption of a progressively unhindered economic unification of the world. The principles of this neoliberal globalization were the unrestricted movement of money, the downsizing of the state, and the creation of an unobstructed global market for goods and services.

A Transnational Capitalist Class

In each of the advanced states, the proponents of globalization constituted the dominant fraction of the capitalist class. But even in third world countries, globalization found strong support among agro-businesses, financial groups, importers, mineral exporters, big export-orientated manufacturers, and subcontracted sweatshop owners. Indeed, the rising influence of these latter elements in underdeveloped countries was noteworthy. As recently as 1980, manufacturing exports represented only 17.7 percent of total exports from underdeveloped countries. By 1998, manufactures constituted no less than 71.6 percent of such exports. In both the underdeveloped and developed countries, a powerful block of economic and political interests had emerged in support of the program of neoliberal globalization.

Documentation of the tentative emergence of a transnational capitalist class—in 2001 there were some 7.1 million individuals worldwide with a total financial asset wealth of $26.2 trillion—can be found in the *World Wealth Report*, a publication of the Wall Street firm of Merrill Lynch. The establishment of this annual report in 1998 indicates both the emerging reality and aspirations of such a class. The Merrill Lynch report endeavors to help the wealthy in each country to begin to see themselves as part of a single class of the global rich. Globalizing institutions—the World Bank, IMF, Bank for International Settlements, Group of Seven, Organization for Economic Co-operation and Development, Trilateral Commission, and World Economic Forum—constitute the maturing institutional framework for this transnational class. The thousands of economic experts and functionaries attached to these organizations compose an emerging international bureaucracy acting as the directorate of this new class. The staggering increase in the number of cross-border corporate mergers and acquisitions over the 1990s lends further credence to the idea of such an emerging transnational class based on the international unification of capital. In this sense, neoliberalism has helped engender an increasingly self-conscious global capitalist class over the last 30 years.

The rapidly increasing number of transnational mergers and acquisitions also underlines the greater importance of financial operations in the workings of even industrial corporations in the globalizing economy. In the English-speaking countries, in particular, stockholder value or short-term return to portfolio investors has become the paramount concern of corporate managers at the expense of the long-term health of enterprises. Manufacturing corporations have become closely linked to the financial community through currency and stock speculation, initial public offerings, buy backs, stock options, and leasing and credit operations—to the neglect of making and selling real commodities. Many global corporations operate according to new organizational principles based on just-in-time inventory systems and outsourcing, which together minimize the cost of raw material inventories and labor. A classic example of outsourcing is the multibillion-dollar Nike Corporation, which owns no factories but contracts with a flexible roster of 900 subcontracting factories in more than 50 countries, which employ 660,000 workers, mainly women, to produce sportswear marketed under its globally recognized label. Increasingly, manufacturers everywhere are dependent on giant distribution chains controlled by firms such as Wal-Mart.

The United States: Champion of Globalization

During the 1990s, the major institutional advance in the direction of globalization was the 1995 creation of the World Trade Organization (WTO), which incorporated and superseded the GATT. The WTO was distinguished from its predecessor by an enforcement tribunal empowered to break down existing trade barriers on the national level. The birth of the WTO opened the way for a more extensive and deeper market with low tariffs and minimal commercial barriers. But it further aimed to advance the free flow of international capital through the implementation of the Multilateral Agreement on Investment.

The multilateral character of these globalizing institutions and agreements ought to be emphasized. Not only did this approach accord with the new ideology of globalization, but also with the internationalist approach pursued by the United States since 1945. Indeed, it was the United States that most enthusiastically embraced and promoted this new ideology during the 1990s. It perfectly harmonized with the multilateral approach that the United States took to international political conflict reflected in the First Gulf War and in the subsequent armed conflicts of the decade.

Despite the fact that the ideology of neoliberal globalization promoted a level playing field worldwide, it was the United States and the other advanced countries that stood to benefit most from its advance. During the 1990s, almost half of the 500 top multinationals were U.S-owned, with more than half of the remainder being mainly in the hands of Europeans. Interest in globalization by U.S corporations was spurred by a massive expansion of overseas investment. As recently as 1982, foreign investment by U.S. non-financial corporations totaled a little more than $200 billion. In 2006, such investment stands at more than $1.5 trillion. Notable was the rapid expansion of direct U.S. investment in Latin America. Indeed, an increasing percentage of top U.S corporations were now earning the majority of their profits overseas.

The leading institutions of globalization, such as the IMF, continued to be dominated by U.S and European experts. For the most part, such economists, monetary specialists, and bankers faithfully reflected the interests of the financial elites of the leading capitalist states. During the 1998 Asian crisis, for example, the repayment of Western banks and investors became the top priority of the experts of the IMF. Their second most important concern appeared to be opening up Asian economies to foreign direct investment, i.e., the buying up by Western investors of depressed Asian capital assets at bargain prices. Furthermore, forceful trade negotiators from the advanced capitalist countries at successive meetings of the WTO and other international trade bodies sought to impose, not a level playing field, but one in which the intellectual property rights and the agricultural products of their countries were protected while the markets of third world states were opened.

During the 1990s, the U.S. economy outpaced that of the other advanced capitalist countries. Growth was especially notable in the latter half of the decade. The relative success of the U.S economy was due in part to the high-tech boom, productivity gains, and a moderate reduction in interest rates. But growth was especially fueled by an enormous expansion of debt, dividends, and stock prices. The continued offensive of capital against labor was also important. The intimidation of labor by ongoing job insecurity and international competition reduced inflationary pressure that might have threatened profits.

The Clinton administration was also able temporarily to reduce the enormous level of government debt, accumulated by the previous Reagan and Bush administrations, by budgetary cutbacks and by banking-enhanced tax receipts. Meanwhile, consumer and corporate debt mushroomed into an enormous credit bubble. The simultaneous bubble on Wall Street and Main Street was based to some extent on enhanced profitability. But it depended even more on deregulation and corporate buybacks, which inflated values. Ongoing U.S balance of payments deficits were made up by a significant influx of overseas investment in U.S stocks and bonds, which further helped Wall Street. Mounting external debt paradoxically compelled overseas investors and exporters to sustain the value of the dollar in order to safeguard their existing U.S investments. Under the conditions of the continued supremacy of the dollar, the ever-accumulating foreign deficit expressed itself as a vast influx of foreign commodities and capital, which resembled an imperial tribute.

Financialization of Economic Life

The ratio of debt—bonds, shares, bank loans, and mortgages—to GDP reached ten times in the United States and in other Group of Seven countries during the

1990s, up dramatically from previous decades. The huge expansion of financial assets became completely delinked from growth in the stock of fixed capital, which, although expanding, tended to lag way behind. Indeed, it seems that the initial ballooning of financial assets came about as a result of the lack of the opportunity for reinvestment of profits generated in the productive parts of the economy. Eventually financial profits were extracted at the expense of profits in the productive economy. In other words, net overall industrial profits were kept depressed over time by the burden of debt and dividend payouts. The progressive deregulation of finance capital, both at the national and the international level, started with the 1971 floating of the U.S dollar by Nixon. Over the succeeding decades, finance capital came to dominate productive and industrial capital. Banks and investment, pension, and mutual funds, whose worldwide economic and political power increased dramatically in the course of the 1990s, held most of this debt.

The Burden of Third World Debt

Mounting levels of private and public debt posed problems for the economic future of first world countries. But in the 1990s, the effects of accumulated debt were felt most acutely in the underdeveloped countries, many of which still labored under the IMF structural adjustment programs imposed during the debt crisis of the early 1980s. The problem of debt was seen by neoliberal economists to be the result of market distortions in the economies of these countries. Loans were conditioned on the correction of these conditions by the introduction of neoliberal austerity measures. Far from eliminating the debt problem in the underdeveloped countries as promised under structural adjustment, the debt crisis worsened over the two succeeding decades. In 1982 the external debt of the underdeveloped countries totaled $500 billion. By the end of the 1990s, such debt amounted to $1.8 trillion.

The mounting debt problem is illustrated by the case of Latin America. At the beginning of the debt crisis in the early 1980s, outstanding external Latin U.S debt totaled $257 billion. By 1998, this total stood at $698 billion. Annual interest payments, largely to U.S. banks, represented a huge drain of capital out of Latin America. In 1995 alone, these banks received $67.5 billion in interest from Latin American countries. Over the decade of the 1990s, they received more than $600 billion. At enormous social and economic cost, 30 percent of Latin

America's total export earnings went to pay this sum. The situation of sub-Saharan Africa was even worse. During the 1990s, the states of this region transferred $105 billion in debt repayments to their major creditors in Europe and the United States. Despite this heavy schedule of repayments, the debt burden increased rather than decreased. The debt of the sub-Saharan states stood at $335 billion as of 2002. Furthermore, 65 percent of the increase in debt since 1988 was due not to new borrowing, but the result of accumulated interest.

Under the aegis of structural adjustment and neoliberalism, the economies of the underdeveloped countries have fared poorly. Excluding China, their average overall growth rate declined from 5.5 percent (1961–80) to 2.6 percent (1981–99). Their average per capita rate of growth over the same period declined from 3.2 to 0.7 percent. Economic growth in sub-Saharan Africa largely stagnated. That region's share of world trade between 1990 and 2000 fell from 3 to 1 percent. The intrusion of Western food and manufactured exports tended to bankrupt local producers. Local or international financing was almost impossible to obtain. Privatization of state industries under structural adjustment provided little capital, while there was an ongoing flight of capital, especially from South Africa. Almost everywhere, educational, health, and social services deteriorated or disappeared.

Crisis in Africa

Under the stress of structural adjustment, the 1990s in Africa were marked by widespread political instability. The massacre of Tutsis in Rwanda, successive invasions of the Congo by neighboring countries, and civil wars in Liberia and Sierra Leone were the tip of the iceberg. Ethnic strife, civil war, and coups troubled Burundi, Chad, Guinea-Bissau, the Republic of Congo, Mali, Niger, Namibia, Togo, Sudan, and Uganda. Soldiers, smugglers, refugees, and migrants increasingly ignored state frontiers as the political capacity of governments withered. Mercenary armies of the pauperized young became a menace to many African governments and the population at large. Economic collapse and political disorder left many governments at the mercy of European and U.S entrepreneurs. The interests of forestry companies and diamond traffickers, for example, lay behind the destabilization of Liberia, Sierra Leone, and Congo during the 1990s. The international oil companies played an increasingly important role in determining the politics of the oil-rich states of West Africa, as well as Sudan. As a result of ongoing political instability, tens of thousands of sub-Saharan Africans were displaced into refuge camps. Close to half of the population lived on less than a dollar a day. High infant and child mortality killed 20 percent of children before the age of five. The spread of AIDS and other tropical diseases threatened the demographic future of the African population.

Most distressing of all, perhaps, was the turn of events in South Africa in the wake of apartheid's end. Its highly developed industrialized economy and great natural wealth had the potential to pull out of poverty not only South Africa's own population but also the rest of sub-Saharan Africa as well. Yet the first act of the interim ANC-dominated government in 1993 was to accept an IMF loan that called for lower import tariffs, cuts in state spending, and large cuts in public sector wages. Joblessness doubled from 16 to 30 percent between 1995 and 2002. Black nationalists took possession of the South African state, while the white upper class and private corporations were left to enjoy complete freedom in the use of capital both at home and abroad. The low incomes of the black majority plummeted, while those of whites rose. Privatization of water and electricity made basic services largely unavailable to millions of black families. Class tensions made South Africa a kind of pressure-cooker society, marked by high crime rates and violence. At the same time, the IMF, World Bank, and the United States used the South African state increasingly as a proxy between themselves and the rest of impoverished Africa. In the early twenty-first century, strikes, indigenous rights campaigns, and local so-called IMF riots in various African states, as well as the growing attachment of African militants and radical intellectuals to the global justice movement, signaled an increasing willingness to resist neoliberal policies.

Impact of Neoliberalism in the Third World

The effects of structural adjustment and neoliberalism on underdeveloped countries were summed up in a report entitled *Structural Adjustment Participatory Review Initiative,* which was published in 2001 by a coalition of some 250 nongovernmental organizations worldwide. It concluded that trade and financial liberalization had devastated local industries. Structural reforms in agriculture and mining had undermined small farms, weakened food security, and harmed the environment. Labor market reforms and the undermining of local labor-intensive activity had caused unemployment, lower wages, and a weakening of workers' rights. Privatization and user fees had reduced access to services such as health and education. Increased impoverishment had especially damaged the situation of women. Many of the supposed benefits in efficiency, competitiveness, and economic growth had failed to materialize. Both current account deficits and external debt had increased.

Structural Adjustment in Latin America

Structural adjustment led to negative economic and social outcomes in Latin America. Under the neoliberal regime, social welfare and protectionist barriers to the operation of the market were largely dismantled. Public assets were privatized and foreign investment welcomed. An influx of short-term U.S investment and direct takeovers of public or private firms produced little capital formation, but dramatically increased the flow of profits from Latin American to the United States.

During the so-called lost decade of the 1980s, overall economic growth in Latin America was only 1 percent per annum. It rose to 2.7 percent between 1990 and 1998 to drop again to 1 percent between 1998 and 2003. The share of wages as a part of national income fell from 40 to 20 percent. Massive unemployment led to the spread of the so-called informal sector or primitive markets. Perhaps 60 percent of the population was poor, with 26 percent living on less than two dollars a day. Despite economic stagnation, the upper class, made up of perhaps 15 or 20 percent of the population, aggregated huge new wealth at the expense of the rest. A substantial fraction of this wealth came from the narcotics trade.

Populist Reaction in Latin America

In Africa, state authority and a sense of class were typically weak. Under such conditions, it has proved difficult to generate an effective response to the ravages of neoliberal globalization. It was otherwise in Latin America. There, state structures and organized class struggle had a long history, and thus the potential existed for a political response to neoliberalism. The postwar period had seen an initial wave of Latin American political and social protest dating from the Cuban Revolution in 1959 until the imposition of military dictatorships in the Southern Cone in the early 1970s. From the late 1970s until 1991, a second wave of unrest welled up in the states of Central America. In the aftermath of these upheavals, the Cuban Revolution and the insurgency in Colombia remained as focal points of ongoing political and military resistance to Washington. The imposition of neoliberal policies in the 1990s generated a third and still wider surge of political protest. The decade saw the proliferation throughout Latin America of a great variety of popular social movements whose thrust was anti-imperialist.

Indigenous and Peasant Revolts

The first to receive international attention was the so-called Zapatista revolt of 1994 in southern Mexico. Based in the southernmost Mexican state of Chiapas, its masked leader, Subcomandante Marcos, demanded recognition of the land rights and political and cultural autonomy of the indigenous peasantry in the face of landowners, the Mexican state, and international capital. In Ecuador, Peru, and Bolivia, peasant movements based on the indigenous peoples also challenged neoliberal governments backed by the United States. Agricultural imports from the latter and the development of agro-business threatened peasant survival. The organizational capacity, endurance, and innovative tactics of these continuing movements were surprising. Entrenchment of peasant power at the grassroots became the springboard for challenges to state power at the national level. Local struggles over immediate grievances such as land or human rights became the basis for national mobilizations and international solidarity campaigns.

The development of the peasant movement in Bolivia culminated in September 2003 in a great uprising that led to the overthrow of President Gonzalo Sanchez de Lozada. Known as the "American President," Sanchez de Lozada spearheaded a drive to sell off Bolivia's huge oil and gas reserves to the United States and other foreign investors. The widespread popular mobilization, in which the majority indigenous population played a prominent part, forced the president's resignation and flight to the United States. The grassroots movement in Bolivia based itself on peasant leagues, coca farmers, and aboriginal organizations. These rural bodies created increasingly close alliances with miners, the poor, and trade unionists in the principal cities. Following the ouster of Sanchez de Lozada, a renewed attempt to sell hydrocarbon assets to private foreign investors led to the development of even broader national protests in the spring of 2005. Carlos Mesa, Sanchez de Lozada's successor, was forced to resign. Many protest leaders demanded the nationalization of all hydrocarbon resources. In December Evo Morales, the aboriginal leader of the Movement Toward Socialism (MAS), was elected president. There were disturbing signs of capitulation to local business and landlord interests as well as to Brazilian and European oil and gas corporations. But Morales in time would have to reckon with the ongoing demands of the popular movements, which have not demobilized.

Ecuador

A parallel evolution was seen in Ecuador where, by the late 1990s, an oil boom had ended in recession amid a runaway inflation. An IMF-imposed stabilization package included privatization, increased prices on basic commodities including fuel, and the adoption of the U.S. dollar as national currency. Mounting popular protest, especially among the indigenous majority, led to a military coup in 2000 that deposed President Jamil Mahuad. Colonel Lucio Guttiérez played a prominent role in the coup and was elected president in 2003 with the backing of left-wing parties. Turning his back on his followers, Guttiérez opted to impose another IMF austerity package, to pass laws threatening indigenous land rights, and to allow the establishment of a major U.S military presence. Renewed nationwide popular protests in April 2005 led to Guttiérez's removal from office and flight to Brazil. By late summer, output of oil was interrupted by popular demands in the oil-producing regions for a more equitable division of the nation's hydrocarbon wealth. Deepening peasant and worker unrest made the future of Ecuador look increasingly like that of Bolivia. The steadily rising international price of oil was creating growing unrest not only in Ecuador, but also in other poverty stricken oil-producing nations. Indeed, the relationship between recent civil conflict and oil and gas resources is widespread, as witnessed in states such as Nigeria, Sudan, Angola, Yemen, Iraq, Colombia, Indonesia, Algeria, and Congo-Brazzaville. Possession of such resources has been correlated negatively as well with economic growth and the reduction of poverty.

Lula in Brazil

In Brazil, as well as in the Andes, peasant unrest spearheaded resistance to the ravages of neoliberalism. By the 1990s, Brazil's Movement of the Landless (MST) had seized many large estates and redistributed the land to tens of thousands of peasant families. The Workers Party also became a national force in the 1990s. Its rise was based on working-class dissatisfaction with an IMF-imposed austerity program that had impoverished millions of Brazilians while only increasing Brazil's staggering external debt. The Workers Party was able to elect a former metal worker, Luiz Inacio da Silva (Lula), as president in 2002. Unfortunately, the election of Lula coincided with the exhaustion of the political energy of the popular movement and a growing debt crisis induced by nervous Brazilian investors. Forced to compromise with regional agro-export interests, the national middle class, and the IMF, the capacity of Lula to redistribute land and income was compromised. He was able to offer only better government within terms laid down by the Brazilian business elite and the IMF. Political activists, trade unionists, and peasant leaders became increasingly critical as Lula's presidency evolved. On the other hand, the Brazilian president has tried to strengthen the Latin American free trade organization known as MERCOSUR in the face of U.S hostility. He has notably extended Brazil's economic and political reach to China, the Middle East, Africa, and Europe and extended a protective hand toward Cuba. Without confronting the United States directly, Lula's aim seemed to be to distance Brazil from Washington's economic orbit and to move it and the rest of Latin America toward playing a much more independent role in the global economy.

Argentina

In Argentina the military dictatorship ended in 1983. But successive governments were forced to deal with a crushing load of external debt under an IMF-imposed structural adjustment program. The official poverty rate went from 8 to 40 percent during the 1980s. Argentina's stock of machinery and equipment shrank by 35 percent during the same decade. Austerity reached its peak during the presidency of the Peronist Carlos Menem (1989–99). Menem sold off state assets, checked the power of organized labor, welcomed foreign investment and imports, and tied the currency to the dollar. Indeed, the availability of credit was directly linked to the ability of the economy to attract dollars. Inequality, unemployment, and poverty increased, while speculators and multinational corporations had a field day. By 1997 Argentina fell into economic depression and Menem was disgraced by the consequences of his policies and by accusations of personal corruption. With poverty levels at 52 percent, massive food riots and a general strike of the middle and working classes and the poor forced the flight of Menem's successor, Fernando de la Rua, and Finance Minister Domingo Carvallo at the end of 2001. Under its new president, Néstor Kirchner, Argentina abandoned its neoliberal policies and distanced itself from further involvement with the IMF. A modest and uncertain economic recovery based on a revival of demand for Argentina's exports has occurred. But the structural problems of the economy rooted in a lack of internal demand and productive investment remain.

Uruguay

Sandwiched between Argentina and Brazil, Uruguay could not escape the economic ills that beset its large neighbors. Liberal democracy based on the two-party system of Blancos and Colorados had been restored in 1984 following an extended period of military rule. But its livestock and manufacturing exports to Argentina and Brazil as well as its banking sector were undermined by the increasing economic difficulties of the 1990s. Uruguay entered a deep slump between 1999 and 2003. IMF-imposed austerity measures, including the privatization of industries, deregulation, and the outsourcing and reduction of public services, undermined the jobs and livelihood of both workers and the middle class. Turning away from neoliberalism and the traditional political parties, Uruguayans for the first time elected a left-wing coalition government headed by Tabare Vasquez in October 2004. Taking a leaf from Lula in Brazil, Vasquez in power proved reluctant to redistribute power and income in Uruguay or to challenge the influence of international capital over the economy. The regime's modest job creation and food relief efforts were little more than bandages to assuage the plight of the impoverished, to quiet them, and to demobilize the organized left. Indeed, the Vasquez government was assuming the shape of a third world version of Tony Blair's social democracy within the parameters of neoliberalism. It seems unlikely that the Vasquez regime could long retain the support of the Broad Front of the Left that elected him.

Venezuela

Like the rest of Latin America, recent decades have seen a dramatic decline in the living standards of the people of Venezuela. The white elite traditionally dominated the black and mulatto majority through its control of the country's wealth and politics. Closely linked with the United States, this elite assured the American economy continued access to strategically vital Venezuelan oil. Despite the fact that Venezuela had enormous oil and mineral wealth, the great majority of the population lived in deep poverty. During the 1980s, falling petroleum prices and mounting foreign debt led to dramatic rises in inflation and interest rates. Most of

the population of 23 million experienced a drastic decline in their already low living standards. Over the 1980s and 1990s, in fact, the purchasing power of the
working class declined by two-thirds.

A junior army officer, Hugo Chavez, succeeded in winning an electoral victory
in 1998, breaking the constitutional stranglehold of the corrupt oligarchy over
Venezuelan politics. Chavez's populist government survived successive attempts
on the part of the elite and the United States to overthrow him. The national oil
company (PDVSA), the key to the economy, was for the first time fully nationalized
after a bitter struggle between Chavez and the oligarchy (2003). The mass of
Venezuelans experienced modest improvements in their livelihood and new educational opportunities. Fifty-eight percent of the population voted in the negative
in a referendum that attempted to remove Chavez from office in 2004. The successive defeat of attempts against his regime enabled Chavez to consolidate the military and political defenses of his government. Venezuela appeared to be moving
toward a radicalization of its revolution, including an increasingly close alliance
with Cuba. Capitalism continued but under the scrutiny of the state, the military,
and the increasingly radicalized labor movement and the poor. Internationally
Chavez was using Venezuela's vast oil resources to further a policy of integrating
the economies of the Latin American states. At the end of 2005, Venezuela became
part of MERCOSUR. Under Chavez the country seemed destined to lead the
charge in defying American attempts to regain control of the Continent.

As a result of the reassertion of Latin American populism during the 1990s,
American control over the region has been shaken to an unprecedented degree.
Especially of concern to Washington is the defiant posture of important states,
such as Argentina, Brazil, and Venezuela, and the concerted nature of their
actions vis-à-vis the United States. The American-backed Free Trade Agreement
of the Americas has become a dead letter. The increasing number of economic
and trade agreements between the Latin American states threatens overall
American control of the continent. Joint military planning and procurement
between some of these states appear to be in the works. A Latin American-based
all-news network rivaling CNN has come into being. On its border, the United
States looks askance at the possibility that Andrés Manuel López Obrador, governor of Mexico City and head of the populist Democratic Revolutionary Party,
may be elected president of Mexico in 2006. Washington has responded by trying to deepen its long established links with the Latin American military and by
increasing the number of its military bases in the region. At the same time, it is

attempting to defuse the populist surge through negotiated compromises with countries such as Brazil, Uruguay, and Argentina. As a substitute for the FTAA, it has concluded more limited accords with the still compliant states of Central America (CAFTA) and Peru. Strengthening local middle classes, forging new links with key groups in civil society, and acceding to minimal populist demands may be part of an evolving U.S. strategy for pacifying Latin America. In the final analysis, it is the strength of popular mobilization in the various Latin American countries that will determine the success or failure of Washington's attempt to preserve its traditional control of the continent.

China and East Asia

Developments in Asia, likewise, have tended to erode American influence over the course of the decade. In contrast to the lackluster performance of most of the economies outside of Asia, China's economy grew by almost 10 percent per annum in the 1990s. Inequality increased, but the number of people in absolute poverty fell. China proceeded with liberalization and privatization, but cautiously. Price controls were dropped, foreign direct investment welcomed, and institutional reforms suitable to the operation of a market economy were introduced. Individual farms replaced agricultural communes in the rural sector. Thousands of small state-owned enterprises were merged, closed, or privatized. Left-wing critics of the regime point to the emergence of a large class of both rural and urban capitalists.

But land, agricultural equipment, and rural enterprises remained, by law at least, under collective ownership. The state insisted that it maintain a majority stake in large enterprises and retained complete control of the top 500 such enterprises. State-run enterprises continued to produce 30 percent of total industrial output, while becoming more efficient and profitable. Private ownership existed, but its extent was relatively small, especially in key sectors such as heavy industry, banking, insurance, and wholesaling. Private firms continued to be hemmed in by significant regulatory, legal, and financial constraints.

Over half a trillion dollars in direct foreign investment, much of it from Asia, was attracted to China over the decade. American or European investment made up only a small percentage of the total. By means of this foreign direct investment, China acquired new technology, access to world markets, and much needed capital. At the same time, unlike the rest of Asia, China restricted the flow of much more volatile portfolio investment that had destabilized many Asian and Latin American economies. China spawned an increasingly prosperous lower middle class. But the infusion of foreign direct investment actually inhibited the development of an indigenous upper middle class.

China to this point is neither socialist nor capitalist, but what may be described as a mixed economy or developmental state. The Communist Party, dominated by technocrats and engineers, retains its political control at the top of society. The leaders of the party rationalize these policies by invoking Lenin's New Economic Policy of the 1920s, which saw capitalist enterprise used to develop the Soviet Union in the context of an overall Communist Party dictatorship. A fundamental difference between the current Chinese policy and that of the Soviets is that China is attempting to pursue this course while progressively integrating itself into the world economy. Such a course is unprecedented and may lead to the overthrow or internal disintegration of the Communist Party. The stakes for China and the rest of the world are enormous.

The growing economic strength of China may be seen in the aftermath of the Asian Crisis of 1998. In American financial circles, the crisis was seen as an opportunity for the United States to eliminate the protectionist and interventionist elements in the South Korean, Indonesian, Thai, and other Asian economies. Indeed, American investors hoped to use the occasion to seize control of some of the strategic sectors in these economies. Strong local reactions blocked most such plans. Indeed, in the six years since the crisis, East Asia has seen growing interregional economic and financial cooperation, with China taking the lead. The economies of many of these states, including Japan itself, have become increasingly reoriented around China as the growth pole of the whole region. Joint initiatives have recently been announced to try to secure the energy independence of the states of the region vis-à-vis the United States.

Russia

Russia began the 1990s as a virtual dependency of its former enemy, the United States. President Yeltsin and his advisers Yegor Gaidar, Anatoly Chubais, and Boris Nemetsov were convinced that the key to a revival of the Russian economy was integration into the capitalist world market. This would be possible only through the fullest possible cooperation with the United States. Legions of American economic consultants, financial specialists, political missionaries, and academics were invited to Russia to advise the government, media, political parties, schools and universities, and trade unions on how to transform Russia into a liberal and capitalist society.

At the beginning of 1992, finance minister Gaidar launched a program of shock therapy that included rapid privatization, an end to price controls and state subsidies, and the convertibility of the Russian currency. Prices rose dramatically, with the ensuing inflation wiping out the savings of millions of Russian citizens. Privatization by vouchers gradually handed control over enterprises to their managers. But in the absence of a real market, most of these enterprises went into a financial and economic tailspin. Industrial production and GDP fell by 50 percent between 1991 and 1995. Shops in Moscow and St. Petersburg were filled with goods, which only 5 percent of the population had the money to buy. The bulk of the Russian people became deeply impoverished. Pensions and salaries went unpaid and social services disintegrated. Whole sectors of the economy fell into the hands of the Russian mafia. Following the secession of Soviet republics such as Georgia and Ukraine, various regions of Russia itself also declared their autonomy. Guerrilla warfare broke out in the separatist territory of Chechnya. In response to growing resistance in the democratically elected Parliament, President Yeltsin dissolved that body. Its refusal to disband caused him to order an army attack on the parliament buildings in the center of Moscow in October 1993. Yeltsin's parliamentary opponents defeated him in the December elections even as his proposal to expand the president's powers gained approval. In 1996 Yeltsin was re-elected amid widespread apathy.

Meanwhile, the economy continued its inexorable downward spiral. The level of internal and external debt rose to unsustainable levels. The one sector of the economy that maintained and even increased production during the 1990s was the newly privatized oil and gas sector. It enabled Russia to continue to earn foreign exchange, finance imports, and pay interest on its foreign debt. In the fall of 1997, investors became increasingly unnerved by the Asian crisis and a precipitous decline in oil prices, which in the winter of 1997–98 jeopardized Russia's ability to continue to service external debt. At the end of August 1998, the ruble finally collapsed, and Russia suspended debt payments. Collapse of the currency marked the end of neoliberal ascendancy over the Russian economy.

The Russian economy that emerged from the upheavals of the 1990s was far removed from American notions of a market economy. It was certainly true that a massive privatization or seizure of state assets by former managers and speculators had occurred. Moreover, market exchanges had become much more important to the economy than hitherto. However, the strong patrimonial state continued to play the predominant economic role. Urban food and fuel subsidies by the state were kept in place through the 1990s. The land was scarcely privatized, with most agricultural production staying in the hands of state farms and collectives. Industrial enterprises and so-called collectives, nominally in private hands, continued to be dependent on state subsidies and, accordingly, remained under its control. Inter-firm relationships based on barter and gift exchange remained much more important than in normal market societies. Wages and pensions may have been in arrears, but employment was largely maintained at the insistence of the state and despite industrial depression. On the face of it, the banks appeared to have been transformed into private businesses. In fact, control of credit and even the personnel of the banks remained under state control. The sector of Western-style private ownership actually stayed quite small.

The ongoing decline and resulting crisis of the Russian economy helped to diminish American influence. The aggressive character of U.S. foreign policy towards Russia weakened it further. During the 1990s, U.S. military advisors were sent into many of the former Soviet satellites and republics of the Soviet Union, and U.S. bases were set up in Romania, Bulgaria, the Czech Republic, Ukraine, Georgia, Kyrgyztan, Uzbekistan, and Kazakhstan. The former satellites, Poland, the Czech Republic, and Hungary, joined NATO in 1999. With the blessings of the United States, many of these former Eastern Europe allies of Russia were invited to join the European Union. The American-led NATO attack on Russia's longtime protege Serbia in 1999 destroyed whatever illusions the Russians had left about American good intentions. Russia was progressively being encircled.

The incapacitated and frequently drunk Yeltsin finally resigned on the last day of 1999, naming his prime minister, Vladimir Putin, as his successor. Under Putin, the authority of the Russian state was strengthened. The increasingly important oil and gas sector and the weak ruble permitted a partial recovery of the Russian economy. Putin's plan was to revive the economy through state-directed investment aimed at modernizing industry and agriculture. The economic control of the so-called oligarchs, the 100 men who controlled a quarter of the Russian economy, was not directly threatened. But indirectly it was. Their freedom of action apart from the Russian state was curbed through the prosecution of the richest of them, Mikhail Khodorkovsky, head of Yukos, the largest oil company, on charges of fraud and tax evasion (2003–05). As Putin envisaged it, foreign earnings from the oil and gas industry would be a key source of finance for his program of economic revitalization. Energy exports to Germany would become an important means by which Russia would integrate itself with Western Europe. Plans were announced to ensure future Russian control over strategically vital parts of the economy. Under Putin, Russia assumed the form of a state-business oligarchy.

The ongoing weakness of the Russian economy limited the reach of Putin's foreign policy. Washington even helped to install pro-American governments on the doorstep of Russia in Ukraine and Georgia (2005). Putin's main goal remained the insertion of Russia into the world economy. Efforts continued to deepen Russia's ties with both China and the European Union, while not directly alienating the United States. In the meantime, Russia embarked on a limited modernization of its armed forces, including its nuclear deterrent, whose credibility is critical to the maintenance of Russian sovereignty. Under Putin the Russian economy seems to be rallying. Its abundance of energy and other natural resources and its well-educated population make it likely that Russia will reemerge as a powerful state.

The Yugoslav Wars

NATO's war against Serbia ended the post-Cold War honeymoon between the United States and Russia. As far as the United States was concerned, the aim of the war was the dismantling of the last remnant of communism in Europe. It was also designed to reassert American leadership over NATO, while extending its mission beyond the defense of Western Europe. But the entry of the United States into the Balkans under the aegis of NATO pointed to something even more significant. It was part of the fundamental redirection of the main thrust of American foreign policy from Europe toward the Middle East.

Until his death in 1980, Marshal Tito ruled multi-ethnic Yugoslavia through a complex balance of external and internal pressures. He carefully maintained neutrality between East and West, while remaining one of the leaders of the non-aligned movement. Within Yugoslavia, he asserted ultimate federal power, while conceding some control to the local republics. By these means, Tito was able to contain ethnic and nationalist rivalries while managing to direct economic resources from the developed north to the less developed south of the country.

Workers control of enterprises was offset by a certain amount of central planning and fiscal oversight. Within this framework, Yugoslavia experienced extraordinary levels of growth in the 1950s and 1960s. Growth rates slowed toward the end of the 1960s. Even so, through the next decade average annual growth remained higher than 5 percent. There was a substantial improvement in the standard of living that by the 1970s took the form of a degree of consumer affluence. Throughout these decades, Yugoslavia tried to balance its economic relationships with the Western and Soviet blocs. It borrowed capital and bought advanced technology from the Western countries. From the East, it acquired fuel in exchange for manufactures, armaments, and construction projects. In accord with its neutralist foreign policy, it made a substantial effort to develop trade relations with other non-aligned states. But over time, economic ties to the non-aligned states weakened. Trade with these states declined from 17 percent in 1958 to 6 percent of overall exchanges by 1971. The increasing need for Yugoslavia to be technologically competitive, meanwhile, required a steady increase in its economic ties to the West. It became more and more dependent on Western technology, spare parts, and trade credits, running a persistent trade imbalance. In common with many other states, the oil crises of the 1970s exacerbated its debt problems.

Following the death of Tito in 1980, the situation of Yugoslavia became more precarious. Growing debt gave Western banks increasing leverage over the economy. Gorbachev's policy of rapprochement with the United States made Yugoslavia's politics of non-alignment seem redundant. The dissolution of the Soviet Union and the other communist regimes at the end of the decade then led to the isolation of this still-communist regime. American policy aimed at putting the regime out of its misery. Initially it supported the installation of a non-communist government over federal Yugoslavia. The newly united German state adopted a more reckless approach aimed at the dismemberment of Yugoslavia and successfully fostered the development of separatist tendencies in Slovenia and Croatia.

IMF-sponsored programs of neoliberal economic reform led to austerity and a deterioration of living standards in Yugoslavia during the 1980s. Unemployment, inflation, and cuts to public services increasingly marked the decade. In turn, economic difficulties fueled increasing tension between the wealthier and poorer republics, as well as between ethnic groups. The better off republics such as Slovenia and Croatia were led to believe that by splitting from Yugoslavia they could integrate with Germany and the European Union. The federal Yugoslav government, led by the pro-U.S. Ante Markovic, responded to the growing crisis by introducing a neoliberal economic shock therapy program at the beginning of 1990. Despite this, a few months later the U.S. government cut off aid to Yugoslavia. Aid could be resumed only if each republic agreed to conduct elections under U.S. State Department supervision.

In 1990, the first multi-party elections in the republics led to victories by nationalist parties in Croatia and Slovenia. In Serbia, meanwhile, Slobadan Milosevic emerged as leader of the Serbian League of Communists. His popularity was based on his resistance to Albanian nationalism in the Serbian province of Kosovo. But he was also admired for his defense of Yugoslav federalism against separatists and his continued commitment to the socialist principles of workers self-management and social property. Tensions between nationalist elements in Croatia and Slovenia and the Yugoslav federal army escalated in 1990–91. Finally, the two northern republics seceded in September 1991, with the all but open support of the European Union and the U.S. government. Serbia and Montenegro remained part of a truncated Yugoslavia.

The Slovenian secession proved relatively bloodless. But in Croatia the future of the large Serb minority in the Krajina and the eastern Slavonian regions led to major clashes between the Yugoslav army and the armed forces of Croatia, led by the ultra-nationalist Franjo Tudjman. Federal Yugoslav troops occupied Krajina and bombarded and razed several Croatian towns before a 1992 UN-mediated cease-fire took effect. In 1995 overwhelmingly strong Croatian forces, armed and trained by the United States and Germany, invaded and re-occupied Krajina. Three hundred thousand Serbs fled, taking refuge in Serbia.

Further south, the republic of Bosnia-Herzegovina was made up of Muslims who constituted 40 percent of the population, Serbs who made up another third, and Croats who amounted to another 18 percent. After the Bosnian republic declared its independence from Yugoslavia in March 1992, the three ethnicities fought a bloody civil war for the next three and a half years. The prolonged battle of Sarajevo was particularly destructive and tragic. In backing the recognition of Bosnian independence, the United States lent its support to Bosnia's ruling Muslim faction under the leadership of the Alija Izetbegovic. American military advisers and equipment helped to strengthen both the Muslim and Croatian military forces. NATO bombardment of the Serbs ultimately forced them to the negotiating table in Dayton, Ohio, in 1995. The subsequent Dayton Accords placed Bosnia under NATO military occupation and the political control of a High Representative appointed by the United States and the European Union.

The conclusion of the Bosnian war in negotiations at Dayton, Ohio, signified that the Americans and not the Germans had assumed the leading role in the restructuring of the Balkans. Their dominance in the subsequent and final Yugoslav conflict in Kosovo in 1999 was even more evident. Led by the United States, NATO bombed Serbia in order to afford humanitarian protection to the Albanians in the Serbian province of Kosovo. Indeed, the Albanian majority in the province had been persecuted and suppressed by the Serbs, but the NATO intervention had purposes other than the protection of Albanians. The American and other NATO governments decided to discredit the Serbian leader Milosevic in order to dismantle the supposedly outdated remnants of the last socialist economy in Europe.

The war against Yugoslavia also gave NATO a chance to redefine itself in the wake of the Cold War. Just prior to the initiation of hostilities in 1999, NATO had been expanded to include Hungary, Poland, and the Czech Republic. A successful war against rump Yugoslavia would eliminate a rogue state on the alliance's new southern frontier. More idealistically, a so-called humanitarian war against ethnic violence opened up the possibility of further NATO missions in Europe and beyond. The guerrilla activities of a militant Albanian nationalist group, the Kosovo Liberation Army, sparked the outbreak of war. Escalating its activities between 1996–99, Kosovo Liberation Army attacks were met by counter-attacks by the Serbian military. Talks to end the conflict were organized at Rambouillet, France in January 1999.

Insisting on the presence of Kosovo Liberation Army representatives at the conference, the United States then proposed a NATO occupation not only of Kosovo, but of the rest of Yugoslavia as well. Yugoslavia's refusal led to a NATO air assault that began on March 24 and continued until June 10. American pilots flew 90 percent of the sorties against Serbia. The bombing did lasting harm to Serbia's civilian infrastructure, while the camouflaged Yugoslav armed forces suffered minimal damage. Western government and media reports of Serb atrocities against the Albanians turned out to be wildly inaccurate if not deliberate disinformation. The June 9 cease-fire mandated that Serbia withdraw its troops from Kosovo, leaving NATO forces to occupy the province. Kosovo became a UN/NATO protectorate within Yugoslavia. The hundreds of thousands of Albanians who had fled the province returned, while about 100,000 Serbs departed. In September 2000, Milosevic was defeated in the Yugoslav presidential election by Vojislav Kostunica who was committed to free market reforms.

The next year Milosevic was arrested and handed over to the United Nations War Crimes Tribunal in The Hague for trial. The state of Yugoslavia was dissolved and replaced by the nations of Serbia and Montenegro.

Throughout the course of this step-by-step dismemberment of Yugoslavia, the United States had presided, acting in a careful, multilateral fashion under the umbrella of NATO and the United Nations. Its direct military intervention in Kosovo was justified in the name of so-called humanitarian war. The Clinton administration continued and expanded on the multilateral successes of the previous Bush administration. The latter had overseen the collapse of the Soviet Union and the organization of an unprecedented broad political and military coalition against Iraq in the first post-Cold War conflict. The Yugoslav campaigns were conducted in a similar manner under the aegis of an increasingly fashionable humanitarian interventionism. The new unipolar world dominated by the United States was to be apparently based on international cooperation and humanitarian principles.

The United States Advances into Central Asia

It was not to be. While the dissolution of Yugoslavia proceeded, the United States in the 1990s was intruding aggressively into Central Asia and further into the Middle East. The oil and gas reserves of the area of the Caspian Sea and the regions to the east have long been known. While they do not quite match those of the Persian Gulf and Saudi Arabia to the south, they are enormous nonetheless. Possible oil reserves in the Caspian basin and the region to its east are calculated to exceed 200 billion barrels. The area has in addition 40 percent of the world's proven natural gas reserves. With the breakup of the Soviet Union, this region was split into the independent states of Azerbajan, Turkmenistan, Uzbekistan, Kyrgyzstan, and Kazahkstan. They were now run mainly by ex-Soviet party chiefs in a highly autocratic manner. They were also breeding grounds for narcotics trading and Islamic militancy radiating from Pakistan and Afghanistan.

The big American oil companies interested in the region—Chevron, Union Oil of California, Amoco, and Exxon—tried to acquire concessions and to strike pipeline deals in the region in the immediate wake of the collapse of the Soviet Union, but they were initially rebuffed. In 1997, the Clinton administration began to dispatch troops and establish bases in several of the ex-Soviet republics. Part

of the logic of such a move was to drive a wedge between these newly independent republics and Russia. Out of its weakness and desperation, the Russian government acceded to the American intrusion, despite deep misgivings. The U.S.
military presence then facilitated the conclusion of a number of important oil and
pipeline deals.

Pipeline agreements included one by Chevron running from Kazahkstan to
Baku to the Russian Black Sea port of Novorossiisk. This project was linked to
the American acquisition of landing and basing rights in Romania, Bulgaria, and,
especially, Kosovo in the ex-Yugoslavia. Since 1999, the Americans had created
an enormous permanent base in Kosovo called Camp Bondsteel. Another
pipeline from Baku through Georgia and Armenia to Turkey's deep water
Mediterranean port of Batumi took form. A third still unrealized oil and gas
pipeline would run from Turkmenistan through Afghanistan to Pakistan, serving
the burgeoning South and East Asian energy markets. None of these pipeline
routes were secure. Chechen rebels, Armenian separatists, the Iranian Islamic
Republic, and Kurdish guerrillas threatened their viability. In the case of
Afghanistan, the Taliban regime, which the Americans had helped to install,
stood in the way. The initial American military buildup in the former Soviet
republics could only be regarded as preliminary to a much larger operation.

The U.S. Military in the Middle East

The American intervention in Central Asia was part of an overall strategy to
assure control over the oil-rich Middle East. The new military bases in the ex-
Soviet republics were seconded by the growing military capacity of CENT-
COM in the Persian Gulf. With the conclusion of the Gulf War, American mil-
itary bases in Saudi Arabia and Kuwait, adjacent to Iraq, were bolstered. In the
course of the 1990s, further American basing capacity was established in the
United Arab Emirates, Oman, Djibouti, Egypt, Israel, and Turkey. The
Americans pre-positioned enormous quantities of military equipment in these
installations. Large numbers of U.S. warships operated in the Persian Gulf,
Arabian Sea, and Red Sea.

Iraq was not the only target. In May 1993, the Clinton administration declared
its Persian Gulf policy to be one of double containment against both Iraq and the
Islamic Republic of Iran. Libya, likewise, was regarded as hostile, Syria somewhat
less so. At the same time, the United States continued to staunchly support the

other repressive governments in the region, such as Egypt and Saudi Arabia, that were considered reliable allies. Where possible, the U.S. government encouraged the implementation of neoliberal economic policies, especially those that favored the intrusion of American trade and investment.

With regard to Iraq, the policy of containment was pursued with determination. The United States and Great Britain maintained the no-fly zones against Iraq by flying thousands of sorties against Iraqi targets. With American help, the Kurds in northern Iraq were able to consolidate an autonomous region in defiance of the Saddam Hussein regime. Above all, at American insistence, the United Nations maintained an economic boycott and a weapons inspections regime—at great cost to the Iraqi population.

Intifada II

American involvement in the region deepened as a result of its efforts to resolve the Palestinian-Israeli conflict. Secret negotiations between the two sides led to the Oslo Accords in 1993. These in turn became the basis of agreements between the Palestinians and Israelis reached in Washington two years later. As part of an ongoing process, the Palestinian Authority was given complete control of seven cities and civil, if not military, control over much of the rest of the West Bank and Gaza. But successive Israeli governments placed roadblocks in the way of implementation of these agreements. In July 2000, Clinton invited the Israeli Prime Minister, Ehud Barak, and the Palestinian president, Yasser Arafat, to Camp David to work out the framework of a final peace accord, but the talks floundered over the perennial issues of the status of Jerusalem and the disposition of the Palestine refugees. The visit of the right-wing Israeli leader Ariel Sharon to the Temple Mount accompanied by 1,000 armed guards at the end of September then set off a second Palestinian Intifada. A cycle of Arab terrorist attacks and brutal Israeli reprisals marked the next years (2000–05). Israel unilaterally withdrew its army and settlers from Gaza in 2005 at the insistence of the United States. Indeed, Israel proved unable to crush the Palestinian resistance. At the beginning of 2006 the Palestinians elected an intransigent Islamic government under Hamas. Despite the appearance of overwhelming Israeli strength, it was by no means clear that it would emerge as the winner in this long-term war of attrition.

Al-Qaeda

American efforts to control the region were further hampered by the rise of the Islamic extremist organization known as Al-Qaeda (The Base). Al-Qaeda grew out of the American effort to overthrow the Marxist government in Afghanistan during the 1980s. Tens of thousands of non-Afghan mujahidin were trained at the jointly run CIA-Pakistan Inter-Services Intelligence training camps on both sides of the Pakistan-Afghan border. The leader of these foreign mujahidin was Osama bin Laden. Son of a wealthy Saudi building contractor, bin Laden not only fought with the mujahidin in Afghanistan, he also successfully lobbied his wealthy relatives and friends to support the anti-Soviet and anti-Marxist campaign in Afghanistan. Indeed, the financial networks he created throughout the Islamic world played a great part in increasing his influence. Bin Laden regarded the 1989 exodus of the Soviet army from Afghanistan as a great victory for Islamic jihad. In the wake of this Afghan triumph, he decided to organize an international network of those who had participated in the anti-Soviet jihad.

On returning to Saudi Arabia, he was dismayed not merely by Saddam Hussein's invasion of Kuwait, but by the intrusion of half a million American troops into Saudi Arabia, site of the holy cities of Mecca and Medina. Indeed, his indignation reflected the alarm felt by Muslims throughout the area at the increasing American military and political presence, to say nothing of its growing economic influence. The intrusion of big American capital, as well as the flow of Western manufactured goods, was seen as an increasing threat by entrepreneurs both large and small in the Islamic world. The anti-Islamic cultural and religious values, as well as the pro-Zionist U.S. foreign policy, reinforced a growing sense of hostility. Such attitudes inspired a flow of recruits and money toward Al-Qaeda.

Hounded from Saudi Arabia in 1991, bin Laden moved to Sudan where he set up various enterprises under Al-Qaeda direction. Al-Qaeda at this time was itself run like a corporation with centralized leadership directing separate departments dedicated to ideology and propaganda, recruitment, finance, arms purchases and military training, and armed operations. During the Bosnian civil war in the early 1990s, Al-Qaeda sponsored about 5,000 Arab fighters fighting on the Muslim side. Al-Qaeda cells operated in Albania, Britain, Lebanon, Malaysia, the Netherlands, Pakistan, Romania, Russia, Saudi Arabia, Turkey, and the United Arab Emirates. It established ties with sympathetic groups in Algeria, Chechnya,

Egypt, Ethiopia, Somalia, Lebanon, Libya, Philippines, South Asia, Southeast Asia, Syria, and Yemen.

In 1996 bin Laden was welcomed back to Afghanistan by the new Islamic fundamentalist government of the Taliban. By the end of the decade, Al-Qaeda had about 3,000 men under arms in Afghanistan and some 4,500 militants operating worldwide. The United States blamed Al-Qaeda for devastating bombings of its embassies in Nairobi and Dar-es-Salaam on August 1998 and the warship USS *Cole* in Aden in October 2000.

WTO and NAFTA

As the threat of terrorism loomed, the U.S.-backed project of neoliberal globalization began to run into difficulty. The centerpiece of this effort was the World Trade Organization (WTO), created in 1995. Through its disputes tribunal, it was empowered to enforce free trade between all countries affiliated with the GATT. Parallel to the creation of the WTO was the inception of talks within the OECD looking towards the conclusion of a Multilateral Agreement on Investment. Moving a step beyond free trade, this accord would have swept away national barriers to foreign investment.

The creation of the WTO had been preceded by the consolidation of three enormous free trade zones: the European Union in 1992, the Association of Southeast Asia Nations (ASEAN) also in 1992, and the North American Free Trade Agreement (NAFTA) in 1994. It was proposed that NAFTA eventually be transformed into the Free Trade Agreement of the Americas (FTAA), which would embrace all the states of the Americas. The WTO was seen in part as an insurance policy against the crystallization of protectionist policies between these three trading blocs.

Rise of the Anti-Globalization Movement

A growing resistance to neoliberal globalization succeeded in exposing the Multilateral Agreement on Investments, which was drafted by the International Chamber of Commerce and its American affiliate, the Council for International Business. Effective lobbying against it by an emerging coalition of anti-globalization organizations helped to make it politically untenable in the advanced capitalist states. But this campaign, although successful, only involved an elite of activists. Major popular protests against the globalization process erupted at the meeting of the WTO in Seattle in November 1999. Hundreds of thousands of protestors including trade unionists, environmentalists, anarchists, socialists, communists, and indigenous people confronted delegates to the meetings in both peaceful and violent protests. At Prague in 2000, Quebec City, Genoa, and Davos in 2001, and Cancun in 2003, subsequent meetings of the WTO and related organizations met with similar mass protests.

More alarming to the participating governments were opinion polls showing rising levels of public support for the protests against neoliberal globalization. The questionable legitimacy of governments pursuing this agenda was reflected in growing complaints about the democratic deficit or lack of popular control over economic and political life. Attendant on the wave of protests was the mushrooming of a multitude of local anti-globalization protest movements. Within the WTO and other international economic bodies, a major split between the developed and underdeveloped countries forced debate on the terms of global free trade. Agriculture and intellectual property rights were particular sore spots. The developed countries were accused of restricting entry to their own markets, while demanding open access to third world markets and investment opportunities.

Grassroots and decentralized organization has been the hallmark of the popular anti-globalization efforts. Coordination has been achieved by means of a highly innovative style of communication using the Internet. The successive World Social Forums at Porto Alegre, Brazil (2001–03), Mumbai, India (2004), and Caracas, Venezuela (2006) have attracted hundreds of thousands of anti-globalization activists. The ultimate effectiveness of these events hinges on whether they can help to strengthen democratic movements against capitalism and imperialism at the local and national level as in Latin America. Otherwise, they will remain as spectacles—symptoms more of the weakness than the strength of resistance at the grassroots. The potential for mass organization at the base of society is central to the political future.

The Stock Market Decline

Efforts to expand neoliberal globalization have continued, but the momentum toward such globalization clearly was slowed at the beginning of the new millennium as a result of these protests and disputes. Compounding these difficulties was the collapse of the stock market boom and onset of a deep recession. The economic boom of the late 1990s had been centered on the U.S. economy. It was nourished by debt-financed personal consumption and a surge of investment in the high-tech sector. Indeed, it has been argued that by encouraging economic concentration, insisting on profitability, and improving the efficiency of capital allocation between economic sectors, neoliberalism did somewhat increase the productivity of the leading industrial sectors of the American economy as well as that of the other advanced capitalist countries. But many enterprises, meanwhile, had been left burdened by unsustainably heavy levels of debt. By the late 1990s, private sector as well as household debt had reached historic peaks. While the boom lasted, such debt helped to sustain the economy. Indeed, the large and increasing American trade deficit and growing overseas debt offset, in part, the contraction attending neoliberalism worldwide. But it also created an enormous financial bubble.

The bubble of accumulated obligations—loans, mortgages, bonds—found its ultimate expression in the stock market mania of the late 1990s. The inflated stock prices that had developed in the Reagan years suffered a deep correction in 1987, but stocks rose precipitously from 1995, reaching a peak in the summer of 2000. Corrected for inflation, stock prices had quintupled between 1980 and 2000. More and more doubts began to surface over the sustainability of those stock market advances beyond any hope of future profits. Accordingly, Standard and Poor's ratings of stocks suddenly began to decline in August 2000, fell precipitously after September 11, 2001, and reached a low in September 2002 that was nearly 50 percent below its peak two years earlier. After the bubble burst, news about accounting scandals and financial malfeasance at Enron, Global Crossing, Tyco, Merrill Lynch, WorldCom, Xerox, Halliburton, and many other corporate giants came to the surface. Economic activity and investment contracted sharply and unemployment rose worldwide. The previous extraordinary level of speculative excess promised a painful period of adjustment.

American Economic Malaise

As the financial and economic center of the global economy, the downturn had grave implications for the United States at the beginning of the new millennium. Already plagued by massive amounts of private debt held abroad, the deep recession required the new administration of George W. Bush—Bill Clinton's successor and George H. W. Bush's son—to drastically cut interest rates and massively increase government spending to stimulate the economy. Suddenly, the accumulated national debt that Clinton seemed to have brought under control loomed once again as a worrisome, indeed enormous, problem. Projected tax cuts by the Bush administration directed mainly at the wealthy only compounded the difficulty. It was a problem precisely because so much of both the private and public debt was held by foreign creditors. The ballooning of deficits and debt threatened to undermine confidence in the dollar whose economic underpinnings had not ceased to weaken. Doubts continued to grow over the long-term competitiveness of the American economy in the face of the outsourcing of not only manufacturing employment, but even research, design, and development work. The value of the dollar in the end was the lynchpin of the continued global political and financial primacy of the United States. More than ever, the United States was dependent on the rest of the world, which it needed to control. Provided that it was not too costly, an aggressive foreign policy that protected the pivotal international role of the U.S. dollar would be welcome to American business.

September 11, 2001

Faced with a conjuncture of problems that included threats to its economic and financial primacy, growing unrest and resistance to globalization in the underdeveloped and developed world, and ongoing problems of the Intifada and terrorism in the Middle East, the United States suffered a devastating attack. The simultaneous air assaults by Muslim fundamentalists on the citadel of global capitalism, the World Trade Center in New York, and the nerve center of the American military at the Pentagon on September 11, 2001, directly challenged the United States. In the Western world, the overall response to this attack was one of sympathy for its 3,000 victims. Elsewhere, especially in the Middle East and the rest of the third world, the reaction was muted or even gleeful. Among the powerless, the globally televised spectacle of 9/11 fostered the illusion that those seemingly without power had, in reality, the capacity to challenge the power of organized capital. Those who held power in Washington came to similar conclusions.

Afghanistan Occupied

The United States labeled bin Laden's Al-Qaeda as the prime suspect and called for an open-ended war against terrorism. The forces of atavistic nationalism and religious fundamentalism were marshaled within the United States by the Bush administration. In the short run this jingoism proved fully a match for the Islamic fundamentalism being promoted by Al-Qaeda. Indeed, with the launching of the war against terrorism, the United States had at last found a new long-term theme for its ambitious global foreign policy that could take the place of the containment of the Soviet threat. At the beginning of October 2001, NATO invoked article five of its charter for the first time in its history, calling for a collective response to an attack on one of its members. Eventually, other states including China, Russia, and even erstwhile Taliban sponsor Pakistan joined the coalition. The bombing of Afghanistan began on October 7, while the United States began to build up its ground support for the so-called Northern Alliance, a coalition of Tajiks, Uzbeks, and Harastas who had continued to resist the Taliban in the extreme north of Afghanistan.

By the first week of November, American troops were present in northern Afghanistan in support of the Northern Alliance. An offensive launched in the following weeks swept the Taliban from Kabul and the major cities. A Pashtun tribal leader and American oil executive, Hamid Karzai, was installed as head of a coalition interim government. With American support, Karzai was able to consolidate control of Kabul. But the outlying areas remained under the control of local warlords. The Taliban retreated to the mountainous border region between Afghanistan and Pakistan and initiated a guerrilla resistance against the new regime and the American-led occupation. By the spring of 2005, amid reports of U.S. prisoner abuse and insults to the Koran, there were signs that the Americans had outworn their welcome in this strategically important country. Many nationalist Afghans appeared no more willing to accept the American project of modernization than they had the earlier British or Soviet versions. Meanwhile, the emerging resistance appeared to lack a positive political project. The future prospect for war-ravaged Afghanistan was one of indefinitely protracted conflict.

Unilateralism and Empire

In the first Gulf War and subsequent Yugoslav conflicts the United States had asserted its hegemony through its traditional policy of multilateralism. It used the United Nations and NATO as its instruments, easily gaining their compliance. In the case of Yugoslavia, the notion of humanitarian intervention gained currency as a theme of American foreign policy. The brief Afghan War was in reality almost entirely a U.S operation, indeed, a campaign by a United States on the warpath in the wake of 9/11. But it was stamped with international approval. The military occupation of Afghanistan extended the notion of justifiable military intervention to terrorism, but continued the policy of multilateralism.

But during the successive conflicts of the 1990s leading to the Afghan campaign, a debate had been unfolding among U.S. foreign policy elites. Bipartisan discussion revolved around how to exploit the fact that the United States was now the only global military superpower. The possibilities of future military intervention to fight drug lords and ethnic violence or to build democratic nationhood were invoked. Discussion of American indispensability, unipolarity, and possible unilateralism were soon enlarged to frank avowals of American primacy, hegemony, empire, and even imperialism. Key foreign policy experts spoke of the necessity of preventive war to block the emergence of possible rivals to American military power. The militarization of American foreign policy was a notable feature of this rhetoric. Such affirmations were made across the political spectrum from Democrats to Republicans. In the aftermath of 9/11 and the Afghan War, an open-ended campaign against terrorism was added to the list of reasons justifying military action.

The emergence of these unilateralist themes was in part the result of the vacuum created by the collapse of the Soviet Union at the beginning of the 1990s. With the end of the Cold War, the concept of containment could no longer serve as the basis of maintaining American hegemony over its allies in Asia and Europe. Indeed, throughout the decade, the United States had been at pains to maintain control of its allies through the United Nations, NATO, and the global trade organizations. The option of unilateralism or, indeed, imperialism emerged as a more tough-minded approach meant to reassert American leadership not merely over its allies, but also to extend and project such control globally. At a deeper level, the new unilateralist foreign policy represented a startling throwback to American isolationism and the aggressive imperialist politics of the so-called China Lobby of a bye-gone era. Under changed conditions there was no question of retreating from the world stage. Instead, the United States appeared to be veering toward a single-minded and predatory imperialism. War against terrorism abroad could also serve to unite the American population, deeply divided both socially and economically, against foreign enemies.

Such a view assumed concrete shape in the new Bush administration. Under the Bush presidency the military-industrial and oil faction of the American elite clearly dominated. Indeed, it was the vice-president, Dick Cheney, former head of the oil conglomerate Halliburton, and the secretary of defense, Donald Rumsfeld, closely tied to the defense industries, who now determined the direction of American foreign policy. Under them, a constellation of civilian-military policy experts including Paul Wolfowitz, Douglas Feith, and Richard Perle ardently championed the notion, not merely of unilateralism, but of American imperialism. Closely connected to the Israel lobby, whose power in Washington is enormous, these advisors, above all, made the case for decisive American intervention in the Middle East.

The attack on the World Trade Center in September 2001, no doubt, represented a tragedy, but it also provided a great opportunity for proponents of a dramatic American move into the oil-rich Middle East. The control of this region was now regarded as central to global strategic dominance. The massive buildup of American forces in CENTCOM and the new military bases in Central Asia provided the means to such an enterprise. Al-Qaeda would be dealt with on its home ground of Afghanistan. But from the beginning it was understood that the domination of Afghanistan was only a first step. Removal of Saddam Hussein through an attack on Iraq must follow. The goal was to respond to terrorism, once and for all, to secure control of the petroleum of the Middle East, and to assert the imperial dominance of the United States. Indeed, the latter goal would be served more by unilateral rather than multilateral action. Conquest and occupation of Iraq would put other states on notice. Long term in the Middle East, the objective would be to reconstruct not only Iraq, but the other nations of the region into stable capitalist democracies friendly to both the United States and Israel. Iraq was only the next step in a military campaign that, if it went well, would extend to Syria and Iran.

This audacious U.S. plan was born out of overwhelming military strength combined with a growing sense of economic vulnerability. On the latter point, American military power and, if possible, control of Middle East oil would enable it to reassert its waning economic primacy while shoring up the dollar. Massive increases in military and reconstruction expenditure in the form of contracts to American companies would help to reawaken the United States economy out of deep recession.

The Attack on Iraq

During the 1990s, the United Nations Special Commission (UNSCOM) on disarming Iraq had superintended the destruction of virtually all of Iraq's weapons of mass destruction. By 1998 Baghdad claimed that it had effectively disarmed itself and demanded an end to UN economic sanctions. Acting in concert with the United States, Richard Butler, the Australian head of UNSCOM, withdrew the inspectors in protest in mid-December 1998. Blaming Iraq for the end of inspections, the United States and Great Britain almost immediately afterwards launched massive air attacks on Iraq as punishment for the exodus of inspectors. In the wake of the successful Afghan campaign, Bush began a propaganda offensive against Iraq. The American president claimed that Saddam Hussein had restarted Iraq's weapons of mass destruction program and that there were links between Saddam and bin Laden. Under pressure, the Iraqi government agreed to readmit UN arms inspectors in mid-September 2002. Despite Iraqi compliance, the U.S. Congress voted Bush war powers in October and an American and British military buildup against Iraq began.

Under a UN ultimatum, Iraq opened itself to a new inspections regime. Rejecting evidence to the contrary, the United States and Britain declared that Iraq had failed to fully comply with the UN ultimatum. Unprecedented mass demonstrations against an imminent American and British military attack on Iraq swept the world, enlarging by many times the anti-globalization protests of the previous years. Over the objections of France, Germany, Russia, and China, the United States and Great Britain commenced military operations against Iraq on March 20, 2003, with a campaign of massive bombing. Meeting only limited Iraqi resistance, American ground troops occupied Baghdad on April 10, establishing an occupation government. Militarily, the campaign was yet another demonstration of American superiority in the kind of electronic and cybernetic warfare that was expected to dominate the next century. But almost at once an increasingly effective urban-based Iraqi guerrilla resistance began to develop. Moreover, the occupiers' lines of communication and the oil pipelines proved open to attack. Indeed, a full-scale insurgency against the United States and Britain began to emerge. The inability of the American and British military to suppress the uprising instilled growing defiance of the United States not only in Iraq, but in neighboring Iran, the states of Latin America, and even as far afield as North Korea. A swarm of Islamic terrorist attacks plagued the Middle East as well as Spain and

Great Britain. In economic terms, it seemed that, in the short run at least, the occupation of Iraq had created more loss than profit to the Americans in the form of higher oil prices and increased budgetary deficits.

The Consequences

The long-term consequences of the American and British occupation of Iraq are enormous. Far from advancing the war against terrorism, the American occupation of Iraq is alienating whatever is left of American support in the Middle East and fueling the terrorist movement there and beyond. The spillover of such attacks into oil-rich Saudi Arabia is, in fact, ominous for the world economy.

During the Cold War, many in the Communist sphere and the third world had opposed the United States. But those in the Western countries who had been hostile to American dominance had always been a minority, even during the Vietnam War. In many Western countries, unease at the United States' unique status as a superpower has grown in the 1990s. The process of neoliberal globalization has fed this disquiet. Even in the countries most closely aligned with the United States, the attack on Iraq has turned public opinion against he United States. As a result of its invasion of Iraq, the United States is now widely and openly perceived as bent on imperialist control of the world. Economic globalization championed by the United States has turned into militarist unilateralism.

War historically has been a catalyst of radical and unexpected changes that have surprised its perpetrators. The Iraq war has been no exception. The anti-globalization movements of the 1990s that had attracted worldwide support have been transformed into an unprecedented global antiwar and anti-imperialist protest movement. From Tokyo to Cairo, London, and New York, a collapse of the international legitimacy of the United States has taken place. Human rights abuses by the American military in Iraq, Afghanistan, and the American prison in Guantánamo, Cuba, only compound the problem. More concretely, the ongoing insurgency in Iraq makes it difficult for the United States to deal with the populist and anti-imperialist upsurge that has swept Latin America. The American political and military preoccupation with the Middle East allows this movement in Latin American to spread and consolidate itself. It will be difficult for the United States to wield a big stick against so widespread a movement.

Multilateralism had been an overarching theme of American foreign policy since before 1945. The United States had not always abided by this approach, particularly with respect to Latin America or Vietnam. Moreover, in the political realm, multilateralism was always a fig leaf hiding the fact of fundamental American political and military global hegemony over the non-communist world. Yet fig leafs are, nonetheless, useful and important in legitimizing the exercise of power. Obtaining the support of allies in practice proved important to the exercise of American dominance both during and after the Cold War. Washington's actions against Iraq left the concept of multilateralism broken. France and Germany are alienated and it is questionable whether they can be brought back into the fold. Indeed, the decade since the collapse of the Soviet Union has seen the consolidation of a Western European political pole of attraction around these two powers. The European Union and an emergent European Corps in NATO potentially challenge future American political and military control. Within NATO and the European Union, these two important powers face a bloc—led by Britain and including the Netherlands, and some Eastern European states—that remains more closely aligned with the United States. This seems to preclude a united Europe emerging quickly as a counter-balance to the unipolar power of the United States. While a blow to neoliberalism, the rejection of the European Union Constitution in the spring of 2005 by the electorates of France and Holland further weakens Europe's capacity to offset American power, at least in the short run. Indeed, divisions within the European Union fit entirely with the American goal of blocking the emergence of any would-be global rival. But France and Germany, together with Russia and China, might eventually constitute a Eurasian power bloc that could offset U.S. power. Since the Iraq invasion, both Russia and China have announced significant upgrades in their strategic nuclear missile programs and have moved toward joint military exercises. Economic ties between these two former comrades are also stronger, with plans for Russian oil and arms to be exchanged for Chinese consumer and other manufactured goods.

Multilateralism, in fact, operates not solely in the realms of political or military power. It is also about economics. Following the Second World War, the United States, preeminently a commercial state, was instrumental in creating a liberal worldwide trading order, which was vital to its own interests. It helped to restore the economies of both its allies and enemies, as they were all indispensable business partners. The IMF, World Bank, GATT, OECD, and G-7, which undergird the liberal trading order, are, likewise, multilateral bodies created largely by the United States. These institutions and similar others have become the framework of a new globalized economy. It remains to be seen whether the Iraq occupation and what it implies has shaken this structure.

Talk of globalization has become increasingly muted and further progress toward liberalization of trade and investment more and more difficult. The December 2005 WTO trade negotiations in Hong Kong reflected ongoing division between the United States and the European Union and increasing capacity on the part of underdeveloped states to refuse unreciprocated access to their markets. The shakiness of the dollar encourages a disturbing trend toward reliance on gold and bilateral and even barter agreements in trade between major economic players. In any case, American unilateralism seems to be in fundamental contradiction to economic liberalization, threatening perhaps even the foundations of the open global economy.

In this context, the American occupation of Iraq may be seen as a kind of atavism from which, sooner or later, the United States must retreat. There are signs that unforeseen political, military, and economic difficulties and growing political divisions within the United States are forcing a rethink among policy makers. If the occupation of Iraq was conceived originally as a blitzkrieg meant to instill "shock and awe" not only among the Iraqis but in the rest of the world as well, the resultant protracted war does not augur well for military adventures elsewhere. Faced with an aroused and hostile public, the willingness of British governments to support further U.S. military adventures is questionable. It may be that unilateral military intervention proves to be an aberration. On the other hand, what has been done may not be so easily undone. Predatory and militaristic behavior may, in fact, be rooted in factors deeply lodged in an American economy in relative decline, in the predisposition of American politics and society, or, indeed, in the nature of the existing global political economy. If so, the American invasion of Iraq marks the beginning of a new period of unpredictable and destructive international rivalry that harks back to the conflicts of the early twentieth century.

Conclusion

In 1945 the American and Soviet victory put an end to the interimperialist rivalries that led to two world wars. The overwhelming economic and military strength of the United States and the weakness of other capitalist states ruled out the possibility of a renewed outbreak of the competition that had characterized the first part of the twentieth century. The real or imagined threat of Soviet communism reinforced this sense of accord. As a result, for more than half a century following the Second World War, the principal capitalist countries co-existed in relative harmony. They remained dependent on the political leadership of the United States, which led the fight against what was considered the menace of Soviet expansionism or communist subversion.

Certainly there were periods of friction in the Western camp. The Suez adventure in 1956 led to a temporary disruption of relations between the United States and its partners France and Britain. During the 1960s, France under de Gaulle was barely a member of the NATO alliance. Yet overall relations between the United States and its allies were relatively harmonious during the decades of the Cold War. In the face of the Soviet and Chinese Communist threats, most of Washington's allies were content to accept its hegemony. Moreover, American relations with Europe were premised on consultation and multilateral agreement, except perhaps with respect to Indochina and Latin America. Political bonds between Europe and the United States were reinforced by mutually rewarding economic ties. By 2003 the branch plants of American corporations in Europe were producing and selling nearly $1.5 billion in goods to European customers. Likewise, the branch plants of European corporations were producing and selling a like amount of goods in the United States. Japan, the United States's main

Asian ally, depended heavily on access to the American market and was the major foreign holder of American debt. While continuing to largely exclude American direct investment, Japan remained a politically docile ally.

Despite such ties, fundamental changes began to affect the relations between the United States and its close friends at the close of the twentieth century. The end of the Soviet threat inevitably tended to weaken the political and military ties between the United States and its allies. Moreover, the decade of the 1990s saw new big players such as China, capitalist Russia, India, and Brazil enter onto the international scene, complicating the architecture of international relations and rendering American efforts to dominate international politics more difficult. These challenges were heightened by the relative economic decline of the United States. The United States remains the largest single national economy in the world with 32 percent of world GDP—double that of Japan, its nearest rival—yet this was a decline of 18 percent from 1950 when the United States had generated more than 50 percent of global product. Since 2004, the GDP of the European Union has become larger than that of the United States. Likewise, the U.S. share of global trade has significantly declined. Even its lead in research and development, while still substantial, shows signs of decline, especially in fields not directly related to the military sector. The deterioration of its public sector, including education, has jeopardized the future competitiveness of the American economy.

There is no doubt that the United States will remain one of the key players in the future global economy. What is notable, nevertheless, is the trend toward relative decline. The erosion of American economic strength and competitiveness is reflected in the half-trillion dollars in debt accumulated in the hands of foreigners, including 45 percent of the outstanding volume of U.S. Treasury indebtedness, 15 percent of U.S. corporate debt, and 12 percent of equities. With its economic primacy crumbling, the continuing dominance of the American dollar, which has given the United States enormous economic and political leverage, is in question.

It is from this perspective that one must view the unilateral American attack on Iraq. Its political, economic, and financial hegemony slipping, the United States responded by playing the card of military adventurism. The object of the Iraq invasion was to achieve a hammerlock on the world's increasingly scarce supply of petroleum resources while demonstrating incontestable American military power. By such means it was believed that the United States could reassert its political and ultimately its economic dominance. But rather than vindicating

American military prowess, the U.S. failure to rapidly suppress the Iraqi insurgency, and the stepped-up nuclear weapons and other military spending by big and small powers, demonstrates that the United States will not be able to assure its dominance through superior military technology alone. It will require many more boots on the ground in order to pacify Iraq, let alone take on other countries. The magnitude of commitment of personnel and resources required for overseas military adventures has been seriously underestimated. Indeed, given the rising level of internal dissent in the United States, further deep modifications of the American body politic will be necessary in the pursuit of empire. Bush Administration attacks on civil liberties and democratic institutions have already taken the United States part way down this road.

In the light of history, it is clear that the resort to unilateral war on the part of the United States risks ending the intercapitalist cooperation that marked the period after 1945. This gamble may be an aberration. The Bush Administration or its successors may decide that a retreat back toward a policy of multilateral cooperation is in order. There are some tentative signals of a change in this direction. Indeed, the American political and economic elite may conclude that a new international order, allowing for more political and economic coordination than previously contemplated, may be necessary to sustain the globalizing capitalist economy. Such a change might entail attempts to reconcile U.S. public opinion and the deep international anger at both American imperialism and neoliberalism. The American reaction to the launch of the Comprehensive Development Framework by the World Bank and the IMF, meant to address the problem of world poverty within the neoliberal framework, perhaps reflects such a shift. While not overtly blessing this initiative, the United States has nonetheless been required to give its grudging assent.

But it is conceivable that as a result of the American invasion of Iraq we may have entered a new period of interimperialist rivalry marked by war and militarism analogous to the first half of the twentieth century. In the United States authoritarianism at home and imperialist adventure abroad represent real temptations to a ruling elite confronted by growing class divisions and social inequality within, faltering economic competitiveness abroad, and an increasing worldwide scarcity of oil and other natural resources. So far the United States has acted militarily against countries with limited capacity to fight back. It is likely, however, that any future aggression against more powerful states would encounter serious resistance.

Growing international tension or even military conflict seems more likely as a result of the continuing weakness of the global economy. The economic downturn of 2000–02 ended with a recovery orchestrated by the United States. The recovery was made possible by the reduction of real interest rates in the United States to near zero and by the creation of unprecedented government deficits. Such as it is, this debt-led recovery has not been enough to fully revive an anaemic job market within the United States or in fact to sustain renewed West European economic growth. New business investment and increases in personal income lag. The recovery has been the weakest since the Second World War. Coupled with dramatic increases in the price of oil, the signs point toward a curtailment of the recovery sooner rather than later and a renewal of economic stagnation. More alarming is the growing volatility and disequilibrium of the substructure of the global market place itself. The last two decades have been marked by the sudden emergence and implosion of one growth pole after another across the globe. There has been a great acceleration in the flow of finance capital from one place to another in search of the highest possible return.

The deregulation of international capital flows is of course part of the process of neoliberalism worldwide, with its insistence on removing all barriers to the movement of goods and money. Deregulation has been paralleled by the global dispersal of production processes to low-wage areas and assaults on the living standards of working people worldwide. The motive behind the neoliberal program was to restore the rate of profit, which faltered by the mid-1970s. It has conspicuously failed to do so. Indeed, it is increasingly clear that neoliberalism has cut the ground out from under the possibility of sustained global accumulation. The global institutional and regulatory framework for such accumulation has in fact been undermined by neoliberalism. While the rate of return on industrial capital appears poised for recovery, for example, further investment and growth seems to be inhibited by the continued demands for high returns and the inconstancy of finance capital. The reduction of real wages globally has caused global production to outrun consumption, resulting in persistent manufacturing overcapacity. American corporations still dominate globally but the lynchpin of the world economy—the United States economy and currency—is increasingly weak in relation to its rivals. These growing global imbalances and problems have been reflected in a mounting series of trade disputes between the major trading states, especially as between the United States and its primary commercial partners. Meanwhile, the more deep-seated problems of energy shortages and ecological limits lurk just over the horizon. The possibility for growth and accumulation under the weight of these growing difficulties appears increasingly bleak.

It is conceivable that what is referred to as a global social democratic solution to these problems might be possible. The United States might graciously accept a devaluation of its currency—and, indeed, a whole new international currency and regulatory order—in order to rebalance the global economy. Re-regulation on an international basis and a deliberate raising of living standards worldwide could conceivably restore stable economic expansion. A new global political order would then be in the offing.

But such a positive outcome is unlikely. It is improbable that the United States would willingly accept such a diminished role unless constrained to do so. Moreover, it is important to realize that such a redistributive program requires someone to pay for it. Ultimately such resources would have to come at the expense of the profits of capital. When one realizes that neoliberalism was itself the product of a profits squeeze on capital in a stagnant world economy, it is difficult to see where the means for such a program would come from. Soberly considered, the short-term future would appear, at best, to be one of increasing international tension and social conflict and, at worst, one of economic crisis and war. The end of history is not in sight.

Bibliography

Achar, Gilbert. *Eastern Cauldron: Islam, Afghanistan, Palestine, and Iraq in a Marxist Mirror*. New York: Monthly Review Press, 2004.

Adams, Nina S. and Alfred W. McCoy., eds. *Laos: War and Revolution*. New York: Harper and Row, 1970.

Agnew, Jean Christophe and Roy Rosenzweig, eds. *Companion to Post-1945 America*. Malden, Massachusetts: Blackwell, 2002.

Allen, Robert C. *Farm to Factory: A Reinterpretation of the Soviet Industrial Revolution*. Princeton: Princeton University Press, 2003.

Ali, S. Mahmud. *Cold War in the High Himalayas: the USA, China and South Asia in the 1950s*. New York: Palgrave Macmillan

Alperowitz, Gar. *The Decision to Drop the Atomic Bomb*. New York: Vintage, 1995.

Anderson, Perry. *Considerations on Western Marxism*. London: Verso, 1976.

———. *The Origins of Postmodernity*. London: Verso, 1998.

Appy, Christian G., ed. *Cold War Constructions: The Political Culture of United States Imperialism, 1945-1966*. Amherst: University of Massachusetts Press, 2000.

Arias, Arturo, ed. *The Rigoberta Menchu Controversy*. Minneapolis: University of Minnesota Press, 2001.

Armstrong, Charles K. *The North Korean Revolution: 1945-1950*. Ithaca: Cornell University Press, 2003.

Armstrong, Philip. Andrew Glyn and John Harrison. *Capitalism Since World War II: The Making and Breakup of the Great Boom*. London: Fontana, 1984.

Arrighi, Giovanni. *The Long Twentieth Century: Money, Power and the Origins of Our Times*. London: Verso, 1994.

Aslund, Anders, *Building Capitalism: The Transformation of the Former Soviet Bloc*. Cambridge: Cambridge University Press, 2002.

Auty, Phyllis, *Tito: A Biography*. Harmondsworth: Penguin,1974.

Azéma, Jean-Pierre. *From Munich to the Liberation, 1938-1944*. Cambridge: Cambridge University Press, 1984.

Barnett, Richard. *The Alliance*. New York: Simon and Schuster, 1983.

Barme, Geremie R. *In the Red: On Contemporary Chinese Culture*. New York: Columbia University Press, 1999.

Batatu, Hanna. *The Egyptian, Syrian and Iraqi Revolutions: Some Observations on their Underlying Causes and Social Character*. Washington: Center for Contemporary Arab Studies, 1984.

———. *The Old Social Classes and Revolutionary Movements in Iraq*. Princeton: Princeton University Press, 1978.

———. *Syria's Peasantry, the Descendants of its Lesser Rural Notables and Their Politics*. Princeton: Princeton University Press, 1999.

Beaud, Michel. *A History of Capitalism, 1500-2000*. New York: Monthly Review Press, 2001.

Beinin, Joel. *Workers and Peasants in the Modern Middle East*. Cambridge: Cambridge University Press, 2001.

Bello, Walden F. *Dark Victory: The United States, Structural Adjustment and Global Poverty*. London: Pluto Press, 1998.

———. *Dilemmas of Domination: The Unmaking of the American Empire*. New York: Owl Books, 2005.

———. *People and Power in the Pacific: The Struggle for the Post-Cold War Order*. London: Pluto Press, 1992.

Berghahn, Volker R. *America and the Intellectual Cold Wars in Europe: Shepard Stone between Philanthropy, Academy and Diplomacy*. Princeton: Princeton University Press, 2001.

Berman, William C. *America's Right Turn from Nixon to Bush*. Baltimore: Johns Hopkins University Press, 1994.

Betts, Raymond D. *Decolonization*. New York: Routledge, 1994.

Bird, Kai. *The Chairman: John J. McCloy and the Making of the American Establishment*. New York: Simon and Schuster, 1992.

———. *The Color of Truth, McGeorge Bundy and William Bundy, Brothers in Arms: A Biography*. New York: Simon and Schuster, 1998.

Birstein, Vadim J. *The Perversion of Knowledge: The True Story of Soviet Science*. Bolder: Westview Press, 2001.

Blight, James G. *On the Brink: Americans and Soviets Re-examine the Cuban Missile Crisis*. New York: Farrar, Strauss, & Giroux. 1992

Blum, Robert M. *Drawing the Line: The Origins of the American Containment Policy in East Asia*. New York: W.W. Norton, 1982.

Boll, Michael M. *Cold War in the Balkans: American Foreign Policy and the Emergence of Communist Bulgaria, 1943-1947*. Lexington: University Press of Kentucky, 1984.

Bonner, Raymond. *Waltzing With A Dictator: The Marcoses and the Making of American Policy*. New York: Vintage, 1987.

Bordne, William. *The Pacific Alliance: U.S. Foreign Economic Policy and Japanese Trade Recovery, 1947-1955*. Madison: University of Wisconsin Press, 1984.

Borstelmann, Thomas. *The Cold War and the Color Line: American Race Relations in the Global Era*. Cambridge, MA: Harvard University Press, 2001.

Boterbloem, Kees. *The Life and Times of Andei Zhdanov, 1896-1948*. Montreal: McGill-Queen's University Press, 2004.

Brands, H. W. *Inside the Cold War: Lloyd Henderson and the Rise of the American Empire, 1918-1961*. New York: Oxford University Press, 1991.

Brinkley, Douglas. *Dean Acheson: The Cold War Years, 1953-1971*. New Haven: Yale University Press, 1992.

Bromley, Simon. *American Hegemony and World Oil: The Industry, the State System and the World Economy*. University Park, PA: Pennsylvania State University Press, 1991.

Brus, Wlodzimierz. *Histoire économique de l' Europe de l'Est, 1945-1985*. Paris: La Deouverte 1986.

Burkett, Paul and Martin Hart-Landsberg. *Development, Crisis and Class Struggle: Learning from Japan and East Asia*. New York: Palgrave Macmillan, 2000.

Caldwell, Peter C. *Dictatorship, State Planning and Social Theory in the German Democratic Republic*. Cambridge: Cambridge University Press, 2003.

Carroll, Peter. *It Seemed Like Nothing Happened: America in the 1970s*. New Brunswick, N.J: Rutgers University Press, 1990.

Caute, David. *The Dancer Defects: The Struggle for Cultural Supremacy During the Cold War*. Oxford: Oxford University Press, 2003.

Chafer, Tony and Brian Jenkins, eds. *France: From the Cold War to the New World Order*. New York: St. Martin's Press, 1996.

Chalmers, David. *And the Crooked Places Made Straight: The Struggle for Social Change in the 1960s*. Baltimore: The Johns Hopkins University Press, 1991.

Chandler, David and Ben Kiernan, eds. *Revolution and Its Aftermath in Kampuchea: Eight Essays*. New Haven: Yale University Press, 1983.

Chen, Jian. *China's Road to the Korean War: The Making of the Sino-American Confrontation*. New York: Columbia University Press, 1994.

———. *Mao, China and the Cold War*. Chapel Hill: University of North Carolina Press, 2001.

Chen, King C. *Vietnam and China, 1938-1954*. Princeton: Princeton University Press, 1969.

Chomsky, Noam et al. *The Cold War and the University: Toward an Intellectual History of the Postwar Years*. New York: The New Press 1997.

Chuev, Feliks Ivanovich. *Molotov Remembers: Inside Kremlin Politics*. Chicago: Ivan R. Dee, 1993.

Clapham, Christopher, ed. *African Guerrillas*. Bloomington: Indiana University Press, 1998.

Clark, John G. *The Political Economy of World Energy*. Chapel Hill: University of North Carolina Press, 1990.

Clayton, William. *Selected Papers*. Baltimore: The Johns Hopkins University Press, 1971.

Coates, Ken S. *A Global History of Indigenous Peoples*. New York: Palgrave Macmillan, 2004.

Cockcroft, James D. *Neighbors in Turmoil: Latin America*. New York: HarperCollins, 1989.

Colby, William. *Thy Will Be Done: The Conquest of the Amazon, Nelson Rockefeller and Evangelism in the Age of Oil*. New York: HarperCollins, 1995.

Cooper, Frederick. *Africa Since 1940: The Past of the Present*. Cambridge: Cambridge University Press, 2002.

———. *Decolonization and African Society: The Labor Question in French and British Africa* Cambridge: Cambridge University Press, 1996.

Crankshaw, Edward, ed. *Khrushchev Remembers*. Boston: Little, Brown, 1970.

Cullather, Nick. *Secret History: The CIA's Classified Account of Its Operations in Guatemala*. Palo Alto: Stanford University Press, 1999.

Cumings, Bruce. *Korea's Place in the Sun: A Modern History*. New York: W.W. Norton, 1997.

———. *North Korea: Another Country*. New York: New Press, 2004.

———. *The Origins of the Korean War*, 2 vols. Princeton: Princeton University Press, 1981-1990.

———. et al, eds. *Inventing the Axis of Evil: The Truth About North Korea, Iran, and Syria*. New York: New Press, 2004.

Davidson, Basil. *The Black Man's Burden: Africa and the Curse of the Nation-State*. New York: Three Rivers Press, 1992.

———. *Black Star: A View of the Life and Times of Kwame Nkrumah*. New York: Allen Lane, 1974.

———. *Modern Africa* (London: Longman, 1989.

Davis, Eric. *Memories of State: Politics, History and Collective Identity in Modern Iraq*. Berkeley: University of California Press, 2005.

Dear, Ian, ed. *The Oxford Companion to World War II*. Oxford: Oxford University Press, 1995.

De Witte, Ludo. *The Assassination of Lumumba*. London: Verso, 2001.

Dezelay, Yves. *The Internationalization of Palace Wars: Lawyers, Economists and the Contest to Transform Latin American States*. Chicago: University of Chicago Press, 2002.

Djilas, Milovan. *Conversations With Stalin*. New York: Harvest/HBJ, 1962.

Dower, John W. *Embracing Defeat: Japan in the Wake of World War II*. New York: New Press, 1999.

———. *War Without Mercy: Race and Power in the Pacific War*. New York: Pantheon, 1986.

Droz, Bernard. *Histoire de la guerre d'Algerie: 1954-1962*. Paris: Seuil, 1982.

Drury, Shadia B. *Leo Strauss and the American Right*. New York: Palgrave Macmillan, 1997.

Dubcek, Alexander. *Hope Dies Last*. New York: Kodansha America, 1993.

Dudziak, Mary L. *Cold War Civil Rights: Race and the Image of American Democracy*. Princeton: Princeton University Press, 2000.

Duggan, Christopher and Christopher Wagstaff, eds. *Italy in the Cold War: Politics, Culture and Society, 1948-1958*. Washington: Berg publishers, 1995.

Duménil, Gérard and Dominique Lévy. *Capital Resurgent: Roots of the Neo-Liberal Revolution* Cambridge, Mass: Harvard University Press, 2004.

Dunkerely, James. *The Pacification of Central America: Political Change in the Isthmus, 1987-1993*. London: Verso, 1999.

———. *Political Suicide in Latin America and Other Essays*. London: Verso, 1992.

———. *Power in the Isthmus: A Political History of Modern Central America* London: Verso, 1988.

Eckstein, Susan. *Back from the Future: Cuba Under Castro*. Princeton: Princeton University Press, 2003.

Edsall, Thomas B. and Mary D. *Chain Reaction: The Impact of Race, Rights and Taxes on American Politics*. New York: W.W. Norton, 1991.

Eisenberg, Carolyn, *Drawing the Line: The American Decision to Divide Germany, 1944-1949*. Cambridge, Cambridge University Press, 1996.

Elliot, W.P. *The Vietnamese War: Revolution and Social Change in the Mekong Delta, 1930-1975* 2 Vols. Armonk, NY: East Gate Books, 2003.

Engerman, David C. et al, eds. *Staging Growth: Modernization, Development and the Global Cold War*. Amherst, Mass: University of Massachusetts Press, 2003.

Erickson, John. *The Road to Berlin*. London: Cassell, 1983.

———. *The Road to Stalingrad*. London: Cassell, 1975.

Evans, Eric J. *Thatcher and Thatcherism*. London: Routledge, 1997.

Evans, Grant. *Red Brotherhood at War: Vietnam, Cambodia and Laos Since 1975*. London: Verso, 1990.

Ewell, Judith. *Venezuela and the United States: From Monroe's Hemisphere to Petroleum's Empire*. Athens, GA: University of Georgia Press, 1996.

Ewen, Stuart. *Captains of Consciousness: Advertising and the Social Roots of the Consumer Culture*. New York: Basic Books, 1976.

———. *PR: A Social History of Spin*. New York: Basic Books, 1996.

Farouk-Sluglett, Marion and Peter Sluglett. *Iraq since 1958: From Revolution to Dictatorship* London: I.B. Tauris, 2001.

Filtzer, Donald. *Soviet Workers and Late Stalinism: Labour and the Restoration of the Stalinist System After World War II*. Cambridge: Cambridge University Press, 2002.

Forster, Cindy. *The Time of Freedom: Campesino Workers in Guatemala's October Revolution*. Pittsburgh: University of Pittsburgh Press, 2001.

Fossedal, Gregory A. *Our Finest Hour: Will Clayton, the Marshall Plan and the Triumph of Democracy*. Palo Alto: Hoover Institution Press, 1993.

Freeland, Richard M. *The Truman Doctrine and the Origins of McCarthyism: Foreign Policy, Domestic Politics and Internal Security, 1946-1948*. New York: Alfred A. Knopf, 1972.

Freeman, Alan and Boris Kagarlitsky, eds. *The Politics of Empire: Globalisation in Crisis*. London: Pluto Press, 2004.

Fulbrook, Mary. *Anatomy of a Dictatorship: Inside the GDR, 1949-1989*. New York: Oxford University Press, 1994.

Fursenko, A.A. *One Hell of a Gamble: Khrushchev, Castro and Kennedy, 1958-1964*. New York: W.W. Norton, 1998.

Gaiduk, Ilya V. *Confronting Vietnam: Soviet Policy Toward the Indo-China Conflict, 1953-1964.* Palo Alto: Stanford University Press, 2003.

Gardener, Lloyd C. *Architects of Illusion: Men and Ideas in American Foreign Policy, 1941-1949*. Chicago: Quadrangle Books, 1970.

———. *Economic Aspects of New Deal Diplomacy*. Madison: University of Wisconsin Press, 1964.

Gavin, Frances J. *Gold, Dollars and Power: The Politics of International Monetary Relations, 1958-1971*. Chapel Hill: University of North Carolina Press, 2004.

Gerhardt, Gail. *Black Power in South Africa: The Evolution of an Ideology*. Berkeley: University of California Press, 1978.

Gerstle, Gary. *American Crucible: Race and Nation in the Twentieth Century.* Princeton: Princeton University Press, 2001.

Gilbert, Marc Jason. *Why The North Won the Vietnam War.* New York: Palgrave Macmillan, 2002.

Gildea, Robert. *France Since 1945* (Oxford: Oxford University Press, 1996.

Gienow-Hecht, Jessica C.E. and Frank Schumacker, eds. *Culture and International History.* New York: Berghan Books, 2004.

Gilman, Nils. *Mandarins of the Future: Modernization Theory in Cold War America.* Baltimore: The Johns Hopkins University Press, 2003.

Ginsborg, Paul. *A History of Contemporary Italy: Society and Politics, 1943-1988.* London, New York: Penguin, 1988.

———. *Italy and Its Discontents; Family, Civil Society, State, 1980-2001.* New York: Palgrave Macmillan, 2003.

Gleijeses, Paolo. *Conflicting Missions: Havana, Washington, Africa, 1959-1976.* Chapel Hill: University of North Carolina Press, 2002.

———. *Shattered Hope: The Guatemalan Revolution and the United States, 1944-1954* Princeton: Princeton University Press, 1991.

Goldberg, Ellis Jay, ed. *Social History of Labor in the Middle East.* Boulder: Westview Press, 1996.

Golsan, Richard J. *Vichy's Afterlife: History and Counter-History in Post-War France.* Lincoln: University of Nebraska Press, 2000.

Goncharov, S.N. *Uncertain Partners: Stalin, Mao and the Korean War.* Palo Alto: Stanford University Press, 1993.

Goodson, Larry P. *Afghanistan's Endless War: State Failure, Regional Politics and the Rise of the Taliban.* Seattle: University of Washington Press, 2001.

Gorbachev, Mikhail Sergeevitch and Zdenek Mlynar. *Conversations with Gorbachev.* New York: Columbia University Press, 2002.

Gorlizki, Yoram and Oleg Khlevniuk. *Cold Peace: Stalin and the Soviet Ruling Circle, 1924-1953.* New York: Oxford University Press, 2004.

Gott, Richard. *Cuba: A New History.* New Haven: Yale University Press, 2004.

Gregory, Paul R., ed. *Behind the Facade of Stalin's Command Economy: Evidence from the Soviet State and Party Archives.* Palo Alto: Hoover Institution Press, 2001.

Halliday, Fred. *Iran, Dictatorship and Development.* New York: Penguin Books, 1979.

———. *Islam and the Myth of Confrontation: Religion and Politics in the Middle East* London: I.B. Tauris, 1996.

———. *The Making of the Second Cold War.* London: Verso, 1986.

Halliday, Fred and Maxine Molyneux. *The Ethiopian Revolution.* London: Verso, 1981.

Halliday, Jon. *A Political History of Japanese Capitalism.* New York: Monthly Review Press, 1978.

Halliday, Jon and Bruce Cumings. *Korea: The Unknown War.* New York: Pantheon, 1988.

Hart-Landsberg, Martin. *Korea: Division, Reunification and U.S. Foreign Policy.* New York: Monthly Review Press, 1998.

Hart-Landsberg, Martin and Paul Burkett. *China and Socialism: Market Reforms and Class Stuggle.* New York: Monthly Review Press, 2005.

Harvey, David. *The Condition of Post-Modernity: An Enquiry into the Origins of Cultural Change.* Oxford: Blackwell, 1989.

———. *The New Imperialism.* New York: Oxford University Press, 2003.

Helleiner, Eric. *States and the Reemergence of Global Finance from Bretton Woods to the 1990s.* Ithaca: Cornell University Press, 1994.

Heller, Francis H. *Economics and the Truman Administration.* Lawrence, KS: University Press of Kansas, 1981

Hinton, Willliam. *Fanshen: A Documentary of Revolution in a Chinese Village.* New York: Monthly Review Press, 1967.

———. *The Great Reversal: The Privatization of China, 1978-1989.* New York: Monthly Review Press, 1990.

Hiro, Dilip. *Desert Storm to Desert Shield: The Second Gulf War.* New York: Routledge, 1992.

———. *The Essential Middle East: A Comprehensive Guide.* New York: Carroll and Graf Publishers.

———. *The Longest War: The Iran-Iraq Military Conflict.* London: Routledge, 1991.

———. *Neighbours, Not Friends: Iraq and Iran After the Gulf Wars.* London: Routledge, 2001.

———. *Secrets and Lies: Operation "Iraqi Freedom" and Afterward.* New York: Nation Books, 2004.

———. *War Without End: The Rise of Islamist Terrorism and Global Response.* London: Routledge, 2002.

Hitchcock, William I. *France Restored: Cold War Diplomacy and the Quest for Leadership in Europe. 1944-1954.* Chapel Hill: University of North Carolina Press, 1998.

Hobsbawm, Eric J. *The Age of Extremes: A History of the World, 1914-1991.* New York: Vintage, 1994.

Hodges, Tony. *Anatomy of an Oil State.* Bloomington: Indiana University Press, 2004.

Hodgkin, Thomas Lionel. *Vietnam: The Revolutionary Path.* New York: Palgrave Macmillan, 1981.

Hogan, Michael J. *A Cross of Iron: Harry S. Truman and the Origins of the National Security State, 1945-1954.* Cambridge: Cambridge University Press, 1998.

———. *The Marshall Plan: America, Britain and the Reconstruction of Western Europe, 1947-1952.* Cambridge: Cambridge University Press, 1987.

Horowitz, Daniel. *Betty Friedan and the Making of the Feminine Mystique: The American Left, the Cold War and Modern Feminism.* Amherst: University of Massachusetts Press, 1998.

Hough, Jerry F. *The Logic of Economic Reform in Russia.* Washington, DC: Brookings Institution Press, 2001.

Huang, Yashang. *Selling China: Foreign Direct Investment During the Reform Era.* Cambridge: Cambridge University Press, 2003.

Hudson, Kate. *Breaking the South Slav Dream: The Rise and Fall of Yugoslavia.* London: Pluto Press, 2003.

Hunter, Allen, ed. *Rethinking the Cold War.* Philadelphia: Temple University Press, 1998.

Iriye, Akira. *Power and Culture: the Japanese-American War, 1941-1945.* Cambridge, MA: Harvard University Press, 1981.

Isserman, Maurice and Michael Kazin. *America Divided: The Civil Wars of the 1960s*. New York: Oxford University Press, 2000.

Jin, Qiu. *Culture of Power: The Lin Biao Incident in the Cultural Revolution*. Palo Alto: Stanford University Press, 1999.

Jones, Owen Bennet. *Pakistan: Eye of the Storm*. New Haven: Yale University Press, 2002.

Kahin, George Mcturnan. *Intervention: How America Became Involved in Vietnam*. New York: Anchor, 1987.

Judt, Tony, ed. *Resistance and Revolution in Mediterranean Europe, 1939-1948*. London, New York: Routledge, 1989.

Kennan, George F. *George F. Kennan and the Origins of Containment 1944-1946: The Kennan-Lukas Correspondence*. Colombia: University of Missouri Press, 1997.

Kennedy, Michael D. *Professionals, Power and Solidarity in Poland*. Cambridge: Cambridge University Press, 1991.

Kennedy, Paul M. *The Rise and Fall of the Great Powers: Economic Change and Military Conflict from 1500 to 2000*. London: Unwin Hyman, 1989.

Kersten, Krystyna. *The Establishment of Communist Rule in Poland, 1943-1948*. Berkeley: University of California Press, 1991.

Khrushchev, Sergei N. *Nikita Khrushchev and the Creation of a Super-Power*. Univeristy Park, PA: University of Pennsylvania Press, 2000.

Kiernan, Ben and Chanthou Boua, eds. *Peasants and Politics in Kampuchea, 1942-1981*. London: M.E. Sharpe, 1982.

Kimmerling, Baruch and Joel S Migdal. *The Palestinian People*. Cambridge, MA: Harvard University Press, 2003.

Klein, Herbert S. *A Concise History of Bolivia*. Cambridge: Cambridge University Press, 2003.

Knight, Amy W. *Beria, Stalin's First Lieutenant*. Princeton: Princeton University Press, 1993.

Kolko, Gabriel. *Anatomy of a War : Vietnam, the United States, and the Modern Historical Experience*. New York: HarperCollins, 1985.

———. *Century of War: Politics, Conflict, and Society Since 1914*. New York: New Press, 1994.

———. *Confronting the Third World: United States Foreign Policy, 1945-1980*. New York: Pantheon, 1988.

———. *The Politics of War: Allied Diplomacy and the World Crisis of 1943-1945*. New York: Pantheon, 1969.

Kolko, Gabriel and Joyce. *The Limits of Power: The World and United States Foreign Policy, 1945-1954*. New York: Harper and Row, 1972.

Kuniholm, Bruce Robellet. *The Origins of the Cold War in the Middle East: Great Power Conflict and Diplomacy in Iran, Turkey and Greece*. Princeton: Princeton University Press, 1994.

Kuznick, Peter J. and James Gilbert, eds. *Rethinking Cold War Culture*. Washington, D.C: Smithsonian Books, 2001.

Lafeber, Walter. *America, Russia and the Cold War, 1945-1992*. New York: McGraw-Hill, 1993.

———. *The Clash: A History of U.S.-Japan Relations.* New York: W.W. Norton, 1997.

———. *Inevitable Revolutions: The Untied States in Central America.* New York: W.W. Norton, 1997.

Lampert, Nick and Gábor T. Rittersporn, eds. *Stalinism: Its Nature and Aftermath: Essays in Honor of Moshe Lewin.* Armonk, New York: M.E. Sharpe, 1992.

Lankov, A.N. *From Stalin to Kim Il Sung: The Formation of North Korea, 1945-1960.* New Brunswick, NJ: Rutgers University Press, 2002.

Latham, Michael E. *Modernization as Ideology: American Social Science and "Nation Building" in the Kennedy Era.* Chapel Hill: University of North Carolina Press, 2000.

Lee, Stephen Hugh. *Outposts of Empire: Korea, Vietnam and the Origins of the Cold War in Asia, 1949-1954.* Montreal: McGill-Queen's University Press, 1996.

Leeson, Robert. *The Eclipse of Keynesianism: The Political Economy of the Chicago Counter-Revolution.* New York: Palgrave Macmillan, 2001.

Leffler, Melvyn P. *A Preponderance of Power: National Security, The Truman Administration and the Cold War.* Palo Alto: Stanford University Press, 1992.

Leffler, Melvyn P. and David S. Painter, eds. *Origins of the Cold War: An International History.* London: Routledge, 1994.

Levering, Ralph B., ed. *Debating the Origins of the Cold War: American and Russian Perspectives.* Lanham, MD: Rowman and Littlefield, 2002.

Levy, Robert. *Ana Pauker, the Rise and Fall of a Jewish Communist.* Berkeley: University of California Press, 2001.

Lewin, Moshe. *Russia–USSR–Russia: The Drive and Drift of a Superstate.* New York: New Press, 1995.

———. *Le siècle sovietique tr. Denis Paillard and Florence Prudhomme.* Paris: Fayard, 2003.

Lievesley, Geraldine. *The Cuban Revolution: Past, Present and Future.* London & New York: Palgrave Macmillan, 2004.

Little, Douglas. *American Orientalism: The United States in the Middle East Since 1945.* Chapel Hill: University of North Carolina Press, 2002.

Litváni, György. *The Hungarian Revolution of 1956.* London & New York: Longman, 1996.

Loewen, Roberta S. *Creating the Cold War University: The Transformation of Stanford.* Berkeley: University of California Press, 1997.

Lomax, William. *Hungary 1956.* New York: Alan and Busby,1976.

Lowe, Peter. *The Korean War.* London: Palgrave Macmillman, 2000.

Madisson, Angus. *The World Economy: Historical Statistics.* Paris: Organization for Economic Cooperation and Development, 2003.

Magdoff, Harry. *Imperialism Without Colonies.* New York: Monthly Review Press, 2003.

MacFadyen, David. *Red Stars: Personality and the Soviet Popular Song, 1955-1991.* Montreal: McGill-Queen's University Press, 2001.

Maier, Charles S., ed. *The Cold War in Europe.* New York: Markus Wiener, 1991.

Majd, Mohammed Gholi. *Great Britain and Reza Shah: The Plunder of Iran, 1921-1941.* Gainesville: University Press of Florida, 2001.

Markovits, Claude. *A History of Modern India, 1480-1950.* London: Anthem Press, 2002.

Matusow, Allen. *The Unravelling of America: A History of Liberalism in the 1960s.* New York: Perennial, 1984.

Mathy, Jean-Philippe. *French Resistance: The French-American Culture Wars.* Minneapolis: University of Minnesota Press, 2000.

Mazower, Mark. *Dark Continent: Europe's Twentieth Century.* New York: Vintage, 2000.

McLoughlin, Barry and Kevin McDermott, eds. *Stalin's Terror: High Politics and Mass Repression in the Soviet Union.* New York: Palgrave, 2003.

Mead, Walter Russell. *Mortal Splendor: The American Empire in Transition.* Boston: Houghton Mifflin, 1987.

Medvedev, Roy A. and Zhores A. Medvedev. *The Unknown Stalin.* New York: Overlook, 2004.

Meisner, Maurice J. *Mao's China and After.* New York: Free Press, 1999.

Menchu, Rigoberta. *I, Rigoberta Menchu: An Indian Woman in Guatemala.* London: Verso, 1984.

Military History Institute of Vietnam, ed. *Victory in Vietnam: The Official History of the People's Army of Vietnam, 1954-1975.* Lawrence, KS: University Press of Kansas, 2002.

Milward, Alan S. *The Reconstruction of Western Europe, 1945-1951.* Berkeley: University of California Press, 1984.

Maclean, Mairi, ed. *The Mitterand Years: Legacy and Evaluation.* New York: Palgrave Macmillman, 1998.

Morgan, Patrick M. and Keith L. Nelson, eds. *Reviewing the Cold War: Domestic Factors and Foreign Policy in the East-West Confrontation.* London: Praeger, 2000.

Morgan, Ted. *A Covert Life: Jay Lovestone, Communist, Anti-Communist and Spy Master.* New York: Random House, 1999.

Myant, M.R. *Socialism and Democracy in Czechoslovakia, 1945-1948.* Cambridge: Cambridge University Press, 1981.

Nitzan, Jonathan and Shimshon Bichler. *The Global Political Economy of Israel.* London: Pluto Press, 2002.

Norton, Anne. *Leo Strauss and the Politics of American Empire.* New Haven: Yale University Press, 2004.

Nove, Alec. *An Economic History of the Soviet Union.* Harmondsworth: Penguin, 1976.

Nzongola-Ntalaja, Georges. *The Congo from Leopold to Kabila.* London: Zed Books, 2003.

O'Brien, Thomas F. *The Century of U.S. Capitalism in Latin America.* Oxford: Oxford University Press, 1996.

Offner, Arnold A. *Another Such Victory: President Truman and the Cold War, 1945-1953.* Palo Alto: Stanford University Press, 2002.

Ovendale, Ritchie, ed. *The Foreign Policy of the British Labour Governments, 1945-1951.* Leicester: Leicester University Press, 1984.

Patricio Silva, ed. *The Soldier and the State in South America: Essays in Civil-Military Relations.* New York: Palgrave Macmillan, 2001.

Patterson, James T. *Grand Expectations: The United States, 1945-1974.* New York: Oxford University Press, 1996.

Peet, Richard. *Unholy Trinity: The IMF, World Bank and WTO.* London: Zed Books, 2003.

Perry, Elizabeth J. and Li Xun. *Proletarian Power: Shanghai in the Cultural Revolution.* Boulder Colorado: Westview Press, 1996.

Pettifor, Ann, ed. *Real World Economic Outlook 2003: The Legacy of Globalization, Debt and Deflation.* New York: Palgrave Macmillan, 2003.

Phillips, Kevin. *Wealth and Democracy: A Political History of the American Rich.* New York: Broadway, 2002.

Pierpaoli, Paul G. *Truman and Korea: The Political Culture of the Early Cold War.* Columbia: University of Missouri Press, 1999.

Plummer, Brenda Gayle. *Rising Wind: Black Americans and U.S. Foreign Policy, 1935-1960* Chapel Hill: University of North Carolina Press. 1996.

Pollin, Robert. *Contours of Descent: U.S. Economic Fractures and the Landscape of Global Austerity.* London: Verso, 2003.

Rabe, Stephen G. *The Most Dangerous Area in the World: John F. Kennedy Confronts Communist Revolution in Latin America.* Chapel Hill: University of North Carolina Press, 1999.

Rees, E.A., ed. *The Nature of Stalin's Dictatorship: The Politburo, 1924-1953.* New York: Palgrave, 2004.

Richani, Nazih. *Systems of Violence: The Political Economy of War and Peace in Colombia.* Albany: State University of New York Press, 2002.

Rioux, Jean-Pierre. *The Fourth Republic, 1938-1944.* Cambridge: Cambridge University Press, 1987.

Rivière, Claude. *Guinea: The Mobilization of a People.* Ithaca: Cornell University Press, 1977.

Robin, Ron Theodore. *The Making of the Cold War Enemy:Culture and Politics in the Military-Intellectual Complex.* Princeton: Princeton University Press, 2001.

Ross, Corey. *The East German Dictatorship: Problems and Perspectives in the Interpretation of the GDR.* London: Arnold, 2002.

Ross, Kristin. *May '68 and its Afterlives.* Chicago: University of Chicago Press, 2002.

Rotter, Andrew J. *The Path to Vietnam: Origins of the American Commitment to Southeast Asia.* Ithaca: Cornell University Press, 1987.

Rowbotham, Sheila. *A Century of Women: The History of Women in Britain and the United States in the Twentieth Century.* New York: Penguin, 1999.

Said, Edward W. *From Oslo to Iraq and the Roadmap.* New York: Bloomsbury, 2004.

———. *Orientalism.* London: Routledge, 1978.

———. *Out of Place: A Memoir.* New York: Vintage, 1999.

Salucci, Ilario. *A People's History of Iraq: The Iraqi Communist Party, Workers' Movements, and the Left, 1924-2004.* Chicago: Haymarket Books, 2005.

Samary, Catherine. *Yugoslavia Dismembered.* New York: Monthly Review Press, 1995.

Saunders, Frances Stonor. *Who Paid the Piper? The CIA and the Cultural Cold War.* London: Granta Books, 1999.

Schaller, Michael. *The American Occupation of Japan: The Origins of the Cold War in Asia.* Oxford: Oxford University Press, 1985.

Schrecker, Ellen. *Many are the Crimes: McCarthyism in America.* Boston: Little, Brown, 1998.

————, ed. *Cold War Triumphalism: The Misuse of History After the Fall of Communism*. New York: New Press, 2004.

Schulze, Reinhard. *A Modern History of the Islamic World*. New York: New York University Press, 2002.

Scott-Smith, Giles and Hans Krabbendam, eds. *Cultural Cold War in Western Europe, 1945-1960*. London: Frank Cass, 2003.

Shalom, Stephen Rosskamm. *The United States and the Philippines: A Study of Neocolonialism* Philadelphia: Institute for the Study of Human Issues, 1981.

Sheng, Michael M. *Battling Western Imperialism: Mao, Stalin, and the United States*. Princeton: Princeton University Press, 1999.

Shlaim, Avi and Eugene L. Rogan, eds. *The War for Palestine: Rewriting the History of 1948*. New York: Cambridge University Press, 2001.

Shlaim, Avi and Yezid Sayigh, eds. *The Cold War and the Middle East*. New York: Oxford University Press, 1997.

Simpson, Christopher, ed. *Universities and Empire: Money and Politics in the Social Sciences During the Cold War*. New York: The New Press, 1998.

Smith, Carol A., ed. *Guatemalan Indians and the State, 1540 to1988*. Austin: University of Texas Press, 1990.

Smith, Neil. *American Empire: Roosevelt's Geographer and the Prelude to Globalization* Berkeley: University of California Press, 2003.

————. *The Endgame of Globalization*. New York: Routledge, 2005.

Smith, Tony. *The French Stake in Algeria*. Ithaca: Cornell University Press, 1978.

Stalker, Peter. *International Migration*. Oxford: Oxford University Press, 2001.

Stavrakis, Peter J. *Moscow and Greek Communism, 1944-1949*. Ithaca: Cornell University Press, 1989.

Stavrianos, L.S. *Global Rift: The Third World Comes of Age*. New York: Morrow, 1981.

Stiglitz, Joseph E. *Globalization and Its Discontents*. New York: W. W. Norton, 2002.

————. *The Roaring Nineties: A New History of the World's Most Prosperous Decade*. New York: W. W. Norton, 2003.

Stites, Richard, ed. *Culture and Entertainment in Wartime Russia*. Bloomington: Indiana University Press, 1995.

Suny, Ronald Grigor. *The Soviet Experiment: Russia, the USSR and the Successor States*. New York: Oxford University Press, 1998.

Taubman, William, Sergei Khruschev and Albert Gleason, eds. *Nikita Khrushchev*. New Haven: Yale University Press, 2000.

Thornton, Richard C. *Odd Man Out: Truman, Stalin, Mao and the Origins of the Korean War*. Washington, DC: Potomac Books, 2001.

Thurston, Robert W. and Bernd Bonwetsch, eds. *The People's War: Responses to World War II in the Soviet Union*. Urbana: University of Illinois Press, 2000.

Tismaneanu, Vladimir. *Stalinism for All Seasons: A Political History of Romanian Communism*. Berkeley: University of California Press, 2003.

Tomson, William. *The Soviet Union Under Brezhnev*. Harlow: Longman, 2003.

Toranska, Teresa. *"Them": Stalin's Polish Puppets*. New York: Harper and Row, 1987.

Vassiliev, Alexei. *The History of Saudi Arabia*. New York: New York University Press, 2002.

Wall, Irwin M. *The United States and the Making of Post-War France, 1945-1954*. Cambridge: Cambridge University Press, 1991.

Wenger, Andreas. *Living With Peril: Eisenhower, Kennedy and Nuclear Weapons*. Lanham, MD: Rowman and Littlefield, 1997.

Weiner, Amir. *Making Sense of War : the Second World War and the Fate of the Bolshevik Revolution*. Princeton: Princeton University Press, 2001.

Werth, Alexander. *Russia at War, 1941-1945*. New York: Carroll and Graf, 1984.

Westad, Odd Arne, ed. *Brothers in Arms: The Rise and Fall of the Sino-Soviet Alliance, 1945-1963*. Washington: Woodrow Wilson Center Press, 1998.

Williams, Kieran. *The Prague Spring and Its Aftermath: Czechoslovak Politics, 1968-1970* Cambridge: Cambridge University Press, 1997.

Wlliams, William Appleman. *The Contours of American History*. New York: W.W. Norton, 1973.

———. *The Tragedy of American Diplomacy*. New York: W.W. Norton, 1972.

Wolf, Eric R. *Europe and the People Without A History*. New York: W.W. Norton, 1997.

Wood, Elisabeth Jane. *Insurgent Collective Action and Civil War in El Salvador*. Cambridge: Cambridge University Press, 2003.

Woodside, Alexander B. *Community and Revolution in Modern Vietnam*. Boston: Houghton Mifflin, 1976.

Yaqub, Salim. *Containing Arab Nationalism: The Eisenhower Doctrine and the Middle East*. Chapel Hill: University of North Carolina Press, 2004.

Yergin, Daniel. *The Commanding Heights: The Battle Between Government and The Marketplace That is Remaking The Modern World*. New York: Simon and Schuster, 1998.

Zalouk, Malak. *Power, Class and Foreign Capital in Egypt: The Rise of the New Bourgeoisie*. London: Zed, 1989.

———. *The Prize:The Epic Quest for Oil, Money and Power*. New York: Free Press, 1991.

Zhai, Qiang. *China and the Vietnam Wars, 1950-1975*. Chapel Hill: University of North Carolina Press, 2000.

Zhang, Shu Guang. *Economic Cold War: America's Embargo Against China and the Sino-Soviet Alliance, 1949-1963*. Washington DC: Woodrow Wilson Center Press and Palo Alto: Stanford University Press, 2001.

Zubkova, Elina. *Russia after the War: Hopes, Illusions, and Disappointments, 1945-1957*. New York: M.E. Sharpe, 1998.

Zubok, V.M. *Inside the Kremlin's Cold War: From Stalin to Krushchev*. Cambridge, MA: Harvard University Press, 1996.

Index